EDEN RENEWED

PETER LEVI

EDEN RENEWED

*The Public and Private Life of
John Milton*

St. Martin's Press ♒ New York

Library of Congress Cataloging-in-Publication Data

Levi, Peter.
    Eden renewed : the public and private life of John Milton
/ Peter Levi.
        p. cm.
    ISBN 0-312-15116-0
    1. Milton, John, 1608–1674—Biography. 2. Poets,
English—Early modern, 1500–1700—Biography. 3. Milton,
John, 1608–1674—Contemporary England. 4. England—
Civilization—17th century.
    I. Title.
    PR3581.L44   1997
    821'.4—dc21   96-45532
    [B]   CIP

First published in Great Britain by Macmillan, an imprint of
Macmillan Publishers Limited

First U.S. Edition: April 1997

10   9   8   7   6   5   4   3   2   1

FOR DEIRDRE AND MATTHEW

Contents

LIST OF ILLUSTRATIONS

INTRODUCTION

JOHN MILTON'S LIFE seems broken-backed: the break is his polemical and public career, of which almost the only monuments are in the deadliest official Latin. He did go on keeping notebooks, and he did go on writing sonnets, which were passionate and many times revised, even in the days of his blindness. But otherwise there is little to connect the wonderful young poet of *Lycidas*, 'L'Allegro', *Comus* and the hymn 'On the Morning of Christ's Nativity' with the blind, majestic old man who wrote *Paradise Lost*, and *Paradise Regained* and it appears *Samson Agonistes* in poverty and blindness. He was a London poet born in Shakespeare's working lifetime very close to a tavern called the Mermaid, which Shakespeare and Ben Jonson frequented, at a time when London was still what we would call a country town. Almost every trace of that London has been obliterated, and Milton's reputation, unlike Shakespeare's, has now no great shrine, no house or tomb to focus it. There is a cottage at Chalfont St Giles where he took refuge from the plague and so escaped the Great Fire of London; there is Christ's College at Cambridge where he studied as a boy; and there are the ruins of Ludlow Castle where *Comus* was acted, but that is all. Even at Christ's the mulberry tree which drew such splendid indignation from Tennyson is only the remotest of legendary links.

Birrell, in his *Obiter Dicta* (1887), still knew Milton's London: 'From Bread Street he moved to St Bride's Churchyard, Fleet Street; from Fleet Street to Aldersgate Street; from Aldersgate Street to the Barbican; from the Barbican to the south side of Holborn; from the south side of Holborn to what is now called York Street, Westminster; from York Street, Westminster, to the north side of Holborn; from the north side of Holborn to Jewin Street; from Jewin Street to his last abode in Bunhill Fields.' Birrell has missed out a few of the addresses, among them the village of Horton, near Datchet, where the poet's mother was buried, the house in Petty France with a gate on to Green Park and the mysterious Hammersmith address that came to light recently. But the house at Horton was gone by 1887, and so was Petty France, where a tablet once recorded that Hazlitt too had lived there. It is probably what Birrell means by York Street and came down in 1877. A year later All Hallows church, where Milton was baptized and which Wren rebuilt after the Fire of London, was pulled down and redeveloped. Number 17, Aldersgate, in the Barbican was demolished in 1864, the St Bride's churchyard lodgings were burnt in 1874, and all the other lodgings were destroyed by Hitler or perished before the bombing. Even St Giles, Cripplegate, where Milton and his father were buried, was bombed to a skeleton. That skeleton has been reconstructed and can be found crouching in a courtyard of enormous modern constructions.

Milton's London is gone, curiously even more so than Shakespeare's. His St Paul's School and the Cathedral, ill-treated under Cromwell, were wiped away by the Fire of London, yet Shakespeare's hoary and blood-stained Tower of London survived, and Paul's towered 500 feet into the air until 1666. The generations of Shakespeare and Milton are closely connected, of course, and without grasping that one has no chance of understanding either of them. An elderly man could easily have recalled the Armada when Milton was eighteen – or, more importantly for Milton, the massacre of St Bartholomew's Day. He could even have been at Cambridge with Christopher Marlowe and seen all the plays and publications of Spenser and then Shakespeare, heard the sermons of Donne and read the poems of George Herbert. He would have been eighty when the King's head came off at Whitehall. He would no doubt have understood the history of his lifetime as one that led almost inevitably to that terrible event: the rise of Puritanism, the rebellion of Essex and the Irish troubles, the entry of the Scots onto the stage, the constant shedding of blood, the resentment of tyrannous government, the Church's worse than the State's, the Martin Marprelate controversy, then the impotence and folly and scandals of the Stuart kings.

It is not surprising, perhaps, that the heady mixture of ideas and violence between the Armada and Inigo Jones should end in a shattering explosion. The Levellers were already active in Shakespeare's Stratford, Machiavelli was an influence in London, and extreme Puritans had taken root, at least in East Anglia, when

Marlowe was a boy at Cambridge. The reason for writing the biography of a poet is to see how the honey of poetry is produced by that writer in a precise relation with his world, his circle and his times. Shakespeare makes that comparatively easy for us, but Milton makes it difficult.

John Milton's early poetry has a beautiful perfection of texture which is almost abstract, almost wholly literary and perhaps artificially learnt, like violin-playing or Latin verse. Then come the passionate statements of his middle years, those sonnets which substitute an astounding clarity for Shakespeare's impenetrable mysteries, and the prose with its alarming range and varying quality. In the final stage, when at last he wrote his two 'epics' (as he thought they were) and his classical tragedy, he had drifted away on his own; there was no poet remotely like him, not Cowley, his favourite modern poet, nor Dryden, and least of all his closer friend Andrew Marvell. Of course, the earlier poet can be discerned sometimes in the later, but no one could have expected the writer of his earlier works to produce *Paradise Lost*. That is essentially blind man's poetry, as we shall see.

Milton's entire career is full of teasing problems, and it may be the absorbing historical questions as much as the poetry itself that make him seem inexhaustible. This book is not meant for professional historians: I certainly have no illusion of having got to the bottom of him. His early biographies were collected by Helen Darbishire in 1932; they set out the limits within which he must be sought, but they are not the end of the matter: we can know more than they did about his family and his education, and about the last salt whispers of the Renaissance, so late to reach these barbarous shores and yet so potent an influence. We can be more detached and more honest about his politics and his theology. We can easily see what rubbish William Winstanley wrote about him in *Lives of the English Poets* in 1687: 'his fame is gone out like a candle in a snuff, and his memory will always stink, which might have ever lived in honourable repute, had he not been a notorious traitor,' etc. In the biography of Milton, the eighteenth century (if one sets aside Dr Johnson for a moment) is the period of steady accumulation, particularly by Thomas Warton; then early in the nineteenth, arguments one might have thought closed reopened with Sumner's edition of Milton's long-lost formal treatise in two books, *De Doctrina Christiana* – or were reopened rather not so much by that learned and fully annotated Latin work as by a very lively reviewer in the *Edinburgh Review* whose first contribution the notice was. This was Macaulay, still a young man and a student at Lincoln's Inn, trying to write his way out of the corner in which he was born.

Controversial views about Milton and the Civil War have swung between judgements that his public career was a great and glorious one, that it was a forgivable aberration and that it was detestable, whether forgivable or not. It is the difficult duty of anyone writing now to take all his political and theological views seriously. He never climbed down, never to my knowledge altered his views once he had developed them and seldom dissimulated except about theology. On that subject his treatise was suppressed by the government and rediscovered by the chance investigation of a Mr Lemon into the contents of a parcel, nearly a century and a half old and covered with dust, in a cupboard that stood among the assorted archives soon to be dignified as our Public Records. Sumner confined himself to one scathing Latin sentence about this; the truth was spelt out by Macaulay. There is no doubt that Milton had intended *De Doctrina Christiana* to be published, but posthumously: its views are surprisingly like those of common sense, although he maintains the fiction, which was all-important to him, that at every stage of his discussion he was closely following Scripture. He was an Arian (that is, he did not think Christ was God) and he was also a Unitarian (that is, the Trinity, he thought, was a figment and the Spirit a metaphor); he accepted both divorce and polygamy. It is surely acknowledged that a great deal of *Paradise Lost* is not to be taken literally, that there is no cure for literal belief in devils more effective than writing an epic poem about them and that the singular freedom Milton showed in scenes like the war in Heaven, where the devils invent artillery and start winning but the angels bombard them with mountains and prevail shows a poet not chained down by orthodoxy.

Milton had always strongly believed in the freedom of writers to say what they chose, and his *Areopagitica* is still the most popular and the most moving of his works in English rhetorical prose. In the 1820s the issue was still a lively one. Leigh Hunt went to Surrey Gaol for insulting the Prince Regent in 1814, and as late as 1831 William Carpenter, then thirty-four and the self-educated assistant to a

Finsbury bookseller, went to prison because he refused to pay stamp tax. Leigh Hunt praised Milton splendidly in his *Feast of Poets* (1814) and expressed disgust at the way Wordsworth and Southey and Coleridge had sold out to the government. Carpenter wrote the best and by far the most stirring of the shorter lives of Milton. It was Carpenter's thirteenth book: as a radical and a close friend of Cobbett, he deserves more attention than he has received.

The biographical tradition offers a bumpy ride and most of the biographers have axes of their own to grind; they are selective. Helen Darbishire offers a subtle guide to the first four and some brilliant insight into John Phillipps. This insight, like much else in Milton studies, has been denied. Almost no useful book about Milton is any longer obtainable, except perhaps for the Pickering 1852 *Poetical Works* in three small volumes, with Mitford's life. The complete prose works are now almost unobtainable: the Columbia edition was the most recent, in the 1940s, but is now out of print, and the Yale edition appeared as slowly as the timidest of snails, a volume every ten or twenty years. Even the Clarendon Press publication, the *Life of Milton* in two stout volumes by W. R. Parker (1968), has been unavailable for many years. The earliest publications on the life of Milton were his own, and some explosions of rage against him, in his lifetime. Aubrey knew him and took methodical notes both from Milton and from Edward and John Phillipps, nephews brought up in his house: soon after his death Aubrey procured the life by John for his employer Anthony à Wood, and the autograph copy is among Wood's papers, where it has survived as Bodleian ms Wood D4. That was first printed by Mr Parsons in the *English Historical Review* for 1902, hesitantly and wrongly attributed to Milton's medical friend Dr Paget. More recently it has been attributed to Cyriack Skinner, but on no real evidence. John Phillipps wrote of his uncle with careful thoroughness, deep affection and great admiration, in a style of crystalline purity. His work was dissolved into Wood's growing and mean-minded account in the *Fasti* of Oxford in the year of his incorporation as an Oxford MA in 1635, a practically useful step taken by many Cambridge graduates at that time. Wood's *Fasti Oxonienses* appeared in 1691. The ingrained nature of his prejudice can be seen in his annotation of the name of Milton in Edward's *Theatrum Poeticum* as 'a great rogue'.

From the Restoration onwards, and even before, more insults have been aimed at John Milton than have ever been collected. Winstanley's in 1687 rank among those, and in the same spirit the young Lord Bridgewater, who as a boy had acted in *Comus*, annotated his copy in Latin 'deserves the bonfire and the author the gallows'. Most of the biographers until Sir Egerton Brydges were supporters of the poet, though Johnson was barely so and still gnashing his teeth with scarcely suppressed rage in 1780. As early as 1750 Johnson had foolishly supported what turned out to be a fraud by a frustrated Scottish schoolmaster called Lauder, who pretended to demonstrate from neo-Latin verse that Milton was a plagiarist on a huge scale, deriving his verse from such characters as the great international lawyer Grotius. Johnson withdrew from this false position swiftly and handled Milton with care in 1780, but as we shall see his fury broke through: he found it far easier to be fair to Cowley, Milton's Cavalier contemporary, but he rightly describes Milton's Latin as being lusciously elegant; his reaction to *Paradise Lost* is clearly honest, and he notices in the poet 'a kind of humble dignity', which is just.

Edward Phillipps produced Milton's life in 1694 in a strange volume of letters with a few really startling sonnets, printed for the first time: the dangerous ones to Cromwell, Fairfax, Henry Vane (executed) and to Cyriack Skinner upon his blindness. In the Trinity manuscript of Milton's minor poems this last is in the hand of John Phillips, who also wrote in the revisions. Its publication had been long delayed because the poet had formerly spoken with such pride of losing his eyesight 'in Liberty's defence, my noble task'. Edward's biography is written in a mixture of styles but is nevertheless moving and was published at a time when John's life of his uncle was thought lost. Edward begins with ancient and modern examples of great biographers, though with no reference to Clarendon. He refers to 'Machiavel', a writer through whom the style of Tacitus was discovered as a historical tool, and pays charming compliments to Walton's *Lives*: Walton had struck a chord that Edward Phillipps sounded. 'Here he liv'd a private and quiet Life, still prosecuting his Studies and curious Search into Knowledge, the grand Affair perpetually of his Life ... he was courted into the Service of this new Commonwealth, and at last prevail'd with (for he never hunted after Preferment, nor affected the Tintamar and Hurry of Publick business) to take upon him the Office of *Latin* Secretary ...' But Edward could not remain long in the cloister of that way of writing, and it is he who gives us a few of the exciting moments of Milton's public career, in which he was for a time his uncle's assistant.

We are now near the end of the witnesses who had known Milton. Dr Darbishire, Principal of Somerville College, Oxford, and a lady of formidable scholarly integrity, goes on to John Toland, editor of the collected prose in 1698, who knew Aubrey, talked to John Phillipps and saw Edward's papers, and to Jonathan Richardson who wrote an introduction to *Paradise Lost* in 1734 and had some claim to access to a genuine though diminishing tradition. One might indeed criticize the last inclusion, since what it adds is mostly unreliable, from a granddaughter and the family of an old servant. Still, it is Richardson who tells us of old blind Milton being led about in the streets of London by Millington the bookseller. We would know a lot more about Milton if we had Marvell's or Dr Paget's account; Dr Paget had found Milton his last wife, a cousin of his own from Cheshire. Aubrey had a promise from Marvell to tell him all about Milton, but he went round to collect this information only to discover that Marvell had died a fortnight before. John Toland in 1698 has at least some sympathy with Milton's known views. (He chose for his epitaph what appears to be a sentence from John Phillipps put into Latin: '*Veritatis propugnator, Libertatis assertor, Nullius autem sectator aut cliens*'.) Toland wrote a distinctly political life: he was the first to notice that the censor threatened even *Paradise Lost*, because of the eclipse, which 'with fear of change/Perplexes monarchs', and to note that Milton as an old man adhered to no Christian sect and held no family prayers. He praised John Aubrey for his handling of the Druids. Toland's book was printed in London, though it purports to have been produced in Amsterdam. His views belonged to the future, and his life of Milton was reprinted by the eccentric Whig Thomas Hollis in 1761.

As the lives of Milton went on they got duller until 1780, and there have been more recent relapses. In 1725 Fenton edited the poems, along with what Johnson rightly enough dismissed as one of 'those honeysuckle lives', and did publish the contract date for *Paradise Lost*, 27 April 1667. Dr Birch (1738) and Bishop Thomas Newton, later the Bishop of Bristol (1749), get honourable mentions from Dr

Darbishire for attempting to tap the half-remembered family gossip, but the time for interviews was over, and the time for scholarship had come: they would have done better to sort through Aubrey's papers. While these are usually regarded as unutterably confused, Dr Darbishire treats him gently and makes it appear that his life of Milton was easier to disentangle than most. If all interviewers rate a mention, then Johnson was one, since he confirmed at least one detail from a man's son.

But all these late writers ignore one strange accusation, which if it were not for H. J. Todd (1801) would be altogether forgotten. Parker mentions it only to dismiss it with scorn. It is a pity the tale is so incredible, since some truth, which if it is accurate is extremely interesting, may lie behind it. Todd had heard a rumour that Milton was 'a principal founder' of the Calves Head Club. Todd knows of a 'secret history' of this bizarre society, which he describes as having been published in 1709. The Bodleian Library offers editions between 1703 and 1707, but an Oxford bookshop had one of 1715, so the 1709 edition may not be a figment: the point is of some importance because the book gets fatter and fuller as its editions go on, so that in the end it has baroque, cartoon-like illustrations of the society meeting with a wood-axe on the wall and the Devil under the table. *The Secret History of the Calves Head Club* is thought to be by Edward Heath (1667–1731), 'not the same as the journalist'. It is certainly an extreme royalist or anti-republican and anti-Whig lampoon, and yet I am not sure the story was wholly invented. Such an assembly is just within the limits of possibility, though as a story of a secret society it sits more happily in the 1700s than in 1650.

The Calves Head Club is supposed to have been founded soon after 1650 as a counter-blast to Anglican devotion to the dead King. The club, it is claimed, always met privately to celebrate the King's death. They venerated an axe, sang anthems which they commissioned (one or two of which have a genuine ring), took an oath of loyalty with a hand on Milton's *Defensio Populi Angli* and sat down to a dinner of calves' heads, a big pike with a little one (for Charles II) in its mouth, a boar's head chewing an apple, a large cod's head and so on; they drank together from a calf's skull 'in memory of the Patriots who killed the King'. In 1705 they met somewhere 'in a blind alley about Moorfields', and some of them frequented the Black Boy in

Newgate Street. Is it absolutely certain this story was complete nonsense and that Milton had nothing to do with any society of the kind?

The long sequence of biographies and criticisms of Milton does seem to touch on some critical changes in popular feeling. Addison, in four volumes reprinted (1788) from his essays, represented a high point, but in general the late eighteenth century belonged to Thomas Warton and the Romantic movement. Brydges in 1835 offered a Romantic attack on Milton, much resented by writers like William Carpenter, who demolished him in 1836. Hayley's *Milton* (1797) is of little consequence to scholars, but it leads in another Romantic direction. Samuel Palmer learnt to worship Milton from his nanny; her edition was Warton's *Minor Poems* of Milton, which she left him. The Scotsman Masson, a mighty respectable figure in his day, spent the last three decades of the nineteenth century working on Milton. He accumulates more information than anyone, but he is deadly dull and full of mad prejudices about Scottish affairs. The most desirable life and poetical works to be produced in the nineteenth century is surely the Pickering three-volume edition of the 1850s. The fuss and the flaring up of new interest created by Sumner's edition of *De Doctrina Christiana* had come more or less to rest in the life by T. Mitford, there reprinted, which is the fullest and most readable.

At the end of the century Milton came into his own in another way with the edition 'with etymological notes' by H. Bradley (1901) and the various works of Robert Bridges, Bradley's great friend. The study of Milton's text was promoted by Beeching, a canon of Westminster, and great textual advances were made by W. Aldis Wright, who issued the facsimile of the Trinity manuscript (1899) and by Darbishire in her treatment of the manuscript of Book 1 of *Paradise Lost*. The modern lives have been light but all enjoyable reading: they are by writers such as Rose Macaulay, Hilaire Belloc (a remarkable performance but wrong-headed) and A. N. Wilson, an excellent guide to an intricate subject. For the poetry I have used the Carey and Fowler commentary, often without acquiescence but with the increasing realization of how formidable they are. The standard life by W. R. Parker published thirty years ago is put together like a suet pudding, and he is no poet, but he has noticed what no one else notices in *Milton's Debt to Greek Tragedy* (1937), in *Milton's*

Contemporary Reputation (1940) and in the *Life* (1968), and the more one reads him the more one likes him. His first volume of the *Life* is 666 pages long, and the second, consisting of notes, adds another 823, that is, 1,489 in all: he is a researcher into minute detail, as Masson was before him. It is not easy to recover a subject from hands like his. Parker is American literary scholarship at its crushing and complete best; naturally one is inclined to rebel a little. Against French's vast collection of Milton documents it would be foolish and ungrateful to rebel. My only hope is to steal from French and from W. R. Parker and Helen Darbishire, and everyone who has written on the subject, but I can rival Belloc only by greater sobriety and heaviness and A. N. Wilson by sheer plod. I am sufficiently elderly to have forgotten by now most of my own research but not to have lost a lifetime's reading of Milton, who has always sustained me and continues to do so. The genesis of this book was a lecture on the young Milton that I gave in the 1980s, 'The Art of Poetry' (Yale, 1991), which I now find much reason to mistrust and to contradict. That is progress of a kind, I suppose.

CHAPTER ONE

BOYHOOD

BRAITHWAITE, the author of *Barnaby's Journey* (1638), wrote of London, which he called 'New Troy':

> Seven Hills there were in Rome, and so there be
> Seven sights in New-Troy crave the memory,
> Tombs, Guild-hall, Giants, Stage-plays, Bedlam poor,
> Ostrich, Bear-Garden, Lions in the Tower.

John Milton the poet was born and brought up among all these, not far from the Mermaid when it was frequented by Shakespeare and Ben Jonson, and well within the sound of Bow bells. His father's house had the best position in a court on the west side of the southern half of Bread Street and would have looked much like the Elizabethan houses of Stratford-upon-Avon. Bread Street runs down to the Thames from Cheapside, not far east of St Paul's, but west of London Bridge and the Tower, and within easy walking distance of all three. A direct walk northwards into the country led to Bunhill Fields. At the corner of Cheapside stood the church of All Hallows, and the city was studded with churches innumerable. John Milton senior owned his house, which was also his place of work; he was a scrivener, that is a drawer-up of contracts, an agent in wheeling and dealing and a party to financial transactions. The profession was a flourishing one and he was rich. In nearby Cheapside there were goldsmiths.

He was a member of the Scrivener's Company, a new rationalization of what had become a most lucrative profession because of its stranglehold on important business through its mastery of documents. London was not an illiterate city; indeed, it was the most literate city in Europe in the early seventeenth century and possibly the one which was expanding fastest, in population at least. This increased from 100,000 in 1550 to some 220,000 in 1600 and to about 450,000 in 1650. However, the extent of the city grew very little. From the

Roman walled town between St Paul's and the Tower it had spread along the north bank of the Thames to include Westminster, though Oxford Street was still a track across fields, a route for cattle; and the long inhabited strip between the Abbey and the Tower, mostly the fortified houses of noblemen as far as the Temple, was only just matched by a thinner area on the south bank, where the brothels and the playhouses and the bear-baiting were, with a slightly larger knob at Southwark. Under James I the city was expanding most swiftly to the north and east; the ward of Cripplegate outside the walls was part of London, but Stepney and Clerkenwell were suburban villages, and St James's Palace stood among parks and fields. The Palace of Westminster was a huge and rambling area at the far western end of London, extending from Parliament and the Abbey nearly to Trafalgar Square. Further west London ended in a huge prison on Millbank. Much of the expansion of the population of London went into the intense life of labyrinthine courts and alleys and passages. London was not yet filthy, but it was terribly crowded. It was the only place in the kingdom where an army could be raised at the drop of a hat, or a navy or a large sum of money.

To say what London thought or felt in 1608 is to generalize unjustifiably. But it had been under Edward VI, and was to show itself again under Charles I, an extreme Protestant stronghold: whether because so many of its people came from traditionally Protestant Essex, or because the poor were swayed by generations of propaganda, or because of the old Church's corruption, or because of the new spread of literacy, it is hard to say. In all England patronage was still important, even all-important, and the court therefore played a role in the city's life, but the City of London itself and its mayor resisted taxes, took a more detached view of the monarchy as time went on, and almost certainly despised the court. What they wanted of the central government was a strong foreign policy that would protect British trade, and most of Milton's time as Latin Secretary would be taken up by negotiations over shipping in trouble abroad.

It is important not to overstress the Renaissance aspect of London. At the time of Stowe's *Chronicle*, shortly before Milton was born, not only the churches and entire districts were unaltered since the Middle Ages but the way of life was largely medieval. Between Cheapside and the Thames, just of Bread Street, lay a house called Gerard's Hall, probably a tall medieval hall where the smoke escaped through a hole in the roof, and certainly one where a giant was believed to have lived. They showed you the ladder they used to feed him.

The Miltons' house, the Spread Eagle, was named after its sign, like a public-house sign, as the custom was in London in those days, and the poet's father had a seal made with a double-headed, stretch-winged eagle on it, which his son cherished after him, so that it has survived. He retained ownership of his father's house too, although he never lived in it as an adult but let it, as his father had done, for many years. It was still his when it was burnt to the ground in the Fire of London.

There is no doubt that the poet's father was a substantial and successful business man, but he had come from the country, like many Londoners. His grandfather had had a good income and a small estate at Stanton St John, quite close to Oxford, and since he was the deputy ranger of Shotover forest, he ranked as a gentleman, though anything we are told of his family origins is vague and probably as unreliable as the precise sum of £500 a year we are given by John Phillipps as his great-grandfather's income. Shotover was the first of the circle of hills that surround Oxford encountered by a traveller towards London, though modern roads avoid it. It lies between Stanton St John and the Henley road: it is still a green, more or less wild hilltop; it was a forest only in the legal sense of being subject to the draconian Norman forest laws which regulated hunting. On the top of Shotover, near Vanbrugh's Shotover House, stands an obelisk recording the spot where Elizabeth I, on a state visit to Oxford, was met by the Vice-Chancellor; earlier still, it was where an undergraduate from Queen's College defended himself against a wild boar with a heavy volume of the works of Aristotle. The poet's grandfather was a fierce, old-fashioned figure, who disinherited his son for disloyalty to the Catholic Church under Elizabeth. A Geneva Bible, in English and presumably with the fierce anti-papal marginal comments that grace its later editions, was found in the young man's room, and the poet's father set off for London, where he became a scrivener through the help of a kinsman.

He married Sarah Jeffrey, daughter of Paul Jeffrey, a merchant tailor of St Swithin's and, it appears, a kinsman of the Bradshaws, one of whom later became the poet's lawyer and a few years afterwards presided at the King's trial and condemnation to death. In 1601 Sarah lost her firstborn child, who was buried unbaptized in the churchyard of All Hallows. John Milton was born on 9 December 1608 and was baptized a few days later. His sister Anne was perhaps a year or two older, since her eldest daughter was born in 1626 and died in 1628, and her eldest son, Edward Phillips, was born in 1630. John's younger brother, Christopher, was born in 1615. If it is true that three other Milton children died in infancy, then John was the only surviving son of the first fifteen years of his parents' marriage. Little is known of his mother except that the poet loved her and that the poor, to whom she was very generous, adored her. We know from a poem of John's boyhood that she was not perfectly orthodox in religion, and we can presume from the success of her husband that she was a good match, with connections that seem to lie in Essex. She is said to have been nine years younger than her husband, who was probably born in 1563. This raises the question of how the scrivener spent his youth, since he adopted that profession only in 1595 and was not admitted to the Company of Scriveners until 1600. If he was about thirty-seven and she was about twenty-eight when they married, the dates which were hammered out in nineteenth-century controversies are at least plausible. The scrivener had been educated at Christ Church, Oxford, where he probably sang in the choir and certainly learnt a good deal about music.

It is here that he would have acquired his Protestantism; although the main push against the old religion came in the 1580s, Christ Church showed the Queen's influence earlier. By 1600 George Abbott, the Vice-Chancellor, was having any religious picture he could lay his zealous hands on publicly burnt. In 1610 Dr Abbott began his disastrous reign as Archbishop of Canterbury. It is likely enough that by the age of twenty-five, in the year of the Armada, the scrivener was determined to break out of the limitations that the old religion imposed on him, and that he was genuinely a convinced Protestant. He was also a composer of music and a kind of poet. The poetry is not to be dismissed, though it is shockingly bad because the influence of Spenser and of Sylvester's translation of Du Bartas, which I will discuss later, would have flourished in the scrivener's shadow; likewise the poet's Italian culture, with all that implied for him, developed under the influence of his father's music.

We have only one example of the older Milton's poetry, a complimentary sonnet addressed to a friend called John Lane. Lane was a Somerset man and proud of it, an effortlessly mediocre poet most of whose works remained unpublished until the nineteenth century: he does not merit very close attention. All the same, Edward Phillipps called him 'a fine old Elizabethan gentleman ... equal to Drayton and others of the next rank to Spenser'. This is the scrivener's poem in praise of him:

Joannes Melton, Londinensis civis, amico suo viatico in poesis laudem.

> If virtue this be not, what is? Tell quick!
> For childhood, manhood, old age thou dost write
> Love, war, and lusts, quelled by an arm heroic,
> Instanced in Guy of Warwick, knighthood's light;
> Herald's records and each sound antiquary
> For Guy's true being, life, death, eke hast sought
> To satisfy those which *praevaricari*;
> Manuscript, chronicle, if might be bought;
> Coventry's, Winton's, Warwick's monuments,
> Trophies, traditions delivered of Guy,
> With care, cost, pain, as sweetly thou presents,
> To exemplify the flower of chivalry:
> From cradle to the saddle and the bier,
> For Christian imitation, all are here.

The manuscript contained a licence to print (1617), but it was not printed until Hunter's *Milton, a Sheaf of Gleanings*, in 1850. The pretentious antiquarianism, the Protestant search for examples for Christian imitation and for 'knighthood's light' and the queer reference to 'prevarication' are all of a piece. Lane's compliment to Milton is not quite as unskilful.

> ... Music conducts,
> Loud organs, sackbuts, viols chime,
> Lutes, citherns, virginals, harpsichords ...
> ... Accenting, airing, curbing, ordering
> Those sweet, sweet parts Meltonus did compose,
> As wonder's self amazed was at the close,
> Which in a counterpoint maintaining *hielo*
> 'Gan all sum up thus, *Alleluiah Deo*.

The scrivener's musical activity is well documented and ambitious. He appeared in anthologies and collections with the best musicians of the day, contributed music to the psalms and to *Oriana* and composed an *In Nomine* in forty parts for which a Polish nobleman gave him a gold chain and a medal. This interests us only as an early presage of the poet's Polish and Russian interest. It is more important to us that the scrivener taught his son a love of music and a skill at it that he never forgot. The boy did not compose so far as we know, but music was his consolation throughout the years of his blindness. He was to keep an organ in his house along with other instruments, and as soon as he began the education of his nephews, who came to him as little boys, he had them chirping away like choirboys.

As for the poetry, Joshua Sylvester's translation of *The Divine Weeks and Works* of Du Bartas (1544–95) into English was an important part of the culture of the day. It has now become too tedious to be read, but Dryden as a boy paid it a more intense worship than even Spenser, and its influence can be perceived in the younger Milton's poetry. Like *The Faerie Queene*, the work was never finished. There is an appalling similarity between the talents of the poet and those of his translator; indeed, the French original struck a chord all over Europe. It was translated into Danish, Swedish, German, Spanish, Italian and Latin, but it is said to have fitted best into English. The French think Du Bartas must be better in translation than in French; Goethe predictably admired him. Sylvester (1563–1618) knew French from his schooldays, but his life was in no way easy; all he ever got by patronage was £20 a year from Prince Henry of England, and for his last five years he had to live in Germany, at Middelberg, where he died when Milton was ten.

In 'The First Day of the Week' Du Bartas begins as he will go on:

> *L'architecte du monde ordonna qu'à leur tour*
> *Le jour suivit la nuit, la nuit suivit le jour . . .*

In twenty or thirty lines he gets to the nine '*doctes pucelles*' that humans are expected to read at night. He wrote sonnets to them too, as the Nine Muses of the Pyrenees:

> Passer-by, what you see is no mountain
> But a great Briareus mounted high

To guard the pass and keep it endlessly
From Spain to France and from France to Spain . . .

As so often happens with naive writing that is bursting its boilers to
impress, it is the finest flourishes, in their tastelessness, that are the
worst. They thrilled poor Sylvester; Dryden's early work is littered
with their debris, as is Milton's; and some of them have a long
afterlife in the language. But it is best to sample Sylvester:

Now where the winter's keener breath began
To crystallize the Baltic Ocean,
To glaze the lakes and bridle up the floods,
And periwig with wool the bald-pate woods . . .

'I am much deceived now,' wrote Dryden, 'if this be not abominable
fustian.'

The velvet peach, gilt orange, downy quince
The scent-sweet apple, and astringent pear . . .
There smokes a castle, there a city fumes . . .

This is charming and amusing enough, but taken in the mass it
becomes inexpressibly tedious. It is important for John Milton,
however, because, although he claims Spenser as his original inspiration when he first decided he was going to be a poet, Sylvester was
his pole star. That makes one understand the lengthy moralizing in
Comus, the reverence he shows for his own vocation and much of his
subject matter.

We must assume that as a child Milton went to catechism classes
three times a week under Richard Stock, the Yorkshireman from
Cambridge who was the rector of All Hallows, an unlovable figure,
one of many who intended to complete the unfinished work of
reformation in the Church of England. He reproved his people for
the dust that gathered on their Bibles and he taught a strong version
of Protestantism. Until the poet was an old man, in despair of politics
and in horror of church politics, he was a loyal supporter of this grim
tendency. His private tutor and one of the strongest influences on
him was Thomas Young, a Scotsman who graduated MA from St
Leonard's College in St Andrews in 1606. Young was born in 1587
the son of the minister of Luncarty in Perthshire; his father signed a
protest against the introducing of bishops into Scotland. That conflict

went on with increasing fury and spread, until it cost Charles I his head.

Young had come to London by about 1612 in search of a living or, as he no doubt believed, as a missionary to the back-sliding, semi-reformed English. In 1622 he went to Hamburg as chaplain to the English colony there, two years after Milton, who I think was ten, had gone to school. Young taught the boy therefore between the ages of eight and twelve, being himself between thirty-one and thirty-five. Young was a passionately serious young man, by no means unambitious. Three years later he sent Milton a present of a Hebrew Bible and in March 1625 was to receive an answer full of shame at years of silence, expressing boundless gratitude to one Milton has 'always seen as his father'. Two years later he got a letter in elegiac couplets. He came home soon after and obtained the living of Stowmarket in Suffolk. We shall meet him again, since he was not a man to rest quiet or to neglect an old pupil as talented as John Milton was. For the time being it is necessary only to stress that he was an intense and well-grounded Puritan, and for John Milton the beginning of many tears.

What Thomas Young taught his pupil was probably not only the elements he should learn before going to St Paul's, but also those languages he would not acquire there. That would explain his remaining with the family for John's first two years of schooling. John learned not only Greek and Latin but Italian, French and Hebrew too. He was a determined student, and his father indulged him in the habits of book-buying and working very late at night in a room high up in the house, with a servant sitting up to wait on him if necessary. Reading the dead languages seemed at that time to be the key to getting on in the world, to elegance and superior knowledge, and to the magic world of pagan poetry and philosophy, even to salvation itself. The Protestant emphasis on Bible reading and on primitive Christianity gave Greek and Hebrew texts and Latin learning a crucial prestige which they scarcely lost until this century.

To understand the little boy's position it is necessary to keep in mind the strangeness of that age. Science as we understand it had scarcely begun, and medicine was largely a matter of the properties of herbs. John Milton's future was certain to depend on patronage, not on commerce. He was destined for the Church, and was already being prepared to attract the notice of those in whose hands patronage lay. This necessitated success and learning, in competition with his peers at school and at university.

Poetry, as it grew in importance for him, was in an unsteady, eccentric condition. At some later time Milton took against the public theatre for doctrinaire theological reasons. As he grew up the masque was dying, and so was the patronage of the court, but as a boy he was certainly conscious of the last works of Shakespeare, about whom he wrote his earliest published poem. Generally, however, the efforts of poets were scattered like minerals in a cavern. Donne as a poet in manuscript did not reach him. He knew Drayton; that is why Edward Phillipps, whose *Theatrum Poeticum* reflects his views, compares John Lane to Drayton. We know Milton had read William Browne (?1590–?1645) because there are notes in his hand in a copy of Browne's works. It is not certain that he knew Herrick or Herbert; his models as he grew were Italian, and it is therefore all the more fascinating that of all the poets under Spenser's leadership who lamented Philip Sidney, Milton should choose to imitate in *Lycidas* the poet lurking under the initials L. B., Lodowick Bryskett, Lodovico Bruschetto.

In a much earlier poem he showed close attention to Edmund Bolton, a poet obscure except for his contribution to *Englands Helicon* (1614). There indeed Milton may have encountered something like a school of English poetry, though it was a school dying when that anthology appeared. To Walton in his *Compleat Angler* it recalled the innocence of a simpler and a lost age. England was really in a state of transition in Milton's youth. His close contemporary as a poet Robert Wild (1609–79) wrote this epitaph:

> Here lies a piece of Christ; a star in dust;
> A vein of gold; a china dish that must
> Be used in heaven, when God shall feast the just.

As a prose writer his contemporary was Thomas Browne, born in London in St Michael's Cheap, close to Bread Street, in 1605, son of a merchant, who died a year before Izaak Walton. There was no settled English prose manner. Sir Henry Saville produced his magnificent Tacitus in Milton's youth, but his style was inimitable; Philemon Holland's was not taken up, nor was North's. In Ralegh's *History of the World* the style is brilliant only in the first part, while it sticks to classical eloquence, but it soon relapses into banality, whose only form is chronology. The English prose that first makes one hold one's breath with excitement is Clarendon's *History of the Rebellion* and perhaps just a little of Milton's own prose when he was an adult.

His preparation for his remarkably full career as a writer began in Latin and in verse: it is as if he had been made to run before he could walk. St Paul's School, near the Milton house, had been founded by Dr Colet for 153 pupils: the miraculous draft of fishes numbered by St John (21:11). The textbooks were Colet's *Catechism* and Erasmus's *Institutio*, and patristic writers in Latin like Lactantius (who had an interesting style), Prudentius and the recent writer of eclogues, Baptista Mantuanus, the famous Mantuan who, being unreadable, is today little read, but who was the first poet to introduce theological controversy into the Virgilian eclogue. Milton follows him without much thought in *Lycidas*. Alexander Gill senior was headmaster and his son, Alexander junior, was his usher. Milton developed a connection with this rather unattractive man, who succeeded his father in the end but lost his job through over-enthusiastic beating of the children.

Old Gill got the school in 1608. He was a Lincolnshire man who left Corpus Christi an MA in 1590. The large schoolroom had a bust of Colet and an inscription recording the foundation. It stood just at the east end of St Paul's, with an anteroom where the smallest boys were instructed. Gill's writings reveal him to have been a ripely eccentric clergyman. An attack on Norwich Anabaptists written in 1597 and printed in 1601 was followed by *Logonomia* in 1619 (second edition 1621) and *Philosophy of Holy Scripture* in 1635. The *Logonomia* is the rioting of a lonely grammarian. He treats Anglo-Saxon, which he ornaments with signs of his own invention, discusses prosody, defends English against Latin and French and speaks of 'Chaucer of unlucky omen', but his syntactic examples are from Spenser, George Wither and Daniel as well as Juvenal and Lucan. On the other hand, Gill is surely the source of Milton's lifelong preoccupation with punctuation, and his queer spelling: an observation that I think Andrew Wilson was first to make. Aubrey tells us that old Gill was a great whipper. 'He had his moods and his humours, and particularly to whipping fits. Often Dr Gill whipped Duncombe, who was afterwards a Colonel of Dragoons at Edge-Hill fight.' His son was at Trinity College, Oxford, and his father's assistant from about 1619.

When John Milton was fifteen and in his last year at Paul's, he was already a poet in Latin and in English. His Greek verse was never any good; in England no one's was. But Latin verse was both an exercise, to learn the language and achieve fluency in reading it, and something more. Excellent Latin verse of a more serious kind was written by Thomas More and has occasionally been written since in England until about 1950. Its best characteristic was always agility, and because that was hard to achieve, it was what everyone aimed at. The most agile verse was always in elegiac couplets; the hexameter in hands not skilled in the lighter metre was often too heavy. It is not surprising that the best (the only) Englishmen to be genuine poets in Latin were usually poets in English too, like Thomas Gray, George Herbert and John Milton. Since modern readers often know no Latin, I can support my opinion of his excellence as a Latin poet, and the further conjecture that his Latin verse was an essential apprenticeship to his English poetry, only by my own faltering translations and by William Cowper's posthumously published smooth and neoclassic versions. At first we cannot tell the difference between verse written as a school exercise and verse written with deeper and more personal ambition. Someone set him an exercise on getting up early and not being late for school: he seems to have attempted it in more than one form. The best version is not only acceptable and impressive as a boy's work; it touches on images and rhythms he will use again in that poem of magical lightness, 'L'Allegro'. He had decided he was going to be a poet at the age of ten, in his first year at St Paul's, an age not as unusually early as people think. It will have been then that he was introduced to the intricate mazes of Latin metre.

When he was fifteen he produced two paraphrases, or loose English verse translations, of psalms. The work will have interested him because his father wrote music for metrical psalms (1621) and because the psalms were central to Christian as well as Jewish religion. But in 1624 he did not know much Hebrew; the result is a certain baroque splutter. In Psalm 114 Sylvester is a likelier influence than Buchanan's Latin verse.

> Why fled the ocean? And why skipped the mountains?
> Why turned Jordan toward his crystal fountains?

Egypt is called 'Pharian fields', an adjective (from the Pharos of
Alexandria) coined by Sylvester; and where Sylvester has 'clear
Jordan's self . . . was fain to hide his head' Milton puts 'and sought to
hide his froth-becurled head': a fine flourish very much in Sylvester's
manner. In the other psalm (136) Milton has this charming and once
again highly Sylvestrian pair of couplets, in which admittedly Spenser
and Shakespeare himself use the same words.

> And caused the golden-tressed sun
> All the day long his course to run.
> The horned moon to shine by night
> Amongst her spangled sisters bright.

This is a pleasant exercise in English versification, and at least as able
as his elegiac verses on getting up early, surely done as a school
penalty in the same year.

The culture of school was oral; that of home was bookish: Milton
commanded both, and undoubtedly he learnt verse skills by ear as
well as by the book. The trick of dropping the first (light) syllable of
an iambic line whenever he chooses is an example. In Latin, however,
he is exquisitely correct. The elegiac couplet is a Greek metre, and it
took the Romans 300 or 400 years to learn to be faultless in it, and
light. The same shadow-footed agility could be mastered by a boy.
His head was so full of Latin verse known by heart that it was (as we
say) coming out of his ears.

> Rise up, arise, shake away your light sleeps,
> the light is eastern, spring from your hot beds,
> the cock crows wake, that winged herald is
> to the new sun and shall our task appoint . . .

It can be seen in this Latin as well as in his earliest English verse
that Milton was under the influence of Shakespeare, who died when
Milton was eight, but whose collected works came out in 1623, the
year before this earliest apprentice poetry of Milton. It must also be
noted that in his day the great mass of the old ballads, once popular
literature, had begun to disappear: Robin Hood was not one of

Milton's heroes, and he must find a substitute in the Bible or in foreign romance 'epic' poetry.

Among his contemporaries, born within three years, are William Habington from Worcester (1605), one of the most underestimated poets, Davenant from Oxford (1606), Waller (1606) and Richard Fanshawe (1608), a poet of towering talent whose works are harder to find even than Habington's; there were also such minor characters as Randolph and Cartwright, who were really only versifying wits. Milton's closest boyhood friend was Charles Diodati, who was his equal academically but perhaps not a poet. Diodati's family for two generations before him had been Italian Protestants and therefore refugees from Italy. Charles was born in 1609 and after St Paul's went on to Trinity College, Oxford. His father was a doctor, and he followed his father's profession; his grandfather and remoter kin were famous theologians at Geneva, still the centre of Calvinist theology from which Isaac Casaubon (1559–1614) had had to escape to become a classical scholar. Charles had also a cousin Elia in Paris, who was a strong supporter of Galileo, whom he visited in old age outside Florence to assure him that his cause was doing well in France. The Diodati family were international intellectuals. Did Milton's father cultivate them for their musical or their medical skills? We know only that the boys were at school together, and luckily we have some of their correspondence, Milton's Latin verse and Diodati's rather accomplished Greek letters: the high-minded records of a genuine friendship.

Unfortunately Diodati's letters in Greek are not dated. He went up to Trinity in 1623 and matriculated on 7 February (BA December 1625, MA July 1628). Milton went to Cambridge only in 1625, matriculating on 9 April. The first elegy to Diodati is addressed to him somewhere near Chester 'on the western bank of the Dee', from Milton in Bread Street. He is already a Cambridge undergraduate; this is no longer a school exercise but a serious attempt at Latin poetry. About the same time, in the winter of 1625, his poem 'On the Death of a Fair Infant Dying of a Cough' was dated in his old age 'Anno aetatis 17', between December 1625 and 1626, though unluckily there has been some confusion over this. As a boy's poem it is a *tour de force* and the first evidence that Milton will be a great poet. The elegy to his friend Diodati offers at least supporting evidence for the same high estimate. Until the age of seventeen Milton had been a schoolboy of a startling brilliance but perhaps no more. But from his earliest days at Cambridge he was, and knew himself to be, a serious contender for an international crown as a poet. He intended to be a successor to Tasso as well as to Shakespeare: he had formed that ambition as a schoolboy.

CHAPTER TWO

CAMBRIDGE

THE CAMBRIDGE THAT MILTON first saw at seventeen was an astonishing spectacle: its medieval and sixteenth-century monuments stood grandly in their places in what was rather a village than a town. The university was like some great public school of twenty houses, each with a chapel of its own; the pupils were younger than they would be today; and grammar schools like St Paul's were like primary or preparatory schools in comparison. Braithwaite tells us that Cambridge's 'Grounds, greens, groves are wet and homely,/But the Schollers wondrous comely.' Milton's college was Christ's, founded in 1442 to teach its pupils grammar; it was moved by Henry VI to make way for King's College chapel and given money, a less enviable position and a new charter in 1505 by Lady Margaret Beaufort, the mother of Henry VII, who left a huge and impressive coat of arms on the front gate, much like the one at St John's, which she also founded. Little else in Christ's College looks quite as hoary and antique today as it did in 1625, but a window or two in the Hall and the Master's Lodge and here and there an old fireplace still gently insinuate the original atmosphere. In the chapel only the vast and ancient brass lectern, with its gloomy brass eagle and its four Beaufort greyhounds, seems to say something about early Protestantism, though in fact the chapel is pre-Reformation, and the stained glass in the north windows is fifteenth-century. The Fellows' Building was not built until just before the Civil War, nearly a hundred years after Serlio's *Libro Estraordinario* had introduced Italian tricks to Europe: this pretty construction suggests the age of Inigo Jones, though it was begun only in 1640. Pevsner calls it the boldest building in England of the mid-century, and it certainly has a neat bravura which was an ideal of Milton's generation, a generation that rather looked forward to the days of Wren than backwards to the jumble of the past.

The Master of Christ's was Dr Thomas Bainbrigge, who was, as the antiquary Thomas Baker (1658–1740) assures us, 'a severe governor'. Baker, a non-juror from Durham ejected from his fellowship at St John's, maintains that Bainbrigge rusticated Milton, so that Milton's prospective fellowship went to someone else by royal mandate; that is, to Edward King for whom Milton wrote *Lycidas*: 'a circumstance, as is supposed, together with his expulsion, that disgusted him against the King, clergy and universities'. Baker collected forty-two folio volumes in manuscript towards an *Athenae Cantabrigenses* that he never finished: half of it is now in the British Library and half in Cambridge University Library. But this story, although it pulls everything together, falls down at several points: it ignores the prose writings that Milton published in his own defence, makes havoc of dates and too obviously imputes to Milton Baker's own feelings about St John's. He was not an eyewitness of Milton's Cambridge career, since it was over twenty-five years before he was born, and the Civil War and, still more, the Restoration had disrupted people's memories.

The grandest old Fellow of Christ's, Paul Baynes, was a Puritan preacher sufficiently fierce to be deprived of a lectureship at St Andrew's church. His later career was happy and successful enough all the same, and he was a frequent and famous visitor to the Puritan gentry until his death in 1617. Bainbrigge ruled as Master from 1620 on, and the Fellows were Power, Siddall, Chappell, Meade, Knowsley, Honeywood, Cook, Tovey, Scott, Gell, Alsop, Simonds and Sandilands. Honeywood died in 1681 as Dean of Lincoln, where he left a fine library, Gell in 1665 as rector of a City parish: his *Remains* were edited in 1676 and turn out to include astrology, apocalyptic sermons, allegories and 'mystical notions'. He appears to have gone quietly batty. Meade did mathematics, philosophy and chronology. He was swarthy and well built, with 'a fat eye full quick and sparkling'. He suffered from a stammer, but 'in private discourse sometimes smiled out his stammering into silence'. In 1626 and again in 1630 he refused the provostship of Trinity College, Dublin. He died in 1638, but until that year he is the best spy into college affairs that we have. Andrew Downes was the Professor of Greek, who called the ancient Greeks 'but hirelings and triobulary rhetoricians'. George Herbert had been the Cambridge Public Orator (1618–19), though now he was gone. Edmund Waller was at King's, Thomas Randolph at Trinity.

Milton's tutor William Chappell was born in 1582, which makes him four years older than Meade; in 1615 he disputed in a showpiece argument before James I, apparently with credit. There is some question of his being an Arminian: that is, an opponent of Calvin, an ally of the Catholics and of Laud. Arminius was the Latin name of a Dutchman called Harmensen who died about the time Milton was born and whose doctrine was condemned at Dort (1618–20): in England it was a theological tendency, popular in Laud's time, rather than a dogmatic system: later in the century there were what were called Arminianizers, but nothing could be found then as precise as an Arminian. (When John Selden was asked by a country gentleman, probably in the late 1630s, what the Arminians held, Selden answered that they held most of the best bishoprics and deaneries in England.) Laud made Chappell Dean of Cashel in 1633, Provost of Trinity and then Bishop of Cork and Cloyne. He left Ireland in 1641 and died at Derby in 1649 after some sufferings in the Civil War. If Milton was ever whipped as a boy at Christ's, as Aubrey conjectured, then it was surely done by Chappell as his tutor.

They certainly quarrelled, and Milton took the extreme step of changing tutors. He moved to Nathaniel Tovey, who had been an orphan adopted by the Lucy Bedford whom John Donne loved; by birth he was the son of a Coventry grammar-school master. (In 1621, Milton's twelfth year, John Donne had just begun the last ten years of his life, at the age of forty-eight, as Dean of St Paul's, but there is no evidence that Milton ever heard him preach or noticed him.) In 1637 Tovey resigned from Christ's, but he was ejected from his parish by the extreme Protestants in 1647; the Earl of Rutland gave him Ayleston in 1656, and there he and his wife died two years later.

Milton prospered well enough under his new tutor. He did not take to theology or to theologians, and his immoderate enthusiasm for the logic of Ramus, which was the new fashion at Cambridge, probably represents a rebellion against the official teaching, which was scholastic, charmingly childish and deadly boring. On 26 March 1625, Milton wrote to Thomas Young from London to thank him for the Hebrew Bible. He apologized for his three years of silence, and remarked that he was not at the moment fenced in by his usual rampart of books. Presumably the carter had taken them to

Cambridge. Next day, King James died, and on 9 April John Milton was matriculated, which means he was formally admitted to the university. Christ's presented Tom Aldridge and Richard Earle, fellow commoners John Milton, Robert Bell and Robert Pory as normal undergraduates and two sizars, Edmund Barwell and Richard Britten, who would work their way through college.

Terms lasted from 10 October to 16 December, from 13 January to the third Friday before Easter and from eleven days after Easter to about 10 July. Hobson the London carrier used to travel to Cambridge from the Bell in Bishopsgate, with an eight-horse wain: he was a maltster and an inn-keeper, with forty horses and bridles, whips and boots for hire. In college, the chapel bell rang at five in the morning, dinner was at twelve and supper at seven, and the college gates shut at nine in winter and ten in summer. Punishment took place, at least in Trinity, in hall on Thursdays every week at seven in the evening. The BA, which was enough for most people, was obtained by scholastic exercises based on Aristotle's *Posterior Analytics*: it took four years from matriculation, a period during which Milton, having started late at sixteen, would attain maturity. Three more years would take him to the MA and another five to a doctorate. But Cambridge was preoccupied with religion, not with real learning, and probably a majority of its students aimed at theology as a profession. They distressed and disgusted Milton, a very serious boy who preferred Puritan ministers to the jollier and more tolerant country clergy being bred up at Cambridge.

On the day of the King's funeral, 7 May, the university presented Latin and Greek verses of lamentation, which were really brief epigrams. The custom of printing them (in competition with Oxford and in the hope of attracting patronage) went back to the funeral of Sir Philip Sidney. On the day of the King's burial, the Provost of King's College preached in the morning and Mr Thorndike, the deputy Orator, in the afternoon: but at Christ's there was a fuss about the allotment of rooms and beds. Sir Martin Stuteville's son had come to be tutored by Meade, and he might have to share a room, which shameful situation led Meade to deep machinations. Milton's 'rooms' were known, 'traditionally' at least, as late as Wordsworth, but we do not really know where he was lodged. Charles, the new King, got married by proxy in Paris in May, and arrived there halfway through

June to collect his wife, in whom ran the blood of the Sforza family. This provoked another salvo of courtly verses in dead languages. But in London there was plague, and it got to Cambridge: in September no eels, no rooks and nothing from Ely were to be eaten. Meade wrote how 'All our market today could not supply our commons for tonight. I am steward and am fain to appoint eggs, applepies and custards for want of other fare'. There was plague also in Oxford; the King dissolved Parliament; and the Cambridge Vice-Chancellor issued a decree against bedmakers, nurses and laundresses. That autumn 35,000 people died in London.

Parliament was to meet in February 1626, and at that time King Charles wrote to Lord Suffolk, the Cambridge Chancellor, an appeal which that elderly peer duly passed on to all heads of house in Cambridge, to 'bring home that long banished pilgrim discipline'. In May, Suffolk died and the King wanted the Duke of Buckingham to succeed him; Cambridge, in a panic, said they wanted Suffolk's son, Lord Berkshire. The Duke's secretary arrived there with Bishop Laud to organize Buckingham's election, so that 'divers got hackneys and fled'. The Duke got in, by 108 votes to 102: among the doctors only Dr Porter of Queens' dared oppose him. There was a tumult of bad feeling, and in June Charles dissolved Parliament. (If, as I much doubt, Milton was ever whipped, it was now. The suggestion is made by Aubrey, who writes gossipy hearsay, with no good source for this period in Milton's life.)

Certainly terrible things had become usual in England. Selden remarks on the ordinary and quite illegal use of torture. In 1614 Bartholomew Legate of Essex was burnt at the stake at Smithfield in London, and another victim at Burton-on-Trent. Abroad the Thirty Years War had started 1620 with wolfish behaviour, and Vorstius, said to have been an Arian, had succeeded to the chair of Arminius at Leyden, to the apoplectic fury of James I. Where resistance was commonest, repression was most savage. The headmaster of West-minster was sentenced to have his ears nailed to the pillory in which he was to stand in Dean's Yard. Luckily the excitement of the crowd was so great he got clean away. Alexander Gill the younger was threatened with the loss of his ears for a drunken and seditious conversation at Trinity College, Oxford, where he was visiting, about Felton, the Duke of Buckingham's assassin. There is no doubt that

Laud, once in power, tried to organize the persecution of Puritans and Anabaptists. Bishop Wren, the uncle of the great architect, was sent to Norwich, where his manuscript notes have survived and suggest an inquisition. Milton was as seriously disturbed by what was going on as one would expect.

The poem 'On the Death of a Fair Infant Dying of a Cough' is passionately unorthodox, as well as extraordinarily beautiful. Milton's metre is close to several that had been used by Giles Fletcher and by Spenser and coincides exactly with that of Spenser's 'Hymn of Heavenly Love' (one of the *Four Hymns*, 1596). Its images, which mix classical allusions with Christian presuppositions quite gleefully, are often astoundingly bold. The last two lines of the poem make it clear that the dead child's mother was Milton's own mother (*TLS*, March 1983). Edward Phillipps thought it was meant for his mother, Milton's sister, but the sister's baby died when Milton was nineteen, and he claims in the title that he wrote it at seventeen. There is really no need whatever for the poem to be about a baby dying at the time the poem was written, and if, as I think, the last two lines prophesy the birth of John Milton (there is a parallel in a poem in Latin to his father), then it refers to the child buried in 1601, his mother's first-born. It deliberately sets out to comfort her with the unimportance of baptism for salvation, a view utterly opposed to the Thirty-nine Articles, and still hotly disputed when I was a theological student in the early 1960s. Milton takes the liberal side. He ends with the splendid boast,

> Think what a present thou to God hast sent,
> And render him with patience what he lent;
>   This if thou do he will an offspring give,
> That till the world's last end shall make thy name to live.

The poem was not printed until 1673, whether because by then Milton had forgotten the close dependence of a few lines on Edmund Bolton or because of its unorthodoxy in which he had not wanted to implicate his mother, I do not know. There are eleven seven-line stanzas.

> O fairest flower no sooner blown but blasted,
> Soft silken primrose fading timelessly,
> Summer's chief honour if thou hadst outlasted

Bleak winter's force that made thy blossom dry;
For he being amorous on that lovely dye
   That did thy cheek envermeil, thought to kiss
But killed alas, and then bewailed his fatal bliss. . . .

So mounting up in icy-pearled car,
Through middle empire of the freezing air
He wandered long, till thee he spied from far,
There ended was his quest, there ceased his care,
Down he descended from his snow-soft chair,
   But all unwares with his cold-kind embrace
Unhoused thy virgin soul from her fair biding-place. . . .

Wert thou some star which from the ruined roof
Of shaked Olympus by mischance didst fall;
Which careful Jove in nature's true behoof
Took up, and in fit place did reinstall? . . .

Or wert thou of the golden-winged host,
Who having clad thyself in human weed
To earth from thy prefixed seat didst post,
And after short abode fly back with speed,
As if to show what creatures heaven doth breed,
   Thereby to set the hearts of men on fire
To scorn the sordid world, and unto heaven aspire? . . .

Then thou the mother of so sweet a child
Her false imagined loss cease to lament . . .

The Latin poem to Diodati may be less moving but it is no less affectionate. (The translation is mine.)

> . . . I will not go back to the reedy Cam,
> will not regret my rooms, forbidden now,
> those naked fields refusing soft shadows
> a place not suiting to Apollo's sons.
> I will not bear with a harsh monster's threats
> and what else my brain will not entertain.
> So if my father's hearth is my exile
> and leisure without care lived pleasantly,
> I will accept to be a wanderer
> and will enjoy my exile in delight.
> I wish the weeping exile of Tomi

> never had anything harder to bear:
> he would not have yielded to Homer then
> nor would you, Virgil, have won greater praise.

The compliment to Ovid at Tomi is unexpected, and the comparative criticism, all but preferring Ovid to Homer or Virgil, is extraordinary, though it shows what kind of poet Milton as a boy had wanted to be. I quote these lines not as the best in the long poem, but to show how clear and candid he is and how he differs from the scholar-wits. He must have sat down to write this long address to his friend in full consciousness of the two whale-spouts of verses that had greeted the death of James and the marriage of Charles the year before. This poem goes on:

> Now time is free to give the pleasant Muses,
> and books which are my life enrapture me.

From this he lapses into a description of theatres and plays, which sound entirely like Plautus and Terence: 'the girl who knows not love, unknowing loves ...', he adds some tragedy which recalls Seneca. He speaks of 'the grove of elms, the noble suburb shade' that he frequents, meaning perhaps no more than Lincoln's Inn Fields or Moorfields. He suggests companies of girls, 'stars that breathe soft fire', and one in particular who might make old Jove young again.

> ... First prize of glory goes to English girls,
> you foreigners be glad to come second.
> City of London, Trojan colony,
> raising your towering head high to be seen,
> you are happy to hold within your walls
> all that is beautiful of the swinging globe;
> those stars that glitter in your calm heaven
> that minister to the goddess of the moon
> are not so many as your lovely girls
> that pass about your streets ...

This is an unusual tone for Milton to take, and it may be he had felt starved of girls at Cambridge, but it is part and parcel of him: it is how he saw himself. The sneering nickname 'the lady of Christ's' is likely to come from outside his college, whether because of his beauty in extreme youth or because he scorned the student wits (all the dirt of the Restoration without any of the wit) we do not know. No weight should be attached to it. For the grotesque to give place to the erotic is normal development. For religion to intervene is equally normal.

In October 1626 he wrote some Latin lyrics on the death of old Dr Felton, Master of Pembroke and Bishop of Ely. They are jolly and striking, but no more: all one can say about them is that their liveliness, which is quite credible in young Milton, would be incredible in any contemporary or senior Latinist. Then there was Dr Gostlin, the Vice-Chancellor of Cambridge and Professor of Medicine, who died at the same time. For him Milton composed a forty-eight-line poem in Horatian stanza form. There is a certain absence of earnestness about it which, while it beguiles and pleases, makes against the apparent purpose of the exercise. Once again, it is becoming difficult to tell his poems from his exercises. This poem has in it a myth of elaborate obscurity, dredged up from Quintus of Smyrna's flat Greek or from the dull recesses of Stephanus's dictionary: yet it works very well. Dr Gostlin has to die because his cures empty the Underworld. The worst lines in this poem are about flowers, a list of 'roses and marigolds and hyacinth with purple face' that is conventional enough, and recurs in *Comus* (849), and in *Lycidas*, but always in lines that he had the good taste to cancel.

Again in the same few weeks, Milton wrote twenty-four lines of elegiac verses for Richard Ridding, the university beadle and mace-bearer whose will was proved in November. He was 'whiter haired than that bird as with Jove sinned'; Death, the last great beadle, has hurried him away. Then suddenly comes a couplet which is like a translation of Shakespeare:

> So in the court of Troy wing-footed stood
> the herald Mercury, then newly lighted
> down from his father's court in upper air.
> . . . O thou great queen of graves, hell's satellite,
> fierce to the Muses and Athene's people,
> take those who uselessly burden the earth,
> who in their thousands cry out for your darts . . .

The prayer was addressed to Hecate, and the entire poem was classical with no Christian overtones. It was possible to write in such a way only about a servant, just as the portraits of jesters and servants, which were beginning to exist at this time, admitted caricature to art, to the vast enrichment of later generations. Milton did write some lines akin to those verses I have castigated and did so, I suppose, because of the example of great men and because he thought it fun as a youth. He addresses Guy Fawkes, wondering if he intended an act of mercy, whirling his victims up into the skies as Elijah was whirled. He wishes Rome to give her monks a heavenward push in the same way; this grotesque thought recurs in *Paradise Lost*. King James, says Milton, nearly suffered the same fate, as a penalty for jokes about Purgatory. He reveals an inexhaustible fund of these uneasy and unwitty witticisms. There is an epigram on the inventor of gunpowder and a long poem of 226 lines of Latin hexameter verse about the Fifth of November. It is almost unreadable, but I have read it and found in it the bee-buzzing noise of Pandemonium in *Paradise Lost*. Abstractly viewed, the poem is not as bad as it might be: the fact is that the grotesque has an attraction for Milton in his first or second year at Christ's. There is a liveliness of enjoyment about him. The story of the poem is, of course, preposterous and worse than the daftest of allegorical paintings, with which it may profitably be compared.

After this a return to elegiacs comes as a relief. What is extremely curious is that Milton, who in English verse was nearly faultless from the beginning, put himself through a tough apprenticeship as a Latin poet. I can only suppose that he wanted to be internationally renowned as a poet and thought that would still be possible for a writer in Latin, like the writers of the Italian Renaissance from Petrarch through Sannazaro to Mantuan. No such reputation was made in his time, as things turned out, nor had it been made perhaps since the early sixteenth century. For better or worse, every nation had by now begun to be conscious of its own language and its own poetry. The elegy on the death of Lancelot Andrewes, the Bishop of Winchester, was written late in 1626, but the death of the Bishop of Ely crowded on its heels, and Ely's poem refers to Winchester. A lot of these Latin poems are hard to date. He labelled them all as having been written at seventeen, which may mean when he was seventeen or in his seventeenth year. Those on people's deaths can be fixed within a few months after that date, in this case 25 September 1626.

It is a spirited set of verses, about ghosts and visions and Death shaking the marble palaces of princes, ending with a serene dawn in the rich gardens of the sun on the Ganges.

> Sudden by me Winchester's Bishop stands,
> the light of stars was shining from his face;
> his vesture white flowed to his golden feet
> a white fillet circled his godlike head.
> As the old man went cloaked in reverence
> earth's flowers trembled at the happy sound.
> Heaven's ranks applauded then with spotted wings
> and the pure trumpet sounded in heaven.
> . . . the winged squadrons laid fingers on their harps,
> and my golden quiet fled with the dark.

The old Bishop dressed like a Druid does not portend well for Milton's relations with bishops; indeed, it is noticeable that all these commemorations of the dead were not addressed to living patrons. Probably by now the poet had given up all prospect of life in the clergy, as he soon would of college life. But this scene of reception into Heaven is daring in detail as well as in conception. The angel's wings are jewelled, that is, spotted with colour, and is it the Bishop's feet or his sandals or his boots that are gold? The gardens of the sun (called Lucifer) seem to derive from Claudian of all people. It is still more curious that in line 22 Milton invented a line just like the one in Ovid that fascinated Tennyson all his life, *miretur lapsus praetereuntis aquae*: Ovid has *desilientis aquae*. How much of this poem is pure fantasy, mere performance? The vision is carefully dressed up as a dream, and I do not suppose John Milton really wept for that old fraud Bishop Andrewes. This is a conventional compliment brilliantly, even dazzlingly, executed. The only living poet it recalls is Gongora: in him and in Milton the Renaissance, which had died at its centre like a rose bush, flowered at its extremest points.

Thomas Young got a long elegy, equally able but less amusing, in the spring of 1627. He was still in Hamburg, though in 1628 he came home to the rich living of St Peter and St Mary, Stowmarket. His entry into public controversy as the sternest of Puritans came in 1639 with a work on Sabbath observance called *Dies Dominica*. Milton's formal and decorous poem marks their relationship: he was showing off to his childhood tutor and expressing a loyalty to the extremes of

Puritanism. His proud display of knowledge, of the yellow sands of the German coast and Hama, the founder of Hamburg, whose brains were dashed out with a Danish club, is dredged out of Stephanus. His tutor is likened to Amyntor's son, Phoenix, and the nymph Philyra's son, Chiron the centaur, the tutors of Achilles.

> Through the Aonian glens I was the first
> to follow him and by the sacred lawns
> of the twin peaks I drank Pierian springs,
> and by favour of Clio I three times
> sprinkled my glad mouth with Castalian wine.
> But three times Aethon saw the Sign of the Ram
> and put new gold upon her snowy back,
> twice Chloris scattered new grass on old Earth
> and twice the south wind bore your wealth away . . .

The boast of being the first is taken from Virgil: Milton is just the first pupil. Aethon was one of the horses of the sun, Chloris is the goddess of green things. The south wind 'bore your wealth away' may refer to the rich shipping of Hamburg, but if one reads *suas* for *tuas*, then it would mean the wealth of Chloris, when the south wind withers up the grass. Castalian wine, where water is normal, is Milton's invention; it may possibly derive from something in Plutarch on the dying away of oracles, which he certainly read and uses in the ode 'On the Morning of Christ's Nativity'. It is of some interest that he refers to England as Young's country. The end of the poem is about the wars of religion in Europe, which he views with horror. They had an important connection with the English Civil War, as this poem suggests and as Defoe's *Memoirs of a Cavalier* (one of Winston Churchill's favourite books) fully demonstrates.

> . . . Lonely and poor upon an unknown ground:
> and on a foreign coast and destitute
> you seek the wealth your father's hearth denied.
> Hard fatherland, wilder than your white rocks
> the waves that foam and batter at your shore . . .

Hamburg is transformed to the lonely sands where Palinurus was flung ashore in the *Aeneid*, and there is some suggestion in these and the following verses of the drift of Puritans to Holland and Germany and New England. But the reference is vague, as is the comfort he offers: Elijah, Paul, Jesus of fishy Gergessa and the biblical victories of God over Sennacherib and Ben-hadad in the second book of Kings. The verses are well turned and becoming to a young scholar. They even contain a line, *Cornea pulvureum dum verberat ungula campum*, to rival Virgil's thunderous hoof-beat, but they are not poetry. Only his most personal Latin poems are that.

His Latin verse 'On Nature Does Not Age' appears to refer to George Hakewill's *Apology of the Power and Providence of God* (1627), which conveyed in its second edition (1630) an account of an operation for phlebotomy carried out by Theodore Diodati, the father of Milton's friend. But this conjecture does not provide a date: the poem was published in 1645. Milton's secular version of the ultimate fire, which is Virgilian and Lucretian in phrasing, is a powerful and convincing bit of genuine poetry. Otherwise the poem is impressively old-fashioned, no more than that. It contains the astonishing doctrine of the spheres of Heaven to which learned men clung long after astronomy had rendered it obsolete: but one would not learn the new science at Christ's College.

> So all things keep to their eternal path.
> So daily slides the world's first circle on
> and heaves the heavens enclosed and balancing;
> Saturn is not slowed, Mars in crested helmet
> glitters his lightnings keenly as ever.
> Flowering Phoebus shines for ever young
> he does not glide downhill to heat tired earth
> but runs with friendly light through circling signs;
> the star that summons in his airy flock
> Olympus whitening and at evening
> takes them out to the grazing fields of heaven
> from the spiced Indies rises beautiful . . .

That was how Milton saw, or how he imagined, the universe at that time. His Latin verses 'On the Platonic Idea' are surely an exercise, an attack on Platonic Ideas for use, apparently, by a fellow of Christ's in a formal university debate at the end of the academic year 1627–8, which he refers to in a letter to Alexander Gill junior on 2 July. There are thirty-nine verses with allusions of gleeful or giggling obscurity, the thrice-great Hermes, 'the Assyrian priest' Hurombalus, Philo of

Byblos and, by implication, Sanchuniathon. These queer persons were known to the great and learned lawyer Selden, whom therefore by the summer of 1628 Milton knew or would have desired to know. The verses were printed on a fly-sheet that nobody bothered to keep, then again in 1645.

That summer came another elegy.

> Spring, and the light on the house roof brought Mayday
> but my eyes still sought night that fled away
> and could not stand the shining of morning.
> Cupid with painted wings stood by my bed,
> the shaking of his quiver betrayed him . . .

The elegy is an extremely general love poem in which nothing really happens, though we may be sure it was communicated to Charles Diodati. 'A Vacation Exercise', perhaps of August 1628, goes with it, which is an academic exercise on the theme 'Playful exercises are not always contrary to philosophy'. There is a prelude in elaborate and, at this date, boring Latin prose to go with it. Milton has been reading the *Corpus Hermeticum*, a collection of gnostic, that is to say, mystical and allegorical documents, a work of great curiosity, value and sometimes beauty, easier to find in our day than in his own, yet less read. Milton's verse speech is exactly 100 lines long and is dry and boring in exactly the manner of his Latin exercises, unlike his personal poems, whether in Latin or in English, which breathe a certain passion.

> . . . How he before the thunderous throne doth lie,
> Listening to what unshorn Apollo sings
> To the touch of golden wires, while Hebe brings
> Immortal nectar to her kingly sire:
> Then passing through the spheres of watchful fire,
> And misty regions of wide air next under
> And hills of snow and lofts of piled thunder . . .

The lack of internal momentum in these lines, the couplet form and the jejune touches of boldness recall the huge influence of Sylvester's translation of Du Bartas on this generation. One may also note that the only intellectual movement Milton was fitted to join after his Cambridge education was that of the Cambridge Platonists, for which

he was some five years too early. At this stage he was nearly twenty
and just coming into flower as a poet, writing in Italian as well as
Latin, and writing sonnets. 'On the Morning of Christ's Nativity'
belongs to the Christmas morning of 1629, when he was just twenty-
one. Many of the dates of his poems so far have been disputed, but in
adopting those adopted by John Carey after many rereadings and a
few wobbles of opinion, I believe I follow the most careful and reliable
order in which they can be put. Even the 1645 edition does not follow
the exact order of composition.

In Milton's third year at Cambridge Christopher Bainbrigge, the
Master's son, and Roger and Edward King, sons of John King, aged
sixteen and fourteen, born in Dublin and at Boyle, Connaught,
entered the college in October 1626 as lesser pensioners under Mr
Chappell. Chaucer was having a revival, at least at Christ's; he entered
into Milton's verses for Bonfire Day, and in February 1627 Meade
sent a Chaucer to Sir Martin that cost thirteen shillings and fourpence.
Alas, we know what Milton and his nephew thought of Chaucer. The
Master and tutors were intriguing busily about rooms for the Master's
kin and who was to tutor whom. The Master was by statute the judge
of his own powers and their limitation. In 1627 George Herbert (long
absent) formally resigned his Cambridge post. In March Buckingham
installed himself as Chancellor and incorporated Laud as a member
of the university. 'If a man did but stir his hat, he should not lose his
labour,' wrote Meade. At Clare Hall library, the Duke said, 'Mr
Doctor, you have here a fine library, but here are two books not very
well bound.' In May the Master quarrelled with Power over his pupil
Justinian Isham, son of Sir John of Northamptonshire: Power was
called a 'Jesuit' and in 1643 was ejected and mobbed. In September
1627 John Cleveland the poet arrived, fourteen years old and the son
of a Leicestershire vicar. At Shrovetide 1628, the King was expected
from Newmarket, and Bainbrigge was Vice-Chancellor. Payments
included ten shillings for a professional jester and special wages to
ushers, pages, grooms and trumpeters. It was the year Parliament
settled on a Petition of Right and the year Thomas Young got the
living at Stowmarket, where the advowson (the right to present)
belonged to James Howecloth, a cousin of John Hampden.

In August Buckingham was assassinated at Portsmouth at the age
of thirty-six. Young Gill's conversation at Trinity, in which he

proposed Felton's (the Duke's assassin) health, took place, and his own arrest followed rapidly. A certain 'Mr Diodat' was obscurely mentioned in the enquiry. Those definitely present were William Pickering, Powell of Hart Hall, Craven of Trinity and a new fellow aged twenty-six, William Chillingworth (who arrived late). This was the formidable theologian, the friend of Lord Falkland and of Hyde, later Lord Clarendon. He was also Laud's godson and his spy in Oxford and therefore, surely, the informer against Gill, who was sentenced to have his ears cut off but later reprieved. Chillingworth (1602–44) merits closer attention if only because he was so sharp a reasoner, accused of infidelity and through his book *The Religion of Protestants a Safe Way to Salvation* very close to Milton, who naturally (given the episode of Gill's ears) never mentions him. But the position Chillingworth took was exactly Milton's: that the Bible was the only acceptable authority for Protestants and that every man had a right to reason about that on his own. It was only in June of that year that Chillingworth was elected at Trinity; when the war came he followed the King and his friends, so he died a prisoner in the bishop's house at Chichester in 1644, soon after the siege of Arundel. Gill was taken by pursuivants at Paul's and imprisoned in the Gatehouse, Westminster. Pickering was searched for. Gill's name was put to some verses against the King by one William Grinkin, MA, of Jesus College.

> And now great God I humbly pray
> That thou wouldst take that slime away
> That keeps my Sovereign's eyes from seeing
> Those things that will be our undoing.
> . . . And then no doubt his royal nose
> Will quickly smell these rascals' savours
> Whose blacky deeds eclipse his favours.

No doubt this piece of tomfoolery is typical of what circulated in manuscript, but it is shockingly bad. Yet compare it with the loyal Latin verses on the King's pimples, the Cambridge *Anthologia in Regis Exanthemata*, on the King's recovery from smallpox (1631).

> Why palest thou Pest? Pustule why swellest thou? . . .
> Grows Death fastidious of plebeian gut?
> And seeks she now a rarer meat to cut?

Crashaw wrote that Apollo had returned 'And his true face, for there his purple lives/And runs as lover in commingling snows'. As Booth of Corpus put it,

> The Muse erupted where the Doctor's been
> In clouds of pimples on the august skin,
> And every pustule has a poet now . . .

The dull levity of these verses, and the ostentatious and idiotic wit, were the sort of thing which had a seriously bad effect on poetry that Dr Johnson never noticed. More precisely, it influenced the young Dryden as a boy at Westminster under Busby, writing on the death of Lord Hastings.

Charles Diodati had been an Oxford MA since July 1628. In March 1629 John Milton became a BA at Cambridge, and that same year Diodati was incorporated at Cambridge, as was the normal procedure. That year Rubens got an honorary degree, and the formal disputes were 'The Rational soul is a new creation', 'Streams come from the sea' and on hereditary versus elective monarchy. The university presented some terrible plays: we have, for example, *Fraus Honesta* by Philip Stubbe of Trinity (1616, revived 1628, ed. 1632), with a final Latin chorus, 'Heigh cuckold, Whup cuckold, let's go to bed'. It calls to mind Milton's furious remark in 1642 about

> young divines, writhing and unboning their clergy limbs to all the antic and dishonest gestures of Trinculoes, buffoons and bawds, prostituting the shame of that Ministry which either they had or were nigh having, to the eyes of courtiers and court ladies . . . There while they acted and over-acted, I was a spectator: they thought themselves gallant men and I thought them fools . . . they mispronounced, and I misliked.

After the comedies the visitors went on to Christ's and heard an oration by Cleveland, which is printed in his works (1677), so Milton was not the only young man to value his university exercises.

In the spring of 1629, when he was still an undergraduate, Milton had written an enchanting set of 140 lines of elegiac Latin verse 'On the Coming of Spring'. 'He speaks holiday, he writes verses . . .' They are intensely reminiscent of Shakespearian spring poetry, though they begin pedantically.

> Time turning in his everlasting spire
> calls back fresh west winds as the spring heat comes,
> earth is restored and puts on her brief youth
> and free of ice the ground is green and sweet.
> And surely power comes back to my songs,
> and it is spring has brought me intellect.

He was a mere boy of twenty, a student getting ready for an examination. Later in life his inspiration famously flowed only in the winter, from equinox to equinox. Now, it led him to no goal the university recognized: he was a visionary and his inspiration was pagan.

> ... Now Philomel hidden in the fresh leaf
> you teach your tunes, and all the grove is quiet.
> I in the city, you among the woods,
> let us together sing and tell of spring ...

The Latin is not perfectly correct, but in all Milton's poetry I have never noticed more than three or four slips in scansion, and those are easily corrected. The poetry is pouring out of him, and he is as passionate and apparently facile as the nightingale itself.

> ... Maybe some shepherd stretching on his rock
> while dewy earth reddens in the dawn light
> cries out, Phoebus you had no girl tonight
> delaying your swift horses ...
> Phoebus, the easy loves cry out courage,
> and the West wind smelling of cinnamon
> claps his light wings, and birds utter goodwill ...

Milton is promoting the Sun's love affair with the Earth

> Jove sports on high Olympus with his wife,
> and calls the servant gods to feast with him,
> now draws dark twilight on, and the Satyrs
> circle the flowering meadows in swift dance,
> Sylvanus crowned with his old cypress crown
> and the goat-god dancing with the god of goats ...

The imitation of Ovid reaches a climax in that last line, which echoes *semibovesque dei semideique boves*, substituting goats for cattle, and arguably improving on what was famously Ovid's best line or his worst: but one should not miss Milton's charming tendency to bring his gods down to earth in English weather (red in the morning) and English fields where the satyrs have become shadowy, transforming themselves into elves.

Somewhere about this time he wrote his first sonnet. To do that he put himself to school under Italian masters. His copy of Giovanni della Casa's *Rime e Prose* (1563) was bought in December 1629; it is full of marginal notes and corrections, and he has copied into it a sonnet from the 1623 edition; this book is now in the New York Public Library. He would study a poet, suck his marrow and move on. We do not always know what he has been reading, so della Casa's book is a bonus. He was, as Carey points out, a follower of Bembo, pleased with intricacy, keen on the startling inversions and syntactic complexities that are to be found in the school of Donne, perhaps from the same influence. In a sense these chiming and cross-chiming rhythms, with the screwing up of sense they demand, are the end of the sonnet form. In England the old, innocent and simple sonnet had gone out of fashion: it survived mostly in women's poetry and in periodicals and albums until innocence came back into fashion, in Bowles and in Wordsworth. Milton's sonnets do not follow Shakespeare's in their metrical scheme: it is possible he had never read them. Tasso was his guiding star.

His first sonnet, as we suppose, because of its closeness to his elegiac verses on the coming of spring, is an imitation of Bembo: *O rossignuol che in queste verdi fronde* . . . (*Rime* 45, Venice, 1564), but it is written with an assurance and perfection of footfall.

> O nightingale, that on yon bloomy spray
> Warblest at eve, when all the woods are still, . . .
> Thy liquid notes that close the eye of day,
> First heard before the shallow cuckoo's bill
> Portend success in love; . . .
> Whether the Muse, or Love call thee his mate,
> Both them I serve, and of their train am I.

The voice is closer to Spenser than Shakespeare, and the poem has perhaps a certain emptiness about it which belongs more usually to an earlier period than Milton's own. The transformation into English is so successful that one is dumbfounded to think it is part of that

Italian culture he inherited from his father. By that same autumn of 1629 he was writing his own sonnets in Italian. As love poetry they are false, and in style they look to us affected, but as performances they are astonishing. At this stage of his life one is not certain when or whether he will settle down to be a great poet in English, but he appears to have an infinite facility in all languages except Greek. The best of his Italian poems is one he vaguely christens a *canzone*, in which girls and boys in love crowd round to ask him why he writes in a strange language.

> There are other rivers, other streams for you
> where the reward, the lasting crown of leaves,
> is sprouting for your head . . .

He replies that his lady has proclaimed it to be the language on which love prides itself. It is a curious fantasy, but he was in love with love and intoxicated with the idea of immortality as a poet.

Somewhere about this time he translated a love poem by Horace (Bk 1, Ode 5) in a version of unequalled brilliance and austerity that is unrhymed and as close as possible in English to the Latin metre.

> What slender youth bedewed with liquid odours
> Courts thee on roses in some pleasant cave,
> Pyrrha for whom bind'st thou
> In wreaths thy golden hair, . . .

At this time English was fertile in fresh stanza forms. The most talented students of Latin poetry, particularly of Horace, were poets rather than professional scholars. Milton's version was printed only in 1673, and used a queer text of Horace: other versions take liberties he would not have taken. Horace had early attracted the notice of Sir Henry Wotton, who had adapted his metre. But two poets in particular should interest us, Marvell who was to be Fairfax's children's tutor and became Milton's close friend, and the virtually unknown poet Richard Fanshawe, born in June 1608, who after Farnaby's school in Cripplegate went to Jesus College, Cambridge, in 1623 and left in 1626. Marvell was born only in 1621 and came up to Trinity in 1633. The wonderful stanza form, which by rhyming is less austere but as an English form more effective than Milton's, which Marvell uses for his *Horatian Ode*, does not derive from Milton's sparkling version, which Marvell may not have known. He was already doing close imitations of Horace on his own account in the winter of 1636–7. The precedence may possibly belong to Fanshawe, whose *Selections from Horace* (1652) include the precise stanza form of Marvell's *Horatian Ode*. Marvell wrote in 1650 but was printed only in 1681; Fanshawe appears to have been writing his marvellous adaptations of Horatian metres ever since Cambridge. He was an unpretentious and unambitious man, though after the Restoration he was Latin Secretary to the government, and died an ambassador. The interest of this digression is that here at least we can match Milton with his contemporaries, yet he is still quite alone as a craftsman. All three are poets into whom Horace deeply entered.

> What stripling now thee discomposes
> In woodbine rooms on beds of roses,
> For whom thy auburn hair
> Is spread, unpainted fair? . . .
> Dissolve the frost with logs piled up
> To th' Mantle-tree; let the great Cup
> Out of a larger sluice
> Pour the reviving juice . . .

These are Fanshawe's, whose Horatianism goes back to Cambridge, including his wonderfully enlivening and amateurish Cavalier style as a translator.

By now John Milton was a poet, a scholar, fit to be a secretary perhaps, or more likely a tutor, scarcely more than a schoolmaster. He had a poet's passion for freedom, to which not long afterwards he gave strong expression. He would not find a patron to support him, and his father's affairs, though they were prosperous, were somewhat ramshackle. His sister had two young children and a husband who was a civil servant with no extraordinary income, and his younger brother was soon due to come to Cambridge. He did not stay there long and went to the Inner Temple to study law after five terms. His friend Charles Diodati was going to Geneva. John would hang on at Cambridge for his MA in 1631; meanwhile his portrait was painted by Mytens, but he knew no one would pull strings for him at court: he was a man without an obvious future.

That Christmas (1629) he wrote his first great and extended

English poem, 'On the Morning of Christ's Nativity'. It must be said that it contains a generous number of jokes: Peor and Baalim, the 'Lybic Hammon', 'sullen Moloch' and the 'Dog Anubis', let alone Osiris the bull, are figures from an entertainment; we know Milton always liked lists of queer gods. These are romantic and not serious, and the baby Christ, like a tiny Hercules, who 'to shew his Godhead true/Can in his swaddling bands control the damned crew' is hardly heavier in tone. Milton was right not to foresee a future in the Church, and a future in the assemblies of the godly was even less likely. Like his brother, he considered the law, where he might have done as well as Selden. His copy of Fitzherbert's *Natura Brevium* (1584) has the inscriptions *Jn Milton me possidet: Det Christus studiis vela secunda meis* ('Christ prosper *my* studies'), and then in another hand the same words but with *tuis* ('Christ prosper *thy* studies'), and then in a third hand, 'John Marston oeth [owneth] this book'. Did Marston give it or leave it to him? John Marston, the poet and satirist, had become a clergyman and died as one in 1634: his father was a lawyer. The link would be an interesting one; Hunter in his *Milton Gleanings* believed in it, but Masson judiciously doubted. What is certain is that Milton had the book, Marston was Shakespeare's friend and colleague, maybe his cousin, since they both used the term or accepted its use with the same local lawyer Francis Green, and in 1630 Milton wrote his sonnet on Shakespeare, printed with the Second Folio in 1632.

The Christmas poem deserves a longer treatment: for its lightness, its run, its sheer sparkle. The stanza form seems to be Italian, as F. T. Prince pointed out. Thomas Warton called it 'a string of affected conceits', but to us it seems rather a fine network of bold images and pleasant jokes. It is not, of course, an expression of unbelief, though no doubt some solemn persons might have thought it so. The introduction is in the stanza form of 'On the Death of a Fair Infant', but one needs not look too closely into the admirable works of Giles and Phineas Fletcher to find parallels to the degree of levity in which Milton indulges: Christmas was still a jolly festival. Tasso's Christmas Day poem (*Rime*, 1621) gave him the idea or offered him the vision. The courts of everlasting day, the awe of nature, the silence of Apollo and his cave and waves, the laurel and the oak, Ammon, even the mooing and lowing of Apis and Anubis are all in Tasso, whose verses go swinging along with true Italian facility. In the language of this remarkably beautiful poem, though, all the echoes are English: Milton's loyalty is to Spenser and to Shakespeare.

> ... So when the sun in bed,
> Curtained with cloudy red,
>   Pillows his chin upon an orient wave,
> The flocking shadows pale,
> Troop to the infernal jail,
>   Each fettered ghost slips to his several grave,
> And the yellow-skirted fays,
> Fly after the night-steeds, leaving their moon-loved maze.
>
> But see the Virgin blest,
> Hath laid her Babe to rest.
>   Time is our tedious song should here have ending:
> Heaven's youngest teemed star
> Hath fixed her polished car,
>   Her sleeping Lord with handmaid lamp attending:
> And all about the courtly stable,
> Bright-harnessed angels sit in order serviceable.

CHAPTER THREE

MILTON'S MATURITY

JOHN MILTON was now at the height of his promise, and it would not be long before its fruits appeared. In the university list for the BA he had come fourth in the whole university, his Latin verse greatly impressed the fellows of his college, and he was popular with them and with his contemporaries. He was elected or appointed to make a speech to the college with broad jests of an obscene tinge in Latin, and carried off his role well enough. His English poetry was dazzling; both entertaining and brilliant. He had duly sworn his BA oath to adhere to the doctrine and liturgy of the Church of England and to affirm the King's supremacy in everything. He tells us that more than one of the fellows hoped he would stay on. Just before his twenty-first birthday, Charles Diodati wrote him a letter to which he replied in ninety lines of Latin verse. Diodati had apologized for his own muse because friends had distracted him. 'But why does your muse challenge mine,/And not leave her to seek her longed for dark?'

> . . . Happy December's ceremonious dinners
> and the feast of that God who ran from heaven:
> its pleasures and the winter country joys,
> the wines of France drunk by a sparkling fire.
> Then why do you complain of poetry,
> as if poetry loved no wine nor feast?
> The song loves Bacchus and Bacchus loves songs,
> Phoebus was not ashamed of green ivy,
> and he among his laurels let it creep . . .

This is light and personal verse: the praise of wine is classical but for Milton it is more sensuous than usual. The only kind of poet who should live frugally is the one whose subject is

> . . . Now in the holy councils of the gods,
> now in buried kingdoms where the dog howls . . .

Milton goes into loving detail about this poet, his diet of herbs and his beechwood water-bowl, his morality and purity

> . . . Like wise Tiresias when his sight was lost,
> like Theban Linus and like Calchas then
> who fled away out of his fated house
> like antique Orpheus in his wilderness
> training the wild beasts in their lonely caves . . .
> . . . The poet is holy, he is the gods' priest,
> both his heart and his mouth are full of Zeus.

The verses are alarming in their prophetic truth, and alarming in the very high view Milton took of his own calling. Of course, the entire poem is rooted in convention, including that of setting out one side of an argument against another, yet even at that level he is unusually capable. But he goes on to record his poem on Christ's Nativity, his Christmas offering to Christ, which came to him and was written, he says, at earliest light. He promises Diodati a look at his Italian verses as well, when they meet. He certainly did intend something serious, and his next English poem, which is not as good as his last, is on the Passion of Christ, written at the end of March 1630. Its eight Spenserian stanzas are in the same form as the brief introduction to the *Nativity*. Its model is doubtless Italian.

> Erewhile of music, and ethereal mirth,
> Wherewith the stage of air and earth did ring,
> And joyous news of heav'nly infant's birth,
> My muse with angels did divide to sing;
> But headlong joy is ever on the wing,
>   In wintry solstice like the shortened light
> Soon swallowed up in dark and long out-living night.

The poem that follows reads like a Roman Catholic meditation of the same period, such as had entered English poetry through Donne and Fletcher. Milton pays a special compliment to 'Cremona's Trump', meaning the *Christiad*, six books of Virgilian Latin verse by Vida, published at Cremona in 1535 and written by request for Pope Leo X. But Milton is a Puritan, and he cannot bear to get too close to those physical realities of the Crucifixion on which Catholic devotion concentrated. Christ in Heaven stoops 'his regal head/That dropped with odorous oil down his fair eyes' to become man: Milton cannot cope with his subject.

> Me softer airs befit, and softer strings
> Of lute, or viol still, more apt for mournful things.

He sees the chariot of Ezekiel and the tomb of Christ, but he finds the whole subject too upsetting. He might go to weep and wail in the mountains, wake their echoes and

> Might think the infection of my sorrows loud,
> Had got a race of mourners on some pregnant cloud.

At this point he found the subject beyond his possibilities, and broke off the poem unfinished. All the same, for what it was worth, it is full of technical interest; he published it in 1645. And now he swiftly dived back into shallower, more Ovidian waters.

The poem 'On Shakespeare', first printed anonymously (1632) in the Second Folio, is dated 1630 in Milton's own 1645 collection. It was an honour that it should get into the Folio, for which Milton may well have written it. He knew at least one of the publishers or booksellers who produced it and could easily have met Ben Jonson. The language is Spenserian with a strong overtone of Shakespeare's own conceits about fancy:

> Then thou our fancy of itself bereaving,
> Dost make us marble with too much conceiving . . .

This is the penultimate couplet of the seven. In all of them Milton takes a high tone – of 'hallowed relics' and a 'star-ypointing pyramid', of Shakespeare as 'son of memory', therefore brother of the muses – and his victorious verses each impress us more than the other. The climax tells how each heart 'those Delphic lines with deep impression took'. The entire poem is an extraordinary boast. Whether it contains an allusion to W. Browne, who called English poets sons of Mercury and wanted Spenser to have a 'pyramis', to seem 'the stars to kiss', is really immaterial. The boast about a poet's memorial taller than the pyramids of kings comes from Horace, of course, and Herrick too uses it. In this poem it is specially effective.

> What needs my Shakespeare for his honoured bones
> The labour of an age in piled stones,

> Or that his hallowed relics should be hid
> Under a star-ypointing pyramid? . . .

In April 1630 there was plague at Cambridge: 347 people died in 839 families, 2,800 people were in distress. Vice-Chancellor Butts is said to have managed the crisis well enough, and the dioceses of London, Winchester and Lincoln sent money. At the worst period, thirty-four died every week. John Milton was in London; indeed the university did not assemble again until the last days of November. In his college, the gardener, the cook, the porter's son and the baker's sons as well as a laundress and a bedmaker had all died. The last death of all was that of the university carrier, old Thomas Hobson, on the first of January 1631, 'who sickened at the time of his vacancy, being forbidden to go to London by reason of the Plague'. He at least was commemorated by John Milton, and this poem circulated in manuscript, among many others on the same subject, although there does not seem to have existed any formal anthology of them. Milton wrote at least two of these poems. He was witty in the manner of the best seventeenth-century epitaphs, but it is a sad wit. Death, he says,

> In the kind office of a chamberlain
> Showed him his room where he must lodge that night,
> Pulled off his boots, and took away the light:
> If any ask for him, it shall be said,
> Hobson has supped, and 's newly gone to bed.

When spring came he wrote an 'epitaph' of seventy-four lines for Lady Winchester, a much lamented lady who was accorded elegies by Jonson, Davenant, Strode and many lesser men. The British Library manuscript Sloane 1446 has a number of them, including what is certainly a deviant and early version of Milton's poem. Lady Winchester and her husband (1598–1675) were Catholics, married in 1620, and she bore his son and successor Charles, the Restoration Duke of Bolton. She died very young, from a mishandled minor operation, the lancing of a boil. We do not know why so many poems were written, unless because she was kin to the Chancellor, Lord Holland. Can it have been because she was 'inclining to Protestantism'? There is something masque-like about Milton's treatment, particularly these cancelled lines:

> . . . Seven times had the yearly star
> In every sign set up his car . . .

The cancellation is due to new and precise information about dates, which is then incorporated with flawless transitions. He borrows Virgil's traditional simile about the dead man like a drooping field flower: 'But the fair blossom hangs the head/Sideways as on a dying bed . . .' It must be said that the verse appears wholly artificial, produced at so much a yard, like hand-made wallpaper.

> Here be tears of perfect moan
> Wept for thee in Helicon . . .

All the same, that neoclassic facility is not to be despised. It is part of the growth of a great poet of another age, who has not been equalled or rivalled in ours. Milton was imitating Shakespeare: 'Gentle lady may thy grave/Peace and quiet ever have . . .'

The date of 'L'Allegro' and 'Il Penseroso' is a puzzle. These two poems may have been written as early as the summer of 1631, but not earlier than Lady Winchester's poem, on which their prosody shows an advance. They might be as late as the period of revision that followed *Comus*. There is a substantial shadow of Cambridge over them, in the humorously grand introductions and the arguments for two opposed views, but that is an old theme in medieval poetry – summer versus winter, for example. Milton did not leave Cambridge until 1632, and even then he did not move at once to the country retreat evoked in 'L'Allegro': after his BA his residence at Cambridge was less strictly enforced, so that he is impossible to trace. His verse does not precisely reflect his whereabouts anyway; it trails long after them. I follow the conjectural date of summer 1631, because it best fits his development as a poet, which at this period shows a constant extension of his powers. The dominant influences are Shakespeare and, to a lesser extent, Spenser.

It may be of some interest to consider here the two letters written to Milton in Greek by his friend Diodati. The first laments bad weather and looks forward to clear skies. The other tells him to relax his severe studies. 'The present state of the weather seems to be opposed to our plans when we parted, being stormy and disturbed two whole days now . . . Cheer up and prepare for a feastday and a brighter day than this. Tomorrow it will be fine, and air, sun, river, trees, birds, the earth and men will feast with us, laugh with us and dance with us ...' 'When days are long, then grounds flower, leaves and blossom sprout, with thrush or nightingale on every branch ... but in human affairs there is always something missing. And you, my dear wonder, why do you despise the gifts of nature? Why such a determined concentration on books and words all night and all day? Live, laugh, enjoy youth and the seasons, and leave off study ...' Is it not possible that the conflict, so far as it is one, between the Joyful and the Melancholy man, with their Italian titles, may derive from what Diodati outlines in these letters? In the long history of melancholy there are some verses by Robert Burton in *The Anatomy of Melancholy* (1628) that are at least equally suggestive. (His 'Abstract of Melancholy in dialogue form' is in Fowler's *Oxford Book of Seventeenth Century Verse*, no. 184.) Wherever the truth may lie, these poems have perhaps always been Milton's most popular English verses, giving more pleasure than the entire works of other authors, and all our criticism has added very little to that enjoyment.

Still, one cannot rely on Milton not having been conscious that the melancholy he exorcises in the introduction to 'L'Allegro' is the sort of gloom discussed by Galen, while the kind he praises in 'Il Penseroso' is the Aristotelian kind, productive of art. We simply do not know how much he had read of what would soon be drawn on in the movement called Cambridge Platonism. The poems are both twilit, whether at dawn or at evening, as Samuel Palmer observed, but Melancholy as the child of Cerberus and the Darkness is just a baroque invention, and Milton did not mean anything in particular by 'night-raven'. 'L'Allegro' gets off to a new and happy start at line 11, with Euphrosyne and her sisters, the Graces. Euphrosyne has a respectably antique name from Hesiod's *Theogony* and Pindar, but Venus and Bacchus figure as parents of the Graces only in an obscurer source, the commentary of Servius printed around the edges of some Renaissance texts of Virgil. The 'some sager' who say their parents were Zephyr with Aurora playing turn out to be Ben Jonson, so all this dictionary-based scholarship is not in the least serious: the poem whirls along in swift and beautiful syntactic eddies, as fast as Milton's new style (of Christmas 1629) could carry it. It is as intoxicating as it was meant to be, and essentially, deeply Shakespearian. None of the

troupe of revellers, Jest, Jollity, Laughter or even the mountain
nymph sweet Liberty, is intended to delay us. Suddenly and in mid-
sentence the scene becomes English.

> Mirth, admit me of thy crew
> To live with her, and live with thee,
> In unreproved pleasures free;
> To hear the lark begin his flight,
> And singing startle the dull night,
> From his watch-tower in the skies,
> Till the dappled dawn doth rise . . .

A lark that rises before dawn is a phenomenon I have not encountered,
but such confusions in the observation of nature occur in poetry.
Things become further entangled when the lark comes to Milton's
window, in an imagined cottage, to wish him good morning.

> Through the sweet-briar, or the vine,
> Or the twisted eglantine.
> While the cock with lively din,
> Scatters the rear of darkness thin . . .

The images are sharply imprinted in their few words; only the
transitions are careless: the impetus of the whole poem is like a
pouring torrent and the syntax matters no more here than the
mythology did earlier. So the full stop after 'eglantine' and the
sentence beginning 'While' are equally acceptable, as 'the hounds and
horn/Cheerly rouse the slumb'ring morn,/From the side of some
hoar hill,/Through the high wood echoing shrill.' It is a sound often
enough heard then, in the unreformed England, and often enough
until recently. As for the muddled language, it is surely the poet not
the cock who listens in line 53 and walks in line 57.

> Sometime walking not unseen
> By hedgerow elms, on hillocks green,
> Right against the eastern gate,
> Where the great sun begins his state,
> Robed in flames and amber light,
> The clouds in thousand liveries dight,
> While the ploughman near at hand,
> Whistles o'er the furrowed land . . .

It is almost impossible to stop quoting the irresistible run of lines. The milkmaid, the mower whetting his scythe, the shepherd telling his tale, that is counting his sheep, all lead up to 'landscape'. The word is Dutch, and means a painting of a view (first in Du Bartas) before it means a view, or the thing in itself, as it does here for the first time. This longish passage is wonderfully like a picture all the same, and the rejoicing but tiny figures in the fields are reminiscent of a seventeenth-century Dutch depiction of a Gloucestershire scene in the Cheltenham gallery. The landscape of 'L'Allegro' is not only inhabited, it is animated, as Milton's early landscapes all are. The girl in the tower 'high in tufted trees' is fantasy, but Corydon and Thyrsis, Phillis and Thestylis are as English as 'the tanned haycock in the mead'.

When he has put his innocent and happy country people to bed, Milton goes out to see the town, 'the busy hum of men', the triumphant courtly life of London in fact, with its jousts and its masques.

> There let Hymen oft appear
> In saffron robe, with taper clear,
> And pomp, and feast, and revelry,
> With mask, and antique pageantry,
> Such sights as youthful poets dream
> On summer eves by haunted stream.
> Then to the well-trod stage anon,
> If Jonson's learned sock be on,
> Or sweetest Shakespeare fancy's child,
> Warble his native wood-notes wild . . .

Milton may be harking back to the Elizabethan age. The association of Shakespeare with the sweet-tongued birds of Warwickshire comes from Drayton probably. But in 1632 William Prynne published his *Histriomastix*, an essay against actors. Unluckily for him, the Queen and her ladies acted in a masque early in 1633, and Prynne was deemed to have attacked them. He was fined a huge sum, deprived of degrees, and had his ears cut off in the pillory. A little later in life, when he offended again in some other way, he got the same gruesome sentence, so they used a saw to cut away the stumps of his ears. I do not think Milton would have written his sweetly nostalgic lines about either the court or the stage after this nasty case, and suggest that we should put the two poems in 1631. The last pleasure of 'L'Allegro' is the most sophisticated:

> Lap me in soft Lydian airs,
> Married to immortal verse
> Such as the meeting soul may pierce
> In notes, with many a winding bout
> Of linked sweetness long drawn out,
> With wanton heed, and giddy cunning,
> The melting voice through mazes running . . .
> That Orpheus' self may heave his head
> From golden slumber on a bed
> Of heaped Elysian flowers . . .

The introduction to 'Il Penseroso' has some abstruse allusions that are not worth explaining: it is beautiful all the same, and gets better as it goes on, like its predecessor. The poem is not Puritanical: its 'pensive Nun', its cloister and 'storied windows', its organ service and performance of a tragedy would none of them meet with approval in old Geneva, or in the England that was coming. The invocation is to Peace and Quiet, Fast and Leisure, 'that in trim gardens takes his pleasure', and soaring Contemplation:

> And the mute Silence hist along,
> 'Less Philomel will deign a song,
> In her sweetest, saddest plight,
> Smoothing the rugged brow of night,
> While Cynthia checks her dragon yoke
> Gently o'er the accustomed oak;
> Sweet bird that shunn'st the noise of folly,
> Most musical, most melancholy!

The pleasure of walking at night in dry grass under moonlight yields to the noise of curfew 'over some wide-watered shore,/ Swinging slow with sullen roar'. The comforts of the melancholy man include sitting indoors,

> Where glowing embers through the room
> Teach light to counterfeit a gloom,
> Far from all resort of mirth,
> Save the cricket on the hearth,

Or the bellman's drowsy charm,
To bless the doors from nightly harm:
Or let my lamp at midnight hour,
Be seen in some high lonely tower,
Where I may oft outwatch the Bear,
With thrice great Hermes, or unsphere
The spirit of Plato to unfold
What worlds, or what vast regions hold
The immortal mind . . .

This was surely the direct descent of the Cambridge Platonists from the mad old demonologists and astrologers and cabbalists and students of the queerest of secret scriptures to a genuine search for Platonic wisdom. When Milton goes on to mention daemons, planets and elements, we conjecture that he is thinking of the old men in his own college. Does he feel the pull of that way of life? He does apparently have some sense of awe at the sheer mystery of Plato and 'immortal mind'. The Neoplatonist movement had started among Renaissance scholars like Marsilio Ficino (1433–99), who hated being dictated to by clergymen, whose learning and wisdom they overleapt at one bound. They were humanists, and the movement spread through Marsilio's commentary on Plato's *Symposium*. The phrases 'spirit of Plato . . . what worlds . . . what vast regions . . . immortal mind' show that Milton has understood it very well. When the shell of religion has smashed itself around him through too much argument, too many words, this version of Platonism will be with him to the end, even in the unpublished treatise *On Christian Doctrine*, though for Milton the *Philebos* of Plato, not the *Symposium*, will be central.

From this vision which so haunted Yeats as well as Samuel Palmer, he moves swiftly on to tragedy, which is Greek 'Or what (though rare) of later age,/Ennobled hath the buskined stage'. For these he turns like a questing and still dissatisfied student of comparative literature to some obscure names from Chaucer's unfinished *Squire's Tale*, as regularized by his father's friend John Lane. He means really the whole of romance literature,

Of forests, and enchantments drear,
Where more is meant than meets the ear.

> Thus Night oft see me in thy pale career,
> Till civil-suited Morn appear,
> Not tricked and frounced as she was wont,
> With the Attic boy to hunt,
> But kerchieft in a comely cloud,
> While rocking winds are piping loud . . .

This brings him into a beautiful passage on the weather and the woods where he shelters from the risen sun; the bees buzz and the poet dreams; sweet music breathes

> Sent by some spirit to mortals good,
> Or the unseen genius of the wood.

He desires to walk in 'studious cloister' with its cross-arched roof, to enjoy the 'dim religious light', hear the organ's pealing and the choir 'in service high, and anthems clear'. Perhaps none of this is meant to be Milton's true self. In old age he wishes, as the custom in his lifetime was to wish, to find himself a hermitage, 'the hairy gown and mossy cell'. There he will learn to know the stars

> And every herb that sips the dew;
> Till old experience do attain
> To something like prophetic strain.
> These pleasures Melancholy give,
> And I with thee will choose to live.

If 'L'Allegro' is the more attractive poem, this one has perhaps more deeply memorable moments.

In December 1631 Milton had his twenty-third birthday. He was a broody young man, and anxious because he was ambitious to scale great heights. As he told Diodati, his Muse wanted and sought for the dark. He had not regarded his Christmas poem as a serious enough success, it appears, and it was not published: can he have thought it dangerous? He wanted patronage and a public, he wanted what only the theatre could give him, but the Puritans were against the theatre, so only the private masque and its patron were open to him, with music perhaps.

> How soon hath time the subtle thief of youth,
> Stol'n on his wing my three and twentieth year!

> My hasting days fly on with full career,
> But my late spring no bud or blossom sheweth . . .

The sonnet is sad, introspective and melodious. It is like the slow dripping of water into the well where Narcissus or where Hylas died. So far as I know it is an entirely original poem, and its subject matter occurs in a carefully rewritten letter of which both versions are in the small manuscript notebook, now at Trinity, Cambridge, in which for the rest of his life Milton kept copies of all his shorter poems. The letter was almost certainly to Thomas Young.

> You are often to me as a good watch man to admonish that the hours of the night pass on (for so I call my life as yet obscure and unserviceable to mankind) and that the day is at hand wherein Christ commands all to labour while there is light, which because I am persuaded you do to no other purpose than out of a true desire that God should be honoured in every one, yet now I will not strain for any set apology but only refer myself to what shall have at any time to declare herself at her best ease. Yet if you think as you said that too much love of learning is in fault and that I have given up myself to dream away my years in the arms of studious retirement like Endymion in the arms of the Moon on Latmos hill, – that you may see I am sometime suspicious of myself and do take notice of a certain belatedness in me . . .

(He enclosed the sonnet written 'some while since'.) That is how poets should excuse themselves when too much pressure is put on them by their fathers in the spirit. The wonderfully long and weaving sentences suggest Milton's potential as a great master of English prose, but at its most intimate, not its most public. The letter raises, of course, questions we cannot answer about the rather dark and not inactive figure of Young on the margins of his life until both their lives became public.

At present John Milton appears determined to pursue his fantasy of a poetic career as that might have been forty years earlier, and to ignore politics with some deliberation. The Petition of Rights and all questions of foreign policy might never have existed. Tom Randolph of Trinity and Edward King of Christ's wrote poems to celebrate the birth of the future Charles II and of the Princess Mary, but not John Milton. The tone of the university was, I think, altering at this time:

Ralph Cudworth came up to Emmanuel, Richard Crashaw to Pembroke, and Henry More to Christ's at seventeen. Recalling Eton,
More wrote how 'Walking as my manner was slowly and with my
head on one side, and kicking now and then the stones with my feet,
I was wont sometimes with a sort of musical and melancholy murmur
to repeat or rather hum to myself these verses of Claudian.' He
summons up a certain bookish brilliance and a world of private ease,
in which Milton might have flourished. But Charles I had already
given up his attempts to co-operate with Parliaments: they were
summoned and dissolved too easily, and now the King had no money.
Queen Elizabeth had already seen in, as Clarendon put it, 'a total
alteration of religion, and some confident attempts upon a further
alteration by those who thought not the reformation enough'. That is
precisely where Thomas Young stood, and in that direction John
Milton would in the end follow him.

At some time, probably his last year at Cambridge, Milton wrote a
poem in Latin hexameters to his father. It was 120 lines long, the
theme was usual but this example was perhaps occasioned by seeing
such a poem by Gill, since they did habitually exchange their verses.
Gill's poem was printed in 1632. What is unusual in Milton's version,
as we shall see, is his conclusion. He begins with a high-flown and
presumably less than serious invocation of the Muse to produce a tiny
work: 'I know no gift of mine can better answer/Your gifts, although
the greatest that I give/Can be no answer, which is empty words.'

> All I have is what golden Clio gives,
> dream-born upon me in the secret cave
> Parnassus shadows and the holy laurel . . .

It is no better and no more personal than the verses for Lady
Winchester, but it reveals anxiety. 'Do not despise the poet's godlike
work . . .' Nothing, he claims, better shows our heavenly origin, the
heavenly seed in us, the mind of man: poetry retains some traces of
the fire of Prometheus. This Neoplatonic view is what has occupied
him at least since 'Il Penseroso'. 'The gods love song, it stirs the
trembling deeps/Of Tartarus, it binds the gods of hell,/Compels hard
ghosts with triple adamant,' and so on.

> When we come home to heaven, when eternal
> ages stand still we shall walk crowned with gold,

> wedding our sweet songs to the breathing strings,
> and star and hemisphere shall echo us . . .

It is a strange scenario to offer to an ageing father, even if he is a musician, and the rapture increases as it goes on. The only Puritan note is to praise the bard's treatment in the good old frugal days before gluttonous feasts foamed with wine. But the bard's song turns out to be alarming, as usually happens when one attempts to outdo Virgil. He sings of chaos and the foundations of the earth,

> Of gods that crawled the earth's floor, acorn-fed,
> and still under Etna the thunderbolt . . .

Milton is using scraps of Ovid which already go beyond Virgil, and the result is impressively hollow. He assures his father of the worth of his poems, which it would be a mistake to despise (he evidently did despise them). The two of them should share Apollo's gifts and each be half a god. If it is true that his father took a light or scornful view of verse, then no doubt he measured it by the products of his friend Lane. John is at least grateful to the old man for Latin, Greek, French, Italian and Hebrew, and for the opportunity to learn, if he should choose, about fundamental science. No father could give better gifts.

> And I who sit now low among learned men
> shall one day twine the ivy with laurel . . .
> . . . And you my young poems and my pastimes
> if you should look for immortality
> and light beyond my fire and funeral,
> preserve these praises and my father's name
> which is the subject of my poetry,
> for an example to an age to come.

It is not a great or perhaps a very good poem, and yet one cannot but feel in its queer Renaissance terms a certain sincerity, particularly in the last few lines. He is quite sure he is going to be a great poet; he suspects that he already is one. Such a state of mind was not and is not uncommon, but it is unusual in a well-educated and self-critical young man of twenty-four. In Milton's case the attempt on Parnassus was deliberate from the beginning, and his apparently God-given confidence in accomplishing his huge design was, in fact, the necessary condition of his fulfilling it. One might go further, and say that almost all the cases of this sense of a strong vocation to greatness as an English poet occur between Spenser and Tennyson.

The fact that Milton puts himself vehemently and at some length above the mob is perhaps less significant. It may be important that he thanks his father for not pushing him into business or the law. 'You have removed me from the city's noise,/Into this deep seclusion where I walk/Beside Apollo, my companion,/Among the pleasures of the Aonian springs.' Does he mean Hammersmith? Or Horton in Buckinghamshire? Certainly not Cambridge, we may be sure. But the highly fantastical language he uses, *Me procul urbano strepitu, secessibus altis/Abductum Aoniae iucunda per otia ripae*, appears to me wholly metaphorical from the fifth word, and I do not think *secessibus altis* means a real place, unless Parnassus is real. His tangle with the law was real, because we have its monument, half an inscription on Harington's *Ariosto*, the cancelled second line of a couplet of which the first is cut away, saying, 'Justinian, goodbye'.

In March 1632 Butts, the Vice-Chancellor, hanged himself on Easter Day: it was not his first attempt. In July John Milton became a Master of Arts and left Cambridge: he was one among 207 masters and two doctors: twenty-seven masters were from Christ's. Once again he swore to the royal supremacy and the liturgy and doctrine of the Church; theses argued included that the Bible was the only rule of faith, that dregs of sin remained after baptism, that there was some culpable defect even in the best works of the regenerated, and that bare assent to divine revelation was not the same as the faith that justifies. Cambridge had gone a long way towards Calvinism, and it may well be that John Milton's escape to the trickling hillside of Parnassus was largely wishful thinking. Still, he learnt to fence skilfully, he bought an Aratus to study the stars, and he had read Euripides. The edition he used has an excellent Latin translation and a reasonable text. When his juvenilia came to be printed at the end of his life he flung in his Latin *Prolusiones* as a makeweight; they are of scarcely any interest except to those interested in decayed scholasticism at Cambridge before the Civil War. The important point is that he worked extremely hard: the Fellows of his college asked him to stay on.

Edward King (1612–37), who had come to Christ's as a boy with his elder brother Roger, got a fellowship at eighteen, in 1630, by royal command. Writers about Milton have often wondered why he was passed over: but King's father Sir John was an important civil servant in Ireland, and that is how royal patronage worked. Had Milton stayed on, maybe a niche would have been found for him but, hard as he worked, he did not want to be a fellow; at least there is no evidence that he ever thought of it. He was far too ambitious to moulder on for ever at Cambridge, and also there was no one offering to pull strings on his behalf.

Edward King was a pious youth, and it may well be that Milton went for walks with him. Edward was also a poet, at least in Latin, fairly bad but no worse than young Gill or a hundred others. So no doubt he talked about poetry to Milton, who knew a great deal about it. It does appear from *Lycidas* that Milton liked Edward King, and it is highly probable that they shared Thomas Young's views about the corrupt Church of England which also surface in *Lycidas*. One would have to be careful what one said in college, so that no doubt is another subject they ventilated as they wandered across the freezing wastes of Cambridgeshire.

It used to be thought that from Cambridge Milton escaped, almost at once, by way of London to an obscure village which even in the eighteenth century had no roads, only tracks, one of which was a lane to Datchet and another to Colnbrook and Brentford. This was Horton, in the south-easternmost pocket of Buckinghamshire, just a mile or so across the meadows from the Thames, more or less opposite Runnymede or Old Windsor. But it now appears from some legal papers found in the Public Records in 1949 by Charles Bernau, and used by J. M. French in his *Life Records of Milton* (Rutgers, 1940–58), that the old scrivener lived at Hammersmith, which may have begun as a suburban refuge from the plague; a number of references in young Milton's Latin poems could be made to fit it. We know of Horton only through Edward Phillipps, who was four at this time, and through the grave of the poet's mother in Horton church. It may represent a flight still deeper into the country than Hammersmith. Between September 1632 and January 1635 Hammersmith seems to have been the principal residence, or was it only an address more convenient for whatever business the old man still did? He was in the process of retiring.

Hammersmith lay then among open fields. We know it was a

thriving suburban settlement, facing Barnes Common and Mortlake on the south bank of the Thames, but upstream of Putney and Fulham, and on a main road out of London. If you kept to the river, Horton was an afternoon's walk away, but that was not easy, because a walker would encounter numerous small rivers and streams: the Yeading Brook, the Brent and the Coln. Beyond Horton another few miles brought you through the lanes to Datchet, and so to Eton and Windsor. We know that a new church was being built at Hammersmith: Sir Nicholas Crisp, to whom Charles I granted a share in the slave-trading monopoly between Guinea and America in 1632, gave £700 for the building of St Paul's, Hammersmith. He had dealings with the scrivener, and his wife was the daughter of a salt merchant in Bread Street. St Paul's was not a parish church, but a 'chapel of ease' under Fulham, served by a curate. It was consecrated by Laud in 1631.

By the time of his twenty-fourth birthday in 1632, if not earlier, the poet had made up his mind against taking orders, and had retired to the country to read, the classics mostly, but as wide a library as he could acquire. Twenty-four was the canonical age for ordination and the letter I have quoted may well be about that subject. In 1634 he buys a Euripides of his own and (of all curious and unreadable, riddling books) a Lycophron. From what Milton reads and quotes, it is evident he had an ostrich appetite and a hard head. This long period of undirected study came to have an influence on him as a poet some twenty or thirty years later. But the Greek drama of which he hoped so much produced in him only the arid structure of *Samson Agonistes*. It is fair to say that the same is true of nearly all students of the classical tragedians: they belong to the ancient world and are embedded in conventions utterly strange to us. For Milton they were alive to an unusual degree: for most people the enlivening element in Greek poetry in Milton's day was in smaller and prettier pieces, particularly in the short poems of the *Greek Anthology*, first made known in its full form to the West by Claude de Saumaise (that same Salmasius with whom Milton was to clash in the 1650s), though Ben Jonson had already taught the English 'Drink to me only with thine eyes'. Milton learnt the essence of that lesson of song, but alas he did not often exercise in it: he must have thought it old-fashioned and perhaps unscholarly.

'Arcades' ('The Arcadians') is undated, but a draft of it begins Milton's Trinity manuscript. It is called 'Part of a masque', then that is cancelled and it becomes 'Part of an Entertainment'. It was never to be a court masque on the grand scale, but a little private performance for Alice, Lady Derby. We do not know how Milton came to be employed: probably quite casually and by word of mouth, through the musician Henry Lawes who was tutor to some of Alice's grandchildren. Carey dates 'Arcades' in the summer of 1633: it was performed out of doors when the leaves were fully out on the trees. The Dowager Countess, who was seventy-two in 1634, had been patroness to Spenser, Marston and maybe Shakespeare; John Davies of Hereford dedicated his *Holy Rood* to her in 1609, and she was Zenobia in Ben Jonson's *Masque of Queens* in that year. She was married to Sir Thomas Egerton, the Lord Keeper before Milton was born, and her daughter was married to his son Sir John Egerton, who in 1617 became Earl of Bridgewater, and is probably the person who commissioned 'Arcades'. But in 1631 the family was struck by the most appalling scandal of the century.

On 14 May Lord Castlehaven was publicly executed for sexual abuse of a flagrant and violent kind. He had been married to Alice Derby's elder daughter: he was a voyeur and had her raped by a servant. He had also interfered with the children, one of whom had gone to the King and complained, the King being his godfather. Castlehaven's household had been a kind of Bluebeard's Castle; his trial was public, of course. It is hard to know quite how this affects the difficult dates of Milton's work for the Egertons, but it is perhaps unlikely that old Lady Derby would undertake a joyful entertainment the same summer. Lawes had been tutor in music to the children since 1626 or perhaps earlier. Old Alice's house was at Harefield, on a low ridge of hills looking towards Uxbridge and the road to Oxford and to Wales, not far from Hammersmith or Horton. We must assume that Milton attended on the Countess, since the entertainment was presented to her 'at Harefield, by some noble persons of her family, who appear on the scene in pastoral habit'.

> Mark what radiant state she spreads,
> In circle round her shining throne,
> Shooting her beams like silver threads,

> This this is she alone,
> > Sitting like a goddess bright,
> > In the centre of her light.
>
> Might she the wise Latona be,
> Or the towered Cybele . . . ?

It does not much matter who these classical divinities were, but Latona was born in the far north, on an island often identified with Britain. The Genius of the Wood appears after four stanzas of this song. He assures the 'gentle swains' they are not only Arcadian, but children of the river Alpheus, which, he and Milton know, stole away under the sea's water 'to meet his Arethuse'. 'And ye the breathing roses of the wood,/Fair silver-buskined nymphs as great and good . . .' He explains his charming functions:

> To nurse the saplings tall, and curl the grove
> With ringlets quaint, and wanton windings wove. . . .
> And from the boughs brush off the evil dew,
> And heal the harms of thwarting thunder blue . . .

His tone is light, and the alliterations and rhymes do not suggest this verse cost him an enormous effort: yet it could hardly be more pleasing or fitter for a summer evening.

> And early ere the odorous breath of morn
> Awakes the slumbering leaves, or tasselled horn
> Shakes the high thicket . . .
> > . . . then listen I
> To the celestial sirens' harmony,
> That sit upon the nine enfolded spheres . . .

Plato only had eight spheres but Dante had nine, like the nine orders of angels. Marsilio Ficino also thought there were nine spheres. They were 'enfolded' like onion skins around the world and their motion was the key to the motion of the universe. Milton was fond of this strange but once popular idea, as if the universe had been a huge mechanical clock. We, as humans 'with gross unpurged ear', are unable to hear this music, as Shakespeare explained in the last act of *The Merchant of Venice*. The Genius of the Wood has now spoken his eighty-three lines, and that is all. Two more songs and the entertainment, or Milton's part in it, is over.

The first song is an invitation, 'O'er the smooth enamelled green/ Where no print of step hath been ... Under the shady roof/Of branching elm star-proof ...' The second song ends, as the first does, with 'Such a rural queen/All Arcadia hath not seen'. It makes amazing music of geographic names. They had deeply impressed themselves on Milton since his boyhood, and later the best atlas money could buy would be one of his luxuries. Greek names lured him and we know that he intended to visit Greece and Sicily when English politics summoned him home from Naples. These Arcadian names would have taken him into the remotest and in his day still the loveliest country in the known world.

> Nymphs and shepherds dance no more
>   By sandy Ladon's lilied banks,
> On old Lycaeus or Cyllene hoar,
>   Trip no more in twilight ranks,
> Though Erymanth your loss deplore,
>   A better soil shall give ye thanks.
> From the stony Maenalus,
> Bring your flocks, and live with us,
> Here ye shall have greater grace,
> To serve the Lady of this place.
>   Though Syrinx your Pan's mistress were,
>   Yet Syrinx well might wait on her.
>   Such a rural queen
>   All Arcadia hath not seen.

The two lines about Syrinx were inserted, and may possibly refer to a Jonson entertainment at Althorp. As a compliment the whole entertainment is almost top-heavy with elaboration, its content hardly exists, but it is exquisite.

'At a Solemn Music' seems to be composed rather than transcribed and then corrected, on the reverse leaf of the end of 'Arcades', in the Trinity manuscript. Milton was imitating Petrarch's *'Vergine bella, che di Sol vestita'*, as F. T. Prince pointed out. The language is consequently high-flown. Here it is the spectacular complication of music that Milton celebrates. There are wonderful phrases like 'the sapphire-coloured throne', which Carey refers to Ezekiel 1: 26, but it may as easily derive from Dante's *dolce color d'oriental zapphiro*, which is turquoise, a milky colour like a May morning, rather than the formidable gleam of our sapphires. The rhapsody ends with a simple, almost Wither-like aspiration.

> O may we soon again renew that song,
> And keep in tune with heaven, till God ere long
> To his celestial consort us unite,
> To live with him, and sing in endless morn of light.

The little rhapsodic outburst 'On Time' may equally belong to 1633, and sounds just as Italian as 'At a Solemn Music'. This poem is really about eternity, which 'shall greet our bliss/With an individual kiss;/And Joy shall overtake us as a flood ...' so that in the end 'Attired with stars, we shall for ever sit,/Triumphing over Death, and Chance, and thee O Time'. The ode 'Upon the Circumcision' is also mercifully short, if irregular, at twenty-eight lines: the three of them form a group. Can they all have been intended for music? The first fourteen lines of the 'Circumcision' ode create a stanza form inferior to Spenser's, and somewhat dull by comparison. The word 'whilere', which is used to rhyme with 'tear', is no doubt intended to recall Spenser: just as Scott, who rhymed it with 'Henry's royal ear' (in *Marmion*) no doubt also intended. It is hardly surprising that Milton found nothing of interest to say about the Circumcision, only surprising that, in the Catholic or Italian manner of these poems, he tried. It is possible we may be quite wrong about their date: they may be earlier than we think.

Poets do not always develop evenly, and we know Milton did not lose his interest in *canzone*, or in the Pindaric ode, or in lyric choral poetry until he had written *Samson Agonistes*, which, I take it, was at the end of his life. It was a subdued obsession of his. The English first learnt how to manipulate the ode from Ronsard, whose Pindaric stanzas are rather like Horatian ones only longer. They are less ambitious than Spenser's intoxicating *Prothalamion* and *Epithalamion*. By the end of the Civil War and Cromwell's Commonwealth, the easy ability to manipulate forms had disappeared, and the state odes that did continue Cowley's tradition are, as it were, exceptions that prove the rule. On the other hand, Milton was brought up with Italian as well as English music, and his ability was always astonishing, although his theory, arising as it does from the academic teaching of his time, is somewhat unhelpful.

He felt he could accommodate the classics most intimately to the Scriptures. In about 1641 he speaks of 'what the mind at home, in the spacious circuits of her musing, hath liberty to propose to herself, though of highest hope and hardest attempting ...' He is recalling the ambitious thoughts he had at Horton, I believe, about epic, 'whereof the two poems of Homer, and those other two of Virgil and Tasso, are a diffuse, and the Book of Job a brief model'. He has measured all this against the usefulness or otherwise of adhering to the rules of Aristotle. He asks 'what King or Knight before the conquest might be chosen in whom to lay the pattern of a Christian hero': dare one find him in our own ancient stories, as Tasso did in his? (He is thinking now not of *The Squire's Tale* but of King Arthur.) Or is it better to teach as Sophocles and Euripides did? (Does he not comprehend the force of Aeschylus?) 'The Scripture also affords us a divine Pastoral Drama in the Song of Salomon, consisting of two Persons and a double Chorus, as Origen rightly judges. And the Apocalypse of Saint John is the majestic image of a high and stately Tragedy, shutting up and intermingling her solemn Scenes and Acts with a sevenfold Chorus of Hallelujah's and harping symphonies.' For this amazing view he relies (as he often does) on the commentator Pareus, a Protestant of the last generation. 'Or if occasion shall lead, to imitate those magnifick Odes and Hymns wherein Pinder and Callimachus ...' Never was the influence of the classics more vigorously felt or more wrongheadedly. Alas, by the time Europe had educated herself to understand this, the inspiration was gone.

'These abilities, wheresoever they be found, are the inspir'd gift of God rarely bestowed ... and are of power, beside the office of a pulpit, to inbreed and cherish in a great people the seeds of virtue and public civility ...' That is what Milton believed at this time as much as in 1641. He goes on to become even more lyrical about the office of poets as moral teachers. He added, since in 1641 he had come back from Italy, a plea for academies, and 'set and solemn Paneguries in Theatres ...' whatever he meant by those. For the moment it is more useful to hold in mind not his mixed feelings about the theatre or about the public uses of poetry, but his strength of didactic feeling about his own verses, because this was the young man who was about to write *Comus*.

CHAPTER FOUR

COMUS

BY SEPTEMBER 1632 the old scrivener was nearly seventy, and that was when he started using Hammersmith as an address. The same summer young Christopher left Christ's College for the Inner Temple, and John left with an MA and no prospect but what poetry offered. Some time in 1635, at seventy-two and irritated by the Chancery cases in which he was involved, the old man began to give his address as Horton. We know that his wife died there in April 1637, because her stone, in blue-black Tournai 'marble', lay in the floor of the church, to be moved to the centre of the chancel only in the nineteenth century, when the building was expensively and wonderfully well restored. It stands now among the oldest and mossiest of sixteenth-century brick walls, some of which must have been familiar to Milton; in his day the top storey of the tower (brick on flint) was freshly built. The western extension to the churchyard is the walled garden of the old manor house, which was demolished in 1785. Today the whole village, with its cowed and queer-shaped little green and its clapboarded inn, is overshadowed by the enormous bulk of the Queen Elizabeth Reservoir, and much ruffled by the sudden roaring of aeroplanes from Heathrow. Its willows have gone; the numerous streams that ran through its wet fields now run underground. There were elms, alders, poplars, some cedars, and big orchards. The nearest to a monument that still survives of Horton in Milton's day is a painting by Linnell: the fields are authentic if not the house. In Masson's time, runnels full of minnows ran beside the lanes or tracks. I could find only one.

There were five or six gentry families in Milton's day and 300 or 400 people altogether. Elisabeth, the daughter of one of the Bulstrodes who were lords of the manor, had married Sir James Whitelocke, a judge with property not far away, and her child was Bulstrode Whitelocke. The Revd Edward Goodall was rector (1631–52). He had once been an assistant to the Puritan Mr Gatacre at Rotherhithe, where he must have been a colleague of Thomas Young. From Horton, London was a five hours' walk; even the plague seldom travelled so far. When it did, it moved from inn to inn. Horton lay lapped in innocence: it was what the public expected of a poet. Dryden in 1699 was right to say, 'Milton was the poetical son of Shakespeare ... Milton had acknowledged to me that Shakespeare was his original'.

Comus, as we call it since an eighteenth-century public-stage adaptation by John Dalton, is not really a conventional masque, although it draws on the masques, or plays within plays, that occur in *A Midsummer Night's Dream* and elsewhere. The subject, which is chastity, is also drawn from Shakespeare, though Shakespeare's emphasis would have been on matrimony and fertility. Is this a matter of personality and the experience of life? Or is it a fault of the times, the tidal drag into Puritanism which is so hard for us to understand? Chastity, after all, is usually assumed to lead to marriage, otherwise it is a peculiar and minority subject for celebration. In *Comus* Milton is what used to be called 'prosy': the speeches are appallingly long, nothing much happens (it is only frustrated from happening), there are no dances, only cavortings, and few spectacular changes of scene. Most of it takes place in the dark: 'dim darkness and this leafy labyrinth'.

We do not know whether the Castlehaven scandal had any effect on the text. John Wain once gave a brilliant lecture in which he argued plausibly that the differences between what Milton allowed to be printed by Lawes and then printed himself in 1645, and what remained a secret, locked away in the Bridgewater library, in a manuscript of *Comus* unknown until the nineteenth century, showed that the family's reaction to the text they were sent had been savage, and they had cut out all Milton's luxuriant references to wickedness, which might have brought Castlehaven to mind. The truth is too complicated to permit such a simple motive as an explanation. What happened is roughly this. The Bridgewater manuscript is a scribe's copy of the Trinity manuscript, which itself was a copy of some lost original working copy. The 1637 edition appears to derive from an intermediary version between Trinity and Bridgewater, made about that time and embodying some of Trinity's corrections. Milton corrected a copy of 1637 for the press in 1645. Facsimiles of all these

different states of the text, with the complex and numerous corrections of the Trinity notebook, were published by Harris Fletcher of
Illinois (1943). It will be clear to anyone who works through a good,
modern edition that the errors of the Bridgewater manuscript are
scribal and not doctrinal. At the same time it is evident that Milton
was intent from the beginning on cutting back his own luxuriance.
For instance, he begins with these pure and perfect lines:

> Before the starry threshold of Jove's court
> My mansion is, where those immortal shapes
> Of bright aerial spirits live ensphered
> In regions calm of mild and serene air . . .

Then he inserts, and later crosses out, lines about

> . . . Hesperian gardens, on whose banks
> Bedewed with nectar and celestial songs
> Eternal roses grow and hyacinth
> And fruits of golden rind, on whose fair tree
> The scaly-harnessed watchful dragon keeps
> His unenchanted eye, and round the verge
> And sacred limits of this blissful isle
> The jealous Ocean that old river winds
> His far-extended arms, till with steep fall
> Half his waste flood the wide Atlantic fills
> And half the slow unfathomed pool of Styx . . .

This tremendous sentence wanders on for ever, through 'strange
distances . . . and unknown climes', until with some trouble he
recovers himself. Now lines 5 and 6 read in a more classic way, 'Above
the smoke and stir of this dim spot,/Which men call earth . . .'

It will not be possible to follow the whole performance in this
degree of detail, but it is important to see how extraordinary Milton's
facility was, and how ruthlessly he cut it back. Some of it he did use
in the concluding part of the entertainment; some looks like the seed
of *Paradise Lost*, where his interest in geography was to erupt with
some force. But to have pruned the profuse blossom of his verses
must mean that he knew what he intended, and brings the plot and
construction into question.

The name *Comus* comes into a masque by Ben Jonson, whose
second folio had just appeared. But Milton's ideas are Neoplatonic,

and in the end their wavering direction is the ascent of the mind to God. The important all-knowing character who opens *Comus* is called in manuscript 'The Daemon', although he is almost the same as the Genius of the Wood in 'Arcades', with an added Neoplatonic emphasis. Milton's Comus, as a character, seems to owe a lot to the Latin prose *Comus* by van der Putten or Puteanus, published in 1608 and reprinted in Oxford in 1634. As a masque what Milton wrote has very little dancing, and in this it resembles W. Browne's Inner Temple Masque of 1615. It is likely enough that doing without elaborate dances and changes of scene was a condition imposed on Milton. The commissioning of the show does sound like old Alice Derby, as she continued to call herself, who was soon to go to her rest under the baroque grandeurs of her remarkable tomb in Harefield Church. It was performed at Ludlow Castle, in the great hall which would be ruined by the end of the Civil War. The Earl of Bridgewater had probably never been there: he was made President of the Council of Wales in June 1631, and Lord Lieutenant of Wales and the Border Counties in July. The second appointment gave substance and authority where the first had been perhaps no more than a subtle step in the hierarchy. As for Milton, he may well have taken a year or two dithering over his first major commission. His Sabrina is the goddess of the Severn, which does not flow through Ludlow: can he have supposed the entertainment would take place in Shrewsbury, which Sabrina so encircles that the town has a Welsh Bridge and an English Bridge? Important magic attaches to her; the name is classical and Milton had found it in the earliest Latin accounts of mythical British history. Drayton and Spenser (*The Faerie Queene*, 2, 10) had already spoken of her with reverence; all the same she was ten miles from Ludlow as the crow flies, and the river at Ludlow is the Teme. It should be emphasized that until after the Civil War the maps that anatomized England did so in terms of rivers, not of roads.

Sabrina is the end of the entertainment, as Lady Derby had been the end of 'Arcades'. The Daemon explains how Comus was born, son of Circe by Bacchus and, alas, not so jolly as Caliban. He has spent his youth, 'ripe, and frolic of his full-grown age,/Roving the Celtic, and Iberian fields'. Now he lives in an ominous and dark forest, waylaying travellers and transforming them with a drink 'into some brutish form of wolf, or bear,/Or ounce, or tiger, hog, or bearded goat ...' They forgot their homes and their friends, 'To roll with pleasure in a sensual sty'. This calamity, which to us sounds more enjoyable than most adventures, is what the Daemon seeks to prevent. He spies upon Comus, who in the metre of 'L'Allegro', with a few diversions into iambic pentameter (for no obvious reason), makes a speech of 52 lines, elaborating 'L'Allegro' and adding some pleasant new passages.

> The sounds, and seas with all their finny drove
> Now to the moon in wavering morris move,
> And on the tawny sands and shelves,
> Trip the pert fairies and the dapper elves ...

The Daemon in blank verse was more impressive, but this amalgam is more Shakespearian. Even here though, in what appears to be an attempt to dazzle his audience with learning, Milton cannot help introducing the 'dark-veiled Cotytto':

> ... to whom the secret flame
> Of midnight torches burns; mysterious dame
> That ne'er art called, but when the dragon womb
> Of Stygian darkness spits her thickest gloom,
> And makes one blot of all the air,
> Stay thy cloudy ebon chair,
> Wherein thou rid'st with Hecat', and befriend
> Us thy vowed priests ...

This nonsense surely touches the verge of pantomime, which indeed has an inherited resemblance to the masque. Comus has twenty-four more lines to transform the scene before the entrance of the Lady, who has lost her young brothers in the dark. She has sixty lines of blank verse: all these speeches contain lines of magical or Shakespearian beauty, but are they not impractically long for performance? She speaks fastidiously of harvest homes:

> Of riot, and ill-managed merriment,
> Such as the jocund flute, or gamesome pipe
> Stirs up among the loose unlettered hinds,
> When for their teeming flocks, and granges full
> In wanton dance they praise the bounteous Pan,
> And thank the gods amiss. I should be loth

> To meet the rudeness, and swilled insolence
> Of such late wassailers . . .

She is a curiously displeasing character of distinctly Puritan colour. To her even the twilight is 'grey-hooded Even,/Like a sad votarist in palmer's weed', where Comus had to disguise 'these my sky-robes spun out of Iris' woof', borrowed from him by the young Cowley later (who got to Cambridge only in 1637) for the robes of Gabriel at the Annunciation. She prays to the angels of Faith, Hope and Chastity (not Charity), observes faint moonlight, and sings to Echo, 'by slow Meander's margent green'. Milton, of course, knew as little about that mosquito-infested river as about the Thracian goddess Cotytto, but the song is charming and clearly intended to be in the manner of 'Arcades'. A manuscript of Lawes songs in the British Library (BM Add. 11518) alters 'and give resounding grace . . .' to the bolder and better line 'and hold a counterpoint to all heaven's harmonies'.

Comus arrives, attracted by the holy sound, and has his best lines in the entertainment.

> How sweetly did they float upon the wings
> Of silence, through the empty-vaulted night
> At every fall smoothing the raven down
> Of darkness till it smiled: I have oft heard
> My mother Circe with the Sirens three,
> Amidst the flowery-kirtled Naiades
> Culling their potent herbs . . .

It does not matter that 'it smiled' was a change later than the manuscripts, since 'she' is not obviously the darkness. The flower-skirted Naiades improve on a vaguer phrase of Homer's, who just says 'daughters of the water-spring and the woods and the holy rivers', since a naiad might be too grand to serve (*Odyssey*, 10, 348). It is the violence of the image for sound which makes it so successful. But when Comus at last encounters the Lady face to face, he questions her and she replies in a quick-fire dialogue of single lines deriving from Greek tragedy. The Lady puts her quandary into a brilliant line which in itself does the work of the whole poem, 'Dim darkness, and this leafy labyrinth', and describes her lost brothers. Now once again Comus has beautiful lines.

> Two such I saw, what time the laboured ox
> In his loose traces from the furrow came,
> And the swinked hedger at his supper sat;
> I saw them under a green mantling vine
> That crawls along the side of yon small hill . . .

The effect is curiously overloaded or heavy-scented. Are there a shade too many adjectives or descriptive phrases? It is the essence of Shakespeare without the substance. At times Milton's Latin cleverness with the iambic pentameter trips him up altogether:

> To find out that, good shepherd, I suppose,
> In such a scant allowance of star-light,
> Would overtask the best land-pilot's art,
> Without the sure guess of well-practised feet.

Mannerism has slid somehow into self-parody.

Comus leads the Lady off to shelter in a cottage, and the two boys appear. They were seasoned actors in their grandmother's entertainments, and that very year they had starred in Thomas Carew's *Coelum Britannicum*. Their speeches are elaborately and deliberately courtly. They would welcome a cottage, and they worry about their sister. The audience, of course, knows that 'a noble peer of mickle trust and power' is expecting their arrival at Ludlow. They discuss vice and virtue in high-flown, abstract terms. Milton has cut a reference to Proserpine in the Trinity manuscript, but it occurs uncut in the Bridgewater copy. No doubt the 'big wallowing flakes of pitchy clouds' are inappropriate to summer. The long and deadly speeches of the two brothers about Virtue, and about Chastity which converses with angels and becomes the soul's essence 'till all be made immortal', last 150 lines, ending in:

> How charming is divine philosophy!
> Not harsh, and crabbed, as dull fools suppose,
> But musical as is Apollo's lute . . .

Sixteen thirty-three was the year that saw the publication of George Herbert: it is a pity that Milton did not know and could not follow his path. Henry More's *Divine Dialogues* were still in the remote future. What then did Milton mean by philosophy? Nothing more than the last foaming and fretting of the Renaissance as the tide receded. It was a word and an idea he had taken from Shakespeare.

The two brothers hear a distant calling, and their language, which is quite vigorously boyish for a moment, is calmed down and made more solemn in the revisions of the Trinity notebook. 'Or else some curled hedgeman of the sword' gets cut, and so does 'He may chance scratch his forehead, here be brambles'. The Daemon, or Attendant Spirit, is coming to the rescue, dressed as a shepherd, not unlike Comus but identifiable as their father's shepherd Thyrsis,

> . . . Whose artful strains have oft delayed
> The huddling brook to hear his madrigal,
> And sweetened every musk-rose of the dale.

He speaks like the spirit of *Englands Helicon*, as these lines suggest, and in a speech of nearly seventy lines he tells them (as a shepherd) of Comus, who was active when 'the chewing flocks/Had ta'en their supper on the savoury herb/Of knot-grass dew-besprent', and of how he met their sister. The knot-grass, a herb with a pink flower, is Shakespearian, and there are more attractive lines in the same spirit. The elder brother, in a fluent reply, demands action. The Spirit tells him at some length about a special herb he knows of from a shepherd boy (Charles Diodati surely?) which he calls haemony, Haemonia being a word for Thessaly, the home of Greek magic. This herb he recommends as a cure against magic: Milton has mixed it up perhaps with buckthorn, an extreme purgative the poets knew vaguely as a protection against enchantment. The boys are to use this when they attack Comus and break his glass. The scene changes to Comus's palace, where the Lady is imprisoned in his enchanted chair but continues to defy him. He offers her a goblet, assuring her 'Not that Nepenthes which the wife of Thone,/In Egypt gave to Jove-born Helena/Is of such power to stir up joy as this'. The wife is an obscure character in the *Odyssey* (4, 219–32) who uses a drug to cheer up Menelaus. The reference sounds more like Jonson than Shakespeare. The Lady is not deceived, however, and remains voluble in moral protest and Puritanic disapproval of pleasure. Comus makes a brave speech against these views, calculated to be mistrusted. She answers him scornfully, and this academic discussion has taken 150 lines.

The boys arrive to rescue her, which they mismanage, but luckily the Spirit tells them he knows of a charm to release the Lady from her chair.

> There is a gentle nymph not far from hence,
> That with moist curb sways the smooth Severn stream,
> Sabrina is her name, a virgin pure . . .

He recounts her legend, how she was Locrine's daughter, Brute's granddaughter, who was running away from her stepmother and dived into the Severn, where the nymphs (out of Virgil's fourth *Georgic*) rescued her, 'till she revived/And underwent a quick immortal change,/Made goddess of the river', where she looks after the cows in the Severn water meadows. The shepherds throw her 'pansies, pinks, and gaudy daffodils'. Sabrina is summoned with a song:

> Sabrina fair
>   Listen where thou art sitting
> Under the glassy, cool, translucent wave,
>   In twisted braids of lilies knitting
> The loose train of thy amber-dropping hair . . .

We now revert to the metre of 'L'Allegro', and the lines are charming, a string of classical allusions like rough gems; it does not really matter what they mean, perhaps not many of the first audience knew, and the knottiest bits sound as good as the rest: 'By hoary Nereus' withered look,/And the Carpathian wizard's hook'. The wizard is Proteus in the fourth *Georgic*, and the hook is his as shepherd of seals. (It is beyond hope that Milton could have known that seals do swim up the Severn.) Leucothea comes from the *Georgics* too, where she is the same as Ino and occurs with Glaucus (*Georgics*, 1, 436–7).

Sabrina rises out of her river singing in a more English manner, 'By the rushy-fringed bank,/Where grows the willow and the osier dank . . .' Her chariot is 'thick set with agate, and the azurn sheen/Of turkis blue, and emerald green/That in the channel strays'. Milton is not on oath here, but 'azurn' means made of lapis lazuli and 'turkis' is the oriental turquoise. Sabrina comes ashore, setting her 'printless feet/O'er the cowslip's velvet head,/That bends not as I tread'. She sets the Lady free, and hastens away 'ere morning hour/To wait in Amphitrite's bower'. The Spirit wishes her plenty of clear water with no floods or mud, but beryls and gold and groves of myrrh and cinnamon.

He will take the Lady to her father's court, there to see what country dancing the Welsh may offer. Milton has surely been told of a morris danced for James I in Herefordshire by ten old rustics whose combined ages added up to over a thousand years. When that is over, the Spirit or Daemon wanders away to the Ocean and everlasting daylight, the gardens of Hesperus, the land of the west winds 'with musky wing' and eternal summer. There the rainbow waters the flowers, more varied than her own variegated scarf,

> And drenches with Elysian dew
> (List mortals if your ears be true)
> Beds of hyacinth, and roses,
> Where young Adonis oft reposes,
> Waxing well of his deep wound
> In slumber soft, and on the ground
> Sadly sits the Assyrian queen . . .

It is possible, and not unlikely, that at the end of this April shower of pretty words and attractive conceptions, Milton is alluding to Plutarch, for whom Venus and Adonis await the ascent of their minds or souls into an unearthly sun. Philosophic souls are supposed to achieve this transition swiftly, but the earthly remain in an Elysium subject to the moon. Cupid and Psyche are mentioned next as the example to follow: she is to give birth to Youth and Joy. Does all this complexity and secret teaching underlie the smooth flow of the lyrics? The only moral of the entertainment is perfectly formulated, it seems to me, by Milton in his last four lines about Virtue.

> She can teach ye how to climb
> Higher than the sphery chime;
> Or if Virtue feeble were,
> Heaven itself would stoop to her.

The 1,022 lines have had their *longueurs*, but they have offered some amazing and quite unexpected pieces of poetry in the Elizabethan manner, thirty years after that age ended and nearly twenty after the death of Shakespeare. It was to Shakespeare's influence that Jonson was turning in his old age, although not as powerfully as this young man, who could now write in his chosen style of English poetry as easily as he could compose Latin verse. What he lacked was any idea of the stage or how to manage it. The long arguments are surely tedious, and Milton seems to have made them more so in revision.

In 1637 Lawes produced the first edition, in which Milton was unnamed, clearly by his own request. He had not finished with it, and his own version appeared only in 1645. The trouble was not only Milton's difficult relationship with the Puritans, though it was also that. He was trying to think through the nature of the masque, or of his masque, the moral and lyrical entertainment as he conceived it. Possibly the family were not best pleased with his compromise; certainly no further commission followed. Probably such capers survived only as long as Alice, who died early in 1636.

The masque as a form was dying out, and only a few were produced under the Commonwealth. Davenant, whose life Milton saved and who is said to have saved Milton's in 1660, persevered, and so did Shirley. But we can sense a certain gloom and its increase in Milton's *Comus*. It is not just the exaggerated formality of his didactic speeches, the neoclassicism that affected him at times like arthritis in the fingers; it was surely a lack of belief in the roses and dew and the pretty speeches of the shepherds. When Shakespeare in a late play suddenly showers everyone with flowers we believe him, and his shepherds are real too, and much less Virgilian than Milton's. It is strange that since the first English translations of Theocritus, which are Elizabethan and excellent though very few, no one dared touch that poet again until Thomas Creech in 1684, during the age of Dryden. Milton has a deep affection for the honey and watermeadows, and the fountains and spirits of Virgil, but Theocritus and the Greeks and Greek nature are really a closed book to him. I wish very much that history had been otherwise, that he had gone to Greece as he intended, and taken Theocritus in his pocket.

He did lavish some fairly bad Greek verse on the younger Gill in November 1634, Psalm 114 in hexameters. He had trouble with the printers too, but however his version is corrected, it is not something one can read with pleasure. This he says is the first Greek verse composition he has attempted since leaving school. It is not a success, and its faintly Theocritean flavour does not help at all. The postscript to his love poems in Latin must have been written after he was twenty

(1628) and in 1645 he stuck it to the end of his 'Elegy 7'. Any date between 1628 and 1645 is possible, but the verses fit the mood of creeping Puritanism that was on him in about 1635: the mood in which he set Psalm 114 to the thumping and not always accurate jollity of his Greek verses may not be far distant. The same concern for chastity that he shows in *Comus* may well have the brief ten lines of Latin verse as a by-product. They are a sort of parody of Puritanic conversion:

> So with a twisted mind and creepy zeal
> I raised this empty trophy to my sin,
> Error and badness carried me away
> and untaught age taught me my wickedness
> until Platonic shadows offered streams
> from Socrates, and I laid down my yoke.
> Now from that time my flames are all extinct
> and my breast hemmed in every way with ice.
> The boy Eros fears frost for his arrows
> and Venus Diomedes' violence.

Bateson was a great admirer of these verses in their Latin originals, and they are in their way striking, but there is always something lacking in a young person's poems about chastity, and in the conversion of young poets from an erotic element that was never very strong in them: Milton was to go on to have three wives and some children, and to write better about love then than he had done in the mid-1630s, when he was between twenty-five and thirty. Before his public life began, he was to write two or three more poems of some importance. The first of these is *Lycidas*, written in the late autumn of 1637, and into which he compressed all the unexpressed passion of his Cambridge years. It is not so much about Edward King, except as an ikon, as it is about youth and the loss of youth, and it is full of frank feeling. As for the way the world was going, which was visible like a small cloud the size of a man's hand in *Comus*, it is a thundercloud in *Lycidas*, dark and dangerous. Did Milton himself know that? I greatly doubt it.

In one important matter he made continuous progress: it is really only by reading a poet's life backwards that one can see what he was up to in the beginning. His progress in technique was steady, undisturbed by any public influence at all. *Comus* was the last time he would scatter flowers with such pantomime generosity, *Lycidas* the last time he would scatter them at all. The verse he was stripping down his technique to write was not going to be the Greek dramatic verse he then envisaged, and would attempt again in *Samson Agonistes* with a stunning degree of success, but it was going to be the muscular moral verse of his sonnets. Tasso's heroic sonnets are not as powerful, and nothing else in English is like them. Milton's progress as a poet was as if the great English political crisis were not threatening: and, when that crisis broke, as if it were not happening. It reduced the time he could spend on poetry, that is all. It did not affect its quality.

His learning also proceeded massively. Already at Hammersmith (if he really lived there) and at Horton he had laid the foundations not only of his prodigious knowledge of the classics but also of his wide knowledge of English history. Here he must to some degree have followed Camden, and Selden's notes on the first eighteen books of Drayton's *Poly-Olbion*, the verse narrative that describes the geography and mythology of Britain. In Drayton he read

> Now Sabrine, as a Queen, miraculously fair,
> Is absolutely plac'd in her Emperial chair
> Of crystal richly wrought, that gloriously did shine . . .
> On her throne: . . . there were engrav'd those Nymphs the god had
>   wooed,
> And every several shape wherein for love he sued . . .
> . . . She in a watchet weed, with many a curious wave,
> Which as a princely gift great *Amphitrite* gave;
> Whose skirts were to the knee, with coral fring'd below . . .

It may be said in general that the peculiar and wide learning of Selden is more striking than the mild charms or slackish power of Drayton's verse. Selden knows about the obscurest chroniclers, the silver horseshoe dug up in his lifetime at Cadbury Hill, and who wrote *Piers Plowman* (which he gets wrong, but from a manuscript source). Milton must have read his *De Diis Syriis* (1617). John Selden (1584–1654), who entered Parliament in the 1620s, had published three books in 1617, the one on the Syrian gods, one on the office of Lord Chancellor of England dedicated to Francis Bacon, and the third and most influential, *A History of Tythes*. It was probably at this time that

Milton got to know him: he had been a friend of the London poets since his boyhood and Ben Jonson paid him flowing compliments. His published *Table Talk* is a mine of dry, laconic humour. 'I never converted but two, the one was Mr Crashaw from writing against plays ... the other was a Doctor of Divinity from preaching against painting ...' (ed. Pollock, 1927).

No one knows who first influenced Milton towards politics. His views until after his Italian journey were too general, too abstract a matter of principle, in fact really too Cambridge-like, to reflect any practical interest in the questions of the day, at least as they were before his Italian journey. Some old friend it was no longer safe to name left him a minor work by Ralegh, which in the end Milton saw into print. The work is interesting if genuine, but unimportant. Was it not by Ralegh, as scholars have suggested? In that case, was it just a manuscript Milton as a young man had picked up somewhere? Sir Henry Wootton had been a friend of Ralegh, so may Selden have been: yet it is hard to see why either of them would have left this minor work to Milton. He had it published by the same bookseller who had recently handled all kinds of late-discovered prose writings of Ralegh, and he contributed a preface himself, entitling the book *The Cabinet-Council, Containing the chief arts of Empire and mysteries of State discabineted in Political and Polemical Aphorisms* (1658).

> Having had the manuscript of this treatise many years in my hands and finding it lately by chance among other books and papers, upon reading thereof I thought it a kind of injury to withold long the work of so eminent an author from the public, it being both answerable in style to other works of his already extant, as far as the subject would permit, and given me for a true copy by a learned man at his death, who had collected several such pieces.

The balance tips towards Selden, who was then four years dead, but the circulation of such a document had been dangerous, so any conjecture we make is based on gossamer. A man stone-blind coming across a lost document among old books and papers and 'reading thereof' does sound unlikely. The work in itself is Machiavellian in tone: 'Of Monarchies Royal with the means to maintain them: First to extinguish the race of him that was anciently prince ...' The examples offered are Naples, Sicily and Ireland. 'The ambition of men is such as rarely they will obey when formerly they have commanded, neither do they willingly accept of mean office having before sat in higher place, yet . . .'

One must remember that it was not only the tidal wave of popular feeling, not only the Anabaptists and the Levellers and the rest who were gathering force, but an intellectual resentment of the settled system of government in England, which had long existed and which shows itself at many points in the life of Shakespeare, that would be ready to break surface if ever it got the chance. Hobbes would soon be writing, English philosophy was at school, and deism, always no doubt more widespread than people admitted, was to emerge in Milton's lifetime. His *Lycidas* would mark the end of an age and not, as he must have hoped, the beginning of a career. Herrick, that very private poet, was born earlier and died in the same year as Milton, but his poetry was all printed by 1648, three years after Milton's. James Shirley (1596–1666), who had public aspirations, produced only a feeble piping.

> Within their buds let roses sleep,
> And virgin lilies on their stem,
> Till sighs from lovers glide and creep
> Into their leaves to open them . . .

Milton outsoared all such poets, even Herrick, though it must be conceded that the lyric did not come naturally to him. Of those few writers who shared Milton's airy Neoplatonic aspirations, his close friend and fellow-poet Andrew Marvell arrived at Trinity College, Cambridge, only in 1633 at the unripe age of twelve and left it in 1641 at twenty. Marvell's *Dialogue between Thyrsis and Dorinda* was set to music by William Lawes, the brother of Milton's composer.

> . . . To the Elysium.
>   O where is't?
> A chaste soul can never miss't.
> I know no way but to our home,
> Is our cell Elysium?

In 1633 the King had visited Scotland to be crowned there, and had begun the long catalogue of mistakes that marked his Scottish dealings. His desire 'to unite his three kingdoms in one form of God's worship and in a uniformity in their public devotions' had disastrous results. The bishops delayed the matter and it was to them the King committed it. Laud, at that time Bishop of London, preached in favour of the King's wishes, but without effect beyond the royal chapel walls. King James had thanked God for the crown of England, because 'it redeemed him from being subject to the ill manners and insolent practices' of the preachers who came from St Andrew's, 'which I could never shake off before'. In this matter I follow Clarendon's account, which the gradual unfolding of the influence of men like Thomas Young with Milton's active co-operation confirms. To bolster the authority of his bishops, the King appointed Spottiswood of St Andrew's Lord Chancellor of Scotland and four or five others Privy Councillors, so that they swiftly made enemies of the nobility.

That autumn saw the death of Abbot, the old and unacceptable Archbishop of Canterbury, of whom Clarendon says, 'he had been master of one of the poorest colleges in Oxford, and had learning sufficient for that province ... of very morose manners and a very sour aspect'. The King at once appointed Laud to Canterbury, and Laud installed his old ally Juxon as Bishop of London. It was Laud who took Dr Wren from Peterhouse to rule Norwich with a rod of iron. When the Earl of Portland, the High Treasurer of England, died, Laud was appointed a Commissioner of the Treasury. His rise had been meteoric, from St John's, Oxford, to St David's which he never even visited, to Bath and Wells, to London and now to Canterbury, and resentment against him was in proportion. By the later 1630s these English circumstances must be set against defeats and reverses in Scotland on an appalling scale: the new Canons of the Scottish Church were issued late, but still before the composition of the liturgy that should have preceded them. They were issued without any kind of consultation and appeared as suddenly as if they were the King's own work. The first Canon gave him the fullest powers imaginable, based on those of the kings of Israel.

In 1636, plague broke out again at London and in spring 1637 it was still spreading. Indeed, it was thought to rise and fall according to the phases of the moon. Between May and August it touched even Horton. The first to die was the innkeeper of the Talbot: after him a tapster, a saddler and a glover died, then a vintner, finally a cobbler

and a judge's daughter. They are all people with some connection or
business beyond the village. On 3 April 1636 the poet's mother died,
though not of plague. It was perhaps her death that made it possible
for John to go abroad to improve himself. His father's affairs at this
time are incomprehensible: a case has been made that he was not
doing well in business, but he seems to have been holding his own.
His old apprentices and assistants were taking over the responsibility
as far as they could. John's sister Anne had been widowed in 1631.
Her husband Edward Phillipps had been a deputy in the Crown
Office in Chancery, and she now married again, to Thomas Agar who
succeeded as Deputy Clerk. Jobs like this depended on patronage or
inheritance, as one may see from the early volumes of Pepys's diaries.

In 1637, when Henry Lawes produced a text of *Comus*, there was
one odd aspect of the publication, even apart from Milton's anxious
anonymity. The motto or epigraph came from Virgil's second *Eclogue*,
and was apparently as near as the poet would go to expressing his
feelings. It was *Eheu, quid volui misero mihi? Floribus austrum perditus*
... ('Alas what was I doing, wretched as I am? Crazy to let the storm
wind at my flowers ...'). But the sentence goes on *et liquidis immisi
fontibus apros*: 'and let wild pigs into my running springs'. Does he
mean he should have kept his mystical doctrines secret? But they
surely do not amount to very much. Or that he should not let the
critics see his precious writing? That may be it, since he clearly
intended to burst on the world in sudden splendour, and did not yet
feel strong enough to do so. He could see that *Comus* was not quite
good enough. Possibly, as we have noted, it had not given perfect
satisfaction to his patrons. But Lawes had circulated his own music
and succeeded in getting the whole affair printed in the year before
Milton went abroad. The book was not a huge edition: only fifteen or
so copies are now known, and five of those are at Oxford and at
London.

It was dedicated to Bridgewater's son.

My Lord, This poem, which received its first occasion of Birth from
your Self, and others of your Noble Family, and much honour from
your own Person in the performance, now returns again to make a
finall Dedication of it self to you. Although not openly acknowledg'd
by the Author, yet it is a legitimate off-spring so lovely, and so much
desired, that the often Copying of it hath tir'd my Pen to give my

severall friends satisfaction, and brought me to a necessity of producing
it to the publike view . . .

The young man is to accept it 'from the hands of him who hath by
many favours been long oblig'd to your most honour'd Parents, and
as in this representation your attendant Thyrsis, so now etc. H.
Lawes'. One is fascinated to see so much made of the boy: 'Live sweet
Lord to be the honour of your Name', nothing of his sister, and very
little of his parents. Does this point to a fact about patronage, and
who actually paid for the printing? Or was the entire enterprise the
children's present to Lord Bridgewater? Milton was pleased anyway,
because when he sent a copy on 6 April 1638 to the Provost of Eton,
he received in reply a most generous letter of praise, which he printed
in the 1645 edition of his poems.

At the end of September 1637, Milton still entertained notions of
entering an Inn of Court, as he wrote in a letter to Diodati; but he
seems to have thought of it only as a quiet way of life, modelled
perhaps on Selden's. All the same Selden had been an MP for more
than ten years, and had been to prison. We know that Milton's time
was already being passed 'in the search of religious and civil knowledge'. His commonplace book confirms this, and his pamphlets assert
it. He read Church history in much the same range as a serious
theological student would read it today, claiming that it took him
some years. He owned such diverse works as the monumental Eton
Chrysostom, and Heraclides Ponticus's allegories on the Homeric
gods. Much of what scholars write about the depth of his learning is
poppycock. His notes, for example, on the views of the Fathers on
secular learning are the jejune observations that have been made ever
since the Renaissance. The relevance of his studies to modern
questions remains highly debatable. His claim to have pursued the
Greeks 'to the time when they cease to be Greeks' is silly and
patronizing. In fact, his pretension to cover universal history, though
it was undoubtedly an ideal of his age, is absurd.

He was still in affectionate correspondence with Charles Diodati.
Charles forbids him to be ill; Milton says he will be if he likes. But
the letter explodes like a firework into Platonic sentiments. He had,
since leaving Cambridge, moved from 'the laureate fraternity of
poets', who appear to be Dante, Petrarch and Spenser, to 'the divine

volumes of Plato' and Xenophon: presumably the didactic works of that most uneven author. Now he feels that friendship should be deeply rooted in the mind and 'should spring from a pure origin' and endure lifelong even without the expression of mutual affection. It is not letters that foster true friendship but 'a lively recollection of virtues'. This surprising opinion is not as priggish as it sounds, though it surely is as Plato's *Symposium* was the essential fine flower of an all-male society.

> Your integrity writes to me instead of you, and inscribes true letters on my heart: your purity of life and your love of virtue write to me: your personal quality writes to me and commends you more and more ... Whatever else God may intend for me, of one thing I am certain: he has instilled in me a mighty passion for Beauty. Ceres never sought for her daughter Proserpine (as the story goes) with more ardour than I pursue this Idea of Beauty, day and night in every shape and form (for many are the forms of the divine) [a quotation from Euripides] and I follow close in its footsteps as it leads me on ... Just let me whisper it in your ear, to spare my blushes, and let me boast for a minute. What am I thinking about? Immortality, so help me God. What am I doing? Growing wings and learning to fly. My Pegasus can only soar on tender wings so far, so my new wisdom must be humble.

The letter expresses the same preoccupations we noticed in *Comus*. The Platonic ideal into which Milton proposes to soar is identical with poetry: he intends to achieve his virtuous immortality and fame as a poet; that is fundamental to him. From this time on he will begin to seek large schemes, not of work or reading but of composition. The fact that his attempt at the great work was to be long delayed by his public career does not alter the certainty that it was already putting down roots. His inclination to Platonism might wither in the atmosphere of public life; it was for him, after all, a boyish affair, more so for him than it was for Shakespeare; marriage would modify it, until it was only a scarcely visible ghost inhabiting the ruins of his Christian beliefs in *De Doctrina Christiana*. His poetry remained a more concrete object, one that was modified only for the better by the world, by life, and finally by his blindness. One could not possibly in 1637 have foreseen his future.

CHAPTER FIVE

LYCIDAS

LYCIDAS IS THE MASTERPIECE of Milton's early period, and makes him Shakespeare's heir. It was written for Edward King, who had been drowned off Anglesey crossing over to Ireland on 10 August 1637. Milton wrote his poem in November, as the last poem in *Obsequies to the memory of Mr Edward King*, the second part (in English) of *Justa Eduardo King naufrago*, a collection of twenty-three sets of verse in Latin and a few in Greek by friends; Milton's part had thirteen poems of which *Lycidas* was the longest and last. As his name too was last, it is likely enough by convention that he organized the English part of the anthology. There is a slight mystery about a poem by Henry King, who is either a kinsman, perhaps a brother, who wrote in both languages, or the bishop who is famous for an elegy to his wife: but the editors of that Henry, who became Bishop of Chichester and is buried there, scorn the attribution. This Henry King was at Christ Church, and Milton may have known him: but their alliance or co-operation would not fit easily into what we know of Milton's life.

The English poems on the whole were as bad as the Latin ones. Isaac Olivier's was one of the worst:

> So should he, so have cut the Irish strand
> And like a lusty bridegroom leapt to land;
> Or else (like Peter) trod the waves; but he
> Then stood most upright, when he bent his knee . . .

Cleveland is, or became, a better-known poet, but this, his first published poem, was little better than Olivier's:

> When we have filled the rundlets of our eyes,
> We'll issue't forth, and vent such elegies,
> As that our tears shall seem the Irish seas,
> We floating Islands, live Hesperides . . .

Milton's poem almost rudely shrugs off, or ignores, the whole context of the little book in which it was to appear. It was both technically and personally deeply pondered, so that although we can see him at work on his improvements, it emerged all but perfect. He took his tone as an English poet from Lodowick Bryskett, or Lodovico Bruschetto, who had written a remarkable elegy in Spenser's book of laments for Sidney. Some of the musicality of *Lycidas* is undoubtedly Italian, and one may reasonably say that where Milton is most deeply English in his language he is also most deeply imbued with the classics and with Italian. Above all, his lovely stanza system, which is both loose and controlled, goes back to Tasso and, indeed, to Dante's advice on mingling long and short lines in *De vulgari eloquentia*. Tasso's *canzone* structure was a lesson that had sunk in. Some traces of the experiments that must have led up to this triumphantly successful poem may be discerned in the little poems 'On Time', and 'At a Solemn Music'. Milton now offers eleven stanzas of varying length and differing rhyme patterns, with occasional unrhymed lines and lines of six or of fourteen syllables contrasting with the usual ten syllables. The reader, however, is never conscious of what precise technical design may underlie the perfect run of Milton's language in this poem. Indeed, we do not possess the notation necessary to analyse exactly how the first ten lines work, with their assonance, internal rhyme, half-rhyme and innumerable devices of rhythm, of which rhyme is only the crudest. This poetry is to be tested in the ear and in the mouth.

We know that it goes back to Theocritus: Lycidas is a character out of the seventh *Idyll*, a contemporary poet disguised as a shepherd or goatherd, as he must be to enter this kind of poem. When Thomas Creech came to translate Theocritus later in the century, Milton was already an inescapable influence, but Creech conveys some of the charm of his author:

> Where were you Nymphs? . . .
> Where were you then when Daphnis pin'd and dy'd?
> On Pindus Top, or Tempe's open plain? . . .
> For not one Nymph by swift Asopus stood,
> Nor Aetna's cliff, nor Acis' sacred flood . . .
> The cruel waves enclosed the lovely Boy . . .

These stray lines are from the first *Idyll*: but what Milton exploited in Theocritus was not phrases; it was an intensity of atmosphere in which love, romantic tragedy, the beauty of nature and the warm, innocent lives of the herdsmen among their animals combine in a way that is as enchanting to read as it ever was. He borrows from Virgil and from *Bion* and Moschus, and from Bryskett (the L. B. of Spenser's book), who in turn adapts Tasso: this is a potent stew, and it is small wonder that it confused Dr Johnson, who reserves for *Lycidas* his severest censures: 'the diction is harsh, the rhymes uncertain, and the numbers unpleasing ... It is not to be considered as the effusion of real passion ... Passion plucks no berries from the myrtle and the ivy ... In this poem there is no nature, for there is no truth; there is no art, for there is nothing new. Its form is that of a pastoral, easy, vulgar, and therefore disgusting ...'

What provoked such an outburst? Johnson is annoyed by the use and neglect of rhymes, and by apparent casualness, which today we find refreshing. His hatred of the pastoral form is simply a fastidiousness about its decadence in the late eighteenth century, a point that appears idiotic if you consider the pastoral scenes in *The Winter's Tale*, or the poems in *Englands Helicon*, or the extraordinary freshness of Milton. Creech's version of a passage late in the seventh *Idyll* of Theocritus conveys the atmosphere of pastorals at their warmest:

> We lay, we wanton'd on a flowry bed,
> Where fragrant Mastick, and where Vines were spread,
> And round us Poplars rais'd their shady head:
> Just by a spring with pleasing Murmurs flow'd,
> In every bush, and thicket of the wood
> Sweet Insects sang, and sighing Turtles coo'd.
> The labouring Bees buzz'd round the purling spring,
> Their Honey gather'd, and forgot their sting:
> Sweet Summer's choicest fruits, and Autummn's pride
> Pears by our head, and Apples at our side
> Lay round in heaps; and loaden Plums did stand
> With bending boughs, to meet the reaching hand:
> To please us more he pierc't a Cask of Wine,
> Twas four years old, and from a noble Vine;
> Castalian Nymphs, ye Nymphs that still reside
> On steep Parnassus, and command his pride,

> Did e're old Chiron, did he e're produce
> For great Alcides such rich Bowls of juice?
> Did Polyphem the vast Sicilian Swain
> That darted mountains o'er the frighted main,
> Drink wine like this . . . ?

Creech conveys the rushing of the syntax, the accumulation and momentum of pleasure. Love, which the pastoral scene already suggests, is never far absent from these poems. I take it to have Milton's silent attention in his poem. His nephew Edward Phillipps tells us of a special intimacy of affection between Milton and the boy Edward King: there were four years between them, and Edward was only twenty-five when he was drowned. The Theocritean Lycidas poem is about a long, hot country walk on a Greek island, with much (disguised) conversation about literature, and that no doubt is as much as Milton's relationship with King ever amounted to. Edward was a religious youth, and as the ship went down and the crew tried to save their own lives, much like the sailors in *The Tempest* no doubt, Edward was seen kneeling in prayer on the deck. A long stanza in *Lycidas* about the corruption of the English Church may represent a stream of opinion that Edward King and John Milton had shared.

Is the reference to the classics as deliberate as I have suggested? In a classical translation of Spenser's *Shepheardes Calender*, Piers the Protestant in the May poem is called Lycidas, and in Sannazaro's long neoclassic poem *De Partu Virginis*, which Milton certainly knew, one of the shepherds at the birth of Christ is called Lycidas. There is even an obscure Lycidas, 'Near drowned in the deep water had his friends/ Not saved him', in Lucan. These examples do not on the whole weigh against the evidence of Milton's repeated quotations from Theocritus. It is almost more interesting that in his *Epitaphium Damonis* for his friend Charles Diodati, who was soon to die, Milton would choose a very similar pastoral convention, which in Diodati's case was in large part realistic rather than conventional. The only evidence we have that Edward King was a poet rests in his contributions to Cambridge anthologies like the one on the King's spots, which Milton scorned. In November 1631, at the age of nineteen, he had issued some Latin verses to the Princess Mary:

> Just as the seed and author of all things
> rosy dawn rises loose-haired from the sea
> delighting the round world with her fresh light,
> making the dark clouds not blush at themselves
> conquered by her bright rays, our little Princess
> Lucina's and the heaven's sweetest care
> comes from the Queen's womb . . .

It is by no means great poetry, but perhaps as a piece of diplomacy, which it was meant to be, it passes muster. It does not explain Milton's intimate affection, or why he chose Edward King for the gift of *Lycidas*. Perhaps after *Comus* he simply felt ready to write it: it was the product of his studies and his meditations. When all the poems were printed in 1638, the Latin and the English sections seem to have been available both separately and together: a hundred years ago both conditions of the *Justa Eduardo King* were to be found, *Lycidas* last with the signature J. M. In November 1637, when he wrote and revised it, Milton started with what look like scraps of notes in the Trinity notebook. Since the notebook, when it came to light in the eighteenth century, consisted of loose leaves and was bound for Trinity by Sir Thomas Clarke, Master of the Rolls, the order of its leaves can have no authority. It was Professor Mason, the Professor of Geology, who discovered it among the 4,000 books left to the college by Sir Henry Newton Pickering in 1691, though it was not catalogued among the other Trinity manuscripts in 1697. It is possible that the gift was negotiated by Daniel Skinner, Milton's last secretary, who was a Fellow of Trinity. Sir Henry's father Sir Adam had been tutor to Prince Henry and altered his name to Pickering on inheriting an estate; that is all we know, and it is not much. Milton had the notebook by him most of his life.

One leaf with seventeen lines for *Comus* had been fastened into it, but that was stolen in the nineteenth century and has not been seen since. Many poems are fair copies, not working copies. The order of poems is not exactly chronological, because a sonnet dating from the Civil War occurs before *Comus* and *Lycidas*, and the numbering of the pages represents at best Mason's judgement. The numbering of the sonnets in particular is queer: Wright, who edited the 1900 facsimile, abandons it in despair and follows Mason's numbering. *Lycidas* begins with a page of scraps or notes, after *Comus* (which ends with 'The End') on a new and empty page, actually a new leaf. Milton never leaves a page empty, so this one was filled up before he wrote out the entire fair copy of *Lycidas*. There are four of these fragments or notes: first the fourteen lines that begin the poem, ending with 'melodious tear' at line 14, the few changes being for reasons of harmony of sound. The second is twelve lines, 'Bring the rathe primrose' (now line 142) down to 'fill their cups with tears' (at line 150). These lines are then cancelled and ten lines substituted in a new version, which is the third fragment. This flower passage is not inserted in the poem at its proper place, but a marginal note in that place refers to the page where it was to be found: this third fragment was nearly but not quite what was printed, and it may have been altered in proof. The suppressed lines were these:

> Bring the rathe primrose that unwedded dies
> Colouring the pale cheek of unenjoyed love
> And that sad flower that strove
> To write his own woes on the vermeil grain . . .

The reason I have dwelt on the manuscript for so long is that I believe the flower piece was not necessarily an afterthought but that it was worked out very early in the composition of *Lycidas*, before Milton knew where it would fit. The imperfection of the lines as they are first given points to that, while the symbol of the flowers was central to *Lycidas* and to Milton's idea of the elegy, as we shall see. The idea of an afterthought has sometimes been used as an explanation of Milton's varied stanza length and an analysis built on the supposition: but the supposition is unnecessary. The fourth fragment at the beginning is the Orpheus passage:

> What could the muse herself that Orpheus bore . . .
> His divine visage down the stream was sent,
> Down the swift Hebrus to the Lesbian shore. . . .

The original version had been based not only on Virgil (the swift Hebrus) and Ovid (the Lesbian shore), but probably also on a poem in the *Greek Anthology* (7, 8) to Orpheus, which asks why we lament our dead sons when the gods themselves cannot keep away death from their children.

> What could the golden-haired Calliope
> For her enchanting son
> Whom she beheld (the gods far-sighted be)
> His gory scalp roll down the Thracian lea.

The last two lines were cancelled first, with the enormous improvement:

> Whom universal nature might lament
> And heaven and hell deplore
> When his divine head down the stream was sent.
> Down the swift Hebrus to the Lesbian shore.

'Gory', which is only just better than 'divine', was the final adjustment.

It is worth dwelling a little longer on the flowers. Until this moment Milton's flowers have been conventional and unimpressive since the primrose he borrowed from Bolton when he was seventeen. One might, after all, come across 'the pink and the lily and daffadown-dilly' in a folksong. The flower that 'strove/To write his own woes on the vermeil grain' is not fresh enough. Milton will have discovered the importance of the flowers in Lodowick Bryskett who left only eleven pages of English verse, all of it addressed to Sidney, but his importance is considerable if only because he translated Cinthio's *Hecatommithi* (1565) into English and so furnished Shakespeare with an important source. As a poet he was musical because in that age one could hardly fail to be, and so conventional that the plainness of the composition has a certain charm. In 'The Mourning Muse of Thestylis' he addresses the nymphs:

> Come forth, ye nymphs, forsake your watery bowers
> Forsake your mossy caves, and help me to lament,
> Help me to tune my doleful notes to gurgling sound
> Of Liffey's tumbling streams . . .
> . . . And straight a cloudy mist his senses overcast
> His life waxed pale and wan like damask roses bud
> Cast from the stalk, and like in field to purple flower
> Which languisheth being shred by culter as it passed . . .

In the poem in question, however, which Mitford in the early nineteenth century already realized lay behind *Lycidas*, and in which I

seem to discern Spenser's guiding hand, Lycon begins the Eclogue:
Lycon is the name for the father of Lycidas.

> Colin, well fits thy sad cheer this sad stound,
> This woeful stound, wherewith all things complain
> This great mishap, this grievous loss of ours.
> Hearst thou the Orown? – how with hollow sound
> He slides away, and murmuring doth plain,
> And seems to say unto the fading flowers,
> Along his banks, unto the bared trees,
> Phillisides is dead . . .

He writes in a kind of *terza rima*, in stanzas of between twenty and
twenty-nine lines; the laurel and the myrtle occur, and 'th' ocean with
his rolling waves/The white feet washeth (wailing this mischance/Of
Dover cliffs)', the sea-gods in their 'moist caves' lament, and we hope
'the Nymphs alway/Thy tomb may deck with fresh and sweetest
flowers'. Milton was determined to make more of the flowers than he
had ever done before. The rathe or early primrose that forsaken dies
is his own 'soft silken primrose fading timelessly' from the *Death of a
Fair Infant*, but 'the tufted crow-toe, and pale jessamine' sound highly
specific. Crowtoe is a name for bluebell, and the jessamine, or jasmine,
keeps him within the limits of the Mediterranean, though not of
English wild flowers. The white pink is as conventional as it could be,
but the paradox pleases him, and the pansy freaked with jet is said to
be his invention. However, tulips were described as freaked and
feathered in the tulipomania of this time, and perhaps it is not an
invention but the use of a word lexicographers have missed. Musk-
rose, woodbine and 'cowslips wan' are in no way difficult, except that
the musk-rose is a garden flower. Amaranthus sounds exotic, as it was
said to grow only in Heaven (*Paradise Lost*, 3, 353–7), and means
'unwithering', but *Amaranthus caudatus* is love-lies-bleeding or the
Floramor. The entire list is as romantic and striking as any in English,
and more musical; it is constantly refreshed with homely words like
'crow-toe' and just slightly elevated with touches of grandeur. The
epithets are chosen with dazzling effect, and with extreme care and
precision.

All these glimpses of the young mature Milton at work add to the
impression of his natural powers as a poet, which appear most strongly

in his powers of revision. Even the Virgilian-sounding laurels and myrtles come not so much from Virgil's *Eclogues* but from the humble verses of Bryskett, whose nymphs and oreads (hill-nymphs) are sulking:

> The pleasant shades of stately groves they shun;
> They leave their crystal springs, where they wont frame
> Sweet bowers of myrtle twigs and laurel fair,
> To sport themselves free from the scorching sun.

It is not any single overwhelming example of Bryskett's influence but an abundance of small touches that make one certain Milton had him in mind. Even the splendidly used word 'constraint', in line 6 of *Lycidas*, occurs in Bryskett (line 41) where, as in *Lycidas*, it seems to mean 'affliction'.

> Yet once more, O ye laurels, and once more,
> Ye myrtles brown, with ivy never sere,
> I come to pluck your berries harsh and crude,
> And with forced fingers rude,
> Shatter your leaves before the mellowing year.
> Bitter constraint, and sad occasion dear,
> Compels me to disturb your season due:
> For Lycidas is dead, dead ere his prime,
> Young Lycidas, and hath not left his peer ...

The introduction is by no means violent; indeed, there is a reserve about it, and a sense of season, which is a marked characteristic of English poetry. The strongest complaint is that Lycidas must not 'float upon his watery bier . . ./Without the meed of some melodious tear'. 'Meed' is an odd word in 1637; it is Old English for 'wages', and had come to mean 'reward' or 'prize'; it is used here as the equivalent of the Greek *geras* which goes back to Homer, the payment to which the dead man has a customary right and which the living have an obligation to give. None the less, it is a particularly cool line, and a restrained expression of impersonal emotion after the warm central lines of the stanza:

> Who would not sing for Lycidas? he knew
> Himself to sing, and build the lofty rhyme.

Twice in the manuscript Milton wrote 'he well knew', and inserted 'well' by hand in a printed copy where it was missing, but finally he dropped it to suit the impersonal coolness of mood, and to make the line run better, as it now does.

The stanza is exactly fourteen lines long. We should remember that the origins of the sonnet are entangled in those of the *canzone*, and that they interested Milton. His own sonnets are not always composed of precise lines: as recently as Shakespeare's time the word 'sonnet' had had a most variable meaning. Milton's stanza form, as we call it, is so loose in *Lycidas* that he can make it up as he goes along, by ear. It could not be imitated or repeated.

That is the first enormous difference between *Lycidas* and classical laments, which have very short stanzas in Theocritus, and a refrain. But elegy is not narrative, and it is hard to answer what exactly happens in *Lycidas*: yet it is not a wild wandering song or meditation. The stanzaic structure is the best clue. The second opens with another Theocritean touch, 'Begin then, sisters of the sacred well [the Muses] ... and somewhat loudly sweep the string. . . .' Milton thinks, as all elegists do though few admit it, of his own death. He will give Edward King what he too wants to be given. In fact, he was given nothing; he was in political disgrace when he died, old, poor and blind. Let *Lycidas* stand, then, for Milton's own elegy as well as his friend's. Indeed, when he says 'we were nursed upon the self-same hill,/Fed the same flock' he is paying a compliment that belongs more to Charles Diodati. His third stanza begins at line 25, 'Together both . . .' The phrase about the 'opening eye-lids of the morn' is a late correction, not made in 1638, for 'glimmering' eye-lids, which is better if one looks only at the half-line but, as he saw, less smooth and a distraction.

The third stanza opens up the bucolic metaphor, bringing satyrs and fauns 'with cloven heel', that is little Pans, into an English landscape where they appear to feel quite at home. Milton probably knew that Horace has 'faun' where Virgil has 'Pan': it is not a difference in mythology so much as a difficulty of scansion, to which Virgil was specially sensitive, as was Milton. But when we are told that 'old Damoetas loved to hear our song' (his name being so spelt in the Trinity manuscript, though in print it gets the odd form 'Damaetas'), scholars have gone off on a wild-goose chase to establish who this old gentleman was. He is a herdsman in Virgil and in

Theocritus, and there is no reason whatever to suppose he was any of the Fellows of the college. He is a figure from the pastoral landscape, that is all. But Sidney's *Arcadia* has a Dametas, a loutish clown, so this Damaetas, they argue, must be someone Milton was concerned to insult. This is absurd. Milton is not specific. The publisher's spelling was more easily pronounced by a seventeenth-century Englishman than 'Damoetas', and Sidney called him 'Dametas' for a similar reason: there is no mystery, no concealed message. The stanza is twelve lines long.

The fourth stanza is a neat thirteen lines, about the distress of nature: permissible now that the pastoral world has been established and, by convention, necessary. Moschus's *Lament for Bion*, which is a Theocritean poem though by a lesser and more rhetorical writer, does the scene fully enough, and even Bryskett does not neglect it. In Milton's version, the flowers 'that their gay wardrobe wear' began life, though one can scarcely credit it, as 'flowers that their gay buttons wear'. Milton, here as elsewhere in the poem, is refining his Spenserian repertory by using Shakespeare: his white-thorn recalls *A Midsummer Night's Dream*.

The fifth stanza is of fourteen lines and introduces a certain complexity of texture, a depth, that might well disappear from the easy surface of a purely pastoral poem. The fourth is charming but conventional: the fifth invokes something more powerful. It goes back to Theocritus and Virgil from the first lines, the complaint to the Nymphs. It asks what the Nymphs could have done, since not even his divine mother, the 'muse', could save Orpheus from his dreadful fate. Here Milton has the full weight of the fourth *Georgic* behind him; his masterly manipulation of the words, and the topographic precision of 'Down the swift Hebrus to the Lesbian shore', make the stanza wonderful.

In a long stanza of twenty-one lines Milton works out his own attitude to poetry, which is rather scornful, and to fame, which with his Italian roots he feels is the crucially important element in the lives of 'noble minds' like his. Fame was indeed the spur and inspiration of the late Renaissance, in which elegance turned extravagant and produced the baroque. Even in religious texts the theme had at that date an amazing importance, and Heaven itself was thought of only as an eternal version of fame. Milton was a deeply ambitious young man. In his poem Phoebus Apollo interferes to assure him that fame goes on for ever in spite of fate: not the fame of worldly reputation but fame in the eye of God. For Milton, fame (since he has never yet known it) is abstract and blazing and ethereal, a fire that never goes out. His first taste of it will be when Sir Henry Wotton reads *Comus*. The present outburst is more revealing than the sonnet on lost time, or the careful letter accompanying it. It is in the logic of his poem too, because the question has been implicit from the beginning: he cannot really imagine the songs of an illiterate goatherd being remembered and rehandled and passed on as treasures for generations, so what can his shepherds hope to achieve by poetry? What kind of immortality? Poets for more than a hundred years have regarded this question with awe or with cynicism, but for Milton it was perfectly real.

For his seventh stanza he goes back to the sea, though it is a highly classicized sea, beginning with 'Arethuse' in Theocritean Sicily and 'smooth-sliding Mincius', Virgil's river, and going on to Neptune and 'the herald of the sea', who might be Triton. It does not matter really who he is; his question is really Milton's own question: what doomed Lycidas? Why did he have to die? If this were a real classical poem, the answer would be a casual sin or a ritual omission: that will not quite do for Milton, but the reply that masks it is in lovely words. 'Hippotades' is Aeolus, the god of the winds, and the atmosphere is still Virgilian.

> The air was calm, and on the level brine,
> Sleek Panope with all her sisters played.
> It was that fatal and perfidious bark
> Built in the eclipse, and rigged with curses dark,
> That sunk so low that sacred head of thine.

At this point the poet chooses to introduce a surprising diversion. Apparently a procession is going by, and the new stanza begins with Camus, 'reverend sire, ... His mantle hairy, and his bonnet sedge', who is followed still more unexpectedly by 'the pilot of the Galilean lake' – Peter with his two keys, or just possibly Christ himself (the ambiguity may be deliberate), who wishes someone else had died – and follows this with a swingeing denunciation of 'blind mouths' who creep into the shearers' feast though they hardly know how to hold a sheep-hook. Their songs are thin and grating; the hungry sheep look up and are not fed; but the wolf (devil or Roman Catholic?) gets them. The stanza is twenty-nine lines long, a fearsome growl, ending in the sincere threat:

> But that two-handed engine at the door,
> Stands ready to smite once, and smite no more.

The engine is a two-handed sword, and I take the threat to be sincere, more against bishops and those who held fat benefices than against the entire clergy. The long stanza has been carefully sewn into the poem, with its shepherds and sheep and shearers' feast. The Galilean lake was enough to indicate the change of gear, and such passages existed in the pastoral poems of the old friar Mantuan, who was much read in English schools. Camus pins the entire scene down to Cambridge. Whatever else may be said, the indignation is real, and Edward King must have shared it. It also includes Milton's equivalent of the sin which classical mythology demanded.

No doubt the rivers and waters figure so often in *Lycidas* because he drowned at sea. Moschus begins with them in his *Lament for Bion*:

> Weep for me, vales and Dorian rivers,
> And cry rivers for beautiful Bion,
> Now gardens groan and forest groves lament . . .

The Sicilian Arethuse comes from this poem (line 10) and so does the Doric Orpheus. It is a later and more bizarre poem than those of Theocritus, and if Milton's classical references are thought strange, this fact must be considered in mitigation. No doubt Milton was fond of the *Lament for Bion* without taking it as a model, even for its stanzas of varying length. He recovers himself from the over-serious rage of his digression by calling on Alpheus, Arethuse's Peloponnesian lover, from whom she fled to Sicily: like Moschus he prays:

> . . . return Sicilian muse,
> And call the vales, and bid them hither cast
> Their bells, and flowrets of a thousand hues. . . .

This leads to the famous list, with the profusion and intensity of a Greek or Sicilian spring:

> Throw hither all your quaint enamelled eyes,
> That on the green turf suck the honied showers,

> And purple all the ground with vernal flowers.
> Bring the rathe primrose that forsaken dies,
> The tufted crow-toe, and pale jessamine,
> The white pink, and the pansy freaked with jet,
> The glowing violet
> The musk-rose, and the well-attired woodbine,
> With cowslips wan that hang the pensive head,
> And every flower that sad embroidery wears:
> Bid amaranthus all his beauty shed,
> And daffadillies fill their cups with tears,
> To strew the laureate hearse where Lycid lies.

The catalogue is weighted on the intellectual and symbolic, therefore funereal, side, and no boys or girls are seen to strew the coffin or the grave. Indeed, there is neither coffin nor grave, because the body that weltered in line 13 is now (line 154 following) further on its journey:

> Whether beyond the stormy Hebrides
> Where thou perhaps under the whelming tide
> Visit'st the bottom of the monstrous world . . .

There follow the amazing and mysterious lines about 'the fable of Bellerus old', in which Bellerium is Land's End, and Bellerus a more harmonious name for Corineus, the Cornish hero Milton had first named. Bellerium he took from a map: but Bellerus he jovially invented, it appears. He is certainly not in the first book of the *Poly-Olbion* or in Selden's notes, where you might expect to find him. The great vision of the guarded mount must be Michael the Archangel on St Michael's Mount, where he appeared to the ancient monks. Namancos is on the Galician coast of Spain, found on maps of the time, where it is a misspelling for Nemancos, and Bayona on the western coast of France. The prayer to the angel is oddly moving, though it is only for the dead body to be blown back to England, unless there is a buried reference to war and the protection of the island, as no doubt there is. The line ending 'Bellerus old' is one that pleases Milton and it becomes part of his epic repertory in his blindness: it occurs four or five times at least.

But the last line of this thirty-three-line stanza, swollen with flowers and flowing with seas, is a sudden stop, and it has been criticized. Dr Johnson mocked it, and Tennyson thought it the only bad line Milton ever penned (he cannot have studied the Trinity manuscript). 'And, O ye dolphins, waft the hapless youth' has been taken by scholars to be a reference to Arion, who was brought safely into Tarentum on a dolphin's back. Indeed, he was often portrayed like that. But Arion was saved alive, like Jonah, and Edward King was dead, so this is nonsense. What about Palaemon in Pausanias (2, 1, 3), of whom Milton would have heard (*Comus*, 876)? He was brought to shore dead and became a patron saint of sailors. This is clever but quite unnecessary. It is only the bones that Milton prays to be brought back to England. Is there any hint of the next stanza's Christian hope in this one line? Dolphins really do clean the sea of the dead: there is plenty of evidence for that, and I do not see that any greater miracle is intended: the dead body has already had a long and battering journey. The line is too short to bear all the weight that has been put on it, from Dr Johnson onwards.

The Christian transformation scene follows at once and is very beautiful. Lycidas has sunk only to rise like the sun. 'Through the dear might of him that walked the waves', and he goes to Heaven, where 'with nectar pure his oozy locks he laves', a particularly Homeric touch. The few lines on Heaven (174–81) are the most convincing that Milton was ever to write on the subject. Lycidas becomes 'the genius of the shore' and is going to be 'good/To all that wander in that perilous flood'. This neatly combines his pastoral or mythical status with his reality in a way that must be inoffensive even to Puritans, and for a moment we believe it. The stanzas at the end of the poem are of decreasing length, so after twenty-one lines comes the last of all, with only eight. It puts the poem to bed with the assurance of Milton's simplest and most tranquil touches, rhyming A B A B A B C C.

> Thus sang the uncouth swain to the oaks and rills,
> While the still morn went out with sandals grey,
> He touched the tender stops of various quills,
> With eager thought warbling his Doric lay:
> And now the sun had stretched out all the hills,
> And now was dropped into the western bay;
> At last he rose, and twitched his mantle blue:
> Tomorrow to fresh woods, and pastures new.

The curious beauty of the end owes a lot to Bryskett and to Virgil (one of the few Roman poets to mention the colour blue), and in a way foreshadows the end of *Paradise Lost*. In the English countryside a blue mantle was a new colour: they were mostly red, but Huguenot refugees had brought in a blue dye, so that it was probably by observing nature in Middlesex or around Cambridge, rather than by spotting a pretty colour in an Italian painting, that Milton thought of his last two lines.

The most striking thing about *Lycidas* is its pinpoint observation and the simplicity of its detail. When we hear of the poet at last as an uncouth swain, we suddenly realize we have not until then imagined him at all. Milton can now do set scenes better than anyone and neoclassic lines like 'Sleek Panope with all her sisters played' as well as Jonson. He can make memorable phrases about Amaryllis in the shade, and the tangles of Neaera's hair; he can manage the construction of a longish poem of 193 lines so that its climax comes with crushing weight; he can take serious things seriously in verse, as few of his contemporaries ever learnt to do. He ought to be on the very brink of becoming a great English poet – indeed, he is one already – but his ideas of great poetry are of an ever more over-toppling kind of grandeur. He will soon reveal he has been considering an epic on the story of King Arthur. He is going to go abroad as soon as he has the chance: unusually late in life at the age of nearly thirty, and in his poetry, while he turns over this and that theme or manner in his mind (manner being the more important choice in his own eyes), he will return to writing poems in Latin. What is more, they will be quite excellent poems, one of them oddly like *Lycidas*.

He is a citizen of the world; both in his religion and his politics he can see that the battlefield in his lifetime will not only be England, it will be all Europe, with repercussions in America. It was still true in 1638 that books written in Latin were more widely available and made their authors more famous than English books. Anyway he was good at Latin; he could become more famous abroad by writing in it than any other English writer. His pride or ambition were fuelling a volcano that scarcely had a stopper. It does not seem as if Shakespeare, who certainly intended his own immortality, ever troubled his head about this question of Latin; his own questions of theme and even manner had to be answered at once, and in the theatre. Milton's best advantage was that he had leisure and intelligence to learn, as no one else has ever done, the art of poetry, but his disadvantage was the opportunity to dither. Fanshawe is the only poet with talents in any way comparable with Milton's who dithered more. The only poetry in English that Milton wrote after *Lycidas* was the translation of fragments, until the King marched on London in 1642: and then it was no more than a charming piece of literature. The one exception was scribbled on the back of a letter from Lawes enclosing his passport:

> Fix here ye overdated spheres
> That wing the restless foot of time.

It is not as much as we had a right to expect from the author of *Lycidas*. Politics were unhappy, and it may be that while that road was blocked, all roads were blocked to him. Laud was finding that the Anabaptists, Brownists and various sectaries, being so poor, were hard to deal with. The emigration of Brooke, of Saye and Sele, Hampden and Cromwell to America was prevented. Dr Bastwick of Colchester, with the Revd Mr Burton of Friday Street, who had been railing against bishops since 1624, went to prison in 1637 and had their ears cut off in the pillory; Prynne, as we have noted, had the stumps of his ears sawn off. Williams of Lincoln was fined £10,000; a letter to him from Osbaldiston, the head of Westminster school, drew a further fine of £8,000 on Williams and £5,000 on Osbaldiston, who removed himself and has never been traced. In April 1638, Hampden lost his case at law against the government. In Scotland stools were flying in 1637, and the Covenant, to which the Scots remained remarkably loyal, began circulating for signatures in 1638. A prudent scrivener might well be pleased that his son was going abroad.

We know that Milton's mother died at Horton on 3 April 1637, and that seems to be when the young man got the money to travel, though his finances are almost as obscure as his father's, and in some matters they acted together. Perhaps, once his wife was dead, the old man became freer-handed. In September, the poet thought of rooms in the Inns of Court, and he invested a small sum at 8 per cent. It was his biographer Toland who first suggested he got money from his mother's will: he does so only by insinuation ('his mother having died': as Wood had written 'his mother dead'), but the disposal of money was, of course, in his father's hands, and it was his father who gave him his permission to travel. For the rest, all he needed was a passport from the Warden of the Cinque Ports, which Lawes obtained for him. His journey is still early in the history of the Grand Tour, which did not swell beyond a dribble until after 1660. Such an expedition was often supervised by a tutor, even in Milton's day, though he was too old for that. The expense could be prodigious, and the road adventurous: John Evelyn, on the same track as Milton a few years later, had a far more dangerous time.

In 1638 Europe was still deeply divided by religion; France was more stable than it had been, but Geneva was the citadel of an orthodoxy quite as fearsome as that of Rome. Mark Pattison casts a lurid light on it in his life of Casaubon, the greatest of scholars, who could become himself only as an exile or refugee. When Casaubon first saw the royal library of the French kings, his heart sank at how much there was to know and to learn. He died in England, a martyr to the lack of sanitary arrangements in the Bodleian Library. The road to Rome was well trodden in those days by Roman Catholic priests, and Rome already supported an exiled English Catholic community of some distinction. To them Milton was to behave with callous ingratitude: it is probable that, like his friend Andrew Marvell, he felt the need to establish his Protestant good faith with sneers. Both Marvell and Donne had tried the experiment of actually becoming Catholics as young men: Milton cannot have been unaware of the temptation, but he never for an instant looks like falling into it. The religious part of his early output as a poet might have suggested a Catholic influence, but it was only that universal influence that followed from the cultural prestige of Italy: a prestige that had arisen from the Renaissance. It was the Renaissance itself, now of course long dead, that Milton was setting out to discover.

It was before he went that he dared to present the copy of the newly printed *Comus* to Sir Henry Wotton, the elderly Provost of Eton. That great school was in those days still a college, with two quadrangles and a gate-house or porter's lodge like many a house then and like surviving colleges in universities, with Fellows who were resident learned men.

Eton's prestige did not rest on its royal foundation (which, since Edward VI, many other grammar schools, or Latin schools as they were called, could rival) but on the distinction of its Provost and Fellows (rather than on its headmaster). Wotton had been a diplomat and, as a youth, involved in the dangerous game of opposition to Queen Elizabeth. His predecessor was Sir Henry Savile (1545–1622), the editor and translator of classical texts and once a royal tutor. Milton was well received by the provost, with whom he dined, in the middle of the day, and Wotton then wrote him a remarkable letter: 'Sir, It was a special favour when you lately bestowed upon me here the first taste of your acquaintance, though no longer than to make me know that I wanted more time to value it, and to enjoy it rightly.' The route Wotton recommended through Europe was by Paris and Marseille to Genoa, 'whence the passage into Tuscany is as diurnal as a Gravesend barge. I hasten as you do to Florence or Siena ... *I pensieri stretti ed il viso sciolto.*' Wotton recommended Milton to Lord Scudamore, who was at Paris as ambassador, and would advise. It was at least as important that Wotton praised *Comus* to the skies. With this entry to a wider and a much grander world than any he had so far known, Milton was, so to speak, afloat. Wotton liked the young man and helped him with introductions to Lord Scudamore and Michael Braithwaite, once his tutor, but his recognition of the powerful greatness of Milton's poetry was expressed only in a footnote, after he had read *Comus*. Had he lived, he might have had more to offer, but he died the next year (1639) at the age of sixty-one.

Milton set off from home with one servant, of whom we hear nothing more. The servant must have cost him something in wages and provisions, but how much must remain a conjecture. He was travelling as a gentleman, as Evelyn would; he took care to create an impression, and he was received like a gentleman everywhere. In 1638 the Thirty Years War was two-thirds over. Turenne was hard at it; Richelieu was in power; the Jardin des Plantes and the French Academy were newly founded; Corneille had just produced *Le Cid* and Descartes his *Discourse on Method*. Both Spain and France had a civilization to boast about: Poussin and Velasquez, Zurbaran and Calderon; Lope da Vega had only recently died (in 1635). In Paris Scudamore's embassy chapel was under Laud's influence, though out at Charenton Protestantism reigned.

Scudamore was outmanoeuvred by Richelieu more than once; he had tried to buy an ancient manuscript of the Emperor Basil, and to send back to England the refugee Lady Purbeck. His Laudian chapel attracted malign attentions; he was a friend of Grotius, ambassador in Paris for the Queen of Sweden, who was trying to get agreements to a union of all the respectable northern Protestant Churches: this would, to Scudamore's pleasure, exclude Puritans and Calvinists, and he tried to interest Laud in it. At home Scudamore was magnificent in entertainment, in the breeding of horses and in the grafting of plums and cider apples. It is to his generosity that we owe the restoration of the church at Abbey Dore, to which he was persuaded by the old antiquary Sir Henry Spelman, and which he made one of the loveliest of all the monuments of English religion. The reader will by now have suspected that Milton had little sympathy with Eton and loathed Lord Scudamore, though he was excited to meet so great an international lawyer as Grotius, and flattered by being well treated by him. He writes:

> I became anxious to visit foreign parts, and particularly Italy. My father gave me permission, and I left home with one servant. On my departure, the celebrated Henry Wotton ... gave me a signal proof of his regard ... The noble Thomas Scudamore, King Charles' ambassador, to whom I carried letters of recommendation, received me most courteously at Paris. His lordship gave me a card of introduction to the learned Hugo Grotius ... whose acquaintance I anxiously desired, and to whose house I was accompanied by some of his lordship's friends. A few days after, when I set out for Italy, he gave me letters to the English merchants on my route, that they might shew me any civilities in their power. Taking ship at Nice, I arrived at Genoa ...

He records what he must about Scudamore to make sense of his story, and no more, and Braithwaite is not mentioned at all. He will not allow Wotton his knighthood or his title of Provost, or Scudamore his viscount's or his baronet's title. He is as mute as a fish about religion in France, but one notes that he did not dare go near Geneva until his return journey, although it was the home of the Diodati family. Because he will not say Lord Scudamore, he calls him 'the noble Thomas Scudamore' which is not his name. It was a mistake of carelessness to call him Thomas instead of John, but at the end of the Civil War, when he wrote this account, it was a scornful negligence. Lord Scudamore would have been next-door neighbour to Milton in

Petty France in the 1650s, but after he was taken at Hereford, his London property was vengefully sold off by the Parliament because of something similar done to Lord Essex, and Scudamore was then kept in prison for four years. When he came out, he devoted himself to the support of the ejected clergy of the Church of England. Milton does not choose to remember him with any pleasure, or the French either.

CHAPTER SIX

ITALY

To arrive in Italy for the first time by sea at Genoa, at an age when one is ripe for the architecture and has some sense of the language, must still today be an unforgettable experience; what it felt like three and a half centuries ago is unimaginable. For Milton it was meant to be the beginning of a long and adventurous journey into distant lands: but he found Italy sufficiently exalting to detain him. The great princes and beautiful cities of the Renaissance had settled into a system where learning and the arts had become more marginal and politics less alarming than they had once been. Slowly the Church had been clawing back her lost supremacy, and the Counter-Reformation, a reactionary movement in politics, with an absolute suppression of science and of theology, was at full blast. We may omit the quibbles and the whys and wherefores that attend on the history of these matters to this day: culturally, Italy had entered a decadence even Milton could not assess. That is the sad subject of the last volumes of J. A. Symonds's *Civilization of the Renaissance in Italy*.

The seventeenth century was an age of academies: private societies of the gentry devoted to the formal celebration of arts that had ceased to flourish. One may sniff some vestige of what these people were like from the 1640s woodwork of the Sienese Accademia degli Intronati, now decorating a library at Eastnor Castle in Herefordshire. It is painted, elaborate, pleasing, highly artificial, and a million miles from great art. It much resembles the sacristy woodwork of some great church of the period. As to why all the arts at once drooped and withered let Symonds be our guide. It undoubtedly had something to do with religion, and the academies may be compared to the Sodalities run by the Jesuits, and the musical academies presented by the Oratorians. The Church was making a frantic last-minute attempt to control the modern world, but everything that it touched withered except architecture, the most abstract and the most irrepressibly worldly of the arts. Into this atmosphere Milton stepped like the sturdy Protestant he was, whistling a private tune: the countenance open and the thoughts reserved, as Wotton had advised him.

From Genoa, with its 200 palaces and no two alike, he went to Livorno or Leghorn, which had a powerful Jewish and a small English colony, and from there by Pisa over the mountains into Florence on 10 September. The journey was thrilling, and remained the same for two hundred years: Edward Lear did it as a young man. At Florence Milton stopped until winter seriously threatened. He is unconcerned in his account with its physical beauty: he has no wish to be overwhelmed by the scents and poisons of a Catholic country. Only years afterwards, vignettes and memories of Florence will swim back into his mind,

> which I have always more particularly esteemed for the elegance of its dialect, its genius, and its taste, I stopped about two months: when I contracted an intimacy with many persons of rank and learning, and was a constant attendant at their literary parties; a practice which prevails there, and tends so much to the diffusion of knowledge and the preservation of friendship.

He felt, in fact, that he had been admitted to a worldwide or at least European *respublica literarum*, and it would be fair to suggest he overreacted with praises and poems to his flattering reception. 'No time will ever abolish the agreeable recollections which I cherish of Gaddi, Dati, Frescobaldo, Culterello, Bonomatthai, Clementillo, Francisco, and many others.'

There were over 500 academies in 133 towns: Bologna had seventy, Rome fifty-six (of which the Accademia dei Lyncei survives), Venice over forty, Naples nearly thirty and Florence twenty. The old Florentine Academy was founded in 1540, and the Academy of La Crusca, a breakaway movement from that, had published an Italian dictionary in 1612, with a second edition in 1632. Bologna had one called the Gelati, founded in 1588, Rome had its Umoristi, its Ordinati and so on. These lists were made by Germans in the next century, but even Italian scholars now take a severe view of the amateurs of Milton's day. Tasso had lived his unhappy life from 1544 to 1595, and Marini from 1569 to 1625. Since that time no great talent had come to light in Italian poetry. The greatest intellectual

presence in Florence was Galileo. He was born at Pisa in 1564 and
served as professor at Padua from 1592 to 1610. He then became
personal philosopher to the Grand Duke at Florence.

Unluckily for him, he used the telescope he adapted from a street-
seller's toy to confirm Copernicus' view that the earth circulates and
spins around the sun. In 1616 he was condemned by Rome, which
felt that science had no business to interfere with nature or the
universe, since on settled views about those matters theology had
come to depend. In 1632 the poor man was condemned again for his
Dialogues, apparently because it was thought that atomic physics (as it
was to become) cast doubt on Aristotle's view of matter and form,
without which the explanation of what happened at Mass, that is, the
transformation of wine and bread to the blood and body of Christ,
would go the same way as the stationary earth. This danger was
thought so important that it was kept a secret, but it was the motive
for the prosecution. Galileo had come home to house imprisonment
in Florence in 1633, and in 1637 he went blind. He lived in a villa
just south of the city at Arcetri: there is a woodcut of it in Samuel
Rogers's poem 'Italy'. There he amused himself with music, often his
own, with poetry and with wine.

The academicians had a sleepy sort of distinction, it must be
admitted. N. Heinsius thought well of them and joined the Apatisti
in 1646: he was a classical scholar, perhaps not great but certainly
useful in his way. Gaddi wrote a work about non-ecclesiastical writers
in Italy. Coltellini had founded the Apatisti in about 1632. Buonmatthai had been a priest who retired: he then wrote a commentary
on Dante, and a *Lingua Toscana*. Malatesti, whom Milton left out, was
a poet and pupil of Galileo and touched on such subjects as censorship
and the Inquisition. Milton enjoyed the Svogliati and the Apatisti,
because he was allowed to take an active part in their proceedings. He
is recorded in the minutes: 'John Milton Englishman read a Latin
poem in hexameter verse, very learned.' It was not long before he left
Florence. Milton referred often to Galileo in his later writings, but it
is not quite certain that he was actually taken to see him (*Areopagitica*
(1644), *Paradise Lost*, 1, 288; 5, 262). He does not show that he
understood or accepted Galileo's view of the world, but no doubt the
exigencies of epic poetry may be to blame. He did go to Vallombrosa,
which he loved: it is eighteen miles from Florence. There were monks

newly established there, but we do not know what he felt about them. Milton left behind him one curious contribution to history: he wrote in a Latin letter to Buonmatthai that the reason for the fall of ancient Rome was the decay of learning. It was as if he had been taken in by the self-importance of the Florentine cult of learned literature.

When he came to publish his poems in 1645, the Latin and Italian section began with complimentary contributions from Francini, who wrote him a long, banal and altogether watery ode in Italian stanzas, and Dati, who wrote a contorted letter in Latin and signed it 'Carolus Datus Patricius Florentinus', as Francini signed his 'Gentilhuomo Fiorentino': it meant perhaps no more than 'esquire' did a hundred years ago. Milton himself goes into contortions of coagulated Latin to explain why he prints this nonsense: after all, complimentary poems were a common enough custom in English: the posthumous plays of Shakespeare in their second edition carry one by Milton, and the second edition of *Paradise Lost* has one by Marvell. But these Italian bits and pieces are really too unserious: 'because this is the manner of praise from distinguished intellectuals there, and friends as well, eagerly to append these writings to their own merits not to the truth; he did not want their outstanding good will to him to go un-noticed, particularly because others persuaded him to print them ...' This probably applies specially to Mansi, whom he met later and who takes pride of place over the Florentines, both in his nugatory complimentary verses and in Milton's own long Latin poem addressed to him.

About Rome Milton remained tight-lipped. 'From Florence I went to Siena, and thence to Rome; where after I had spent about two months in reviewing the antiquities of that renowned city, where I experienced the most friendly attentions from Lucas Holstein, and other learned and ingenious men, I continued my route to Naples.' Holstein had a good Protestant name, and had been in England for several months not long before, at the Bodleian Library: he was now a librarian at the Vatican; his real name was Lukas Holste. Milton wrote him a letter of thanks, in March 1639, for getting him invited to a musical evening given by Cardinal Barberini: where he had heard a performance of Rospigliosi's opera, *Chi sofre, speri*. It was once thought that it was there that he heard Leonora Baroni singing and wrote her some Latin verses. But the occasion was too public, and

women were not allowed to sing in opera at Rome. The intricacies of
Roman anti-feminism are not perhaps worth penetrating: we suppose
that Milton did hear Leonora only because he wrote the verses.

The point of those verses is the purely Italian compliment to a
fashionable *diva*. This lady's mother Adriana had an entire book of
poems to her by various hands published in 1623, *Teatro della gloria
d'Adriana*. Her daughter was born in about 1610 at Mantua, and a
volume of *Applausi Poetici alle glorie della Signora Leonora Baroni*
appeared in 1639, collected by a certain Costazuti: it was surely on to
this bandwagon that Milton desired to climb. Perhaps his Latin
elegiacs were too stiff for the Italians and he failed, but he published
them in 1645.

> Each has his angel (O believe it, Sirs)
> Winged from the ranks of heaven for him alone:
> But Leonora's glory must be more,
> For in thy voice we hear the voice of God,
> Since God, or the Third Mind of empty heaven
> Creeps through your throat in secret bringing it:
> Creeps, brings and sweetly teaches mortal hearts
> How to be used to that immortal sound.
> But if all things are God poured out through all,
> In thee alone he speaks, dumb in all else.

The Third Mind refers to a letter formerly attributed to Plato, and
Marsilio Ficino handles the subject. The verses are grossly flattering,
but they are certainly no way to make friends or influence people in
Counter-Reformation Rome. Even in England they would have raised
some eyebrows if the obscurity of Latin had not veiled them. It
appears that Milton had heard his *diva* singing sacred music: that
would be possible in a church, but likelier at some more private
entertainment. A second poem to her refers to Torquato Tasso, in
love with another Leonora and famously driven out of his mind: also
to her mother's golden lyre strings: she played the theorbo. A third
poem to the *diva* is just as extravagant but turns more definitely to a
Neapolitan theme.

> Credulous Naples, why boast your liquid
> Singing Siren, Parthenope's famous shrine:
> The naiad dead upon your sands you gave

To burn at Naples in the holy flames?
She lives and now for Tiber's lovely wave
Leaves thy rough mutterings, Pausilippo:
Here favoured with the applauses of all Rome
She sings enchanting men and gods with song.

This little poem, light thing as it is, adds to Milton's extravagance only his old obsession with geography. The relation of the mouth of the Tiber at Ostia with Capri and with Naples underlies the seventh book of Virgil's *Aeneid*, and it will appear later in Milton's work that he had explored it, probably during his journey to Naples, which he performed on foot. He did not go further south, since the coast was swampy and the tracks were unfrequented. Before he went Milton tossed off some verses to a Roman poet called Salsilli who was ill, a member of the academy of Fantastici who had contributed verse to an anthology of theirs in 1637. He gave Milton a complimentary verse, saying he was a better Homer and Virgil and Tasso. Did Milton print this rubbish out of pride or, more probably, because he liked Salsilli? They must have discussed poetry in some detail, since Milton wrote to him a charming poem in *scazons*, an unusual metre, peppered with learning from Ovid and Livy and Virgil. Most of Milton's poem to Salsilli is about topography, like that of the last one to Leonora. Without it, Salsilli would be unknown.

The charm of the *scazons* to Salsilli is real enough, but it is antiquarian or neoclassic, like that of the elegiacs to Leonora. It depends not wholly on allusions to classical mythology or topography but, unusually for Milton, on reproducing with a sensitive Virgilian nostalgia the 'oak woods of Faunus, and you friendly hills/Bedewed and vinous, mild Evander's seat'. But Milton's transposition of the *Aeneid* into another metre gives him novelty and wit. He shows exactly the skills of a modern prize poem, so it is hardly worth translating the dark groves 'where in eternal happy idleness/Numa lies gazing on Egeria,' which, though not precisely from Virgil, are in the same spirit: there is a neoclassic stillness and deadness about them.

His next poem was the set of full-scale hexameters to the Marchese della Villa, G. B. Manso (1560–1645), to whom Tasso's book of friendship had been dedicated. He was Tasso's and Marino's friend and entertainer, and the founder of an academy called the Otiosi, which met in his house. Milton was recommended to Manso by what he calls a hermit, perhaps a friar of some kind, whom he met on the road from Rome. From 1570 to 1586 Tasso had been locked up at Ferrara, but in 1586 he published *Il Manso*, the treatise on friendship. Tasso was entertained then, and twice in the early nineties, at Naples: the last time, in 1594, he seems to have finished *Gerusalemme Conquistata* there, the year before he died. It was when Tasso died that Manso took up Marino. When he was in his forties and again ten years later (1608 and 1618) Manso had himself published dialogues on love and beauty, then a life of Tasso the next year and last a volume of poems at seventy-five (1635). He was genuinely and usefully friendly to Milton, and the little verses he supplied for the 1645 book are the merest crumbs from his table, the equivalent of an autograph. 'If your religion were like your mind, your beauty, your appearance and your manners, you would be an angel not an Englishman.' He was seventy-nine, and had assured Milton he would have done far more for him if only he had been more discreet in conversation. Manso was scarcely dead when there was a revolution at Naples.

> During my stay, he gave me singular proofs of his regard; he himself conducted me round the city, and to the palace of the Viceroy [Naples and Sicily were Spanish possessions] and more than once paid me a visit at my lodgings. On my departure he gravely apologized for not having shown me more civility, which he said he had been restrained from doing, because I had spoken with so little reserve on matters of religion ... While I was on my way back to Rome, some merchants informed me that the English Jesuits had formed a plot against me, if I returned to Rome, because I had spoken too freely of religion.

This cannot be ranked as a lie, highly improbable as it may be: it is just the vaguest of rumours. His name was beginning to be mentioned, a thought quite chilling enough to a young man alone in a foreign state, where a hostile religious authority was as all-powerful as it appeared unpredictable. It was something to boast about later.

It is sad that so great a poet as Milton was turned back from Sicily and Greece by other rumours he seems to have picked up, from English merchants in Naples, about the Civil War brewing in England. The information which we are given in the most imprecise form appears most questionable, since the King's action was first directed at Scotland. Did Milton think the English would join in at once? If so, can he have heard from Thomas Young? It is really impossible to say, any more than one can imagine what good he thought he could do by returning. Anyway he did not hurry – he wasted most of a year – and when he did get back his first decision was to do nothing. He was a short man, and slimly built, and his ability with a rapier would not have been effective against a dragoon. Did he know what he was missing in Greece? *Paradise Regained* suggests that he did, and in it he wrote the most beautiful lines in English about Athens, far better than Byron's fiery lines.

We must turn for consolation to *Paradise Regained*, but more immediately to the Latin poem for the Marchese della Villa. '*Fra cavalier magnanimi, e cortesi/ Risplende il Manso...*,' as Tasso wrote and Milton quoted. Manso had also apparently given Milton a present, which the poem describes. No one has been so deserving of praise since Maecenas and Gallus. Why Gallus? He is a poet whom Virgil complimented; not a line of his work survived until twenty years ago, when four lines turned up on a scrap of papyrus, and they were shamefully bad. To Milton his very obscurity added charm, and he did fit into the line: 'Gallus in ash, Etruscan Maecenas'. Milton is searching in this poem for a grandeur of tone still unattained: 'Thou too', he writes in a somewhat comic adaptation of the eighth *Eclogue*, 'Thou also if my Muse's breath have power/Among the conquering ivy and the bays/Shalt sit ...' You were Tasso's friend and Marino rejoiced to be your disciple: that is the gist of it. He ignores the view of Masson's generation that Marino was 'the most contagious corrupter of taste'; perhaps it is unthinkable to Milton, whose poetry must rest on Italian foundations. Many of the same technical lessons he could, of course, have learnt from Spanish, and some from French. But his loyalty is firmly anchored in Italy as a classical country and cradle of the Renaissance: no doubt it originated in the Italian musical fever of the 1590s. We hear less about music during the Italian journey, for the reason, I suppose, that so much of it was heard in church.

> Then the knowing Muse
> Brought you Marino, pleased to be your pupil,
> Who sang the Assyrian passions of the gods

And soft in song amazed the Ausonian nymphs.
. . . We see him smiling in laborious bronze.

By its sixteenth line the poem has gathered momentum and to a
certain dreamy coldness has superadded a humane gravity. What it
commemorates is Manso's own commemoration of the dead poets.

> . . . Not enough: your ceremonious offices
> End not in the grave-mound but to preserve
> Them whole from Orcus and the hungry Fates:
> Their ancestry, lives, actions, gifts of art,
> Rivalling him born on high Mycale
> Whose eloquence brought back Smyrniot Homer.

He means Herodotus, who was believed to be Homer's biographer.
The Latin is more resonant than this enfeebling version, and there is
something pleasing about Milton's play with topography, though
what he writes is 'Aeolian Homer' and 'Athene's gifts'. As for Mycale,
it was a cliff-guarded promontory north of Halicarnassus. English
merchants knew such places: Randolph, who was one, had written a
kind of guide: but what Milton knows is in classical texts or on the
map. He goes back to the story that he is 'a wanderer and young,
from the north pole', *Hyperboreo iuvenis peregrinus ab axe*, come to
bring greeetings from Clio and Apollo (because Hyperborean Apollo
had a cult at Delphi):

> You are too kind to spurn a foreign muse
> Now newly reared under the frozen Bear,
> That rashly dares to fly through Italy.
> We too have heard the swans of the river
> Make music in midnight's obscurest shades
> Where silver Thames pours out from his pure urns
> A flood to wash the grey hair of Ocean.
> And Tityrus has trodden our sea-coast.

The poem wanders off here to talk of stars in the conventional but
still moving classical manner. The reference to Virgil's Tityrus as a
wanderer recalls the first *Eclogue* of Virgil, and perhaps Spenser. The
swans are in Spenser too, and in Leland and Ronsard and Ben Jonson:
all the same British Tityrus looks lonely in his line of one sentence,
and I do not really know where Milton got him or what he is doing

in this poem. The Druids as priests of Apollo are to be found in Selden on the *Poly-Olbion*.

> We serve Apollo and send him our gifts
> Baskets of yellow quince and white corn-ears
> Sweet-breathing crocus (or the ancients lie)
> And choruses of girls of Druid race
> (The Druid race did the gods' ritual
> And sang of heroes and taught men their deeds).

This, he explains to his possibly bemused friend, is how it came about that girls in their Greek way on grassy Delos commemorated Loxo daughter of Coryneus (of Cornwall), prophetic Upis and yellow-haired Hecaerge, painting their bare breasts with Caledonian woad. The mythology takes some unravelling because it combines the woad-painted noble savages Caesar found in Britain (and the British more recently in America, which excited them greatly and brought tattooing back into fashion) with a Delian ritual myth to be found in Herodotus and Drayton's useful Corineus after whom Cornwall could be named, the son of Brutus, the wandering Trojan. After this curious diversion Milton returns to Virgilian lines about Tasso, using him as a transition to the easier myth of Apollo keeping cattle, and the favour of the gods as an explanation of Manso's long life.

> So the slow flower of your long old age
> And the long lingering of your green years . . .
> . . . May it be my lot too with such a friend
> Who knows so well Apollo's men's reward,
> Should I recall our native kings in song
> And Arthur's wars fought in the underworld,
> Or tell of the round table's company
> Unconquered, those great heroes (grant me life)
> And break the Saxon lines with British war!

This passage combines themes of some interest. It is the declaration of a serious intention to write an epic about Arthur. The wars the king wages in the Underworld are a foretaste of Milton's fascination with Satan's wars, his still gloomier lurking-place and his splendid war with the angels. Finally there is a hint of European war, that is of the Thirty Years War, in the last line, which in Latin makes a noise like Gogmagog chewing iron.

He brings his poem to an end in exactly 100 lines, like a holiday task. It has been his best Latin poem so far, and although it falls away here and there it has remarkable images and an unusual degree of sincerity. The climax is a sort of apotheosis of the poet:

> May he lay my limbs freed from livid death
> Softly down into my small grave-urn.
> And maybe my head too in marble carved
> Will twine the Paphian myrtle in its hair
> And the Parnassian bay, and I sleep well.
> Then if there is faith, if there is reward,
> I in remote air of the heavenly gods,
> Where labour, fiery virtue and pure mind
> Lead on, shall see from somewhere in heaven
> (If the fates will) and my whole mind at peace
> Shall smile and bathe my face in brightest light,
> Applaud myself and joy in high heaven.

The second last line is sometimes translated as a blush, but the poet shows no such modesty: *purpureo* means extremely bright, not purple or pink. The last line, *plaudam mihi laetus*, is sufficiently extraordinary to be untranslatable with any credit to the author. The whole passage reveals a remarkable and unusual degree of ambition. Milton wants a patron generous enough to commission a head in marble with those Roman leaves in its hair, and he will rest happy. What he will see from some private spot in Heaven or the heavens is his own merit recognized in the marble head. That and that alone will make him happy with the life he has led.

Italy had an unforeseen effect on Milton after all. Poets undertake journeys of that kind in order to transform themselves or to be transformed, and that is what happened. He had entered fully into the world of academies, where one is commemorated with a bust in bronze or in marble: if not in one's lifetime, then after death. He had met a great nobleman who had invited him home to stay but who treated him as an equal in a way he could not expect in England. He had been flattered very deeply by an atmosphere in which lavish compliments were easily exchanged: he could step out (he felt) in that minuet. Remember, it was in his generation that the English aristocracy saw Italy, and resolved to remake England in its image, architecturally and in subtler ways. In Rome he paid compliments to Leonora Baroni with the best; he was in the height of fashion, writing the same kind of towering trifles, redeemed only by their frivolity, as we might expect from Suckling or Lovelace. This was a new John Milton, the poet of *Comus* without its crushing morality or the tedium of its Neoplatonism, or the poet of *Lycidas* without its appallingly serious climax in that lengthy stanza about Cambridge and ecclesiastical politics. He had taken a holiday from all that: whether Italy would do him good or harm in the long run we have still to see.

Parker is certain that Milton received news of the death of his best friend Charles Diodati while he was at Naples. What Milton said was, 'The sad news of the English civil war recalled me; for I thought it shameful, while my countrymen were fighting for their liberty at home, that I should be peacefully travelling after culture.' At least that is what he wrote later. Meanwhile he seems to have visited the old Diodati house at Lucca, and when, after a leisurely progress, he got to Geneva, he must have found out from the boy's uncle that Charles had died and been buried in London late in the August of 1638. Neither this fact, which must certainly have come as a shock to him, nor the preliminary rumbles of the Civil War furnish a sufficient explanation for his long and happy dawdle up Italy. Some writers say he got the news in Florence; A. N. Wilson thinks he got it only in Geneva, which is plausible, but by then, of course, it was old news, and his rushing home would comfort no one. This small mystery should not distract us from the main fact, that the climax and chief expression of his Italian journey was his Latin poem to Manso.

Slowly he moved back towards England, stopping in Rome, then in Florence for a time to read 'some noble Latin verses' to the Academy of the Svogliati and then in Venice, where he sent off the books he had acquired, by sea, to England: one was music by Monteverdi. He himself stayed for a little while in Geneva, bookless and blameless, with old Professor Diodati, the Calvinist theologian, uncle of his friend. Charles Gustav of Sweden had once been a pupil in his house, which stood two or three miles outside the city on the southern bank of Lac Léman. There are prints of it 160 years later, as the plain and charming Villa Diodati which Byron rented. In that house one must assume that Milton also stayed. The only trace he left was a line or two of *Comus* and a line of Horace in an album in

June. Soon after he got home to England, doubtless in a mood transformed by Geneva and by his friend's death, the poet expressed himself in the autumn of 1639 in a pastoral poem of deep grief, his 'Epitaph' (or funeral elegy) for Damon. Scholars discuss a range of classical and later sources, including the *Alcon* of Castiglione, but Milton was now his own man, and took his own decisions. It is likely that this last and longest of his Latin poems (if we except some queer 'Pindaric' verses to Bodley's librarian), at 219 lines long, is deliberately a larger construction than *Lycidas*, as Tillyard has pointed out. The Argument announces:

> Thyrsis and Damon, shepherds of the same region, followed the same studies and were the best of friends from boyhood. Thyrsis went abroad for his mind's sake and there got news of Damon's death. Later when he got home and found it to be true, he grieves for himself and his own loneliness in this song. Damon is to be understood as Charles Diodati, by paternal ancestry from Lucca in Etruria, otherwise English, a young man outstanding while he lived for talent, knowledge and other most shining virtues.

> Daughters of Himera, Nymphs that recalled
> Daphnis and Hylas and sad Bion's fate,
> Sing in the towns of Thames Sicilian songs:
> What words what murmurs grieving Thyrsis uttered
> And with what lamentations filled the caves,
> Rivers and wandering springs and forest lairs,
> Grieving for Damon taken; deepest night
> Must hear his grief and solitary paths.
> Now twice the corn had grown up to a head
> And twice the yellow grain in granaries
> Had rested since Damon in shadow ended,
> Yet Thyrsis was not here, because sweet love
> Of the muse kept that shepherd in Tuscany
> . . . Go home unfed, you lambs, your master fails you.

The texture of the Latin is silver-gilt, and lovely; the lament is conventional enough in its beginning. No doubt he wrote in Latin because it had been his habit with Diodati, but no doubt also this poem is the work of one who in Italy had written nothing else, and, since his return, no English poetry.

Who shall go by my side as you would go
In the hard cold over hoar-frosted ground
Or when the swift sun blights the droughted grass,
To see the distant lion rear his head
Or fright the wolves away from folded sheep,
Then talk and sing and send the day to sleep?
Who now shall have my heart, who teach to soothe
My biting cares, cheat long nights with sweet words,
And while the soft pear whispers in the flame
And the black chestnut crackles on the hearth,
And the storm wind thunders into the elm?
Go home unfed, you lambs, your master fails you.

Milton's world as well as his poem is decorous, but it celebrates reality as effectively: even when reality has to be dressed up in classical allusions.

In summer when the day twists on the pole,
And Pan lurks under oaken shade to sleep,
And the Nymphs under water where they sit,
And shepherds hide and Hodge snores under hedge,
Who will bring back your sweetness or your laughs
Or your Athenian, educated wit?
Go home unfed, you lambs, your master fails you.
. . . Tityrus and Alphesiboeus call,
Come to the hazel wood, to the ash trees,
Aegon calls from the willows, lovely Amyntas
Calls me to rivers: here are cold fountains,
Here are grasses and moss, the Zephyrs here
And the arbutus sighing from the waves.
They sing to the deaf, I went to the brambles.
Go home unfed, you lambs, your master fails you.

A biographer is bound to note the first touch, however slight, of that conventional homoeroticism for which pastoral poetry in the classical period was famous. It is innocent enough, as their lives obviously were, and if it were absent, one might wonder what was being hidden or suppressed. The point to notice is that however transfigured into the classical landscape they were, Milton is honestly and beautifully describing the happiest hours of their lives. This is a more intimate monument than *Lycidas*. The cold springs and soft

meadows of Virgil's tenth *Eclogue* come from a context of passionate
love. At this point (line 75) a new character appears, 'Mopsus who
knew the stars and spoke with birds', and the landscape soon fills up
as if for the death of Daphnis, with Hyas and Dryope and Baucis,
daughter of Aegle; their consolations are useless. Chloris by the
Idumanian stream appears to be an allusion to Ptolemy by way of
Camden's *Britannia* on Essex, where he says it means Blackwater Bay.
These odd bits of information may be disregarded; the names and
places are chosen for a poem like this only for their harmonious
sound and vague resonance. There are references to Tasso's *Aminta*
and Guarini's *Pastor Fido*, works which melt on the tongue or in the
ear. Milton pulls himself together in a longer stanza which is a serious
complaint about human loneliness (lines 93–111). You are lucky, he
says bitterly, to find one true friend among thousands.

> What wandering error drew me to that coast,
> To tread the airy rocks and snowy Alps?
> To see Rome buried, was it worth all that?
> The same Rome Tityrus visited once
> Leaving his sheep and his own countryside
> But to have lost a friend so dear as you,
> Putting deep seas and mountains between us
> So many woods and rocks and sounding streams . . .

His grief becomes passionate again, but the poem is none the worse
for being controlled by its refrain. He calls on the Tuscan shepherds,
'youths exercised in arts', because Damon was a Tuscan. He still has
their gifts, baskets and a pipe, and he remembers Dati and Francini
by name (line 137). Dati was about twenty years old at this time.

> These things the dewy moon gave me to write
> While I closed up my tender kids alone
> You were dark ash, and I so often said
> Now Damon sings, he spreads his net for hares.

He longs to be together again, by the Colne, on Cassivelaunus'
ground (which the Thames bounded to the south, as Caesar says). He
longs to be told again of the medical sap of plants, of hellebore,
humble crocus (meadow saffron?) and the bluebell leaf, 'what grass

this marsh has, and what art to heal . . .' His flute is broken; he played it too loud.

> I will tell Trojan ships in Kent waters,
> And the old kingdom of Queen Imogen
> Daughter of Pandrasos, and lord Brennus,
> Arviragus the lord and old Belinus,
> Armoric farmers under British laws,
> And Iogerne made pregnant with Arthur
> By fatal fraud, Gorlois's stolen arms
> And Merlin's trickery and change of face,
> If life is long enough . . .

This amazing rigmarole, which I have toned down or made smoother, is, of course, more of the projected epic about Arthur. It is not surprising that it was never written: it is a debt Milton once thought he owed to the antiquarian tradition represented by the mighty Camden. One objection to it is that the names are unpronounceable, even in Latin. Iogerne passes, but how is Gorlois declined? The names of rivers out of Ptolemy are equally troublesome: we come, in the next few lines, on Camden in Hampshire and in Yorkshire, and what I called Kent is in Latin *Rutupina*, because, Camden says, Rhutupiae was the mouth of the Wantsum at Richborough. All this holds out little hope for the epic.

> It will be my reward
> If Ouse should read me, of the yellow hair,
> And Alaun's drinker, Abra mountainous
> All the forest of Trent, and firstly Thames
> And dark Tamar metallic and the far
> Waves of the Orkneys shall read my poem.

The catalogue of rivers is much more elaborate in Drayton, where it has a genuine regional charm, and lovelier in Spenser; this is the feeble foretaste of an epic style in which Milton never really wrote in English. Before the time came his style had altered; as an idea it is captivating, but oddly ghostly, as if the humming of the sea and the mountainous surf were distant from us, not heard. Usually the strength of Milton's Latin verse is that one can sense in it even the most English of its detail. This passage was determinedly English all the same, so he follows it with an excursus in the manner of

Theocritus on the two pots he was given by Manso. It is possible that the pots stand for Manso's *Erocallia*, his Platonic dialogues, and for a work of his which contained a translation of the *Phoenix* of Claudian: who knows?

> Centre: the Red Sea and the scented spring,
> Long Arab beach and balsam-sweating woods,
> The Phoenix, godlike bird alone on earth
> Blue gleaming of his vari-coloured wings
> Watching the dawn rise in the glassy waves . . .

'Here too is Love,' he goes on, 'and quivers painted in the clouds . . . and arrows touched with gold' (*tincta pyropo*, a most unusual but classical word from Propertius, indicating an alloy of gold and bronze, which Milton probably took to mean gilt). The transition from the baroque back to Damon, from Italy as he now richly knew it back to Charles Diodati, is in the next stanza.

> And, Damon, you are here, or hope deceives,
> You are here surely, where else should it go
> Holy simplicity and snowy virtue?
> It was not right to seek you with the dead,
> No tears for you, and we shall weep no more,
> No tears more, then, for Damon in heaven,
> In heaven's pure air, treading the rainbow down,
> Among the souls of heroes and the gods . . .
> Heaven's Diodotus, Damon in the woods . . .
> And on your shining head a glittering crown
> And in your hand a shadowy palm-branch,
> You celebrate the everlasting marriage:
> With singing and the lyre and happy dance
> And Sion's thyrsus and her mysteries.

The peculiar amalgam is as close as Milton will go to the Christian ending which had been so effective in *Lycidas*. What he means by 'Sion's thyrsus' we cannot tell, but he seems always to have wanted to place a Christian interpretation on the god Bacchus, or if not always, then at least since *Comus* – or was it only since Italy? Diodati, he points out, got the honours reserved in Revelation for those who preserve their virginity. Modern readers may find that a peculiar point to make as Milton does the very climax of a poem about a dead friend, much of it written with real feeling. It would be more acceptable in a Catholic or Italian poem of that age, and in fact the entire ending of *Damon's Epitaph*, at least from the introduction of Manso, has a contemporary Italian colouring.

The Rome where Milton had just been was not only the centre of a Jesuit spider's web; it was the seat of the papacy in the full blaze of its Counter-Reformation glory: it was the only city in the world where the ruler, Urban VIII, in Milton's lifetime wrote better Latin lyrics than he did. It was where the old Jesuit Kirchner, Milton's contemporary, combined the antiquarian skills of Spelman and Camden and Selden with the scientific curiosity of an early member of the Royal Society and the same labyrinthine Neoplatonism that flourished at Cambridge: fed in his case with a nourishing supply of Egyptian obelisks. When one considers the phoenix and Love's gilded arrows and Charles Diodati's virginity, it is possible to wonder whether Shakespeare's 'The Phoenix and the Turtle' may have been at the back of Milton's mind. However that may be, he did continue to feel some strong emotion about the imaginative world of Manso, and about the phoenix, which reappears at the end of his life (if one accepts the consensus dating) at the end of *Samson Agonistes*.

He was distracted from his warm and glowing dream, and from the long pastoral image of his own life as well as his friend's, by Thomas Young, who at this point was active and vehement against the bishops who were trying to impose the newly achieved Scottish reformation as a model on the Church of England. It was believed by such people that the Reformation in England had not gone far enough, but had hesitated and stood still before its work was done. Exactly at what point it would have ended if Young had his way we do not really know: his party was not blessed with foresight. The bishops were busy addressing the problem of almost uncontrollable fanatics and of a Bible interpreted in any way any man wished.

Some of these ways were very eccentric indeed; the centre of the wildest preaching, the most extreme and novel heresies, of fanaticism and of she-preachers, some of whom announced themselves to be pregnant with the Messiah, was Coleman Street in London, a very short walk north of Bread Street. The fire of 1666 obliterated it, but with its alleys and courts, its chapels as well as its church, it was a most spirited place, which any historian of the time should keep an eye on. Milton acquired friends among these people: he was, in fact, a natural Nonconformist. Outside London the centre of the anti-episcopal clergy was in East Anglia and more particularly in Essex. Whether this was due to Dutch influence, to ill-treatment, to marshes or to some ancestral grudge I have never understood, but certainly in the 1630s trouble was being stirred up by the clergy and by Scottish missionaries like Thomas Young. In the end all the same the Bible was responsible.

They had never liked the Authorized Version, and that great and solemn book did not become popular or widely accepted until the Restoration imposed it. The strong Protestant party preferred the Geneva version, which had been available in roman type since 1560, although the Authorized Version was first printed in black-letter. The Geneva version was clearer and stronger and better, but late in the reign of Elizabeth it was produced with Protestant marginal notes of terrible ferocity: they made it into fighting words, of which Cromwell's 'Soldiers' Bible' is an epitome. It was antinomian in tone, and particularly severe on the kings of Israel, whom the King of England at this time took for his constitutional model. The hatred of Roman Catholics was another sensitive issue: if one began with the official hatred, suspicion and disapproval, there appeared to be plenty of evidence that their influence was widespread and increasing and tolerated by the King, and Milton had certainly swallowed the anti-papalism. Of all Catholics, the English in the 1630s were most terrified of the Irish, because they had treated the Irish unbelievably badly already, and both sides to the quarrel were now about to behave with a scarcely credible inhumanity.

The King, 'upon the compulsion of misfortune, called a Parliament', as Milton put it. This was to be the famous Long Parliament. The second Scottish expedition or Bishops' War had broken out in 1638. Lord Hamilton, aged thirty-one, was first sent north, and the Scottish bishops, who had taken refuge in Bath, were sent after him, but when Hamilton got to Holyrood, 20,000 Covenanters and 500 clergy confronted him, so he hid the King's declaration and began to play for time. The King, with misplaced cleverness, encouraged Lord Antrim to invade Argyll, Antrim being a Catholic married to Buckingham's widow. Peace and war now stood upon a knife-edge in Scotland, and the bishops once again fled south in fear of the

Assembly of the Church, which met in November in Glasgow, determined to govern, while Hamilton could only shuffle with an attempt to substitute a milder kind of Covenant. If all this appears to be tinctured with farce, perhaps the reason was the remoteness of Scotland. The Assembly was dismissed, but it still would not dissolve; in fact, it sacked the bishops.

The war was set to begin from York on 1 April. Lords were to send twenty horse each or £1,000 in lieu: Lord Worcester commendably sent both money and horsemen, and his own son as well. Bridgewater offered twelve foot-soldiers for six months or £1,000 if preferred: the money was preferred. Only Lord Brooke and Lord Saye and Sele refused on principle; the clergy responded well but not the City. England and Wales produced 43,152 infantrymen and 3,599 cavalry. On 18 June peace was agreed, and in about July John Milton came home; early in August King Charles was back in Whitehall. Thomas Young published a stern Lord's Day Observance treatise in Latin called *Dies Dominica* as from Luncarty, Perthshire (*PhiloKyriaces Loncardiensis*). Before his son's death, old Dr Diodati had been active in the Welsh border counties, where Lady Brilliana, Lord Conway's sister, wrote in February 1638 he was 'merrier than ever I saw him. His man told Phoebe that his mistress is with child; if it should be so, sure there is ground of his mirth. Your ancient friend Mrs Trafford is very big with child, and Dr Deodato does something fear her. He tells me he was almost in love with her when she served me, but now he cannot fancy her.' Charles Diodati died in London that August.

When the poet had got home and written out his grief in 'Damon's Epitaph', he took lodgings in St Bride's churchyard, near the bottom of Fleet Street, in a tailor's house, and began at once to tutor his two nephews: Edward Phillipps had died in 1631, leaving a young widow, the poet's sister, with one child, Edward, a year old and the other, John, still in the womb. She lived in the Strand and after about two years married Thomas Agar, an office colleague of her late husband, when he became a widower, to whom she bore two daughters, Mary and Anne. Edward when he was not quite ten and John at not quite nine were sent to lodge with their uncle John and be taught by him. It has been said on most tenuous evidence that he treated them harshly, but we need not believe it. What he did, and at once, was to teach them music and have them singing. As for his private work, the

Trinity notebook yields some pages of notes that probably belong here. He reread Holinshed and Speed for the history of pre-Conquest Britain, and took notes on about ninety-nine themes for epic or for Greek-style dramatic treatment, sixty-one of them biblical and thirty-eight from British history. They all appear alternative to the idea of Arthur based on Geoffrey of Monmouth. Some are playful, like 'Cupid's Funeral Pile, or Sodom Burning', and 'The Sheep-shearers in Carmel, a Pastoral', but the one mostly fully worked out in dramatic terms is *Paradise Lost*, which has three drafts, two crossed out, and then a page or two later a fourth draft called 'Adam Unparadised'. The classical intention is evident in 'Thamar Kuephorousa', 'Samson Pyrsophoros' or 'Hybristes', 'Comazontes' or 'The Rioters' (Judg. 19, 20, 21), 'Theristria', a pastoral out of Ruth, and 'Solomon Gynaecokratoumenos', or 'The Thysiazousai', suggesting an ominous view of women which cannot be said to be unbiblical.

They make an alarming list, though not without light relief: 'Imbres' or 'The Showers' (1 Kgs. 18, 19), 'The Quails', 'The Murmurers', and attempts at trilogies involving the poet in 'Elisaeus Hydrochoos', 'Hydrophantes', 'Achabaei Kynoboromenoi', 'Hezekias Poliorkoumenos'. After these resounding and largely denunciatory subjects, which introduce Samson very much as an outsider, we get eight lines on the Baptist, and turn to British history, where Milton specialized in barbarous names of appalling obscurity: Sigher, Jarumang and the like. 'The slaughter of the monks of Bangor by Edelfride, stirred up as is said by Ethelbert and he by Austin the monk, because the Britons would not receive the rites of the Roman church' sounds like a Protestant pamphlet written in verse in 1820. But 'a heroical Poem may be founded somewhere in Alfred's reign whose actions are well like those of Ulysses' is better, although un-Miltonic. 'Edward the Confessor divorcing and imprisoning his noble wife. His overaffection to strangers the cause of Godwin's insurrection. His slackness to redress the corrupt clergy and superstitious pretence of chastity' foreshadows the future. Of all these seven pages of notes, *Paradise Lost* takes no less than one and a half.

Milton was an active reader, and we can see him here spitting with fury as he reads: as much against Old Testament monarchs as against Catholic saints. He absorbed the grimness of Greek tragedy, whether now or later, until it altered the cast of his mind. *Samson Agonistes* is now generally accepted to be the work of an old, blind man. (Only the weighty opinion of Parker ever disturbed it from that position.) How utterly different it is from *Lycidas*, or from 'Damon's Epitaph'. It was to be Milton's life that would determine that difference, for which the tragic, Greek form was the only means of expression. We shall deal with *Paradise Lost* and *Samson Agonistes* at the end of this book, but it is of interest here that *Paradise Lost* was begun about this time as a Greek drama, with an excessively long monologue by Satan.

CHAPTER SEVEN

CIVIL WAR

MILTON NOW ENTERS a world of conflicts in which one thing leads to another with a certain inevitability which was hidden from him. It is not to be thought that he abandons poetry either: in the next ten years he will achieve the strength of line that he needs for his epic, and he will find it in the sonnet. As for the conflicts, they are already in full progress, as we have seen. Cowley, who was a royalist writer, wrote later that when the King ruled without a Parliament 'not a drop of blood was shed except for two or three ears', but with whatever regret one must reject that view. How the storm built up is better analysed by Clarendon. It is also useful to consult Masson's *Life of Milton*. Masson was one of those learned Scots in the nineteenth century who make one's heart sink with their unremitting seriousness and still more unremitting obsessions. The many volumes of his *Life of Milton* are largely about Scottish history and the Scottish Church, but it is true that Milton was drawn into the whirlpool as an ally of a Scottish missionary to the English. John Hutton, an old apprentice of Milton's father, now a scrivener in his own right, was one of those who were searched and questioned in 1639 over collusion with the Scots. When a Scots deputation reached England in 1640, Henderson, Baillie, Blair and Gillespie were at once in touch with Cornelius Burger of St Magnus and of Watford, and with the five-headed conspiracy called Smectymnus, whose name disguised five clergymen: Stephen Marshall of Finchingfield, Essex, Edmund Calamy of St Mary, Aldermanbury, East London, Thomas Young of Stowmarket, Suffolk, Matthew Newcomen of Dedham, Essex, and William Spurstow of Hampden, Bucks. 'The root of episcopacy,' wrote Blair in his comradely style, 'will be assaulted with the strongest force it ever felt in England.'

In 1640 the King called for a new subsidy, to which Lord Wentworth, now Strafford, contributed £20,000. Bridgewater tried to get £5,000 out of the scriveners, but he could not in the end produce £500 from them. Another peer heard that the King expected £10,000 from him and offered to raise £7,000 on a manor or two. Laud got Convocation to promise £20,000 a year for six years. The King despaired of many of his sources of revenue. Meanwhile the rack was still in use in the Tower, and men were hanged, drawn and quartered. In 1641 Strafford was executed for treason on the decision of Parliament. Laud followed him later to the block: his removal from office at an earlier stage might have made a difference.

John Milton moved to 'a pretty garden house' with more room for books, 'in Aldersgate Street at the end of an entry', that is, outside the gate tower of London, and at the bottom of a courtyard of houses opening on to the road north. It was well placed, 'few streets in the land more free from noise', as Edward Phillipps remembered it, and the garden was a luxury which Milton sought wherever he was, as Aubrey was the first to observe. Aldersgate itself was a four-storey fortified entrance with two castellated towers, and two statues of King James: on horseback on the north face, and enthroned on the south: it had been rebuilt in 1617. Howell (1657) says the street was like an Italian street. A few houses away Alexander Gill now kept a private school; the other neighbours were a weaver, an attorney, Mrs Paravicini who was kin to Oliver Cromwell, Prosper Rainsford, gentleman, Sir T. Cecil, with his wife and four servants, and Dr Theodore Diodati, brother of Charles. John Milton had one servant, called Yates. Further up the street lived the earls of Thanet and Kingston, and in the Barbican nearby lived the Earl of Bridgewater. It was an upper-class area, but Edward Phillipps remembers hard work and spare diet. Once every three weeks or so, Miller of Gray's Inn and Thomas Alphry, 'the beaux of those times', used to carry Milton away. Milton says, 'I betook myself happily enough to my intermitted studies, committing the issues of affairs to God in the first place, and to those (next) to whom the people gave that duty in trust ... As soon as the liberty of speech began to be granted, all mouths began to be opened against the Bishops'.

The debate broke open that winter, and Smectymnus issued a pamphlet against Bishop Hall (1574–1658), who had been at Emmanuel College, Cambridge: he had been a satirist in the old century and in trouble for it, but had also written an elegy on Sir Horatio

Pallavicini, 'An Italian's Dead Body stuck with English Flowers' (1600). He attacked the Brownists, preached three times a week, and caused Laud some worry with his *Divine Right of the Episcopacy*, which Laud felt not strong enough against foreign Protestants and Sabbath observers, and too severe against the Pope; Hall accepted every one of his suggestions. In 1640 the bishops were assailed with 140 furious and diverse pamphlets. Hall had answered for the bishops in *A Humble Remonstrance to the High Court of Parliament* (1641), a forty-two-page pamphlet, and drew in Smectymnus in March, with twenty pages against him, mostly written by Thomas Young. At the same time a Bill against the secular activities of bishops was delayed by the trial of Strafford. The air was thick with petitions of all colours from the counties, and reform had become bogged down by the early summer.

Milton wrote *On Church Discipline*, ninety pages of small quarto, anonymously attacking Hall, Ussher, Prynne and speeches in the Commons. He had also begun to write notes for the use of Smectymnus. He was published between June and July by Thomas Underhill of Wood Street, Cheapside, just a step from his father's door. The British Library has a copy signed by Milton as author. His argument is the simple one that what Luther started had not gone far enough in England. He made fun of Ussher's pleasingly mad view that the Angels of the Churches in Revelation means their Bishops, and he cited Dante, Petrarch, Ariosto and Malvezzi, an editor of Tacitus. Smectymnus published a *Vindication* against Hall, which the printer said was delayed by the great press of pamphlets. Between June 1641 and February 1642 Milton wrote and published *Reformation*, *Prelatical Episcopacy*, *Animadversions*, *The Reason of Church Government* and his *Apology for Smectymnus*, and all this with an unknown number of private pupils, including the Earl of Barrymore and Sir Thomas Gardiner of Essex. He was thirty-three, and very busy.

He had become a kind of journalist, to this day not an unusual or disgraceful course, often taken by those who begin as poets. But he was always more than a hack, he thought seriously about what he wrote, and his style was remarkable. (The greatest admirer of Milton's prose works in modern times has been an intellectual not wholly unlike him, a man of outstanding brilliance but also of deep dottiness or naïvety, the old aristocrat Bertrand Russell. What he admired in Milton's prose was the combination of reason and passion. No one today except Christopher Hill, perhaps, has mastered that war of pamphlets.) Nor was Milton driven back to poetry only by blindness or political failure; as times goes by his poetry never ceases to improve.

The prose is different. He could write it in huge quantities, and at its best it is as wonderful as Bertrand Russell thought it was. But it is mostly too heavy, as Johnson's is, and unprogressive. For its best, one should consult the eight pages of description that begin his history of Russia, a thrilling subject that seizes Milton and becomes for him a kind of romantic dream that leads him to the borders of China. He makes you smell the spice from the old Russian markets, not unlike, maybe, the smell of Musk Street, which is a continuation of Bread Street. It is as good as his poetry, and written simply; maybe it shows the influence of Hakluyt's *Voyages*, which every boy in London in his generation must have read. It is finer even than his enjoyable *History of* [Dark Age] *England*. But for the moment he was close to being what Yeats called 'a coarse-witted pamphleteer', and the air was full of hundreds of similar productions.

His first sentence is of thirteen lines, containing a long disquisition on God and man and the Redemption, expressed so oddly that it sounds heretical: in fact, from Milton's later writings one can see that it is. But the objection to it is that it lies like lead on the stomach. It begins well: 'Amidst those deep and retired thoughts which with every man Christianly instructed ought to be most frequent, of God and his miraculous ways and works amongst men . . .' But then comes the bit about Christ 'suffering to the lowest bent of weakness in the flesh, and presently triumphing to the highest pitch of glory in the spirit, which drew up his body also, till we in both be united to him'. It does make a kind of sense, in its rickety theological manner, but not much: what undoes him is his contrast of body and spirit, so that one draws up the other 'till we in both be united to him'. It sounds like a conjuring trick, and it clogs his prose. Then he goes on in the very manner of a Puritan reformer, and the second sentence is eighteen lines long, no less. Its points are in sharp phrases like 'new vomited paganism of sensual idolatry', but they are strung together with parentheses. The Latinisms can make his phrases vigorous, but he is not deeply enough a Latinist to marshal his syntax, at least in this work. Clarendon and Savile were better.

When he gets his teeth into liturgical questions he improves, at least in humour:

> They began to draw down all the divine intercourse betwixt God and the soul, yea, the very shape of God himself, into an exterior and bodily form. Urgently pretending a necessity and obligement of joining the body in a formal reverence and worship circumscribed, they hallowed it, they fumed it, they sprinkled it, they bedecked it, not in robes of pure innocency, but of pure linen, with other deformed and fantastic dresses, in palls and mitres, gold and gewgaws fetched from Aaron's old wardrobe, or the flamen's vestry.

The superstitious man is an atheist: 'Then was Baptism changed into a kind of exorcism . . .' Next, in a sentence of nine or ten lines, comes the Reformation: a purifying and essentially an English movement that began with Wycliff. But now the English are forced to disbelieve in Protestant ministers on the Continent because they are not ordained by bishops, and Romish ceremonies have dragged the Church of England sliding back to Rome. It cannot be said that his essential argument differs from the common-sense view taken by many English people.

He goes on to offer an explanation of the obstacles to the continuing Reformation in England by a view of history under Henry and Edward VI which his readers would not be likely to dispute. The prelates were worldly, and 'the least wry face of a politician would have hushed them'. 'We all know by example that exact Reformation is not completed at the first push.' It was the bishops who undid the clergy by 'settling in a skinny congealment of ease and sloth at the top'. As for the Elizabethan clergy, 'surely they were moderate divines indeed, neither hot nor cold', and the Queen was 'brought to believe' that putting down bishops would be a loss of her prerogative. It was this central difficulty of a monarch ruling both Church and State that forced the reform party into using the considerable pressure boiling up in the Church against the monarch, and brought Charles I to the scaffold. But Milton in this early exposition of his views is respectful to Protestant monarchs, even when he differs from them. He counts the opposition to his party as either Antiquarians, or Libertines, or Politicians.

His best passages are invective: there is something a little unnatural about them, like a joke in a sermon. They are not an integral part of his pamphleteering. They are witty enough, but they recall the manner and the lack of manners of pamphlets under Queen Elizabeth. Worse was written, often so bad it could not be printed at all, in this period just before the war, but some of Milton's jokes are indefensible by modern standards:

> The people of God ... are now no better reputed than impure ethnics and lay dogs. Stones, and pillars, and crucifixes have now the honour and the alms due to Christ's living members. The table of communion, now become a table of separation, stands like an exalted platform upon the brow of the quire, fortified with bulwark and barricado to keep off the profane touch of the laics, whilst the obscene and surfeited priest scruples not to paw and mammock the sacramental bread as familiarly as his tavern biscuit.

From this he returns to his learned discourse, though we have caught here a whiff not only of change but also of an embittered revolution in Church arrangements treated honestly only by A. L. Rowse.

In 1644, one William Dowsing was employed by Lord Manchester, the parliamentary General, to smash all the stained glass he could find in East Anglia, whitewash the wall paintings and pull down the painted angels stuck to the rafters like beautiful moths. He did it for six shillings and eight pence a church, and where he could not reach the angels he tried shooting them to pieces. At Blythburgh there are still shot-marks in those that survive. His record was eleven churches in a day, at Ipswich. At Haverhill, for which his notes survive, 'we beat down a great stone Cross on top of the Church, and destroyed a hundred paintings'. He was called the Smasher. It is a question whether Milton's prose was not a deliberate incitement to such people.

In Milton's *Animadversions*, a more particular defence of Smectymnus against the old controversialist Bishop Hall, he is very funny, but the style is that of Cambridge, and he should have outgrown it. Meanwhile the Lords threw out Sir Edward Dering's anti-episcopal Bill, so the Commons impeached thirteen bishops. Laud was fined £20,000, and others between £1,000 and £10. Milton's books therefore were about a burning public issue and had practical consequences. The King went off to fight the Scots again, and an appallingly ugly massacre of Protestants took place in Ireland, of up to 1,000 victims a day, twenty-two burnt at Kilmare and seventeen flung in a bogpit, 717 babies or young children hanged at Dungannon, and one fat Scot murdered, whose grease they melted down to make candles. In November the King was back in London, faintly and hopelessly hoping to impose a moderate conservatism. The Parliamentary Guard was dismissed by the King, 'And now what hope have we but in God, whenas the only means of our subsistence, and power of reformation is under Him, in the Parliament?' That is from a petition presented early in December. A petition from the City was presented on 11 December which had 5,000 signatures and was twenty-four yards long. At the end of that month Laud appeared at a window to welcome his colleagues to the Tower.

It was a time of furious tumults: the terms 'Cavalier' and 'Round-head', which have kept their meaning for three and a half centuries, were coined then. On 3 January the King attempted and failed to arrest the five Members whom he suspected to be ringleaders in the House of Commons: the next day he took the Speaker's seat, attended by 400 or 500 supporters, and the armed mob, perhaps 140,000 strong, began to organize against him. Old Captain Skippon taught the dangerous arts of pike and musket and of fencing to whoever came, in the Artillery Gardens, north of London: one is now Moorfields, and by the other, further east, Milton was later to settle among the Nonconformists, who had their burial place there. Mean-while the women, the sailors and the street porters of London petitioned against the bishops. The case is still clear enough: Milton's party wanted the King to accept the rule of law, but he would not; if he had done, then the bishops would have been swept away, and with them a large part of what the monarch felt to be his by divine right. On 10 January, just a week after the farce of the five Members, he withdrew to Hampton Court and soon afterwards to embattled Windsor. On the 13th he yielded over the bishops, while the Queen, who was a French Catholic with Sforza blood, went to France to raise money. In this pause the King's daughter Mary became engaged to William of Nassau; she was to be the mother of William III of England.

In England there was a quarrel over the control of the militia and its armaments. The King extracted a poll tax for his army in the north, but Milton, Alexander Gill, Mrs Paravicini and Dr Theodore Diodati were all defaulters. The poet did give £4 to a public fund for the Irish Protestants, which was twice as much as anyone else in his ward. That should be remembered later when he takes an equally strong line about other Protestants in trouble. By March the King was at York, and John Rothwell printed *The Reason of Church Government*, by John Milton, a small quarto of sixty-five pages. A certain Henry Rothwell had been Milton's father's apprentice in 1631, and John Rothwell had been the publisher of Smectymnus. In November 1641 Lord Brooke wrote a pamphlet, *On the Nature of Episcopacy*, which Milton complimented later. At this time, in 1641, Milton wrote against *Certain Brief Treatises*, defending Ussher but not Laud. The argument is arcane if only because it touches on the even queerer opinions of Lancelot Andrewes, and those of Ussher on the Seven Churches of Asia. The Civil War was starting.

The preface to Book 2 of *The Reason of Church Government* is autobiography, to which Milton felt pricked. There was, no doubt, a certain amount of useless pride or vanity in his make-up. He begins ponderously:

> So, lest it should still be imputed to me, as I have found it hath been, that some self-pleasing humour of vain-glory hath incited me to contest with men of high estimation, now while green years are upon my head, from this needless surmisal I shall hope to dissuade the intelligent and equal auditor, if I can but say successfully that which in this exigent behoves me; although I would be heard only, if it might be, by the elegant and learned reader, to whom principally for a while I may take leave to address myself.

For a combination of snobbery, pomp and verbosity, this scores high. But as usual, when he has cleared his throat and has something to say, he improves.

> If I hunted after praise, by the ostentation of wit and learning, I should not write thus out of my own season when I have neither yet completed to my mind the full circle of my private studies ... For although a poet, soaring in the high region [reason is a printer's error] of his fancies, with his garland and singing robes about him, might, without

apology, speak more of himself than I mean to do; yet for me sitting here below in the cool element of prose ... I must say therefore that after I had for my first years, by the ceaseless diligence and care of my father – whom God recompensed – been exercised to the tongues, and some sciences, as my age would suffer, by sundry masters and teachers both at home and at the schools, it was found that whether aught was imposed me by them that had the overlooking, or betaken to by mine own choice in English or other tongue, prosing or versing, but chiefly by this latter, the style, for certain vital signs it had, was likely to live.

Persuaded by the Italians and 'an inward prompting which now grew daily upon me', he thought 'that by labour and intense study, which I take to be my portion in this life, joined with the strong propensity of nature, I might perhaps leave something so written to aftertimes, that they should not willingly let it die.' That he undoubtedly accomplished.

What is missing is the Svengali role of Thomas Young. We know that his arguments and by now quite elaborate positions are close to Baillie's: all these people were in touch. But Milton wanders on in his sea of glory like a solipsist. Knowing he could never be the greatest writer in Latin,

> I applied myself to that resolution, which Ariosto followed against the persuasions of Bembo, to fix all the industry and art I could unite to the adorning of my native tongue ... to be an interpreter and relater of the best and sagest things among mine own citizens throughout this island in the mother dialect.

He goes on to let the reader into his own mind, evidently with honesty:

> Time serves not now, and perhaps I might seem too profuse, to give any certain account of what the mind at home, in the spacious circuits of her musing, hath liberty to propose to herself, though of highest hope and hardest attempting; whether that epic form whereof the two poems of Homer, and those other two of Virgil and Tasso, are a diffuse, and the book of Job a brief model: or whether the rules of Aristotle herein are strictly to be kept, or nature to be followed, which in them that know art and use judgment is no transgression but an enriching of art: and lastly, what king or knight before the Conquest might be chosen, in whom to lay the pattern of a Christian hero.

These are the things that were really close to his heart as the trumpets played and the war began. He was a poet, and these problems were real to him, the most real. Had he found a patron in Italy or in the Alps, we would have a more mainstream 'epic' Milton, closer to Tasso, but he was intellectually too original to bow for long to Tasso's influence, and we must bear with an English Milton, a Milton of his time in England to some degree, or with one half of his head, while the other wandered off along paths where only critics follow him. 'The Scripture also affords us a divine pastoral drama in the Song of Solomon, consisting of two persons and a double chorus, as Origen rightly judges.' I am sure one would have found Milton's version convincing, but alas, he never produced it. He goes on to suggest the Apocalypse as 'a high and stately tragedy', with solemn scenes intermingled with a sevenfold chorus of harp and 'Hallelujah'. The point of these divagations was to find some dramatic subject so holy that the extreme Puritans might have accepted it. It is important to notice that nothing Milton wrote suggests that at this time he was in any way influential.

The state of England might reasonably be compared with that of Russia in the same years. The Russians had just passed through a long crisis over who was to be Tsar, and then how to get rid of the Poles. Parliaments had met in 1598 and 1613, to decide on the disputed succession, but once that was settled, they showed no interest at all in extending their power. They put no conditions to the Tsar and reserved no powers over the succession. The Tsar was part of the Orthodox religion, which was sacrosanct. The deputies regarded their functions as burdensome duties. As Prince Mirsky puts it in 1927, 'The monarchy needed all the support of the classes that had restored it. To this end a succession of parliaments was convoked. Their influence on affairs was almost unlimited.' With the civil code of 1649, by which the tenants of the civil-servant class became more like serfs or slaves, the work of parliaments was done; they had their wish, and were content to be dissolved. The Russian Church was still in the rich and grand state of the English Church in the first year of Henry VIII. It will be seen that the difference was huge, and rested on the Church, which in England had lost public confidence. The Russian parliament was not unambitious, but the Tsar, Michael Romanov, did not torment it or try to arrest its members. Meanwhile both England

and Russia, and one might add Spain, were expanding beyond all proportion or expectation. The troubles of England were partly religious troubles, but also partly imported from Europe: can Charles I have seen himself as another Henry IV?

Bishop Hall was in the Tower in 1642, but he or his son had turned on Milton in an angry pamphlet, calling him a carping poetaster; in March or April 1642 Milton reacted. This son Robert, now a canon of Exeter, was two years senior to Milton at Cambridge, and this or some other circumstance led Milton to write about a 'suburb sink' or 'rude scavenger', and to use other scurrilous phrases. It was as if Milton was carrying on a private slanging match while paying no attention to the real world. Henry King became Dean of Christ Church while the King was at York in March, and then battering in vain at the gates of Hull, which contained a mass of militia armaments. In mid-May Edward Hyde left Parliament and escaped north to the King, carrying with him the last hope of moderation: his friend Falkland soon followed. By the end of May only forty-two of the Lords were left in London and thirty-two were with the King. The Commons were supposed to number 500, though 300 was generally thought a full house: now there were seldom as many as 200 and in July the number had sunk to 100. This means that even if we allow for laziness, self-interest and lack of concern with the quarrel as it then stood, the King's party had at least as much support in Parliament as had the opposition. Nevertheless, the biggest vote that July was 125 against forty-five, for raising militia.

In June, arms came to the King's party from Holland, where the Queen had sold the Crown Jewels to pay for them. Nobles were to raise armed horsemen for him, and the universities to send their gold and silver plate to be melted down. On the Parliament side the soldiers were inclined to make demands for bread on Roman Catholic houses. At Hillingdon, a mile from Uxbridge on the road from Horton to Harefield, 'the rails being gone, we got the surplice to make us handkerchers, and one of the soldiers wore it to Uxbridge. This day the rails of Uxbridge were with the Service book burned.' These were a parliamentary force under Nehemiah Wharton, a recruiting colonel. The upper classes juggled or reshaped their alliances; Bridgewater said he was ill, for example, but his son married a daughter of the royalist Newcastle. Arundel died abroad. There were young men also who knew they would die, like Sir Edmund Verney, who was twenty-five and assured Hyde of his black future. At the end of the year came the first set battle, at Edgehill, which happened so suddenly that it surprised everybody and both sides claimed to have won.

John Milton is not named in the ranks of those in arms against the King. Edward Phillipps says they thought of making him adjutant-general to Waller, but that is unexplained. A different John Milton, of St Dunstan's in the East, was quarter-master to Colonel Pennington, the MP for Hungerford, but Phillipps would probably not confuse them. At the time of his first war sonnet, 'Captain or Colonel or Knight at arms', it is plain that John Milton had not the least intention of fighting. In 1640 his brother Christopher was called to the Bar; he soon married and began to have daughters. By 1641 Christopher was in Reading, nicely placed for a careful man between the King in Oxford and Parliament in London. His father stayed with him until the place was besieged, and then made his way to his other son John in London. He found John married, but here again one senses compromise. It is, of course, possible though unlikely that young Christopher was really a royalist, but he appears to have played both sides against the middle quite easily all his life; he ended up as a judge under James II. John had married Mary Powell, daughter of a family to which he and his father had lent money, and from which he had taken land at Wheatley, Oxford, at the end of June in 1640. The Powells were royalists and they had been Roman Catholics down to Powell's grandfather, who was still alive in 1601. Mr Powell was now a justice of the peace at Forest Hill, very near the Miltons at Stanton St John.

This implies an old family entanglement or alliance, which the poet chose the strangest of moments to renew. His father had always done what business he could do with this part of Oxfordshire. Richard Powell had been married for twenty years or more, and his wife's mother, an Archdale from Staffordshire, brought him money (£3,000) and Oxfordshire property: perhaps the land at Wheatley which he had mortgaged and lost to the Miltons. He held Forest Hill on a twenty-year lease (1621) from Edward Brome, extended in July 1623 to 1672, and when Brome had died in 1628, Powell was his sole executor, Forest Hill being valued at £270 a year and Wheatley at £40 a year. No doubt he had other interests also, but he was no man

of business, and somewhere in this tangle must lie the reason why
John Milton wandered off to the country (that is, his grandfather's
country) in the spring or early summer of 1642, and married Mary
Powell. Seventeenth-century marriage arrangements never cease to
amaze one. It may perhaps be read as a purely romantic experiment;
in that case, one must admit that it failed. But the ups and downs of
this marriage correspond to the swaying of the balance of war. And if
the marriage were really a romantic experiment, why did the father
permit it? If Milton was exercising a kind of blackmail over Powell,
why did Powell not call for soldiers from Oxford to be rid of him?
Edward Phillips tells us:

> About Whitsuntide it was, or a little after, that he took a Journey into
> the Country, nobody about him certainly knowing the Reason, or that
> it was any more than a Journey of Recreation. After a Month's stay,
> home he returns a Married-man, that went out a Batchelor; his wife
> being Mary, the Eldest Daughter of Mr Richard Powell, then a Justice
> of Peace, of Forrest-hil, near Shotover, in Oxfordshire; some few of
> her nearest Relations accompanying the Bride to her new Habitation;
> which by reason the Father nor anybody else were yet come, was able
> to receive them; where the Feasting held for some days in Celebration
> of the Nuptials, and for entertainment of the Bride's Friends.

This party then returned to Forest Hill and left her behind, 'not
much to her satisfaction, as appeared by the Sequel; by that time she
had for a Month or thereabout led a Philosophical Life (after having
been used to a great House, and much Company and Joviality)'. Her
family begged to have her back for the summer, and she was duly sent
with orders to return by Michaelmas. Edward maintains that at this
time the poet 'made it his chief diversion now and then in an evening
to visit' Margaret Lee, the daughter of James I's President of the
Privy Council; Margaret Lee and her husband Captain Hobson,
neighbours and Parliamentarians, were both very fond of Milton, and
the sonnet to Margaret Lee is not easily dated in any other way: the
copy in the Trinity manuscript is only a fair copy and no help. This
sonnet, on the other hand, does pretend (for the first time in Milton's
life) to an accurate knowledge of the world, which is by no means to
be taken at its face value.

Margaret's father, James Ley (1550–1629), was Lord Chief Justice

(1622), Lord High Treasurer (1624) and Earl of Marlborough (1626), then President of the Council (1628), resigning each post as he got a higher one. He borrowed money from judges as Lord Chief Justice and tried to repay them as Lord High Treasurer by paying the wages only of those judges. He died, suggests Milton in these fine Horatian lines, because of the scandalous end of the Parliament in 1628, when the King had demanded an adjournment on 2 March but the Speaker was then held down in his seat by Members while resolutions about the King's crimes were read out: nine members were sent to the Tower and on 10 March Parliament was dissolved. The 'good Earl once President', however, had resigned as President on 14 December 1628 and died on 19 March 1629. He was a vile old man, at his worst in Ireland, where one of his specialities was to make Roman Catholicism a Star Chamber offence and another never to let the accused person see the charges against him. It is most doubtful whether he cared twopence about the dissolution of the Parliament in 1628; he became President only when it had gone. Milton admits he himself was 'later born, than to have known the days/Wherein your father flourished', but he offers the old man's ghost lofty praises, if only by comparing him with Isocrates, whose reputation stood high.

No doubt the sonnet is heroic in the Italian manner, which makes its Horatian touches second-hand, but it is a fine poem, although Milton does not know what he is talking about. This is not his only sonnet to a lady: another follows of which the date is not known, nor is the person to whom it was addressed. It is an admiring poem to a young woman, 'that in the prime of earliest youth,/Wisely hath shunned the broad way and the green'. He reproves the persons, once again unnamed, who 'fret their spleen' over this girl, wanting her to marry, it seems. The sestet is lovely.

> Thy care is fixed and zealously attends
> To fill thy odorous lamp with deeds of light,
> And hope that reaps not shame. Therefore be sure
> Thou, when the bridegroom with his feastful friends
> Passes to bliss at the mid-hour of night,
> Hast gained thy entrance, virgin wise and pure.

It is not easy for any poet to sustain such a long undertow of a rhythm on such a coolness with such warmth. He can do it only by the slight dislocations of word order and the formalities of syntax this poem shows. It is all a remarkable and perfect control of breath, and a precise selection of the simplest words to create an effect which seems beyond their powers. The 'feastful friends' recall the circumstances of Milton's own marriage.

The Powells had eleven children, the eldest of them, another Richard, born in 1621, James the next year and Mary the next, so she was eighteen or nineteen when the poet married her. Young Richard and James were at Christ Church, where in November 1642 the King arrived like a peacock among pigeons. As for Mary, Aubrey says 'she went from him to her mother'. Toland says:

> Whether it was that the young woman, accustomed to a larger, jovial family, could not live in a philosophic retirement, or that she was not perfectly satisfied with the person of her husband, or lastly that because her relations were all addicted to the royal interest, his democratic principles were disagreeable to her humour (nor is it impossible that the father repented of this match upon the prospect of some success upon the King's side who then had his headquarters at Oxford) . . .

This is interesting only as near-contemporary speculation. She may well have been shocked by Milton's opinions, his gloomy life, or simply his attempts (of which we know nothing) at sex, or the awful prospect of London life as an intellectual's or scholar's wife: and maybe he made too little allowance. She did not come back from the country that year.

On 1 June 1642 the Westminster Assembly was convened to govern the Church without bishops: it was a widely based body that included, for example, Lord Falkland among MPs, though it did not actually meet until July of 1643. This was the way in which the Puritans proposed to exercise power, and Thomas Young was, of course, a leading member. From Milton's point of view it was both a bulwark and a force for good: but as soon as it came into existence he began to distrust it, until in the end he found himself opposed to the Puritans, as Cromwell did, because they were bishops without the funny hats. Meanwhile the armies pursued their manoeuvres. London was still the only city that could raise an army, and when the King left London he lost that resource; so his first tactic was to try to get back there, which he almost accomplished. These are Machiavellian or modern terms in which to see the early part of the war; Clarendon saw it in religious terms, and so did Thomas Young. Clarendon thought Queen Elizabeth had seen 'a total alteration of religion and some confident attempts upon a further alteration by those who thought not the reformation enough': he felt nothing could explain what now followed but 'a general combination and universal apostasy in the whole nation from their religion and allegiance'.

King Charles did not really have the necessary strength of purpose for the hazardous courses on which he had embarked. When he raised his standard he had no arms, no men, only drums and trumpets which banged and blew. A storm knocked down the standard, and it could not be restored for the three nights that the storm lasted: that was in August 1642. A message to Parliament asking for a truce 'was indeed received with unheard of insolence and contempt', just as he foresaw. His friends advised him to go at once in person to Parliament, now when he was not expected. He would stand more chance like that 'than by any army he was like to raise'. But Parliament issued this declaration: 'It is this day declared by the Lords and Commons, that the arms they have been forced to take up, and shall be forced to take up, for the preservation of the Parliament, the religion, the laws and liberties of the kingdom, shall not be laid down, until His Majesty shall withdraw his protection from such persons as have been voted by both Houses to be delinquents ...'

The King wandered about England trying to persuade cities to welcome him. Hull refused, he lost a chance of Coventry, Shrewsbury took him in, he hoped for Worcester and even for Chester, which would be a plum. Essex, the Parliament commander, who at least had an army while the King had scarcely a regiment, dithered as badly or worse for lack of orders. The common soldiers believed the propaganda, and thought the King was merely surrounded by wicked advisers, and would be happy to come over to the Parliament side. All over England places were declaring for Parliament, and Portsmouth surrendered. Taunton and Dunster declared for Parliament. Noblemen who were King's men were captured in their houses or castles, until the prisons of London were full, and 'very many persons of good quality, both of the clergy and laity, were committed to prison on board the ships in the river Thames, where they were kept under decks, and no friend suffered to come to them, by which many lost their lives'. Property was sequestered or simply plundered, until one of those general fits of furious envy spread across England that was seen later in France, and general looting followed.

All this left John Milton tranquil in his ivory tower until, in November 1642, when Christopher Milton was on the Reading muster-roll as a King's soldier (if necessary), an assault was intended against London. The Earl of Essex was at Warwick, after the disconcerting brush with the King at Edgehill, and the King, having no particular plan, advanced on London. Had he taken the city, the situation would have entailed much changing of sides, possibly by Milton among others.

> Captain or colonel, or knight in arms,
> Whose chance on these defenceless doors may seize,
> If deed of honour did thee ever please,
> Guard them . . .
> And he can spread thy name o'er lands and seas . . .
> The great Emathian conqueror bid spare
> The house of Pindarus . . .

The poem is like a nightingale singing in a garden many miles from the war and is exquisitely modulated. But as a practical measure it is, of course, absurd. The rhyme scheme is particularly ornamental, like the trickle of an Italian fountain. The 'great Emathian' is a piece of showing off; it is an epithet used by Ovid for Alexander, but the touch of mystery it adds to Pindar's house, when that poet was more than a hundred years dead in Alexander's time, all adds to the pleasing sense of unreality. We are told, and may well believe, that there was panic in London. What were called the Trained Bands, a sort of Home Guard, met the King at Brentford. Both sides were sensibly terrified of fighting, and the King withdrew. One is tempted to say that in this way he lost London, and the war, and his crown, and his head. The poem's title, in a secretary's hand, was 'On his door when the City expected an assault'. This is erased and Milton writes, 'When the assault was intended to the City, 1642', then 'the' before 'assault' is erased and the date crossed out. He has realized what an absurd figure he will cut. As for Brentford, it is not far from Horton.

'I have heard many knowing men, and some who were then in the City regiments say,' writes Clarendon, 'that if the King had advanced and charged that massy body, it had presently given ground, and that the King had so great a party in every regiment, that it would have made no resistance. But it had been madness, which no success could have vindicated, to have made that attempt . . .' The King moved south 'to Kingston, which the rebels had kindly quitted', and spent that night and the next day at Hampton Court. He then went to Oatlands and then to Reading, so as not to look threatening while a treaty might be negotiated, but it was not. And so things continued.

That winter 'the kingdom felt the sad effects of war'. Parliament took Chichester, and the King took Cirencester. 'The town yielded much plunder, from which the undistinguishing soldier could not be kept, but was equally injurious to friend and foe.' The King now had a small camel's hump of England, extending from Oxford as far as Worcester.

CHAPTER EIGHT

PROSE

THE FIRST PUBLIC UTTERANCE that John Milton made, as the
war continued like some futile game of chess until at last sheer
bitterness begot a professional army, was his pamphlet *The Doctrine
and Discipline of Divorce*, which appeared on 1 August 1643, with no
obvious reference to his own case. It could not have appeared while
the bishops were in power. He pleaded like a public benefactor, but
at the same time like an ecclesiastical lawyer, 'and then I doubt not
with one gentle stroke to wipe away the tears out of the life of men'.
He thought Scripture gave men the right to change partners or have
more than one, and in a day when Scripture weighed heavily his view
was startling. It did not occur to him that women had any particular
rights in the matter; in fact, he was all for demeaning them still
further. Yet he had a case: earlier Protestantism had been freer, and
the views of theologians more liberal, than the current English
position appeared to allow. James Howell, who was in the Fleet prison
for debt, commented on this pamphlet in comic horror, and so did
Hall: 'Woe is me! to what a pass is the world come!'

Milton published anonymously for fear of the tumult he might
(and, in fact, did) arouse, though the next year he said God was trying
him to see if he would stand alone for a cause. As his style immediately
revealed him, he abandoned his anonymity in his second edition early
in 1644. This time there were eighty-eight pages, increased from
forty-four; he dealt in a learned and sophisticated way with the fable
of Eros and Anteros, and he quoted Paul Fagius, a Cambridge
professor of a century earlier, Bucer his colleague, Paraeus who had
died in 1622 at the age of seventy-four and John Selden who was
concerned with the legal aspect of divorce in this decade. That year
Selden was fifty-nine and Milton thirty-five; he writes from this time
as Selden's disciple, with affection and admiration. Selden had been
one of the nine Members of Parliament sent to the Tower in March

1629, then sent to the Marshalsea prison in the swamps near Southwark and finally to the Gatehouse at Westminster until May 1631, when Arundel and Pembroke secured his release because they needed to pick his legal brain. He does not seem to have minded much: he took an active part in the Inns of Court masque in 1633 which vented disapproval of Prynne's *Histriomastix*. In the Long Parliament he was a Member for Oxford. In 1642 the King, who had observed his formidable talent, thought of making him Lord Chief Justice, or at least of tempting him to York.

In 1643 he sat in the Westminster Assembly, where he would confute the ministers of religion much as he had confuted King Charles. He was a God-given ally to Milton who resented the claims of presbytery as he did those of episcopacy. Fuller in the *Church History* says shrewdly of Selden that he used his copious learned ammunition and power of reason more 'to perplex than to inform' the Assembly, his purpose being 'to humble the jure-divinoship of Presbytery'. In 1643 he became archivist at the Tower, where all the older state records were, and, in 1645, a Commissioner of the Admiralty. He was offered the Mastership of Trinity Hall, Cambridge, but refused it, and later £5,000 in damages but refused them too (or so it appears). He procured Archbishop Bancroft's learned library for Cambridge, and did a lot for individuals as a judge of appeals against the Visitors at Oxford. In 1635 he had published the English case in a fishing war with Holland in his *Mare Clausum*, against the *Mare Liberum* of Grotius (1609).

Selden is a shadowy figure in Milton's life; he turns up only in quotations in the controversial pamphlets, yet there is no doubt they knew each other, and if so it is certain that his influence pulled in a different direction from Thomas Young's. The pamphlet on divorce in 1643 is the first time Milton fired off a salvo on his own: whether from timidity or from modesty, he had until now been a sniper from the ramparts of Smectymnus, as Auden put it.

> Our snipers sniping from the walls
> Of learned periodicals
> Our fact defend,
> Our intellectual marines
> Landing in little magazines
> Capture a trend.

His success was by no means immediate, but after the Restoration, when he was in disgrace, and when the first long, slow divorce case, that of Lord Roos, was being fought through the House of Lords, Milton was consulted as an expert. He was brooding on the loss of his wife in October 1642; it is probable enough that the breakdown of his marriage led him to his public utterances on divorce, the second (February 1644) so much longer than the first (August 1643). From this he turned to writing about education (June 1644) and on Bucer's opinion about divorce (6 August 1644).

His persistence on the subject, sweetly reasonable as it seemed, finally earned him notoriety. On 13 August he was attacked in a sermon before Parliament by one Herbert Palmer, and ten days or so later the Stationers petitioned against him. Palmer (1601–47) was a gentleman's son from Kent who had been a Fellow of Queens' College, Cambridge, of which unhappy institution Lord Manchester made him Master; he filled it with German and Hungarian refugees and ruled it with a rod of iron. His emaciated and gloomy visage ends in a straggling beard. He was one of the seven daily preachers who kept up a barrage in the Abbey that was nearly continuous, and Baillie called him the best catechist in England. He can have had no particular reason to attack Milton, but since he was a member and became an assessor of the Assembly, his influence was powerful. Milton's initial attack had been on custom as 'being but a mere face, as Echo is a mere voice ... Hence it is that Error supports Custom, Custom countenances Error, and these two between them would persecute and chase away all Truth and Solid Wisdom out of human life, were it not that ...' and there the fourteen-line sentence gets the bit between its teeth. His basic argument is that God cannot have intended us to be as unhappy as absolutely indissoluble, monogamous marriage can make us. To most people this now appears to be common sense, but in 1644 it was going too far: it must have seemed Milton was doing away with the Church and the sacrament, and relying on his own reason. The fact that he quoted Scripture was no defence, and the Protestant theologians were too obscure to make him respectable. In fact, with one blow Milton had put himself into the opposition. He would never now be a head of college like Herbert Palmer or Thomas Young, who got Jesus College. He had become suspect in the Assembly.

Yet Milton, free of the apron-strings of Smectymnus, is bolder and more eloquent, even at times touche things with a strange beauty that recalls nothing else in his prose or poetry apart from *Comus*, with its cult of purity. 'Truth is as impossible to be soiled by any outward touch, as is the sunbeam.' And he was proud of his performance, his originality. 'Me it concerns next, having with much labour and faithful diligence first found out, or at least with a fearless and communicative candour first published, to the manifest good of Christendom, that which, calling to witness everything mortal and immortal, I believe unfeignedly to be true.' He makes the crucial point that marrying is like swearing allegiance, and if to a bad government or to the wrong person, then in both cases there must be some remedy. As Selden said in his *Table Talk*, 'He that vows can mean no more in sense, than this, to do his utmost endeavour to keep his vow.' Milton's arguments are disciplined and well marshalled, and employ better English, being nervous and more practical, than his earlier work. His radical temper pushes him so far as to claim that the antinomian extremes of Protestantism 'may proceed from the undue restraint of some just liberty', which he thinks the best of reasons for rejecting any such harmful discipline. This puts him where Cromwell is, among what now came to be called the Independents.

Love, if he be not twin born, yet hath a brother wondrously like him, called Anteros; whom while he seeks all about, his chance is to meet with many false and feigning desires that wander singly up and down in his likeness: by them in their borrowed garb, Love, though not wholly blind, as poets wrong him, yet having but one eye, as being born an archer aiming, and that eye not the quickest in this dark region below which is not Love's proper sphere, partly out of the simplicity and credulity which is native to him, often deceived, embraces and consorts him with these obvious and suborned striplings, as if they were his mother's own sons; for so he thinks them, while they subtilly keep themselves most upon the blind side. But after a while, as his manner is, when soaring up into the high tower of his Apogaeum, above the shadow of the earth, he darts out the direct rays of his then most piercing sight upon the impostures and trim disguises that were used with him, and discerns that this is not his genuine brother, as he imagined; for he has no longer the power to hold fellowship with such a personated mate: . . . this is no mere amatorious novel.

The argument derives ultimately from Plato's *Philebos*, and possibly more nearly from Marsilio Ficino, but it is a most amazing outburst of the pagan world that underlies his education, designed to explain the free and guiltless wanderings of youth, and (in Plato's *Symposium*) the conversion of the homosexual lover to the love of God himself. How personal it may be to his own feelings one is not told. 'Thus mine author sung it to me . . . This is a deep and serious verity.'

Milton was careful: nowhere did he suggest that desertion by a wife might be grounds for a divorce. Yet in 1651, when the hounds were really out after Milton, a lawyer scribbled on a petition of Mrs Powell, his mother-in-law, that 'Mr Milton is a harsh and choleric man . . . turned his wife away heretofore for a long space'. He was accused by a royalist writer in 1652 of turning her out because of jealousy, and a Restoration writer in 1660 said it was 'because your waspish spirit could not agree with her qualities, and your crooked phantasy could not be brought to take delight in her'. But these insults are all to be ignored. I do not think many people today would blame Milton if he had made the mistake he delicately sketches in his Eros and Anteros parable, and we do not know that he wronged his wife in the slightest: we know only that she went home and stayed there, and that within the year the Powells were doing 'intelligence' work for the King. The paragraph I have quoted about Love and Anteros is more or less unique in Milton: it is not reflected in his laborious note-taking, and of all the famous Renaissance subjects, love is the only one on which he preserves a stubborn silence, until this passage.

The alternative, he stoutly maintained, was 'to grind in the mill of an undelighted and servile copulation'. Unluckily for him, his pamphlet was greeted with enthusiasm by creatures of low comedy, like Mrs Attaway the Griddletonian she-preacher of Coleman Street, who ran away with William Jenny, her fellow-preacher. There were sectaries like the Ranter John Robins for whom Milton expressed compassion, who changed his own sexual partner and encouraged his followers to do the same. But Milton made no good impression on Thomas Young and his friends. Young advised the House of Commons in a sermon in February 1644 to do nothing to advance the legalization of what he called bigamy. In September of that year Prynne attacked Milton in an onslaught on 'many Anabaptistical, Antinomian, Heretical, Atheistical opinions as of the soul's mortality, divorce at leisure etc, lately broached, preached, printed in this famous City, which I hope our Grand Council will speedily and carefully suppress'. That was no moment for a quiet, liberal, high-table sort of discussion of a subject like divorce. The House of Commons was preoccupied with the much more fascinating question of the idolatrous images of Westminster Abbey; a party was sent to smash them all on 24 April 1643. In March the Rubens altarpiece from Somerset House had been flung into the Thames. Milton was living in Cloud-cuckoo-land: when his father arrived as a refugee from Reading, we are told that he lived with his son in perfect tranquillity and retirement with his studies and devotions. In June the poet published another pamphlet, this one about education: yet that was not the most burning issue of 1643. He thought perhaps he should have written about divorce in Latin, as Selden had done.

The progress of the war in 1643 was delayed by 'the old superstition of not going out of the county' which prevailed among the Trained Bands or local militia. It is Clarendon who calls it a superstition, but it was a solidly grounded prejudice. It prevailed in Gloucestershire among militia regiments until the end of the nineteenth century. At times there was a shortage of ammunition, and 'when they were clouded with that want at Tavistock, some gentlemen of Cornwall who adhered to the rebels, and were thereby dispossessed of their country, made some overtures that a treaty might be entered into, whereby the peace of those two counties of Cornwall and Devon might be settled, and the war removed into other parts'.

At the same time the rebels continually told one another that if they should win, then the King or his son would still be King, but if they lost, they would be hanged. Now that he despaired of Parliament, the King set up a counter-parliament in the city of Oxford. That year the rebels lost John Hampden, who was popular enough to have governed England, while the King's side lost 'very many officers and persons of quality' at Lansdowne, and the earls of Sunderland and Carnarvon and Lord Falkland at Newbury. Arundel and Basing House fell after tremendous sieges; the latter had been newly and thoroughly fortified, but its owner, Lord Winchester, a Catholic, was never recompensed for his vast losses. The end of it all began in summer of 1644 with the triumph of Cromwell and Fairfax and their iron cavalry over Prince Rupert and Newcastle at Marston Moor. The Parliament had at last raised and trained a professional army.

It was in that army that Independents spread like an epidemic: Baillie calls Cromwell the 'Great Independent'. It was suspected that Independents could not swear to what they would believe in the future, a quality that Selden might have found endearing but Herbert Palmer, who was an expert at getting people to swear to things, would have deeply distrusted. Baillie disapprovingly noted that the English lacked a solid Presbyterian system and were 'inclinable to singularities'. Pamphlets began to appear against religious toleration. That spring at Cambridge the Puritans ejected half the Fellows of colleges and eleven out of sixteen heads of house. The Master of Christ's and three of his colleagues took the Covenant and were safe, but Queens' was a clean sweep. At Clare Hall Ralph Cudworth, who was twenty-seven and a Fellow of Emmanuel, the old storm centre, took over, and Whichcot, another Emmanuel Fellow, got King's. Thomas Young and his friend and fellow-Smectymnian Spurstow also got colleges: Cambridge had been taken over by the Westminster Assembly. Young retained his seat there and also his vicarage at Stowmarket, though he did resign Jesus College a year or two later. The Assembly was all for these new heads of college keeping their seats; they 'desired that their brethren be not withdrawn'.

Marston Moor left 4,150 dead. It was an Independent rather than a Presbyterian triumph, and certainly not a Scottish victory. Baillie was shocked by the tolerance displayed by these people, even in the city of London, where Goodwin of Coleman Street had no quarrel with Turks, Jews or Papists. Goodwin's principle was that if no natural Church exists, there should be absolute liberty; if there is a natural Church, there can be toleration all around it, and anyway there can be limited toleration. This brought the irate Thomas Edwards into print with his deadly boring *Antapologia*. It also elicited Dr Featley's *Dippers Dipt*; Edwards's *Gangraena* is more comprehensive. The sorts of view he attacks are that Scripture is all an allegory or a code and the Old Testament a dead letter, that God is the author of sins, that the soul dies and only God lives, that the sun, moon and stars are gospel enough, that we know more than the Apostles, that women may preach, that psalm-singing is wrong, that it is wrong to shed blood, even a chicken's. The list is a strange one but one can discern in it the faint sunrise of English Nonconformity and the intrusions of anti-religious common sense: that Adam's sin is imputed to no man, for example. And it includes Milton among the divorcers. What with Anti-Sabbatarians, Soul-Sleepers, Anti-Scriptures and Sceptics, one is tempted to linger in this playground or inferno, as if anything Baillie and his creatures opposed must be better than the Presbytery. In spite of Cromwell's ascendancy and some ingenious politics, however, Parliament adopted the Presbyterian system.

The reorganized army had ten regiments of horse (6,000), ten companies of dragoons (1,000), and some 14,000 foot in regiments of at least 1,200: they all cost £45,000 a month. In 1645 Laud was executed after three years in the Tower. Old Wren of Norwich lingered on there, in spite of an attempt to release him, in which his nephew Christopher, the architect, was intermediary, but the bishop refused to leave: when he did leave at the Restoration, he calmly went on with building Peterhouse chapel.

And now Milton published his pamphlet *Of Education*, addressed to Samuel Hartlib. Hartlib was a fellow-pamphleteer, the author of *Some Observations and Annotations*, with its formal answers and clear, forcible views against the Westminster Assembly line: he lived in Westminster close to Samuel Pepys, who knew him later on. He was half English, half a Prussian Pole, a merchant since about 1628, well connected by marriage, a friend of John Donne, who quotes him in letters, and of Comenius. Hartlib had written pamphlets about education in 1637 and 1638. Comenius was a Hussite exiled to the mountains of Bohemia, then to Poland. He published a *Janua Linguarum* in Sweden in 1638, with the *Janua Rerum* in reserve. His *Great Didactics* is so dull as to make one dizzy: he talked of a Christian Pansophia to come. In 1642 he and Hartlib were together in England to forward their cause, but Comenius then withdrew to Uppsala in Sweden, while in England the trial of Laud figures Hartlib as a witness. Bishop Hall had been excited about Comenius; Milton thought him a bore (think of the clash of two such egos) but he still liked Hartlib, so now, induced by his 'earnest entreaties and conjurements' he addressed him in sentences of mandarin length.

Milton counsels his pupils to learn swordsmanship but also wrestling and, while 'unsweating' themselves, music: organ or symphony, the lute, and religious, martial or civil song. In spring 'when the air is calm and pleasant, it were an injury or sullenness against nature not to go out and see her riches and partake of her rejoicing with heaven and earth'. He would have them 'ride out in companies with prudent and staid guides to all the quarters of the land', observing fortifications, building methods and soils, harbours and ports. They should go to sea to observe the navy, and get 'practical knowledge of sailing and sea-fight'. One can observe in several of these provisions the influence of the war, the growing fascination of the sea for Milton, and everywhere how he adapts and slightly varies an existing syllabus. He attacked the dismal and decadent scholasticism of the universities, quite rightly, but it is not clear what he seeks to substitute. He rightly attacks the barbarous English pronunciation of Latin and of Italian: the English should learn to open their mouths.

He supports the study of politics with special urgency 'to know the beginning, end and reasons of political societies, that they may not, in a dangerous fit of the commonwealth, be such poor shaken uncertain reeds, of such a tottering conscience as many of our great councillors have lately shown themselves, but steadfast pillars of the State'. He sounds like a Cromwell supporter, but he is far too careful openly to maintain anything of the kind. Milton was certainly happier arguing from his own intellectual background of Greek and Latin than he was in the world of the 1640s. Even his 'spacious house and ground about it fit for an Academy' in every city in the land, each to hold 150 persons, twenty of them servants, is the merest dream. Or does he have it in mind to confiscate the grander country houses? I imagine so.

The world does touch him again in July 1644, in his *Judgment of Bucer Concerning Divorce*, a few weeks later than his essay for Hartlib. It is an appendix to his early work, since he appears to have read Bucer, who was burned under Mary, only in that year. But while in the past he had tried addressing Parliament and the Assembly together, now he spoke only to Parliament, because nothing more was to be hoped from the divines. Parliament for 'some reasons which I shall not here discover' had favoured him, where the Assembly had not. In a post-script he now announces (or, rather, hints) that action against him is now imminent and he may any day be censored and stopped. This lends an excitement to his performance, of course, and there is no doubt that the Assembly had merely to advert to him and action would be taken. The great protester-general to the age was poor old Prynne after all, who was in and out of many prisons. He had published some twenty-two pamphlets before 1640, another twenty-two between 1640 and 1645 and about two hundred altogether; small wonder that he got into trouble. And Milton had no public power base. He was not a lawyer, an MP or a divine. He held no position but that of a schoolmaster or tutor. He was not even a playwright, and he was virtually unknown as a poet. In August 1644 the Assembly denounced sectaries, and his was among the eleven undistinguished names; that was when Palmer attacked him.

Roger Williams, who taught Milton Dutch and whom Milton taught in return until in 1654 he left with letters from Cromwell and orders to protect Narragansett from its New England neighbours, was luckily in mid-Atlantic, but his book was burnt by the public hangman a few days before Palmer's sermon. 'If any plead Conscience for the lawfulness of Polygamy, or for Divorce for other causes than Christ and his Apostles mention (of which a wicked book is abroad and uncensored though deserving to be burnt, whose Author has been so impudent as to set his name to it and dedicate it to yourselves); or for liberty to marry incestuously – will you grant a toleration for all this?' In the *Petition of the Stationers*, Milton's pamphlet on divorce was first just an example of an illegal book; then they petitioned to 'enquire out the author, printer and publisher of the Divorce pamphlet', and those of another pamphlet that said the soul is mortal. But the House of Commons had a Committee for Printing: in 1641–2 it consisted of hard cases like Dering, Vane and Pym. The new Ordnance for Printing of June 1643 provided for licensing by the Great Usher, the Lord Serjeant of the Commons and the Deputies and Wardens and Master of the Stationers. They could search out illegal presses and carry out arrests. This arrangement was as cumbrous as it sounds, and Milton's wings remained unscorched.

For general literature Sir Nathaniel Brent, John Langley the head of St Paul's and Farnaby, the successful private schoolmaster, were the censors, but as they mostly censored Mercuries, the news-sheets of the day, Milton ignored them: his divorce book in August had been anonymous and unregistered, as all his attacks on the bishops had been, only 'Printed by TP and MS in Goldsmiths Alley'. The second edition was just the same, except that Milton now signed his dedication JM. Only the *Bucer* pamphlet conformed with the law. All this tangle led to the most remarkable of all his prose works, the best written and the most uplifting. It inspired Blake, and is indeed a noble piece of writing.

He called it by the thunderous title *Areopagitica*, which means a speech made before the grandest of the ancient Athenian courts, which met on the Hill of Mars, the Areopagus. In this he was already taking very high ground; St Paul was said to have addressed that assembly.

The book was a small quarto of forty pages, published on 23 November 1644. It was unlicensed and unregistered but headed 'A speech of Mr J M' with a quotation from Euripides, and addressed 'To the Parliament of England'. There is a certain solemnity and stillness about the prose as he winds into his argument and discusses the limits of the civil liberty that may be hoped for. He is clearer now about the side he is on. 'And men will then see what difference there is between the magnanimity of a triennial parliament and that jealous haughtiness of prelates and cabin counsellors that usurped of late, whenas they shall observe ye in the midst of your victories and successes, more gently brooking written exceptions against a voted order, than other courts ...' Within three pages he claims to rest on classical and humane precedent rather than 'a Hunnish and Norwegian stateliness', and fires off the example of Dion of Prusa's speech to the Rhodians. After this bewildering point, he lays out his argument: the loathsome origins of licensing, what reading is, and how the law misfires. Finally, it will increase ignorance, blunt ability, and hinder advances 'in both religious and civil wisdom'.

The Athenians worried only about blasphemy and libel. Pope Martin V started the evil custom (Milton does not notice that the invention of printing has anything to do with it) and Milton gleefully quotes Roman imprimaturs and notes the imitative quality of English ones. 'We have it not, that can be heard of, from any ancient state, or polity, or church, nor by any statute left us by our ancestors elder or later; nor from the modern custom of any reformed city or church abroad; but from the most Antichristian Council, and tyrannous Inquisition that ever enquired.' Moses, Daniel and Paul, he points out, read widely and freely. He conceives that when God set man free from dietary laws, so he did from intellectual diets also. To have virtue, you must know vice. 'I cannot praise a fugitive and cloistered virtue unexercised and unbreathed that never sallies out and seeks her adversary, but slinks out of the race where that immortal garland is to be run for, not without dust and heat. Assuredly we bring not innocence into the world ... that which purifies us is trial ...'

Milton goes into his subject deeply, into Plato's *Laws*, into 'Utopian and Atlantic politics' and views on Adam and original sin. 'God therefore left him free . . . Wherefore did he create passions within us, pleasures round about us, but that these rightly tempered are the very ingredients of virtue?' He speaks in the end personally, in a *cri de coeur* from his own seriousness.

> When a man writes to the world, he summons up all his reason and deliberation to assist him: he searches, meditates, is industrious, and likely consults and confers with his judicious friends; after all which done he takes himself to be informed in what he writes, as well as any that wrote before him; if in this, the most consummate act of his fidelity and ripeness, no years, no industry, no former proof of his abilities, can bring him to that state of maturity, as not to be still mistrusted and suspected, unless he carry all his considerate diligence, all his midnight watchings, and expense of Palladian oil, to the hasty view of an un-leisured licenser . . . it cannot but be a dishonour and derogation to the author, to the book, to the privilege and dignity of learning.

He remembers Italy: 'There it was that I found and visited the famous Galileo, grown old, a prisoner to the inquisition, for thinking in astronomy otherwise than the Franciscan and Dominican licensers thought.' The Italians admired English liberty extravagantly and bemoaned the sad fact that 'nothing had been there written now these many years but flattery and fustian'. One cannot be quite certain except by this passage that Milton really did speak to Galileo; others did at the time, including Elia, the Paris cousin of Charles Diodati, so it is possible. As for Milton's moments of eloquence, they come and go in flashes. On the average Englishman who does not care a penny for theology, he says 'There be delights, there will be recreations and jolly pastimes, that will fetch the day about from sun to sun, and rock the tedious year as in a delightful dream . . . What a fine conformity would it starch us all into! Doubtless a staunch and solid piece of framework, as any January could freeze together!' He becomes more inflamed as he goes on.

> Who can discern those planets that are oft combust, and those stars of brightest magnitude that rise and set with the sun, until the opposite motion of their orbs bring them to such a place in the firmament where they may be seen evening or morning? . . . It is not the unfrocking of a

priest, the unmitring of a bishop, and the removing him from off the Presbyterian shoulders, that will make us a happy nation ... We have looked so long upon the blaze that Zwinglio and Calvin have beaconed up to us that we are stark blind.

It is when he addresses himself to England that he really takes fire. God is beginning 'the reforming of Reformation itself; what does he then but reveal himself to his servants, and as his manner is, first to his Englishmen?' He sweeps us along in clouds of eloquence. 'Methinks I see in my mind a noble and puissant nation rousing herself like a strong man after sleep, and shaking her invincible locks. Methinks I see her as an eagle mewing her mighty youth, and kindling her undazzled eyes at the full midday beam; purging and unsealing her long-abused sight at the fountain itself of heavenly radiance ...' There are several more pages, but he has come to the crest of his argument. There is a radical quality, a serious reasoning quality, about Milton which is far ahead of his time. The recurrence of metaphors about blazing light and blindness may reflect anxieties about his own eyesight, which was vulnerable. About this time he lost the sight of one eye.

In December 1644 he was named in an enquiry of the House of Lords and apparently summoned by them. These were the early fruits of his new fame. He was named with Woodward, the author of seven pamphlets (Milton had now written nine). Nothing is recorded about anything that happened to Milton: Wood confirms that the Assembly, 'impatient of having the clergy's jurisdiction invaded ... did cause him to be summoned to the House of Lords, but they did soon dismiss him'. He is certainly likely to have got the better of any argument with their lordships or their advisers. In 1645 Prynne attacked him over divorce, and Dr Featley, now a prisoner in Lord Petre's house and so a neighbour, uttered a growl of his own on the subject. Milton did not relent; he brought out his *Tetrachordon* in March and *Colasterion* too, neither of them licensed or registered. The first consists of texts applied to his case and written with a concentrated bitterness, with no reference to his own case but severe swipes at Palmer and poor old Featley. In the *Colasterion* he attacks Prynne and Caryl, a Lincolnshire preacher. The third victim was an ex-waiter, now a lawyer. 'I mean not to dispute philosophy with this Pork; this clod groom, rank pettifogger, an idiot by breeding ... no antic hobnail at a morris but is more handsomely facetious ... odious fool, varlet, unswilled hogshead ... the noisome stench of his rude slot.'

Cheered no doubt by this jolly pamphlet, Cromwell and Fairfax went on winning the war, which tightened around Oxford. In June they won at Naseby, taking 5,000 prisoners and all the guns; the King fled to Wales. Fairfax took Taunton, Bridgewater and Bath in July, Sherborne in August, Bristol, Devizes, Laycock and Berkeley (which had to be stormed) in September. The war was over really, and in December of that year Essex, who already had a vote of £10,000 a year, was declared duke, Fairfax a baron with £5,000, Cromwell and Waller received £2,500 each, Skippon £1,000. Pamphlets appeared, including one called *Arraignment of Persecution*, printed by Martin Claw-clergy for Bartholomew Bang-priest, in Toleration Street opposite Persecution Court. But Best, the Independent, was imprisoned and Goodwin ejected from Coleman Street and Burton from Friday Street nearby. Lilburne, who was Cromwell's admirer, was imprisoned for libelling the Speaker. At this point the Assembly was remodelling itself for the government of London and of all England.

The complicated intrigues that followed cannot be recorded here, and need not be, because it is not certain now much Milton knew about what was going on. It is for the same reasons, the abundance of material and Milton's own marginal position, that I have not more fully recorded English history in his period. I have paid least attention to Scotland and the Scots, because to them Milton paid the least. He now found himself alienated from the Scottish Presbyterians in the Westminster Assembly, and he did not share in their triumph or in its fruits. We know only that in September 1644 his sight had begun to trouble him, but *Areopagitica* is a work of extraordinary and triumphant energy. In 1645, he was considering another marriage, with a daughter of his friend Dr Davis. But the war was over, his wife returned to him and a reconciliation was arranged: he wanted a wife and legitimate offspring. He moved into a bigger house in the Barbican, perhaps in September, and his *Poems* were registered for publication in October 1645, and published in January of 1646, though they are dated 1645.

He was still all the things he had been when the war started, still a classical scholar who could turn a bit of Euripides, with that author's precise flavour and tone, into English blank verse and, in *Tetrachordon*, a bit of Horace into English satire with a deadly point, once again in blank verse; he was still savage in controversy, still elegant in compliments, still ambitious in his Greek comic verse on his own portrait, which, he justly complained in Greek, was not good, and surprising in Latin 'lyrics' to the Oxford librarian in a stanza form he unluckily invented. His *Poems* came out from the same publisher who had just produced Edmund Waller's, an undertaking more likely to succeed now after the war than during it, when Waller's position was difficult. He was two years older than Milton, was at Eton and King's, had an estate with fine trees near Beaconsfield and had been an MP from the age of sixteen. He was kin to Sir W. Waller and to John Hampden, and his sympathies were at first on that side, but he had been to Oxford as an ambassador to the King in 1642, and 'Waller's plot' to take over London for the royalists had followed and failed.

Soon after the appearance of the *Poems* Milton wrote a sonnet to Henry Lawes (9 February 1646) for the publication of his *Airs and Dialogues*. However, Henry's elder brother had died in battle in Chester, fighting on the King's side, and Henry's *Choice Psalmes* were published instead, in memory of his brother and dedicated to the King in prison in 1648; Milton allowed his sonnet 'To my Friend Mr Henry Lawes' to be included in that sad memorial. The *Airs and Dialogues* appeared only in 1653. It will be seen that in 1646 a compliment to an old musician friend with court connections struck Milton as quite innocent; by 1648 he might have had qualms, but then it was too late. There are three drafts of this sonnet in the Trinity notebook: it has been particularly heavily corrected, though not for political reasons. Midas was given donkey's ears for preferring Pan's music to Apollo's, and Milton feels the English are like that in 'committing short and long'. The Lawes *Choice Psalmes* carries a note that Milton means to praise William Cartwright's 'Complaints of Ariadne', of which Lawes's setting was published in his *Airs*, and which Milton thought set a new standard. I prefer in line six of the sonnet 'and gives thee praise above the pipe of Pan' to 'praise enough for envy to look wan'. But this sonnet would be a light piece if it did not end with the two lines about Dante (*Purgatorio* 2, 76f.): 'Than his Casella, whom he wooed to sing/Met in the milder shades of Purgatory'.

The passage in the *Purgatorio* is a curiously moving one. Dante has just landed on some sort of dream island or perhaps a transformed

Italy, where the Tiber runs out into the sea, where Aeneas landed. There in the Purgatory of his poem his first encounter is with Cato of Utica, a sage with a flowing white beard who is a kind of warden of the place. Since he was a famous suicide, he might be expected in the Inferno, but he seems to be here because he fought and died for liberty. Casella is the first human ghost Dante meets, and he is described with unusual sweetness and assigned no particular sin: he is recently dead. He was a musician and singer who had made settings of Dante's poems, and he now begins to sing him a *canzone* of his about *Amor che nella mente mi ragiona*. It is as if Milton were repairing bridges or preparing to go on with his career where he had left off.

There followed a sonnet in a very different mood; an early version of it is on the same page as the Lawes sonnet. It was provoked by 'the detraction which followed' his divorce writings. He had been classical: he had appealed (no mention of Christianity now) to 'the known laws of ancient liberty' and been mobbed by 'owls and cuckoos, asses, apes and dogs', who mean licence when they say liberty. 'For who loves that must, first be wise and good;/But from that mark how far they rove we see,/For all this waste of wealth, and loss of blood.' The sonnet was not published of course until 1673; it is not as if he were attacking the Independents and extremists: the lines 'That bawl for freedom in their senseless mood,/And still revolt when truth would set them free' point straight at the Assembly, his usual target now. The last line about the 'waste of wealth, and loss of blood' indicates a mood of despairing sadness and war-weariness, such as usually follows great national conflicts, and suggests again that he thinks it is over. It was not, and the mood of both sides between 1646 and 1649 became more deeply embittered. The King tried, and his friends made continuous and devious attempts, using the Irish as well as the Scots, to redress the verdict of the war; the army became even more powerful and the end more inevitable.

In January 1645 Parliament had adopted what they called the Directory for Public Worship, and in August 1646 they drew up the rules for ordination by Presbyteries. The King was captured by the English army only in early June of 1647, and somewhere between 1646 and 1647 probably, Milton fired off a sonnet 'On the New Forcers of Conscience'. The Trinity manuscript notes it should come after his *Tetrachordon* sonnet (1647) but before his Fairfax sonnet of

1648. It was what the Italians called a sonnet with a tail, *caudato*, a form used by satirists. Milton's sonnet has two tails, and is indeed savagely satirical against Stewart (A. S.) and Rutherford, Scots divines, *Gangraena* Edwards and 'Scotch What-d'ye-call', presumably Baillie, who attacked Milton on divorce in 1645. He accuses them of all the excesses of the old clerisy and the Council of Trent, and of pluralism.

In December 1646, his good friend Mrs Catherine Thomason died. Her husband George was a bookseller who built up an extraordinary private collection of pamphlets of this period, now in the British Library, in which Milton's are often marked in Latin 'gift of the author'. His wife had a library too, as well as nine children, but nothing much is known about her. From its first line, 'When faith and love which parted from thee never . . .', to its last, 'and drink thy fill of pure immortal streams', there is a certain masterly sweetness and tranquillity about Milton's poem, to be read I suppose by George. The sonnet is like enough to his early complimentary Latin verses to clergymen, with its handmaid's love and faith dressed like angels 'with purple beams/And azure wings' to waft her to heaven, for it to seem a formal exercise. And yet how very well he does it, and how confidently bold he is in his Counter-Reformation Italian mode in English. It could be said of the exquisite Italian perfection of his earlier sonnets that in them he attained a special music which Shakespeare would never have bothered his head to attain, but here it is not only the music which is foreign and yet looks perfectly at home.

On 23 January 1647 he sent a complimentary Latin poem to John Rouse, Bodley's Librarian at Oxford since 1620 and now seventy-three. When Oxford fell, Fairfax saved the library from probable destruction by posting sentries there, abetted and spurred on by Rouse, who was a formidable figure. The library had lost Milton's poems, it appears, and Rouse had asked him for another copy. Milton sent eleven pamphlets, a complete collection, and also, of course, the poems. His longish Latin poem to Rouse has been pasted in: scholars believe that it is written in too formal a hand to be Milton's autograph, but he did make a list of the books he was sending.

Rouse would have known what Milton's pathetic critics in the nineteenth century did not, that his neo-Latin stanza form followed Italian Latin examples. Milton used it again with an explanation of his metrical intentions, like the one he appended to Rouse's poem, in

Samson Agonistes – like it, at least, to the extent that it uses the same technical terms. This Latin poem is a joyful expression of pent-up feelings, a virtuoso celebration of the end of the war.

First it is a picture of Milton's young self, a laborious but not too great a poet, wandering and playing among Italian shadows and the green places of England: a poet in Latin as in English, and thrilled to be one. There is truth in that portrait, surely. Yet when he says the book was sent 'to Thames's the blue father's cradle, where the clear springs of the Muses ...' he does not really mean high in the Cotswolds, alas, nor the Gloucestershire Colne, nor Cirencester where it rained so hard during the siege that two royalist armies failed to find one another: he only means Oxford. 'Let whatever god punished us for soft luxury and degenerate leisure remove civil war, call back study and the muses now pensioned off more or less all over England.' The 'filthy birds with threatening claws' are certainly the Presbyterians; the compliments to Rouse are very grand. So go to Oxford, to the pleasant groves of the Muses, he tells his book: which surely means to the college gardens, which were full of courtiers and court poets. Into his book's asylum no rabble noise will penetrate, and perhaps the children of another and better age will read him. Once again, this is the expression of pent-up feelings.

On the first day of 1647 his father-in-law, a ruined man and a refugee in London, died. Milton may have become reconciled with his wife, but his attitude to her family was less kindly, though for a short time he took them in too, when they arrived in London. They owed him money, however, and he was determined to get it back. The debt was complicated by their being on the losing side, being malignants and delinquents and subject to sequestration and so on. Milton was deliberate, careful and not unsubtle in his action over the Powell family property. His lawyer was his own kinsman Bradshaw. The Powells escaped from Oxford when the siege was over, on 24 June on generous terms that infuriated Baillie, but Sir Robert Pye took Forest Hill for a debt of £1,400, their goods were sequestered and sold to a London agent, Matthew Appletree, for the small sum of £335. It is no surprise to discover there was an Appletree on the local Oxford committee that sold them. The Powells must have lost £3,000 over the war, and had come to London to see what could be recovered. When Richard Powell died, John Milton showed considerable coolness.

When Anne Milton was born old Mrs Powell stood godmother. John Milton wrote carefully in her Bible that she was born on 29 July, the day of the Monthly Fast, between six and seven. In later life she was a cripple; Edward Phillipps says that as time went on 'she grew more and more decrepit'. That April Christopher Milton had been made to 'compound' or pay a percentage of his property. He hastily agreed to take the Covenant. He lived at this time with the Widow Webber. It was 6 August before Powell's petition came before the tribunal, and Christopher Milton's followed on 7 August. Money was a serious issue, because the army wanted their pay before they would disband: they also wanted toleration and the dissolution of the Lords, the Levellers were rearing their embarrassing heads, pamphlets that had been written in prisons were spreading in the ranks. There were riots in London until Fairfax took the Tower. Lilburne, a prisoner there and now the head Leveller, wrote that the Law of God made no exception of kings, and the lords were no natural issue of lords but mushrooms of prerogative. Cromwell was much displeased with all this, and he and Fairfax quelled their mutinous regiments by arresting fourteen, trying three and shooting one man. Meanwhile Parliament was busy with laws for the suppression of blasphemy and heresy, and John Milton was teaching more and more pupils, and corresponding with Carlo Dati in Florence. He was indignant about the war: 'What safe retirement for literary leisure could you suppose given to one among so many battles of a civil war, slaughters, flights, seizures of goods?' he wrote in Latin.

Meanwhile, now or about now, he wrote the sonnet that defends his intemperate *Tetrachordon*, 'now seldom pored on'. Is the title a difficult word? 'Why is it harder sirs than Gordon,/Colkitto, or Macdonnell, or Galasp?' He means Montrose's army, it appears, in which case Gordon is Lord Huntly's son, Colkitto is Coll Keitache whose son Macdonald was Montrose's deputy and sometimes used his father's name. Galasp was Gillespie, an Assembly Scotsman and a Covenanter. The sonnet, all the same, is not really about ecclesiastical politics; it is about the preposterous ignorance of his enemies who ought, he feels, to know more Greek. Much as one may sympathize with this idealistic position, he is unduly flippant about Scots names. But his indignation about Scots intruding into English affairs goes back, of course, to his earlier sonnet. The amazing thing about this light piece of verse is the deadly stillness and awe-inspiring perspective of the last line about old Cheke, tutor to Edward VI: 'When thou taught'st Cambridge, and King Edward Greek'. Both French and Masson, a strong combination, take Milton to mean 'Thy age hated not learning as ours hates it, worse than toad or asp.' If they are right, as I fear they are, the dislocation of Milton's syntax is awful, and makes the end of the poem almost unintelligible.

> Thy age, like ours, O soul of Sir John Cheke,
> Hated not learning worse than toad or asp;
> When thou taught'st Cambridge, and King Edward Greek.

In April 1648, Milton seems to have entered the battle to produce a metrical version of the Psalms that could be set to music. Parliament was divided: the Commons liked the version by Francis Rous, revised in 1646, but the Lords preferred William Barton (1644). Milton follows the common metre that Rous used. There were, of course, many other English versions; they sprouted by wind-blown seed from Geneva and had been doing so for a century. Scholars have argued interminably over Milton's version and its roots in other versions, but it hardly seems worth it. The point is that Milton was working for, or else against, a committee of the Westminster Assembly set up in 1647 and then again in April 1648. The Psalms under this committee had four sections, and the third section began at Psalm 80. No doubt he intended a private contribution to the subject: he was not a member of the committee, and one may assume that his hostility to the Scots remained unabated. He published in 1673, using italics to mark paraphrase and with some fiddling notes about the Hebrew. Some passages are not bad, but the jogging metre ruins it all. Might he have undertaken this uncharacteristic task to please his father? That is quite possibly at the root of the matter, but on 13 March 1647 his father had died, and John, to whom he left Bread Street and 'a considerable Estate', had him buried at St Giles's in Cripplegate.

> *Psalm 80*
> ... The *tusked* boar out of the wood
> Upturns it by the roots,
> Wild beasts there browse, and make their food

Her grapes and tender shoots.
Return now, God of Hosts, look down
From heaven, thy seat divine,
Behold *us, but without a frown,*
And visit this *thy* vine. . . .

Psalm 83
. . . Giddy and *restless* let *them reel*
Like stubble from the wind.
As *when* an *aged* wood takes fire
Which on a sudden strays,
The *greedy* flame runs higher and higher
Till all the mountains blaze . . .

These lines are not like the work of a young and vigorous poet, but the mild warblings of some retired old schoolteacher.

Of course he did teach: Edward Phillipps until he was sixteen and John until he was fifteen. Edward went to Oxford two years later, to Magdalen Hall, and John was or became a remarkable young poet. Milton taught Richard Heath, with whom he corresponded for years; Aubrey Packer, who became a Doctor of Padua; Cyriack Skinner, the most brilliant of his pupils; Sir Thomas Gardiner; Richard Barry, Earl of Barrymore, whom he attracted by means of Robert Boyle's sister, the Earl of Cork's daughter; and her own son, Richard Jones, Lord Ranelagh. Meanwhile Parliament voted Sam Hartlib £300 and a post at Oxford, of which nothing came. Hartlib was thrilled with the Invisible College (which became the Royal Society) and corresponded with Robert Boyle about airguns and a universal kind of writing; he wasted his thoughts on things like submarines and aerial chariots. Dati had asked the poet to contribute with N. Heinsius and I. Vossius to a learned tome in honour of F. Rovai, a great honour which he ignored. From this list we can deduce that John Milton was not isolated or without connections. In 1647 he gave up the Barbican to move to a new house, smaller and without pupils, having inherited his father's money. The house was in High Holborn, backing on to Lincoln's Inn Fields, and he must have been newly installed there in November 1647 when the King was moved to the Isle of Wight.

CHAPTER NINE

REGICIDE

JOHN MILTON still looked forward to a poet's career of some kind when the war was over, but one must notice that he was now a different kind of poet. The influence of *Englands Helicon* and Browne's *Pastorals* had receded. He had thought over the possibilities, and at about this time he proposed to revive classical tragedy in England. Of all that attempt we have only a few lines cannibalized for *Paradise Lost*, and perhaps some sketchy ideas of *Samson Agonistes*, or rather some ideas about tragic poetry on a scriptural theme which would in the end come together as that play. But his head leaked sonnets on an Italian model, and they were of astonishing perfection. More recently he had thrown off a couple of mordant squibs or satires, in a different but still un-English satirical taste. He was perfecting a strong, clinching style of phrasing which owes something also to his polemical prose and is almost over-muscular. A lot of his prose sentences are of inordinate unstructured length: only in poetry did he attain perfect discipline.

In his new house 'he liv'd a private and quiet Life, still prosecuting his Studies and curious Search into Knowledge', Edward tells us. In 1648 we know little about him, except for the birth of his daughter Mary in October, and yet that was his most important year. With his pupils he had always been circumspect, but it was probably now that he first sketched that brilliantly lucid and trenchant Latin document, modelled on a Dutch catechism, *De Doctrina Christiana*, in the usual version of which by now he almost totally disbelieved. He was not an atheist, but he had quarrelled radically with the Church in all its roots and branches. He accepted the Bible as Chillingworth had proposed it, as the only sure guide to salvation, but of that large library of little books he was his own interpreter. It was at this time also that he drew close to the great men of the new government: we do not know to whom, except his kinsman and lawyer Bradshaw, or Lawrence maybe and Selden – that is, the civilians. Did he know Cromwell? It is to be doubted, because Cromwell's days are well documented. At the same time, someone must have drawn him to the great man's attention. As the avalanche began to rumble, Milton was writing his careful defence of Cromwell's position, and when the King was executed early in 1649, his book, the *Tenure of Kings and Magistrates*, was ready to print.

In 1648 the so-called 'second civil war' saved England from the imposition of really bone-crushing, organized Presbyterian discipline, in which the entire country would have been held down parish by parish, with the right of excommunication vested in local committees. Late in the year, when Milton's *Tenure* must have been nearly finished, and Bradshaw was ready to go to work on the King, Milton addressed a sonnet to Fairfax which was not printed until Edward Phillipps edited the State Letters in 1694, and secondly when Toland's *Life of Milton* came out in 1698. In 1673, when the second collected poems came out, it was still too strong for the public. The siege of Colchester was particularly embittered, and the noblemen among the prisoners when it fell were in the end mostly executed, though mercy had been promised. The siege, conducted by Fairfax, lasted from 11 June to 27 August. Cromwell was a practical man, and he observed that his old friend Lord Capell was simply too dangerous in the King's cause, and too magnetic to be left alive. Clarendon gives a speech by this lord, who had escaped from the Tower but was recaptured after four days, being betrayed by a waterman who had carried him from the Temple to a securer hiding-place on Lambeth Marsh. He was beheaded outside Westminster Hall, having made his speech from the scaffold. Let it stand here for the royalist point of view, as Clarendon gives it:

> As soon as he had ascended the scaffold, he looked very vigorously about, and asked whether the other lords had spoken to the people with their hats on, and being told that they were bare, he gave his hat to his servant, and then with a clear and a strong voice he said, that he was brought thither to die for doing that which he could not repent of: that he had been born and bred under the government of a King whom he was bound in conscience to obey, under laws to which he had been always obedient, and in the bosom of a Church which he thought the best in the world: that he had never violated his faith to either of those,

and was now condemned to die, against all the laws of the land; to which sentence he did submit . . .

That speech was delivered in March, when Charles I was in the grave and Charles II was carrying on the war with even less success than his father. Milton's sonnet to Fairfax, a heroic poem on the Italian model, asks the sharp question 'What can war, but endless war still breed,/. . . In vain doth valour bleed/While avarice, and rapine share the land.' He still hates the Presbyterians, and in spite of a small success last November, is still enmeshed in their appallingly corrupt arrangements for property: in his case the property of the Powells, who still owed him for pre-war loans of money and for his wife's dowry. He wants to see 'public faith cleared from the shameful brand/ Of public fraud . . .' and a more ideal settlement than looked likely. But the main point of the sonnet was to hail Fairfax as the new ruler of England. So he might have been, but he retired in June 1650 to Nun Appleton in the flat part of Yorkshire between the Humber and the sea, where Andrew Marvell was his children's tutor. It is possible, though I argue otherwise, that Andrew Marvell acquired the metre of his 'Horatian Ode' to Cromwell from the Fairfaxes, since John Ashmore's *Certain Select Odes of Horace Englisht* (1621) in duller metres than Marvell's contains several epigrams addressed to them. Fairfax was a great Yorkshire aristocrat, but now he was certainly tired and perhaps disillusioned: it was Cromwell's energies that carried on the state. The Fairfax sonnet was probably written in August or September while Cromwell was away fighting the Scots.

The *Tenure of Kings and Magistrates* is more formidable, if only because it understands what is happening. Its thesis is stated as a subtitle: 'Proving That it is Lawful, and hath been held so through all ages, for any, who have the power, to call to account a Tyrant, or wicked King, and after due Conviction, to Depose, and put him to Death, if the ordinary Magistrate have neglected or denied to do it. And that they who of late so much blame Deposing, are the Men that did it themselves'. People should be governed by reason, says Milton, and not by 'Custom from without and blind Affections within'. Only the good can love freedom; the others love licence, which, of course, flourishes under tyrants. This view goes back through his anti-Scots sonnets, and its roots are already evident in *Comus*. Most people like 'civil wars and commotions as a novelty, and for a flash hot and active', but if they win they want to stick to 'that old entanglement of iniquity, their gibberish laws'. Or they relent, and 'protest against those who talk of bringing him to the trial of justice, which is the sword of God'. One must pay no attention to these 'apostate scarecrows'. By these he makes it plain that he means the Presbyterians with their pluralism, their corruption and their hunger for tithes (which Milton, like Cromwell, wanted abolished).

His learning is amazing. From a deadly sentence by Aristotle he moves to the Bible, to Demophoön in a tragedy by Euripides, Dion on Trajan and Theodosius in the law-code of Justinian. Then '. . . the King or Magistrate holds his authority of the People, both originally and naturally for their good . . .' Kingship is 'a human ordinance' (1 Pet. 2: 13, etc.). Finally he impales us on a quotation from Seneca, from *Hercules Furens* ('Mad Hercules').

> There can be slain
> No sacrifice to God more acceptable
> Than an unjust and wicked king.

Though I have not always noticed the scraps of verse translation that Milton puts into his prose writings, they are getting better all the time. The best of all perhaps are in his *History of Britain*, done in February and March 1649, four books of which were written before he was appointed Secretary for Foreign Tongues, which happened on 13 March. Hartlib's notebook for 1648 says Milton is writing a history of England. It might be thought reasonable to assume that he did not start on the *History* until after his important *Tenure of Kings and Magistrates* appeared, that is, until the King was safely dead, yet it may well be that the *Tenure* interrupted the peaceful *History*. The *History* includes two lovely bits from Geoffrey of Monmouth.

> Goddess of shades, and huntress, who at will
> Walk'st on the rolling sphere, and through the deep,
> On thy third reign the earth look now, and tell
> What land, what seat of rest thou bidd'st me seek,
> What certain seat, where I may worship thee
> For ay, with temples vowed, and virgin choirs.

The other piece is addressed to Brutus the Trojan, foretelling a new Troy in England: 'Sea-girt it lies, where giants dwelt of old,/Now void ... And kings be born of thee, whose dreaded might/Shall awe the world'. It is curious to think that with one side of his mind Milton was lapped in these luxurious, masque-like, patriotic verses about English kings and with the other pursuing his bloody argument with Charles I. From a technical point of view, it is worth noticing that Milton translates a piece of Old English or Anglo-Saxon verse without losing its alliterative quality – 'in a mead of kine under a thorn ... Kenelm king-born'. But his radical streak was now ascendant, and there was no holding him back in the *Tenure*. 'Neither did Samuel, though a prophet, with his own hand abstain from Agag ... "As thy sword has made women childless".' In Christian times his rhetoric becomes superabundant, with Byzantine emperors, Matthew Paris, Gildas and then the sixteenth-century Reformation, on which he lingers long: it is a more popular argument and one about which he knows a great deal.

It is all sawdust: the essential argument could have been succinctly given on half a page. The decision to execute the King was Cromwell's, and it shook and saddened the English. Fairfax disapproved and went home, and young Marvell, writing a praise of Cromwell in 1650, reserved at least a dignity to the King.

> That thence the royal actor born
> The tragic scaffold might adorn:
> > While round the armèd bands
> > Did clap their bloody hands.
> *He* nothing common did or mean
> Upon that memorable scene:
> > But with his keener eye
> > The axe's edge did try:
> Nor called the gods with vulgar spite
> To vindicate his helpless right,
> > But bowed his comely head,
> > Down, as upon a bed. . . .

Marvell's poem, which perhaps owes something metrically to his royalist contemporary Fanshawe, and certainly to Horace, is not as clear as Milton's prose: Milton discusses the trial which he surrounds with biblical mumbo-jumbo about Ahab and Antiochus and Meroz. He addresses the Presbyterians with more calmness than before, and

more in sorrow than in anger. He points out telling instances of
modern monarchs who contrived to be restored to their thrones, only
to inflict the most savage punishments on their old enemies: and it
was, of course, this fear that led Cromwell to see the King tried. At the
trial, Charles refused to admit that this or any court had jurisdiction
over him; he therefore did not defend himself but went to his death
wrapped in his own superciliousness. Still, there have been worse
deaths and worse poems about them than Marvell's. Milton does not
let the moment go by without a sound thrashing for the Assembly. He
has already said, 'I believe very many Presbyterians to be good and
faithful Christians,' but now he tears the Assembly to pieces as 'a pack
of clergymen by themselves to bellycheer their presumptuous Sion'.
He brings down upon their heads and upon the King's all the great
Protestant fathers, Calvin, Zwingli and his old favourite Paraeus, and
likens his opponents to the priests of Bel. In spite of this personal
venom, he has treated the case somewhat abstractly, and the King is
never named. Nor is any other target, except that one of them can only
be Laud, just as the King can only be Charles I.

In those days the year ended in March, so Clarendon ends his
eleventh book with the death of Capell, just after the King's. When
he quotes Latin I have substituted a translation.

> So ended the year of one thousand six hundred forty-eight; a year of
> reproach and infamy above all years which had passed before it; a year
> of the highest dissimulation and hypocrisy, of the deepest villainy and
> most bloody treasons, that any nation was ever cursed with or under; a
> year in which the memory of all the transactions ought to be rased out
> of all records, lest, by the success of it, atheism, infidelity, and rebellion
> should be propagated in the world, and of which we may say, as the
> historian [Tacitus] said of the time of Domitian, *As the old age saw what
> the full flowering of liberty was, so we have seen the full flowering of slavery,
> since inquisitions have taken away the powers of speaking and of hearing,*
> etc., or, as the same writer says of a time not altogether so wicked,
> *Their minds were in a state where the worst of crimes would be dared by a
> few, desired by many, and suffered by all.*

Milton was now committed in direct opposition to this view. Clarendon never mentions him, either because Milton was insignificant or
because he did not like to be hard on poets, or because the poet was

blind. Yet Milton had burnt his boats, and went on to compound his offence by taking employment as a Latin Secretary to the government, which employment he continued throughout the ten years of the Commonwealth.*

In May 1649 the Levellers were put down as mutineers at Burford, and Fairfax and Cromwell got honorary doctorates at Oxford. Milton was employed as Secretary at the same wage as Charles I had paid his predecessor, about £288 a year, with lodgings in Whitehall. He always had two assistants, but at first he was constant in attending all meetings of the Council of State. Later on he found he could take work home and do it there. The Order Books of the Council of State record his labours: they are quite unfit for a poet, and it is not clear whether he was sacrificing himself in the service of the new state or being rewarded for his very able performance in *Tenure*: my own view is that in his opinion it was the former, but in Cromwell's the latter; one cannot know. One afternoon in May he was checking letters to the Senate of Hamburg, and preparing his comments on a book called *England's New Chains*, of which the second part had just appeared. The Hamburg correspondence was about shipping, as most of his Latin letters over the years were: they were in protection of English interests, sometimes ships that were arrested, sometimes individuals who were in trouble in foreign ports. But the need to comment on a book makes it clear that Milton was employed both as an official propagandist for the state and because he had some expertise in foreign affairs of which we now hear officially for the first time.

He printed a little pamphlet about Irish affairs, in which he stoutly maintains that Parliament had confined Irish Roman Catholics 'to the bare enjoyment of that which is not in our reach, their consciences'. He speaks of 'blockish Presbyters' and 'Clandebay ... a barbarous

---

* Wecklein, the man whom he succeeded in his job of Latin Secretary, and who in turn succeeded him on his blindness, is one of the best German baroque poets. Milton's colleague and, in the end, assistant was Marvell, a poet of genius. At the Restoration Fanshawe, who then succeeded, was a poet of astounding powers who had his roots in Horace (learnt at Cambridge), a potent influence on Milton as on Marvell. Like Marvell, Fanshawe was an 'amateur poet', and he seems to have given up too early, but his talent is fit to be named with Marvell's and Milton's. Taken together, this cluster of names affects our view of the history and continuity of patronage under the Stuarts and Cromwell.

nook of Ireland', and is indignant: 'What mean these men? Is the presbytery of Belfast a small town in Ulster of so large extent that their voices cannot serve to teach duties in the congregations they oversee, without spreading and divulging to all parts far beyond the diocese of Patrick or Columba, their written Representation?' This rebuke, which followed Cromwell's interest into Ireland, is a brief piece, a trifle of twenty pages. In 1649, he published *Eikonoklastes* and, in 1650, a second edition much enlarged. That was a more precisely aimed piece of writing against *Eikon Basilike*, a work purporting to be the authentic record of the last days of Charles I, who was now venerated as a martyr. 'I never knew that time in England when men of truest religion were not counted Sectaries ... And since there be a crew of lurking railers, who in their libels and fits of railing up and down, as I hear from others, take it so currishly that I should dare to tell abroad the secrets of their Egyptian Apis ...' He has Thomas Browne's obscurity without his charm and is up to his neck in the most furious quarrelling.

As things went on, Milton's work became harder. He was now to examine letters, mostly about the sale of prohibited goods. He was to view Mr Small's papers as a censor. A letter to Hamburg was sent back to him by Parliament, because the Senate of Hamburg was in no mood to hear it. At last Mr Hall was paid £100 a year to answer pamphlets, and did answer Prynne in Latin. But Milton still had to view the books and papers of Mr Walker, newly arrested for his *History of Independency*. Walker's *History* did not spare Milton, who figured in it as 'a libertine that thinketh his wife a manacle, and his very garters to be shackles and fetters to him too'.

His lodgings at Whitehall, which materialized in November, had been those of an old knighted Member of Parliament. Milton even got some left-over bits of tapestry of the King's which he requested to cover the walls: the best had been bought for Cardinal Mazarin in Paris. But his job was onerous; decisions were real and a good deal depended on them. By the end of November ships in the river were being searched for a great blast against Milton's masters, *Defensio Regia* by Claude de Saumaise, known as Salmasius, who was a classical scholar of some importance and should no more have taken part in the idiotic quarrel that followed than Milton. On 8 January, the Council of State desired Milton to see to the printing of a polemic on

Ireland, and to answer Salmasius and bring his work into the Council to have it checked for political correctness. He was now therefore something lower than a hack.

His Latin letters were at least more dignified: one to Hamburg to complain of a Scottish royalist called Cochrane, some credentials addressed to the King of Spain, and a warning to the King of Portugal about the fleet of Prince Rupert, for example. On 23 December it was agreed he should print his answer to the *Defensio Regia*. Salmasius, Milton's antagonist, was not easily dealt with, being prodigiously learned and a specialist in obscure authors like Florus and the later Roman historians. He had been born in 1588 with twenty years at least of advantage over Milton (what is worse, the sight of Milton's left eye had gone, and the doctors feared the other might go too). Salmasius had written about Greek dialects and about Hellenistic Greek; he had also attacked Grotius. Venice and Oxford and the Pope had all wanted him, but he had settled in 1631 at Leyden. As for his *Defensio Regia pro Carolo Primo*, it has twelve chapters, and only in chapter 8 do we reach England, only in chapter 10 modern times. Chapter 11 deals with the formalities of the King's trial, and chapter 12 with the late King's character. Milton, in his *Church Government* in 1642, had even complimented him.

In Milton's reply to Salmasius, *Defensio pro populo Anglicano*, he expresses 'the consciousness of not having been found at all wanting, as far as in me lies, to this most noble cause, and most worthy of the memory of all future ages'. That was surely his motive in government service. We read in the Order Book at least one intervention in his own hand in 1651: 'That Mr Chambers in the Gatehouse be released upon his own engagement and twenty nobles given him for his relief'. Milton was still writing letters about the Powell debt: he was stern but scrupulously just over valuations, and considerate to Mrs Powell personally. But in his book he lets loose a rage disproportionate to its slightly ridiculous subject: 'this insane sophist who sets up as the leader and coryphaeus of the rest'. His basic principle is set out more clearly and acceptably than ever. 'Among Christians there will either be no King at all, or he will be the public servant.' On the King's behaviour with Buckingham he is savage, and on the theatre surprisingly indecent: he appears to know women actors, who seem as unlikely in London as in Rome. He attacks Salmasius's wife, sends him a joke of stupefying silliness in Latin modelled on Persius and calls him 'a French half-man with your man-wife'. That is enough about this disgusting book.

It was a success all the same; it was apparently just what was wanted. The Queen of Sweden liked it, and Vossius wrote to N. Heinsius about it, implying that Salmasius had a tiger by the tail. The scholarly world salivated at the thought of the feast of insults in dead languages that might follow. 'Who *is* this J M? ... amusing about Graswinkel ... he'll be in worse health if he takes on this English mastiff ...' Salmasius's fury was rumoured before it erupted into print. In June the Council, who had already defended Milton's lodgings against some knighted committee men, congratulated him on the success of his book and offered him £200, which he refused. Graswinkel was stopped from replying by authority, but Salmasius was rampant. Vossius heard that Milton's book was officially burnt at Paris, and remarked that men came into the executioner's hands mostly for depravity and crime but books for their worth and excellence. Yet John Milton was sick at heart. In March 1651 his son John was born and died an infant: he blamed the nurse. On 19 November he signed an album in Greek, 'I am perfected in weakness' (2 Cor.: 12, 9). The quotation is inexact: it is a motto he has adapted for himself out of the closing chapters of that moving epistle.

At least the news was better. An Irish settlement of some kind was in sight. The army was still costing £80,000 a month and the navy £40,000. In December estimates of value were made for Windsor and its park, for the cathedrals and for palaces and royal forests. Ireton had died: his widow was Cromwell's daughter, and one may imagine her in that large, austere town house, in a row with the houses of the other victorious generals on Highgate Hill, still called Ireton House. There was a General Oblivion: there were schemes to reform the law, to suppress the abominable cheat of astrology, to propagate the gospel overseas. Anything seemed possible, even tolerance, and Williams, the New England delegate, remarked that old England was suddenly turning new, while New England grew older. Cromwell became the effective dictator of England: he wanted toleration but such matters were considered by a committee, and compromise was likely. In April 1652, Parliament voted that tithes should continue until some other way of paying the clergy should be devised. Milton wrote a sonnet to Cromwell that May, which hints at the complete dissociation of Church and State: Cromwell wanted at least freedom of opinion, but Milton wanted the clergy not to be paid by the state and to exercise no secular power.

> Cromwell, our chief of men, who through a cloud
> Not of war only, but detractions rude,
> Guided by faith and matchless fortitude . . .
>   . . . new foes arise
> Threatening to bind our souls with secular chains.
> Help us to save free conscience from the paw
> Of hireling wolves whose Gospel is their maw.

The poem is strongly worded, certainly: it rejoices in the river Darwen near Preston, red with Scots blood, and the equally bloody victories of Dunbar, with 3,000 Scots dead and 10,000 prisoners and of Worcester, and it ends in a snare. But one must remember what comfort it must have given to many Nonconformists (Milton already uses the word) in those dark years they were to pass before they emerged into sunlight in the nineteenth century. Milton was felt to burn with a pure white flame: that is as noble a reputation with the people as a poet has ever had, and Milton deserved it.

In June he wrote the last of these political and 'Horatian' sonnets: they are really more Italian and 'heroical', and Horace's influence on them is filtered through Tasso. Milton addressed this one to Sir Henry Vane, and sent it to him on 3 July 1652. That interesting statesman had emigrated as a boy to America in 1635; at the age of twenty-two he was Governor of Massachusetts, but by 1637 he was back in England and in 1639 Treasurer of the Navy. He joined the Council of State in February 1649, and in March he was a member of the Foreign Affairs Committee, where he met Milton if he did not know him already. He was to break with Cromwell in 1653 over the dissolution of the Long Parliament and go cheerfully to his death by hanging in 1662. The sonnet is tranquil, and yet it is another desperate attempt to cement a friendship with someone in a powerful position on Church matters: this time it is only a compliment. Milton praises Sir Henry, 'young in years, but in sage counsel old', for being as good as a Roman senator, and skilful in unfolding 'the drift of hollow states, hard to be spelled'. This refers to Holland, with whom war was imminent but had not yet broken out, so the meaning must be disguised. Vane had spent June composing a letter to the Dutch after an action in the Downs off Dover, which accused Tromp of trying to destroy the fleet by surprise. Vane also gets praised for knowing that iron and gold are the nerves of war: Milton has noted this in Machiavelli (Machiavelli, however, says iron and not gold is the nerve of war; something similar is to be found in Ovid). Finally Vane understands the difference between military or civil power and spiritual power.

There is a stream of these sonnets, all more or less personal, only one or two on great public themes. They are not light pieces: it was as if all Milton's dormant powers as a poet were gathered up and used to the bone in each one of them: they are powerful utterances. The landmark that closes this period is the sonnet on his blindness. Scholars have argued in sophisticated ways that the phrase 'how my light is spent,/Ere half my days' can be used to date the poem, but that method is insecure. Milton went completely blind when he was forty-three in 1652, and calculations based on his father's death at eighty-four do not fit, and anyway Milton might mean only half his working days. The tragedy of his blindness was complete. He was still interviewing visitors, and had an allowance for entertaining them: in December 1651 he wrote to Mylius, who had been in London since August, and Paw, the Dutch ambassador, later claimed to have been his friend. At this time he moved into a house in Petty France that gave on to St James's Park, where Hazlitt and Jeremy Bentham lived later.

In March 1652, he was given the assistance of Wecklein, the German who had served Charles I, and in March and April papers had to be sent to him. He himself said more than once that it was the strain of writing his defence against Salmasius that undid him. We know the detail of his eye disease exactly, because he corresponded with a specialist in Paris about his symptoms: he was told there was no hope. There is no doubt he was blinded by a disease, and one not caused by reading too much. It was not a stroke or the result of any mental disturbance, just something that happened to him. He wrote presumably in 1655, since the evidence is that he lost his second eye's sight early in 1652, a sonnet about it to his friend and pupil.

Young John Milton.

Old John Milton.

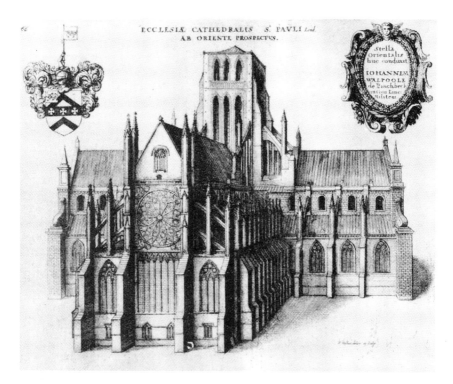

St Paul's before the Fire of London.

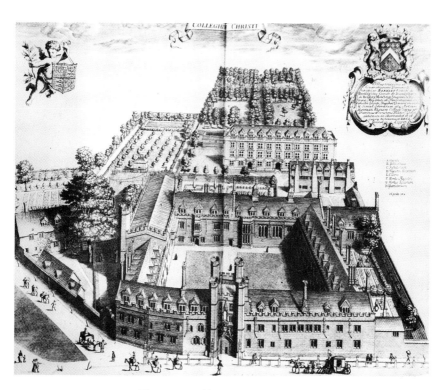

Christ's College, Cambridge.

Left. Detail from Stokesay Manor, carved for a mayor of Ludlow about the time of *Comus*.

Below. Pembroke College, Cambridge: on the right the chapel.

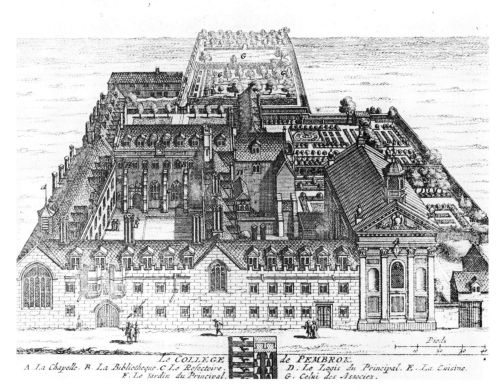

Le COLLEGE de PEMBROK.
A. La Chapelle. B. La Bibliotheque. C. Le Refectoire. D. Le Logis du Principal. E. La Cuisine.
F. Le Jardin du Principal. G. Celui des Associez.

Above. Horton Church, where Milton's mother is buried.

Right. Sir Thomas Fairfax, third Baron Fairfax of Cameron.

Above. House in an English landscape soon after Milton's death.

Opposite. Oliver Cromwell.

Above. The King beheaded.

Left. Andrew Marvell, Fairfax's daughter's tutor.

> Cyriack, this three years' day these eyes, though clear
> To outward view, of blemish or of spot;
> Bereft of light their seeing have forgot,
> Nor to their idle orbs doth sight appear
> Of sun or moon or star throughout the year,
> Or man or woman. . . .

He means it when he says that his good spirits arise from knowing that he lost his sight 'in liberty's defence'. That sonnet could not therefore have been printed until 1694, in the *Letters of State* edited by Edward Phillipps. In the Trinity manuscript it is in a hand that might be Cyriack Skinner's. What he wrote earlier and more immediately, apparently in 1652, was a poem of remarkable religious tranquillity. Whatever his theological opinions may have been, and whatever his political activities were at this time, however furious the battles of his life, it is always true of John Milton that he had a deep reserve of peace that can only be called spiritual; it could flow easily out into his poetry. That is one of the most remarkable things about him. In this crisis he writes like George Herbert.

> When I consider how my light is spent,
> Ere half my days, in this dark world and wide,
> And that one talent which is death to hide,
> Lodged with me useless, though my soul more bent
> To serve therewith my maker, and present
> My true account, lest he returning chide,
> Doth God exact day-labour, light denied,
> I fondly ask; but Patience to prevent
> That murmur, soon replies, God doth not need
> Either man's work or his own gifts, who best
> Bear his mild yoke, they serve him best, his state
> Is kingly. Thousands at his bidding speed
> And post o'er land and ocean without rest;
> They also serve who only stand and wait.

Milton's description of his symptoms is clear and detailed:

It is ten years I think, more or less, since I noticed my sight getting weak and dim, and my spleen and whole belly shaken by flatulence. Even in the morning if I began to read I noticed my eyes hurt deep inside them so I stopped; later I felt better after moderate exercise. When I looked at a lamp, a sort of rainbow seemed to obscure it. Soon a mist gathered in the left of the left eye (the one that clouded over some years before the other), and I could see nothing on that side. If I shut my right eye, things further in front of me seemed smaller. The other eye failed slowly and gradually over nearly three years, some months before I lost my sight altogether: everything I could see while I sat still seemed to swim, now to the right and now to the left. Permanent vapours seemed to have settled on my temples, which pressed on my eyes with a kind of sleepy heaviness, particularly in the afternoon.

He saw amazing lights when he lay down to sleep, but the mist that hovered over his eyes night and day was more white than black, and when his eyes turned he saw a tiny crack of light.

A. N. Wilson, in his *Milton*, cites a Dr Lambert Rogers who reported to the Cardiff Medical Society (*Proceedings*, 1955) that Milton had chiasmal arachnoiditis, which comes of a growth (or cyst or tumour) of the pituitary gland. Dr Rogers used to cure patients by removing their cyst, but if he was too late, they went blind. If he failed, the patients became extremely bad-tempered, which they had not been before, as a result of the terrible pain. Andrew Wilson points out that 'Though Milton's darker nature – his capacity to anger and scorn – continued for some while after his blindness and had more than purely physical causes, it is striking that the most vitriolic of his writing corresponds precisely to the period when he was likely to have been in the most acute physical pain.' He wants to go further and to blame the pituitary infection for his fragile and girlish appearance. This I do not believe, but great pain is an explanation for the savagery of his quarrel with Salmasius.

The *Life of Milton* in the Bodleian Library attributed by Helen Darbishire to John Phillipps, Milton's first private secretary and a believable witness, says:

> While he was thus employ'd his Eyesight totally fail'd him; not through any immediate or sudden Judgment, as his Adversaries insultingly affirm'd; but from a weakness which his hard nightly study in his youth had first occasion'd, and which by degrees had for some time before depriv'd him of the use of one Ey: And the Issues and Seatons, made

use of to save or retrieve that, were thought by drawing away the Spirits, which should have supply'd the Optic Vessells, to have hasten'd the loss of the other.

A 'seton' is a silk thread or a bristle, and comes from medieval Latin and medieval surgical practice. The skin was pricked with a special needle and a thread drawn through it as in sewing. It was obviously a treatment with considerable potential for inflicting pain. Thevenot, Milton's French eye doctor, is supposed to have done it by first cauterizing the skin of the brow and then using a thread dipped in egg yolk. It did no good, of course.

The next year Milton tried to get a job for Fairfax's children's tutor, Andrew Marvell, which he did by applying to his kinsman the old lawyer and regicide Bradshaw. Marvell was a brilliant poet, set by one of the Lawes brothers years ago, who had lived abroad while the war went on and written the unforgettable Horatian ode in praise of Cromwell. Marvell was not appointed to the Assistant Secretaryship Milton sought for him, but he remained a faithful and admiring friend of Milton until the end of his life. Marvell went to live in John Oxenbridge's house at Eton to tutor William Dutton, who was being considered as a future son-in-law to the Protector. Marvell ended in the House of Commons, but other poets had a harder time. James Shirley, who was a Roman Catholic convert and intermittently a schoolmaster, and William Davenant, who claimed to be Shakespeare's bastard, kept musical drama alive between them, and Shirley helped Ogilvie the translator of Virgil with his Greek and Latin, until the Restoration made him rich as a printer of road maps. Young Dryden was a nephew of Colonel Pickering, a friend of Cromwell and a kinsman of Oxenbridge; Sir Gilbert Pickering helped him to a place, first as clerk to Thurloe, Cromwell's most efficient master-spy. The network of patronage was largely a family network, and it operated in this period as it did during the changes of 1660, as one may see from the first volume of Pepys. But Cromwell turned out the old and foolish Parliament in the end, and at that point Milton, blind as he was, disapproved of his action and said so. In 1660, he called the restored Long Parliament the 'recoverers of our liberty', and the time of their absence from power 'a short but scandalous night of interruption'. If that is really how he felt, his darkness must have been deep indeed.

In February 1652 Parliament had had the Rakov Catechism burnt. Milton had been interested in it and in August 1650 left a note in his hand as one of its examiners. It reflected the beliefs of one Fausto Sozzini, the younger Socinus (1539–1604), whose idea was to construct a systematic statement of Socinianism, but in England the very name was almost a swear-word and this Catechism was edited in English only in 1818, by Thomas Rees, FSA. Milton's fourth child Deborah was born in May: Anne was five and Mary three at that time. Three days later his wife died and, a month or two later, his baby son. Milton continued hard at work. He guided Walton and Walton's Polyglot Bible to the House of Commons; Walton served as a curate at All Hallows, Bread Street, under Mr Stock, so they were probably old friends. It was in June and officially that Milton found himself beginning his correspondence with the Greek Philaras, with the kindest and most complimentary brush-off letter about English intervention in Greek affairs. The Greeks were desperately trying to interest Europe in restoring their independence, but that is a story too long to tell here. In November Durie, who was Milton's assistant, was rewarded for putting *Eikonoklastes* into French: it appeared *revue par l'auteur*, so it appears that Milton knew French, though he was strangely uninterested in any French poetry except *La Semaine Sainte* or in the French theatre.

Madame de Salmaise really hated him: 'I will move hell to ruin him.' In August 1652, *Regii Sanguinis Clamor*, or *The King's Blood Cries Out to Heaven for Vengeance*, suddenly appeared as a counterblast to *Eikonoklastes*. It was written secretly by Pierre du Moulin, a clergyman who was in hiding in England, but the plot to protect him from revenge now involved Morus, or Alexander More, a professor of Greek in Ghent, and some weighty insults from Virgil's description of Polyphemus, which irritated Milton quite disproportionately. The seduction or rape of a maid in a Dutch barn by Morus played an enormously big part too: lawcourts sat on it, elders met to decide on it, Milton made hay of it and scholars thoroughly enjoyed it. The Council of State in England ordered Milton to reply in kind to this mysterious new onslaught. He did so, but whatever he was told he could not believe Morus was innocent. In 1653, Salmasius died, his death perhaps hastened by the controversy; but he was an elderly man, nearing his seventieth birthday. It was not until May 1654 that Milton's *Second Defence* was at last published.

I hope I have not made Milton appear harsher than he was. We know very little, for example, about his first wife's married life or her death, which presumably was because of childbirth. There is nothing in his writings beyond the most chilling reference to 'two domestic griefs' refrigerated still further by Latin. Yet Milton did have real feelings all right. There is a moving sentence in his divorce pamphlet, 'The pining of a sad spirit wedded to loneliness should deserve to be freed'. There is only one sentence in that whole old controversy that might be thought to fit Mary Powell, and yet I do not think she entered his head when he wrote, 'Who knows not that the bashful muteness of a virgin may ofttimes hide all the unliveliness and natural sloth which is really unfit for conversation?' or when he asserted that a man 'chancing on a mute and spiritless mate remains more alone than before'. Milton must have been distressed by his son's death; he says nothing about that either. He wrote most deeply about his view of marriage when he noted that 'Moses tells us that Love was the son of Loneliness, begot in Paradise by that sociable and helpful attitude which God implanted between man and woman.' Of that we shall hear more quite soon.

He was being slowly driven from his work. He allowed John Phillipps to reply to a pamphlet, which he did with verve and success. N. Heinsius was back in Italy and wrote that Milton had been rather disliked there because, far from being lax, he was terribly severe about morals and about sex. He would freely discuss religion and hit out hard at the Pope on any occasion. It was agreed now that he could do other work but no longer attend on ambassadors. The State transactions have a diversity that suggests almost jollity. The British send the Dutch a bill for £1,681,816 and 15 shillings, carefully itemized. Andrew Sandelands, an old Fellow of Christ's, Cambridge, more recently an ejected vicar from York, tries to sell Milton Scottish naval timber. Huntley's and Mar's forests on Loch Ness and Abernethy on the Upper Spey are what he has in mind. In January 1653 came a plea for 'the skull of my honourable patron Montrose', which had been for three years on a spike over the Tolbooth in Edinburgh, and was to remain there until 1661. A little later, 'Argyll has forty-four bronze cannon buried within seamark' on the coast of Kintyre.

Between April and December 1653 there was political trouble of a classic kind. Cromwell sat during that time with a Council of a dozen lieutenants, who belonged to his tiny Parliament of 144; then the Council of State was enlarged to thirty. Lilburne, that old thorn in the side, was now kept a close prisoner in Jersey, having rather surprisingly been acquitted of sedition. In December both Parliament and Council collapsed, having nearly divided themselves into two equal halves on the troublesome question of a State Church and of its payment by tithes. Cromwell was now probably less radical about the matter than Milton, certainly less than he had been in the past. Parliament resigned, and nothing was left of the State but the Lord Protector. In April Milton had approved Cromwell's action; now he printed a pamphlet 'to a friend in the country', possibly Marvell. He is confined by his infirmities, he writes, and not a member of their Councils: but the authorship of these twenty pages has been disputed. Milton does write a warm official letter to the Swiss cantons, and is frequently visited by Roger Williams, the New Englander.

For eight months Cromwell had issued eighty-two 'ordinances' or decrees a week, and created his own knights and his Lords of the Council at £1,000 a year each. Milton worked less than he had done, yet until April 1655 he still got his £288 a year: Thurloe by comparison got £800 as Secretary of State. Milton's main work was no doubt concentrated on his *Defence*, 173 octavo pages that appeared at the very end of May 1654. It dealt fully with scandals, and as a piece of clangorous Latin invective it will have satisfied the connoisseurs. Its serious argument is well stated, and it is rich in autobiography; its quibbles about metre and vocabulary are justified, and the passages of Euripides it quotes on blindness are effective (*Orestes*, 793, and *Hercules Furens*, 1398, 1402). Had he perhaps begun to plan *Samson Agonistes*? The Phillipps brothers say they never heard of it. Milton included in his *Defence* splendid eulogies of the Queen of Sweden, of Bradshaw, Fairfax and Cromwell, and a number of others, as if he had meant once to write them all a sonnet each. But Vane was now left out: Milton's only reservations about Cromwell would seem to be based on his own violently anti-clerical views. Milton sent three copies of the *Defence* to his friend Marvell, one for him, one for Oxenbridge and the third for 'My Lord'. Was that third copy for Fairfax maybe?

Cyriack Skinner pops up close to Marvell, and Milton envies him. He has been a frequenter of Petty France and a young man of admirable perversity, as many of Milton's friends were. Even Oxenbridge had been flung out of Magdalen in 1634 and died in the end in New England. Overton, much praised in the *Defence*, was recalled from Hull for an enquiry into whether he had favoured an Anabaptist revolt in Scotland, though he replied sturdily enough. Milton was learning by necessity to rely on the younger generation of his friends. The Phillipps brothers, apart from their obvious ability, have been dismissed as hacks: however Edward was a useful writer, his history of English poets, *Theatrum Poeticum*, being full of what look like Milton's own most interesting views, and John was brilliant. He was faithful too as a secretary to his uncle. The worst that can be said of him is that he is said in later life to have been somehow entangled in the Titus Oates plot.

Morus had been acquitted by a court and whitewashed by the elders over his seduction case. He now tried in vain to get Milton's attack on him suppressed, but the Dutch ambassador wrote to him saying the English refused. As Professor of Sacred History now at Amsterdam, Morus was in a panic about his dignity and about Milton. In April 1654 Milton's Greek friend Philaras had been replaced at Paris on the orders of a new Duke of Parma, and Mazarin tried to have him arrested and disgraced as a spy, because (or so it was rumoured) 'they have found a letter of civility Mr Milton had writ to him'. In fact when his papers were examined he was declared innocent, and the Duke tried to reinstate him. In September of 1654 he actually came to London and visited John Milton. A new Parliament had just assembled, though without Vane or Selden. It agreed to toleration for everything but popery, prelacy, licence, atheism or blasphemy. So far Baptists and Anabaptists and Quakers were within the law. Fifth Monarchy men (Coleman Street millenarists), Ranters and Muggletonians flourished. But in January of 1655 Cromwell dissolved parliamentary government and continued to rule this lively ship's company as Protector with his State Council. It is perhaps at this time, consciously or not, that he ensured the restoration of Charles II as soon as his lifetime was over.

None the less, for the time being the army troubles and the poor Levellers with their wild wishes presented no serious threat. The royalist attempt to stage a coup at Salisbury was farcical, as Clarendon describes in all its pathetic detail: neither side was ruthless enough, neither side seriously wanted to fight a battle. Meanwhile there was appalling trouble in the Romansch-speaking part of Switzerland, where the Duke of Savoy let loose the most savage local persecution against the Protestant Vaudois, a separate sect since Peter Valdes, and formally Protestant since 1215. The Duke's action occurred in late April and left 1,700 victims ripped, impaled, roasted, hanged or hacked to death, the heads of a number boiled and eaten. Among the soldiers who participated some were Irish. In May Cromwell protested, and a treaty with France restored the *status quo*, but Cromwell was not placated, and nor was Milton.

> Avenge O Lord thy slaughtered saints, whose bones
> Lie scattered on the Alpine mountains cold,
> Even them who kept thy truth so pure of old
> When all our fathers worshipped stocks and stones . . .

When Milton speaks of 'the bloody Piedmontese that rolled/Mother with infant down the rocks', he is putting it mildly. The remnant of this remote mountain community had lived, by right of a recent treaty with the Duke, confined to the upper villages of their mountains, but in 1655 they were expelled by Savoy's servant, the Marquis of Pianezza, from the lower and pursued into the upper villages. The hangings were at Torre Pellice bridge. Milton probably wrote his infuriated sonnet in May, when he had the task of composing a letter from the Protestant states of all Europe, who were equally horrified, to Savoy, to be delivered by a special ambassador. This is one of few examples of a poem that arose directly from his work; indeed it is unique in this as it is in the strength of its genuine anti-papal rage.

About this time (it is impossible to determine when) he wrote his sonnet to Edward Lawrence: Carey suggests 1653, because we know that young Lawrence, the son of a President of the Lord Protector's Council of State, used to visit Milton soon after his blindness. The

young man was an MP in 1656, but died in 1657 at the age of twenty-
four, so Carey's date is not unlikely. His father had opposed the
King's trial, to Oliver's annoyance. The last we hear of young
Lawrence alive is when Milton's German friend, Oldenberg, sends
him best wishes in the June of the year of his death. The poem is
charming, and genuinely Horatian. Since it must have been dictated,
it shows a remarkable and new sweetness, as well as great powers of
concentration.

> Now that the fields are dank, and ways are mire,
> Where shall we sometimes meet, and by the fire
> Help waste a sullen day . . .

Milton speaks as a man who has retired and has no worries about
immediate business, and the occupation he proposes recalls the old
days with Damon. He looks forward to 'The lily and rose, that neither
sowed nor spun', to a light lunch as was his custom to the end of his
life, and to some lute music 'or artful voice/Warble immortal notes
and Tuscan air'. It is a charming poem that suggests a country outing.
It may be all the more moving because of its newfound or newly
regained confidence. Milton had praised the elder Lawrence in his
Defence, but one would sooner have this lovely sonnet with its classic,
rather Latin hardness, under which one can sense the juice flowing
from line to line: yet it is temperate, even frugal in its words as
well as in its proposed arrangements. It is the acceptable face of
Puritanism.

> What neat repast shall feast us, light and choice,
> Of Attic taste, with wine, whence we may rise
> To hear the lute well touched, or artful voice
> Warble immortal notes and Tuscan air?
> He who of those delights can judge, and spare
> To interpose them oft, is not unwise.

In 1653 Milton started again to translate the Psalms: the first one
into couplets, the second in August into *terzetti* or *terza rima*. It is not
improbable that in these versions he is experimenting with the task of
dictating his poetry, which cannot have been easily learnt. Even in
the couplets his sentences are not short and the rhyming seems to me
ingenious.

> He shall be as a tree which planted grows
> By wat'ry streams, and in his season knows
> To yield his fruit, and his leaf shall not fall,
> And what he takes in hand shall prosper all. . . .

His task in the second psalm is far more complicated, and it must have been prepared and its scheme chosen before ever he began to dictate it.

> Be taught ye judges of the earth; with fear
> Jehovah serve, and let your joy converse
> With trembling; kiss the Son lest he appear
> In anger and ye perish in the way
> If once his wrath take fire like fuel sere.
> Happy all those who have in him their stay.

No doubt these verses read like experiments just because they adapt phrases from existing versions, and because they are translations of a text so traditional it has established its own kind of cliché, like 'perish in the way', but in their choices of metre and in many details they are bold.

The third psalm is in a six-line stanza form which works against all expectation, and must certainly have been elaborately worked out in his head. As a form it is new. Again and again in this handful of psalms one feels something personal of Milton's, even if it is only a tone or an emphasis. 'Speak to your hearts alone,/Upon your beds, each one,/And be at peace within. . . .' is in the fourth psalm, which is in another but a haunting stanza form. The most striking lines are in the sixth psalm, inserted in the consciousness of his personal plight.

> Wearied I am with sighing out my days,
> Nightly my couch I make a kind of sea;
> My bed I water with my tears; mine eye
> Through grief consumes, is waxen old and dark
> I' the midst of all mine enemies that mark. . . .

But that mood, if it was a mood, and not a mere side-effect of translation, passed swiftly enough. In about 1655 he was taking with Cyriack Skinner the same tranquilly happy line that he had taken with Edward Lawrence. He wrote Skinner a sonnet telling him 'to drench/In mirth' his deep and studious thoughts.

Let Euclid rest, and Archimedes pause,
And what the Swede intend, and what the French. . . .

The sonnet has the simplest of messages: the old, blind teacher is telling his pupil not to fret. It is not quite as cheering as young Lawrence's, but the second sonnet to Skinner, about Milton's intimate feelings, or those he would admit to, about his blindness, is perhaps a greater compliment still. And yet all these poems were written within three or four years of his going blind.

In November 1656 an event occurred that must mark the end of his greatest intimacy with his young friends: Milton married a girl called Katherine, the daughter of Captain Woodcock of Hackney. The marriage must have been arranged, so he can never have seen her. His financial situation was secure: in April 1655 (early in the new year in the old style) his £288 a year was commuted to a pension of £150 a year for life. He could lend £500, taking a mortgage in Kensington as security in 1658, and he had money in the bank at the Restoration. It looks as if he wanted a son: the wedding was on 12 November 1656, and his wife gave birth to a daughter on 19 October 1657. But the second Mrs Milton died the following February and little Katherine on 17 March. Milton wrote a sonnet which is both classical and poignantly personal.

Methought I saw my late espoused saint
Brought to me like Alcestis from the grave,
Whom Jove's great son to her glad husband gave,
Rescued from death by force though pale and faint.
Mine as whom washed from spot of childbed taint,
Purification in the old Law did save,
And such as yet once more I trust to have
Full sight of her in heaven without restraint,
Came vested all in white, pure as her mind:
Her face was veiled, yet to my fancied sight,
Love, sweetness, goodness in her person shined
So clear, as in no face with more delight.
But O as to embrace me she inclined
I waked, she fled, and day brought back my night.

The myth at the beginning is the one Euripides treated, of Alcestis brought back from the grave by Hercules. The allusion at the end is to visions in Virgil. Parker, with the perversity and curious learning that were his trade mark, thought the poem might be about Mary Powell because she died within the purification period decreed in Leviticus. This ignores Milton's blindness, to which he refers, and the hand of Jeremy Picard, the secretary who wrote this sonnet in the Trinity manuscript and also entered Katherine's death and her child's in the Bible. This was the last sonnet Milton wrote, and it is one of the most moving.

CHAPTER TEN

THE KING RESTORED:
PARADISE LOST

THE WOES OF A BIOGRAPHER of Milton differ from chapter to chapter. So far, Milton's life, slowly at first but in the end intricately, has been bound up with public policies. We do not know whether his *Tenure of Kings and Magistrates* was inspired or not: if not, it must have seemed a godsend to Cromwell and his friends, but he was probably encouraged or begged to write it. For the next few years his life became a struggle: attacks came from all sides, a consequence of his propaganda writings, which had all been in prose, never in verse. Meanwhile his sonnets, from the satiric snarls against Scotsmen to the final heavenly suspiration of his sonnet to his dead wife Katherine, opened a form that no one else until Wordsworth was fit to use: it was all but confined to the women's magazines, and to a model quite without that reality that made Milton's such an impressive body of work. But from the time of his blindness his life gradually unwound and relaxed from public life.

He is like a man slowly entering a state of trance, because he is going to write *Paradise Lost*. He knows it and most carefully prepares it. If he wrote ten or twenty lines a day on five days a week he might finish 5,000 lines in a year, and the whole poem has 10,565 lines in its second, perfected edition, so that once he knew where he was going he might finish his entire poem in something between two and four years. He could not have found the time to brood or to concentrate his energies if he had not been blind. Some scholars who think he must have needed a long time suggest that he had begun it in 1655, and we know that he had a copy before the Great Fire of London (1666) and published in 1667. The speed with which he wrote *Paradise Regained*, which is a little more than 2,000 lines, in three years including the planning, was impressive, but it suggests 1,000 lines or so a year: if *Paradise Lost* had taken that long, as it might have done, then it would have taken all his time from 1655 to 1666, allowing a year for the shock of the Restoration, for the stream of his prose publications, then his imprisonment, his loss of all his savings in the collapse of a government bank, and his search for a new house in a different neighbourhood.

Nevertheless, poems of a few hundred lines do not necessarily or always take longer than a month to write, though 5,000 lines a year would exhaust any serious poet. As for the planning stage, that can be spread over a long period of time. We know that Milton had contemplated a great work since his time in Italy, that he relied perhaps all too much on research, and therefore wasted years reading all about King Arthur and Anglo-Saxon history, and that he approached his true theme with fear and veneration. His first notes were written before he was blind, but the introduction to Book 2 shows us Milton lamenting his blindness. Changes of plan, so far as we can see them, happened when he turned to address himself directly to his poem, in about 1655 at the earliest: but I harbour the suspicion that he wrote *Paradise Lost* between 1660 and 1666, in four or five years. If he had written any of it before 1660, then it was probably the first books, with their concentration on the grotesque splendours of the satanic Underworld.

We need not examine carefully his State letters early or late: they are of value to historians, but to students of Milton they demonstrate only the linguistic ability we knew he had. They are all patriotic and some verge on the triumphalist. But his personal letters were also preserved in some numbers, and I have quoted them in earlier chapters: the best probably were to his friend Diodati. 'You promised to come here but no. When will you come? How long are you going to stay with those Hyperboreans? I heard you had been in London; do come.' 'I think of migrating to the Inns of Court, where the walking is shaded and pleasant ...' Later he writes in the same intimate spirit to the young men who had been his pupils. To Richard Jones he writes, 'You say you like Oxford but you don't show you have learnt anything ... You are a philosopher and must not praise victories too much.' To Emeric Bigot in 1656, he writes thanks for a visit: 'I am glad you believe in my tranquillity of mind in blindness and my comity and care in receiving strangers. Even letters don't

worry me or your book on the holding of Parliaments. I need some
Byzantine historians: Theophanes, *Chronicles* of Manasses.' To H. de
Brass, 'You are the right philosophical kind of traveller. Sallust is the
best historian, Tacitus is acceptable but best where he imitates Sallust.
I gave your love to Lawrence. Anyone to whom Sallust appeals is
already a historian.' In 1659 to Oldenburg, 'Yes, I too fear the allied
enemies of religion and liberty ... I hope the Synod goes well (as no
other Synod ever has).' He enclosed a brief encouraging note to R.
Jones. It will be observed that as a blind man he is writing like a wise
old politician or a retired ambassador. To Peter Heimbach, counsellor
to the Elector of Brandenburg, in August 1666, 'There has been so
much death and plague, I am glad you worried about me. God kept
me well in the country ... What you call my politics is piety to my
country.' That he never ceased to feel.

All these years until 1660 he was busy with friends and studies and
correspondence. Pierre du Moulin was a source of continuing irri-
tation: he claimed to have been the origin of *The King's Blood*, though
undoubtedly Morus, who now produced testimonials to his character,
had adapted it. The Revd Dr du Moulin had had a difficult war: he
was a Yorkshire vicar who lost a chimney by cannon fire while
sheltering in York in a cellar. His brother was an Oxford don, and he
settled there in 1654, and often preached at St Peter's in the East. As
for John Phillipps, who answered him in 1652, a report from Mr
Sandelands to Thurloe says he was in Scotland in 1654, but 1655 saw
the appearance in London of Phillipps's pleasing *Satire against
Hypocrites*, about churchgoing.

> Are these the men that would the age reform
> That *Down with Superstition* cry, and swarm
> This painted glass, that sculpture to deface,
> But worship pride and avarice in their place?

The poem is not long, but it must in its sharp way recall Milton's
own opinions. It is a pity the whole poem has never been reprinted.

In 1656 Cowley issued his collected poems in London: Milton
admired his work, but it would be interesting to know whether he
used Cowley's 'Davideis', which has a number of humorous touches,
and whether both of them were not under the influence of Giles
Fletcher or just Ovid. There was a streak of jokiness in Cowley that

was felt discreditable in the new age; certainly from the time that he died in 1667, Cowley began to'sink in reputation, and no doubt it was partly *Paradise Lost* that sank him (see Levi, *The Art of Poetry*, 1991, pp. 154–9). Cowley was a royalist diplomat arrested by mistake for another person in 1655 and bailed for £1,000 until the Restoration. He had thought of conforming, and of creeping across the Atlantic. He says that by 1656 his appetite for his poems had gone, so he printed them. His *Cutter of Coleman Street* is an unusual monument to some ripely comic characters. Milton loved Cowley and named him alone among contemporary poets. Commonwealth Oxford created this still neglected poet MD, and he went happily off to Kent to compose a huge botanical poem in Latin. Some years ago his excellent Civil War poem, an epic in couplets, was published at last (A. Pritchard, Toronto, 1973), and one would be surprised if Milton had not read it in manuscript. Whether by suggestion or counter-suggestion he seems conscious of passages like this:

> Here rebel minds in envious torments lie;
> Must here forever live, forever die.
> Here Lucifer the mighty captive reigns,
> Proud midst his woes, and tyrant in his chains.
> Once general of a gilded host of sprites,
> Like Hesper leading on the spangled nights;
> But down like lightning, which him strook, he came
> And roared at his first plunge into the flame.
> Millions of spirits fell wounded round him there;
> With dropping lights thick shone the singed air . . .

Edward Phillipps, like his brother, was now registering and publishing works of his own: among the Miltonian variety of literary tasks to which he put his hand was an edition of that admirable poet Drummond of Hawthornden. He or his uncle was a friend of John Scot of Scotstarvet, who came to London in 1654–5 to have a fine reduced, and accomplished it. The preface to Drummond (1656) speaks of 'the effects of a genius the most polite and verdant that ever the Scottish nation produced. Neither Tasso nor Guarini nor even the choicest of our English poets . . .' was to be preferred. Can this be close to Milton's own opinion?

The only news in the last two or three years of Cromwell's reign was of Cromwell himself: he was now as grand as a king, with a golden sceptre and a purple robe, titles, lifeguards and the rest of the paraphernalia. Richard, his thirty-one-year-old son, was promoted colonel and Henry (twenty-nine) Lord Deputy. Elizabeth (twenty-eight) had married Lord Claypole of the cavalry, and Ireton's widow (another daughter) married the more important Fleetwood in 1657, when Mary (twenty-one) married Lord Falconbridge. William Dutton married Lord Scudamore's daughter, the widow of Thomas Russell of Worcester. Cromwell's sisters married John Wilkins of Wadham and Colonel Jones. Since Oliver's father's sister had been Hampden's mother and so kin to the poet Waller, a very rich landed gentleman, the Cromwells were now well placed whichever way politics should go. Oliver was champion of all England because he was the only contender left on his feet. Lord Lambert resigned on £2,000 a year to grow tulips in Wimbledon. Only rumours of rebellion disturbed him, though he must have been perplexed when Buckingham's heir stepped across from France at the age of thirty and married Fairfax's only child, who was nineteen: Cowley had known him at Cambridge and was best man. York House in London and a huge estate in Yorkshire were therefore handed back to Buckingham, while the Council discussed his arrest with Cromwell. Conspiracies like 'the Sealed Knot' continued, but none of them stood any chance. Some travelling players were arrested near Newcastle and whipped as beggars.

In August 1658 Cromwell was ill, but he recovered and went riding at Hampton Court. George Fox, the Quaker, came to see him, but 'saw and felt a waft of death go forth against him, and when I came to him he looked like a dead man'. Buckingham was sent to the Tower, all but the last act of Oliver's reign. At his State funeral in the Abbey, conducted by a King of Arms, blind Milton, young Dryden and Andrew Marvell walked together behind his coffin. No king of England has been so well attended. The transition was oddly without incident because everyone was so cautious. Monck came down from Scotland to fill the vacuum, and altered his policy little by little as he saw how public feeling lay. This drove Milton frantic with anxiety, and as London exploded in fireworks, so Milton exploded in pamphlets. He was already in touch with that short-lived institution the Rota Club, which would meet in Miles's tavern, the Turk's Head, in

New Palace Yard, although it cannot be shown he ever attended its meetings. On occasion Cyriack Skinner, now about thirty, took the chair; discussions were about the theory and form of the State; they all knew Hobbes's *Leviathan* (Milton disliked him); and Harrington was a member and probably the convener. After discussions there would always be a vote, which was carried out with meticulous fairness. The members in 1659 were these:

Harrington	John Hoskins
H. Neville	John Aubrey
Cyr. Skinner	Dr Will Petty
Major Jn Wildman	Max Petty (Tetsworth,
Ch. Wolseley, Staffs	Oxfordshire)
Reg Coke	Mic. Mallet
Will Poulteney (future knight)	Ph. Carteret (Guernsey)
Ed Bagshaw (Christ Church,	Fra. Craddock (merchant)
Oxford)	Hen. Ford
Rob Wood (Lincoln, Oxford)	Major Venner
James Arderner (future Revd)	Thos Marriett (Warwickshire)
Henry Croone (doctor)	

Anthony Powell in his *Life of John Aubrey* makes as much as can be sensibly made of these fascinating but mysterious people. It was Bagshaw, for example, whom Aubrey called 'my fanatique friend' of Bunhill. Many of them were young men in 1659, and probably more than I have traced lived into the eighteenth century. But in 1660, events overtook them. If another civil war were to be avoided, armed intervention was ruled out, and not even Milton did want war. The discussions therefore came to nothing practical. Perhaps it is worth emphasizing that when the poet was a young man there were no such discussions anywhere, just as there were none in France or in Italy, because repression would most surely have attended on them. These early conversations about an ideal state are one of the greatest achievements of the Commonwealth, as they were of the Athenian democracy. Once contracted, the habit of freely exchanging opinions about the State or God or anything else is hard to suppress: the Whigs inherited what these men planted.

Milton and also Marvell, who since 1657 had been going downriver in a State barge to receive ambassadors and bring them to Whitehall steps, and was now Assistant Secretary, continued on the payroll for the ridiculous episode of Richard Cromwell's brief reign. In October 1658 Milton's *Defence* had a new edition with a postscript about Roman examples. There are only two pages of this postscript, but it contains a boast that recalls the Latin letter to Manso long ago: it promises 'the accomplishment of yet greater things if I have the power – and I shall have the power'. This must be the first public foretaste of *Paradise Lost*.

Then came his *Civil Powers in Ecclesiastical Causes*, an argument based entirely on the Bible but proudly addressed 'To Parliament, in the process of rising from its ashes': 'To the Parliament of the Commonwealth of England, with the Dominions thereof, Showing that it is not lawful for any Power on Earth to Compel in Matters of Religion ... I have prepared, supreme Council, against the much expected time of your sitting, this treatise ...' It continued in the same grave style, every word well weighed and compelling attention. 'But some will object that this overthrows all Church Discipline, all censure of errors.' But what it forbade was 'violence upon the conscience unconvinced'. The Restoration was to ride roughshod over this impudent high-mindedness, and yet Platonic Milton had lighted a candle that was not to be put out. It would go on until the whole society took light from it, and until it looked as it looks now and has done for 150 years, like pure common sense. 'The brevity I use, not exceeding a small manual, will not therefore, I suppose, be thought the less considerable, unless with them, perhaps, who think that great books only can determine great matters.' His book was twenty pages long. Roman Catholics were still to be outside the law because they were 'a Roman principality, endeavouring to keep her old dominion', a view which Gibbon later gleefully embroidered.

In May 1659 Richard Cromwell abdicated. John Milton had, as Massey puts it, shaken hands amiably with the old Republican party in his last pamphlet. But so far as we can determine, he went on writing foreign letters in Latin for the Parliament. Petitions for the disestablishment of the Church now came pouring into that less than august body in their dozens. Milton produced a swollen second edition in August, and then *Considerations to Remove Hirelings out of the Church*, a new work, though one that still concentrates on his old opinions. It is perhaps in the controversies of these years that his powerful *De Doctrina Christiana* solidified. Parliament is now 'next under God the authors and best patrons of religious and civil liberty that ever these Islands brought forth . . .', a large and unusual claim. Milton was hostile to all tithes and taxes, he thought universities unnecessary for the production of ministers, and that ministers' libraries should cost them £60 rather than £600 (today perhaps £600 and not £6,000). 'Let the state but erect in public good store of libraries.' He was centuries ahead of his time here, though what he suggested had been inevitable since the spread of printing: that is, since about 1600.

In October 1659 in a letter 'To a friend' (printed in 1698) he compared the troubles of the State to an infantile disturbance of the bowels. He disapproved of Lambert and his attempted coup, and of the 'sad dishonour of that army lately so renowned for the civilest and best ordered in the world, and by us here at home for the most conscientious'. Had he been fed with propaganda, believing this ever since 1642? He tentatively considers annual elections, but finally he settles for a Council of State, and another of officers. He desires liberty of conscience and resistance to monarchy, that is, he opposes all one-person sovereignty. This letter was circulated in manuscript, but not printed. The Rota doubtless read it and perhaps influenced it. It is not certain to whom it was addressed, but it could have been Cyriack Skinner, who survived until 1700. But Monck was already talking about 'fanatics', by which he meant people opposed to a State Church (which Parliament had voted for) and all anti-Presbyterian people. By February 1660 rumps of oxen were being roasted in the streets of London and Milton's pamphlet was stopped.

About 3 March, Thomason the bookseller got hold of John Milton's *Ready and Easy Way to Establish a Free Commonwealth*. It is a curious contribution, and has been compared by A. L. Rowse to a shipwrecked sailor frantically gesticulating from the shores of Patagonia as the big ships go by. Milton's confusion is well expressed in his first sentence:

> Although, since the writing of this treatise, the face of things hath had some change, writs for new elections have been recalled, and the members at first chosen readmitted from exclusion; yet not a little rejoicing to hear declared the resolution of those who are in power,

tending to the establishment of a Free Commonwealth, and to remove, if it be possible, this noxious humour of returning to bondage ... Before so long a Lent of servitude they may permit us a little shroving-time first, wherein to speak freely and to take our leaves of Liberty ... What I have spoken is the language of that which is not called amiss *The good old Cause*.

This pamphlet appears to be purely political, but his old theme of liberty of conscience and the interrupted Reformation lies at the bottom of his argument. He now wants one perpetual Parliament with life membership and a General Council of the ablest men: a very high-minded suggestion. The chief gentlemen of every county should be called to London at once, and it should be explained to them how dangerous and confusing it would be to go back to monarchy. If Milton's Council is unpopular, we should try *Rotation*. (Once again, one sniffs the presence of that remarkable debating club, the Rota.) This pamphlet circulated widely and caused fury. 'John Milton their goosequill champion ...' 'Milton is so much an enemy to usual practice he will be the first man to demand to be taken to Tyburn in a wheelbarrow.' A royalist burlesque came out called *Censure of the Rota on Mr Milton's Book*. This rather good-tempered mockery was something new in English journalism.

All the same Livewell Chapman, who printed these last two of Milton's publications, was prosecuted at the end of March; the journalist Needham was sacked at last, after many vicissitudes, and so was Milton. This did not stop the old fellow: he issued *Brief Notes on a late Sermon* by Matthew Griffith, a royalist who had been a protégé of Donne's, and since then had been in and out of prison four times. Meanwhile *The Dignity of Kingship* appeared, which not only answered Milton's early anti-King writings but placed his head squarely on the block. It had become very much a question whether he would survive the next few months, though that did not worry him. At the same time as the *Notes* on the royalist sermon, which called Griffith a pulpit-mountebank, he answered the Rota burlesque in a second edition of his recent *Free Commonwealth*. On 7 May 1660 he drew £400 from Cyriack Skinner by a bond which Skinner cherished. Somewhere it may still exist, since in 1877 it belonged to Lord Houghton, Richard Monckton Milnes, Tennyson's friend.

At Breda, on the verge of his coming to England, Charles II was being petitioned against the Common Prayer and against bishops: but the rest is history. By the Act of Indemnity Milton's books *Eikonoklastes* and the *Defence Against Salmasius*, as well as Goodwin's, were burnt by the hangman. Palmer, the Attorney-General, began proceedings against the pair of them, but on Saturday, 16 June, the House of Commons picked the twenty persons to be excluded by name from the Act of Indemnity, and Milton's was not among them, though Goodwin's was. Of those twenty, some fled to America, some to Europe, and some suffered a nasty fate, including Henry Vane, who must be the only Governor of Massachusetts to be hanged for a crime he did not commit: he had never been a party to the King's death or approved of it. There were nine bishops left alive, including Henry King, about as many as long before had survived into the reign of Elizabeth. Of the members of Smectymnus, Calamy and Spurstow were active and successful under Charles II. Newcomen was alive, Young and old Marshall dead.

Milton had taken refuge in Bartholomew Close, in the arch approaching St Bartholomew's from west Smithfield. By 11 July eleven of the regicides had sensibly made themselves scarce. In August the Lords sent Vane, Haselrig, Lambert and Axtell to their deaths, but they were gentler over the other sixteen. A pamphlet of this time says Milton was struck blind by God, like old Dorislaus Ascham, an alderman from Hoyle, who hanged himself: but the Lords never named him. On 13 August booksellers must surrender Milton's and Goodwin's books for burning, but 'the said J. G. and J. M. are both fled, or so obscure themselves that no endeavours used for their apprehension can take effect'. In principle they were to be tried and punished. When the Royal Assent was given to the Bill on 29 August, Goodwin was only 'incapacitated for office', and Milton was still not mentioned.

Who protected him from death? Edward Phillipps had not the least idea: he says it was managed by Marvell, but managed how? Richardson was not born until 1665, but he did have some trickles of the truth. In his *Life of Milton* in 1734 he thought it was Secretary Morrice and Sir Thomas Clarges who 'managed things artfully in his favour, they or somebody else'. That is too vague to be credible. Massey cleverly suggested the Earl of Anglesey. Warton says Mr T. Tyers (1726–87) told him that when Milton was on the run, he had a mock funeral that made Charles II laugh when he heard about it. As we have noted, Davenant said Milton had saved his life (which I believe), so he saved Milton's (which I do not). That was the story Pope got from Betterton. Lawes was alive: could he have helped? Milton cannot have been just forgotten. The only British monarch there has ever been with enough sense of humour and human compassion to let him alone was Charles II: could it have been the King's doing?

James Norfolk, the Serjeant-at-Arms, did catch him, no one knows how or when, and he was imprisoned at Westminster in the Gate-house. On 15 December he was released, complaining that the fees he was told to pay were too high; Marvell made a fuss in the Commons and they were reduced. His seconders were Colonel King (Great Grimsby) and Colonel Shapcott (Tiverton). Milton was released to Holborn, to Red Lion Fields, Red Lion Square, though he still lived in fear of assassination or 'mugging'. In September 1660 Salmasius's reply at last appeared. It was very long-winded indeed and today has become quite unreadable.

The vicar of St Giles, Cripplegate, was Samuel Annesley, a cousin of the Earl of Anglesey and later, through his youngest daughter, grand-father of John and Charles Wesley. That was the direction in which Milton was led (and in the end he was buried there). He had never frequented church or chapel in Coleman Street, and recently there had been hangings there. From about this time he let himself off church altogether. For some time he was in Jewin Street, north of Aldersgate Street, then Red Cross Street, close to St Giles and the Barbican. Today the Methodist headquarters, with its palatial eighteenth-century chapel, stands overlooking the old Nonconformist burial ground at Bunhill Fields. It was in that street that John Milton settled at last among friends, opposite the Artillery Ground to the south.

Most of his clerical allies lost their jobs, down to his old pupil Richard Heath, assistant to Walton's Polyglot Bible, ejected from Shrewsbury. Even his enemies did not all prosper. Morus came to England hopefully in 1661 but the opportunity of employing or rewarding him was let slip, and he died in the Duchesse de Rohan's house. Gauden, Bishop of Exeter in 1660 and author of *Eikon Basilike*, called his promotion a banishment and pursued Clarendon with well-penned whines. At last he got Worcester, when Morley moved to Winchester, which Gauden had longed for. Du Moulin, the true author of the attack for which Milton had blamed Morus, did not remain unrewarded: he became a prebend of Canterbury.

It would be wrong to call Milton's daughters his enemies, but they were hostile and dangerous, and Edward says that Milton had himself to blame. Anne, who was seventeen in 1662, was lame and had a speech defect; Mary, now fifteen, and Deborah, eleven, could read and write, but they complained of not being taught languages, and yet being condemned to read and pronounce exactly 'all the languages of whatever book he should at one time or other think fit to peruse'. They stole books and sold them, conspiring with the maid, and at least as adolescents expressed contempt for the old poet. Who knows what the truth is? There was a question of their being taught trades: one of them successfully became a lacemaker. It does not sound a happy household, and yet Milton's last years became tranquil after his third marriage.

Every two days Dr Nathan Paget came to see Milton about his gout. He was the Coleman Street doctor and a sincere and lasting friend. He had known Milton for years, and it was he who arranged his last marriage. It may have been through this doctor that Milton met such friends as Thomas Ellwood, a Quaker born in 1639 and twenty-one at the Restoration, whom Milton used to teach. Ellwood's father was a friend of Isaac Pennington, the son of an alderman who was a regicide; Isaac married Lady Springett (Giulielma) as her second husband, and so came into possession of Chalfont St Peter on the London edge of the Chilterns in about 1658, and the Ellwoods, father and son, got to know them there about a year later. They lived at that time at Chinnor, some fifteen miles away from Chalfont. Isaac had then been a Quaker for about a year, but the elder Springetts and Penningtons were furious: Gulielma, on the other hand, was probably a principal attraction of Quakerism to Isaac. The alderman died in the Tower, awaiting execution, in December 1661. The link of the Ellwoods with Milton came about because Dr Paget knew Isaac Pennington and introduced Thomas to the poet. The social and kinship links of these early and intrepid Nonconformists are fascinating, and they survive through Thomas Ellwood's *Life* by himself, which appeared as soon as he was safely dead, in 1714.

Milton instructed young Ellwood in Latin, as the poet Shirley instructed Ogilby. After six weeks Thomas had a kind of breakdown, so he went into the country for a holiday, and then resumed work. He was arrested by a magistrate raging for conformity, and in October 1662 he spent three months in Bridewell and then Newgate, where a kind of hole next to his cell contained the heads and quartered bodies of George Phillips, yeoman, Thomas Tongue, distiller, and Nathaniel Gibbs, feltmaker. The nasty relics had lain rotting there since they had been hanged for 'conspiracy' on 22 December 1662. In January 1663 Thomas was out of prison and back with the blind poet for more Latin lessons; in the end he became a tutor in the Pennington family. The whole of his account of his experiences is well worth reading if only for his transparent sincerity, but the time in prison in 1662 is particularly unusual, and relevant here because he will certainly have told John Milton every word of it.

> When we came first into *Newgate*, there lay (in a little By-place like a Closet, near the Room where we were Lodged) the Quartered Bodies of three Men; who had been Executed some Days before, for a real or pretended Plot: which was the Ground, or at least Pretext, for that Storm in the City, which had caused this Imprisonment. The Names of these three Men were *Philips*, *Tongue* and *Gibs*: and the Reason why their Quarters lay so long there was, The Relations were all that while Petitioning to have leave to bury them: which at length with much ado was obtained for the Quarters; but not for the Heads, which were Ordered to be set up in some Parts of the City.
>
> I saw the Heads, when they were brought up to be Boyled. The Hangman fetch'd them in a dirty Dust Basket, out of some By-Place; and setting them down amongst the Felons, he and they made Sport with them. They took them by the Hair, Flouting, Jeering and Laughing at them: and then giving them some ill Names, box'd them on the Ears and Cheeks. Which done, the Hangman put them into his Kettle, and parboyl'd them with *Bay-Salt* and *Cummin-Seed*: that to keep them from Putrefaction, and this to keep the Fowls from seizing on them. The whole Sight (as well that of the Bloody Quarters first, as this of the Heads afterwards) was both frightful and loathsom; and begat an Abhorrence in my Nature. Which as it had rendered my Confinement there by much the more uneasie: so it made our Removal from thence to *Bridewell*, even in that respect, the more welcome. Whither we now go.
>
> For having (as I hinted before) made up our Packs, and taken our Leave of our *Friends*, whom we were to leave behind; we took our

> Bundles on our Shoulders, and walked, Two and Two a Breast, through
> the *Old Baily* into *Fleet-Street*, and so to *Old Bridewell*. And it being about
> the Middle of the Afternoon, and the Streets pretty full of People; both
> the Shopkeepers at their Doors, and Passengers in the Way, would
> stop us, and ask us what we were, and whither we were going. And
> when we had told them we were Prisoners, going from one Prison to
> another (from *Newgate* to *Bridewell*) *What*, said they, *without a Keeper!*
> No, said we, for our Word, which we have given, is our Keeper.

There is no doubt that the poet greatly liked these people, as he
would have liked Bunyan if he had met him, for who would not?

We shall meet Thomas Ellwood again. But one must remember
that, in the conditions of those days, many natural allies simply never
met each other. Mr Biddle, for instance, whose experiences in the
Civil War and Commonwealth made him the first Unitarian, was
born in 1616 and a minister of religion in London, but I have found
no evidence that he and Milton ever met: and yet their opinions
coincide even more closely than Milton's do with the early Quakers.
Milton was on his own now, because of the necessity of secrecy and
because of his blindness. He was often visited by Skinner and Marvell
and by Lady Ranelagh and other old friends, and on occasion by the
Earl of Anglesey, by Dryden, and until his lamentably early death by
Abraham Cowley, but he did not go much about; he had found an
area of London where he could feel safe and in touch with like-
minded people, outsiders to the Restoration, and there he settled and
made himself a life and wrote his poems.

The same doctor Nat Paget, as we have said, found him his third
wife, Elizabeth Minshull. The Minshulls were Cheshire people, from
Wistaston near Nantwich, and the doctor's cousins. Elizabeth was
born in December 1638: when they met she was in London on a visit,
and twenty-four years old: her father, who was a gentleman with
money, had died in 1657. So John Milton, gentleman, of St Giles,
Cripplegate, was to marry Elizabeth Minshull of St Andrew's, Holborn; the marriage to take place in St George's, Southwark, or St
Mary, Aldermary. The maid at home said, 'I hear your father's going
to be married again.' Mary said, 'That was no news to hear of his
wedding, but if she could hear of his death, that was something.' The
wedding was at St Mary's, where the vicar was Dr Robert Gell, an old
Fellow of Christ's, most interestingly, and a preacher in mystical

terms, who was never ejected by the Presbyterians or the restored Anglicans: he seems to have gone on peacefully weaving his mystical web of words.

The marriage was a success. Even Aubrey liked Mrs Milton, 'a gentle person, of a peaceful and agreeable humour'. She could sing, and the poet thought she had a good voice but a bad ear. They would migrate together to Artillery Walk, when Edward Phillipps went as tutor to John Evelyn's children. Evelyn notes he was 'not at all affected by Milton's principles though he was brought up by him'. Milton now had more garden than before in Jewin Street, soon to be famous as Grub Street; he had four hearths or fireplaces, which sounds like the simpler kind of London tradesman's house, 'two up and two down' and an attic, so common until 1939 and now so desirable. There were bigger houses nearby, some with 'five or six hearths'. Here at last Milton settled down to finish *Paradise Lost*, which he wrote mostly in winter between the two equinoxes, when the nights were longer. He composed in his head, lying alone in bed, so that he would have some twenty or forty lines ready: he would then send for his daughter 'to secure what came: as many as forty lines as it were in a breath, and would then reduce them to half the number'. The method of dictating his poetry is, of course, what produced the splendid unrhymed verse of *Paradise Lost*, with its long, dangling sentences, its long, dangling syntax. It can be seen in its perfection in the introduction to Book 3:

> Hail, holy Light, offspring of heaven first-born,
> Or of the eternal co-eternal beam
> May I express thee unblamed? since God is light,
> And never but in unapproached light
> Dwelt from eternity, dwelt then in thee,
> Bright effluence of bright essence increate.
>   ... Thus with the year
> Seasons return; but not to me returns
> Day, or the sweet approach of even or morn,
> Or sight of vernal bloom, or summer's rose,
> Or flocks, or herds, or human face divine ...

The long sentence of thirty lines wanders on, and one can feel it pouring out of him. In fact the full stops at the end of lines 6 and 36 are quite unnecessary; it might all go sweeping onward, self-echoing, warbling and musing on its mighty theme, until line 55. The repetitions of words not only serve the purpose of emphasis, as with the word 'light', but also they suit the way he now composes, with endless pendent clauses in little more than apposition to each other. All this is very like the parataxis, as it is called, of popular storytelling, and of the speeches in Greek comedy that correspond to the Messenger's speech in tragedy, where it is elaborately syntactic, but that is not where Milton got the idea. It is the resource of a blind man, and of blind poets or poets before the invention of writing. Because of his blindness, Milton has employed the original oral technique of epic poetry, and by using it he has rediscovered some of the freshness of the ancient epic.

He knew nothing of any contemporary epic, of what there was at that moment alive in Ireland or in Crete and scarcely dying in Spain or in Serbia. He was classically trained, and he knew enough Greek to have learned much from Homer, to this day the best place to learn it. Only a poet as well read as he was, a diligent student for half a lifetime who then went blind, feeling himself unfulfilled until he had written his great poem, could have stumbled on the secret. Consider only how different *Paradise Lost* now is from its first form as notes. There are four drafts of the plan of the poem in the Trinity manuscript, all of them, it appears, dating from before the Civil War.

DRAFT I

The Persons
Michael
Heavenly love
Chorus of angels
Lucifer
Adam ⎫
Eve   ⎬ with the serpent
Conscience
Death
Mutes: Labour, Sickness, Discontent,
    Ignorance (with others)
Faith
Hope
Charity

This is some kind of Morality play evidently. 'Heavenly love' is surely what we usually call the Son of God. He and Michael converse, the chorus does what such beings do, and the only action is between the serpent and our ancestors. The remaining characters are abstract: Conscience and Death with a chorus of Mutes, and then the three theological virtues. It is by no means clear that there is any Redemption or any Christ. No doubt this scheme would have been thought orthodox at the time.

DRAFT 2

The Persons
Moses
Justice, Mercy and Wisdom
Heavenly love
Hesperus the evening star
Chorus of angels
Lucifer, Adam and Eve
Conscience
Mutes: Labour, Sickness, Discontent,
    Ignorance, Fear, Death
Faith, Hope and Charity

There have been important changes, mostly making for jollity. Moses, with Justice, Mercy and Wisdom, now balances Conscience and her Mutes, with Faith, Hope and Charity, and this throws emphasis on a future for mankind. Death has become a Mute. Hesperus has an obscure part to play; the rest is as before. In Act 2 of the third draft Hesperus leads to a marriage song and 'Heavenly love' is apparently involved, but as we have not yet met Adam and Eve.

DRAFT 3

The Persons
Moses speaks the prologue, recounting how he assumed his true body, that it corrupts not because of his [being] with God in the mount declares the like of Enoch and Eliah, besides the purity of the place that certain pure winds, dews, and clouds preserve it from corruption whence he hastes to the sight of God, tells they cannot see Adam in this state of innocence by reason of their sin

Justice, Mercy and Wisdom, debating what should become of man if he fall

Chorus of angels sing a hymn of the Creation

Act 2
Heavenly Love
Evening star
Chorus sing the marriage song and describe Paradise

Act 3
Lucifer contriving Adam's ruin
Chorus fears for Adam and relates Lucifer's rebellion and fall

Act 4
Adam and Eve fallen
Conscience cites them to God's examination
Chorus bewails and tells the good Adam hath lost

Act 5
Adam and Eve, driven out of Paradise, presented by an angel with Mutes, to whom he gives their names: Labour, Grief, Hatred, Envy, War, Famine, Pestilence, Sickness, Discontent, Ignorance, Fear, Death (entered into the world). Likewise Winter, Heat, Tempest, etc.

This elaborate charade calls for music, a very large cast, and a Presbyterian audience. The point of the mystical second act is that Adam and Eve are naked, so they must be invisible; they can appear only when dressed and fallen. It appears to be planned as a kind of opera.

DRAFT 4

Adam Unparadized
The angel Gabriel, either descending or entering, showing since this globe was created his frequency as much on earth as in heaven, describes Paradise. Next the Chorus showing the reason of his coming to keep his watch in Paradise after Lucifer's rebellion by command from God, and withal expressing his desire to see, and know more concerning this excellent new creature man. The angel Gabriel as by his name signifying a prince of power tracing paradise with a more free office passes by the station of the chorus and desired by them relates what he knew of man as the creation of Eve with their love, and marriage. After this Lucifer appears after his overthrow, bemoans himself, seeks revenge on man, the Chorus prepare resistance at his

first approach, at last after discourse of enmity on either side he departs. Whereat the chorus sings of the battle, and victory in heaven against him and his accomplices as before, after the first act, was sung a hymn of the creation. Here again may appear Lucifer, relating and insulting in what he had done to the destruction of man. Man next and Eve, having by this time been seduced by the serpent, appears confusedly covered with leaves. Conscience in a shape accuses him, Justice cites him to the place whither Jehova called for him: in the meanwhile the Chorus entertains the stage, and is informed by some angel the manner of his fall: here the Chorus bewails Adam's fall. Adam then and Eve return, accuse one another, but especially Adam lays the blame to his wife, is stubborn in his offence. Justice appears, reasons with him, convinces him; the Chorus admonisheth Adam, and bids him beware by Lucifer's example of impenitence; the angel is sent to banish them out of Paradise, but before causes to pass before his eyes in shapes a mask of all the evils of this life and world; he is humbled, relents, despairs. At last appears Mercy, comforts him, promises the Messiah, then calls in Faith, Hope and Charity, instructs him, he repents, gives God the glory, submits to his penalty: the chorus briefly concludes.

This fuller scenario is still for an opera, but the word 'mask' has now appeared for the first time. There is a certain originality about it, but it is vulnerable to many arguments, and *Paradise Lost*, as Milton wrote it, is a more powerful construction altogether. Still, certain elements from these drafts, particularly from this last one, do reappear in the poem he wrote: I will leave the reader the pleasure of observing which ones. This is the chief reason for reprinting these rather pathetic and unusable drafts here.

He had read his classics and knew his Bible with the banal commentaries; Spenser was deep in him; he had read *Adamus Exsul* by Grotius (1601) and *L'Adamo* by Andreini (1613); he knew Tasso's *Seven Days of Creation* (1607) and he never got Du Bartas out of his system: but none of this, not even the sum of it, is at all equivalent to *Paradise Lost*. The Italian anologies are innumerable but not close. Even his English was by this time an amalgam which was unique. The best book about his language, so far as I know, is still F. T. Prince's *The Italian Element in Milton's Verse* (1954), and the standard commentary is still Alastair Fowler's (1971) (which does, however, exhibit some alarming eccentricities).

CHAPTER ELEVEN

THE GREAT POEM

EDWARD REMEMBERED that when he was a boy he had heard at least one bit of *Paradise Lost* recited before his uncle went blind, if we are to take 'twenty years ago' literally, and when the plan of the vast structure was as we saw it in the last chapter. In this version it was part of a prologue spoken by Satan. The speech he refers to occurs now near the beginning of Book 4, where Satan, who has been described in the first thirty-one lines of the book, addresses the sun. His speech is indeed like the stiff classic verse of a tragedy, though *Paradise Lost* is hardly that unless Adam is its hero: his sin is no mere tragic fault, and he is inactive compared to Satan. Was the play Satan's tragedy? Maybe Satan was based, as scholars suggest, on the wicked heroes or anti-heroes in the tragedies of Christopher Marlowe. Scholars have further conjectured that Milton was copying a prologue of Aeschylus, from the *Prometheus*, but the two have nothing serious in common.

Milton grew more interested in Satan as he worked first on his unfinished tragedy and at last on his epic: there is no place for a prologue by him in any of the four drafts, but it is in this fourth book of *Paradise Lost* that the drafts come most to life, so the prologue to the sun probably represents another intermediate stage. The stiffness and formality of the speech does seem earlier in technique than the first books of *Paradise Lost* as we now have them. The prologue to *Samson* is also quite different: it is written in a vernacular that only the verse formalizes, and is modelled on the manner of Sophocles in *Oedipus at Colonus*, or Euripides (*Phoenissae*, 834–5). This earlier piece of epic sounds like the opening not so much of a tragedy as of a morality play.

> O thou that with surpassing glory crowned,
> Look'st from thy sole dominion like the God

> Of this new world; at whose sight all the stars
> Hide their diminished heads; to thee I call,
> But with no friendly voice, and add thy name
> O sun, to tell thee how I hate thy beams
> That bring to my remembrance from what state
> I fell, how glorious once above thy sphere;
> Till pride and worse ambition threw me down
> Warring in heaven against heaven's matchless king . . .

It is all one sentence, as usual with Milton: in fact the sentence is not quite over where Edward's memory breaks off. It must always have been a speech intended for Satan; it would fit no other character. This is the book that introduces the innocent sleep of Adam and Eve, and then the war between angel and devil: it also introduces the puzzling character Heavenly Love, which the drafts had mentioned. 'Here Love his golden shafts employs, here lights/His constant lamp, and waves his purple wings . . .' (763–4); what is more, a few lines earlier, 'heavenly choirs the hymenean sung', as in Act 2 of draft 3, and Adam discusses the songs of angels in the night with Eve (677–88): 'Millions of spiritual creatures walk the earth'. The entire love scene is firmly embedded in the classics, as Hesperus and the Hymeneal suggest, and Pan, Silvanus and Faunus (707–8) confirm. The fact that 'the unwiser son/Of Japhet' has a biblical sound does not contradict this, or remove him from Hermes, Jove and Pandora, because Japhet is Iapetos and we are speaking of Epimetheus: the identification was normal at the time. It is interesting that Milton feels it necessary to mention the kind of entertainment to which his operatic entertainment had veered: 'court amour,/Mixed dance, or wanton mask, or midnight ball/Or serenade,' all of which he repudiates with scorn. Yet they are present somewhere in the origins of this scene and this book. However that may be,

> These lulled by nightingales embracing slept,
> And on their naked limbs the flowery roof
> Showered roses, which the morn repaired. Sleep on
> Blest pair; and O yet happiest if ye seek
> No happier state, and know to know no more.   (771–5)

It is not possible for a biographer to unpick the labyrinthine tracks of Milton's mind; we do not even have encyclopaedic access to the queer things he knew, such as the names of angels, which are not always biblical. A lot of his reading has only been roughly mapped out, and even his gardening is a curious mixture of real flowers, like the irises of varied colours, and ones that come from other poets. When he says 'on either side/Acanthus, and each odorous bushy shrub/Fenced up the verdant wall' (695–7) we do not really know how exact he felt he was being, and so the commentators thrash about in vain. But I do not think there is any doubt that the central scene in this book came early in the long development of the poem; in its way it is the centre of the epic and from it other things come. It was Milton's central arcanum and his inner shrine.

In the third book of *Paradise Lost* Milton has the idea of tracing Satan's journey through the universe. Not only was space unexplored and scarcely mapped, but various conflicting ideas buzzed about in people's heads, nor was a classical authority like Manilius, whom Milton taught his unhappy pupils, of much practical use. The universe is thought of as having a hard skin or shell.

> . . . he then surveyed
> Hell and the gulf between, and Satan there
> Coasting the wall of heaven on this side night
> In the dun air sublime, and ready now
> To stoop with wearied wings, and willing feet,
> On the bare outside of this world, that seemed
> Firm land imbosomed without firmament,
> Uncertain which, in ocean or in air. . . .   (69–76)

This is a bold attack on the problem certainly, but it is not easy to understand, perhaps because Chaos was by definition a confusion. The lines that follow begin to make a joke of a sardonic kind, but let us concentrate on Satan's journey:

> Mean while upon the firm opacous globe
> Of this round world, whose first convex divides
> The luminous inferior orbs, enclosed
> From Chaos and the inroad of darkness old,
> Satan alighted walks: a globe far off
> It seemed, now seems a boundless continent . . .   (418–23)

The globe is surrounded by 'Chaos blustering round, inclement sky'. The place, 'this windy sea of land', is now uninhabited but, after the

Fall 'up hither' will flow the waste of the world, to form Limbo. To confuse things further, Satan is like a vulture flying over the Tartar wastes who lights on the plains 'Of Sericana, where Chineses drive/ With sails and wind their cany wagons light'. This pleasing reversal recalls his history of Russia: the Russians had got to the borders of China overland only in Milton's lifetime. From the abortions, monsters and unsatisfied souls Milton has put in his obscurely placed wilderness he goes on to discuss the inhabitants of the moon who, he reckons, are translated saints or middle spirits. He is Dantesque but more ridiculous than Dante, because the attempt to map the universe is ridiculous. He takes the opportunity to set about friars and pilgrims: Dante, if he had chosen, would have been far more savage, but not somehow so provincial. A violent crosswind blows them all away 'into the devious air', and into the Paradise of Fools 'o'er the backside of the world far off'. Satan then sees a staircase leading to Heaven (510) just above the site of Paradise (527). He flies down into the 'first region' (562) through the heavens of happy isles (567) to come 'By centre, or eccentric, hard to tell,/Or longitude' (575–6) to land at the end of a long, sleepy sentence not untypical of dictated epic verse.

> . . . where the great luminary
> Aloof the vulgar constellations thick,
> That from his lordly eye keep distance due,
> Dispenses light from far; they as they move
> Their starry dance in numbers that compute
> Days, months, and years, towards his all-cheering lamp
> Turn swift their various motions, or are turned
> By his magnetic beam, that gently warms
> The universe, and to each inward part
> With gentle penetration, shoots unseen,
> Invisible virtue even to the deep:
> So wondrously was set his station bright.   (576–87)

(I have a little emended lines 585–6, where I conceive that someone taking dictation, or the poet himself giving it, had nodded off and made unmetrical nonsense.) The whole conception here is in fact quite clear again, and even the devil finds his feet. Satan is a heroic figure, rather than grotesque as in Dante. This is because Dante, who mocks him and renders him monstrous with the terrifying trumpet-

call of the devil's fart, really believes in him but Milton does not.
Milton's Satan is a fiction and, to sustain an epic poem, must be
heroic and terrible. That is the main difference between the two great
poets, and the main force pushing *Paradise Lost* in the direction in
which it goes. That is why we begin in Hell and spend such a long
time in the early books in the not very entertaining company of Hell's
inhabitants. This poem is in a certain sense sublime, and grotesque
only in the allegorical characters, left over from the masque of the
mutes, Sin and Death. We must look at them in their context: but in
order to do that we must look at the entire scheme or plot as it turned
out.

We should begin by stressing, as Dennis said, that Poetry being an
art must have rules but that Genius may break them: and this will be
found true of Milton's *Paradise Lost* whichever way we look at it. At
the centre of this perception lies another, stated in three words:
'Milton renew'd Eden'.

The first, lesser, question is why in its second edition *Paradise Lost*
has twelve books and not ten. The uncertainty Milton felt about the
end of his poem suggests that the two last or, as they are now, the
four last books had swollen in composition and were the last to be
written. The other small additions confirm this. In Book 1, lines
504–5 are the merest adjustment, a small revision. In Book 8, lines
1–4, he adds three lines to make a pause; in Book 11, lines 485–7 he
adds some splendid plagues to a list already long, and in lines 551–2
he adds a line of resignation. All these are minor adjustments. Only
in Book 5, lines 636–9, is there a substantial improvement as he adds
a few lovely new lines.

> On flowers reposed, and with fresh flowerets crowned,
> They eat, they drink, and in communion sweet
> Quaff immortality and joy . . .

Of course, ten is the classical number of books, dear to Milton no
doubt because of Virgil's *Eclogues* and Luther's admission of only ten
epistles of Paul as canonical. Equally, twelve books is the number in
the *Aeneid*, and Milton's last two in the first edition were terribly
swollen, with 2,293 and 1,550 lines, where no other book had many
more than a thousand and most had less. The epic traced Satan's
victory, so that the silly hopes of Book 1 are apparently fulfilled.

Milton began, it seems, in packets of about fourteen lines, the length of a sonnet, but his stride soon lengthened victoriously. The extent of the last two books does not in any degree alter their content or the impetus of the whole work; the very short alterations were only to insert little connecting passages of a few lines.

The first book begins austerely by setting out the theme and mingling Milton's two worlds of classical imagination ('the Aonian mount') and of the Bible ('Oreb' and 'Sinai'), but in fact the worlds are already silently mingled in 'that shepherd, who first taught ...', which sounds like Hesiod but means Moses. The invocation to the Spirit is followed by the fall of the angels, whom God

> Hurled headlong flaming from the ethereal sky
> With hideous ruin and combustion down
> To bottomless perdition, there to dwell
> In adamantine chains and penal fire ...

Satan soon spots his friend Beelzebub, 'weltering by his side', and breaks the 'horrid silence'. It is a curious fact that this bit of Satan's speech inspired Tennyson.

> What though the field be lost?
> All is not lost; the unconquerable will,
> And study of revenge, immortal hate,
> And courage never to submit or yield ...

Behind both lies the Ulysses of Dante perhaps. Beelzebub answers in a lengthy harangue and Satan continues. We are told about his enormous bulk, a tale embellished with alarming anecdotes. Heaven has left him free to damn himself still further (210–20), which he does with a clear head. 'The mind is its own place, and in itself/Can make a heaven of hell, a hell of heaven.' Beelzebub encourages him to move shorewards, and Milton describes Satan's shield as being like the moon seen through Galileo's telescope. Another of Milton's Italian memories can be found in the beautiful image, 'Thick as autumnal leaves that strew the brooks/In Vallombrosa, where the Etrurian shades/High overarched imbower ...' (302–4). Satan now addresses his troops, who respond (331). Among splendidly well-chosen metaphors a line or two (371–2) suggests Milton's sympathies are not where they ought to be: 'the image of a brute, adorned/With gay religions full of pomp and gold', a line that reminds me of '*gli ornamenti barbarichi e le pompe*'. The Muse is invoked to tell us the names of the devils: 'first Moloch' (there are a dozen, but thirteen if you count Beelzebub), Chemos or Peor, then Baalim and Ashtaroth, for spirits (these gods or devils) can change sex as often as they choose. Then comes Astarte, then Thammuz who has the loveliest lines of all:

> Whose annual wound in Lebanon allured
> The Syrian damsels to lament his fate
> In amorous ditties all a summer's day,
> While smooth Adonis from his native rock
> Ran purple to the sea, supposed with blood
> Of Thammuz yearly wounded: the love-tale
> Infected Sion's daughters with like heat,
> Whose wanton passions in the sacred porch
> Ezekiel saw . . .
>
> (447–55)

The parade continues until it turns, after all its exquisite and stream-like wanderings among Greek and Latin and British gods and Cabbalism, into a full regimental review, with a standard like a meteor (537) and 'sonorous metal blowing martial sounds', and an antique band of flutes and recorders. Satan reviews the troops. Milton tries to cheer up the parade with references to more recent romance heroes, and those who 'jousted in Aspramont or Montalban' and the day 'when Charlemain with all his peerage fell/By Fontarabbia'. No one knows of this day, which sounds like a confusion or a very obscure poem. It cannot be an intended insult to Charles II, who went to Fuenterrabia in 1659, because no one noticed it was, just as no one but the idiot censor noticed that an eclipse perplexing monarchs (597–9) could be anti-monarchic. Satan at last addresses his troops (622), and Mammon opens a mine in a volcano, so that 'a fabric huge/ Rose like an exhalation' (710–11). It is a temple with Doric pillars, frieze and architrave, bronze doors and a dome and thousands of lamps. Hephaistos (here called Mulciber) built it, though to me it sounds exactly like St Peter's at Rome with the lamps that Edward Lear recorded. Hephaistos was

> thrown by angry Jove
> Sheer o'er the crystal battlements; from morn

To noon he fell, from noon to dewy eve,
A summer's day; and with the setting sun
Dropped from the zenith like a falling star,
On Lemnos the Aegaean isle . . .   (741–6)

This is so close to the *Iliad* it could be called a translation, so Milton assures us that the account is 'erring'. The place is named Pandae-monium and Satan and his peers summon a parliament there. In 1642 Henry More had written in a poem, 'wiser men/May name that fort, Pandaemoniothen' (Fowler, *Oxford Book of Seventeenth Century Verse*). It is like a great bee-hive. With some beautiful lines about fairy visions the book is suddenly over. Perhaps the most surprising thing in it is the relaxation of its grim beginnings into a variety that I still find surprising after many rereadings. One is also surprised by the number of jokes which, it gradually becomes evident, Milton has put in for fun.

Yet the abundance of Book 1, which is a kind of shop window of amazing effects for the whole epic, does raise a question about the momentum of this kind of poetry. Milton is more variegated than any of his models, even Homer. But the curious thing is that all the most excellent pieces of verse, the fall of Mulciber and the pantomime transformation scene at the end, Vallombrosa, Thammuz and the Tennysonian courage of Satan, are, so to speak, against or aside from the main current of the narrative. That may be pursued by reading the brief prose paragraphs at the head of each book, the Arguments, but a poem is more than its argument, and this poem very much more. Whether the passages I have mentioned, most of which are similes, are a remote inheritance from the Homeric metaphor or simile is a question to which the answer 'yes' has only a probable and uncertain quality. At the same time the impetus of the epic itself does in the end take over, as it should, rather like a stream that surmounts all obstacles.

The second book begins with a wonderful formality:

High on a throne of a royal state, which far
Outshone the wealth of Ormus and of Ind,
Or where the gorgeous East with richest hand
Showers on her kings barbaric pearl and gold,

> Satan exalted sat, by merit raised
> To that bad eminence . . .

The discussion between the chief devils of the council may very likely be based on the style of the State Council at which Milton had sat. Milton's is not a simple mind, however; he would have learned from the long debates in Homer, where the speeches convey the speaker's character, though character is scarcely Milton's chief concern in *Paradise Lost*. Satan begins (11–42) with an invitation to discussion, and 'Moloch, sceptred king' replies: his Homeric title does epic wonders for him, though the brief account of him that follows is from another, more modern style and world: 'My sentence is for open war: of wiles,/More unexpert, I boast not . . .' He wants to storm Heaven, 'armed with hell flames and fury', and makes a fine cannonade of a speech in which one can hear and feel the artillery that Milton probably never heard unless as a distant thudding. Here it is 'mixed with Tartarean sulphur, and strange fire'. He refers to the lake of Hell now not as a thing of fire out of Dante, but a kind of Lethe: 'if the sleepy drench/Of that forgetful lake benumb not still'. It is as if Lethe had mingled into Phlegethon. 'He ended frowning', and Belial, with no Homeric epithet but 'in act more graceful and humane', answers him. This devil 'taketh the form of a beautiful angel . . . he speaketh fair' as early as 1584, and the opposition of the two characters may reflect an argument in Tasso. His speech is a long one (119–225), and he appears to know *Hamlet* (145f.), but the voice is always Milton's, a style so personal, so inimitable, that it has never been successfully copied or parodied.

Mammon (229–83) answers and gains a great growl of applause from the devils that no one but Satan himself with his trumpets has yet aroused. Milton was a famous roller of the letter 'r'.

> such murmur filled
> The assembly, as when hollow rocks retain
> The sound of blustering winds, which all night long
> Had roused the sea, now with hoarse cadence lull
> Seafaring men o'erwatched . . .   (284–8)

The debate is tending towards peace, so at this stage Satan's second in command, Beelzebub, gets to his feet,

> Majestic though in ruin: sage he stood
> With Atlantean shoulders fit to bear
> The weight of mightiest monarchies; his look
> Drew audience and attention still as night
> Or summer's noontide air . . .   (305–9)

Satan is the inspirer of most of Beelzebub's measured speech (310–78) which suggests Paradise as an easier project: 'There is a place . . . another world, the happy seat/Of some new race . . .' The form of introducing Paradise is an oddly persistent way of telling a story which Milton takes from Virgil and captures at once the excitement and the epic quality of the revelation. But the substance of his plan is

> to confound the race
> Of mankind in one root, and earth with hell
> To mingle and involve, done all to spite
> The great creator . . .   (382–5)

The root, the botanic metaphor he uses, runs throughout *Paradise Lost*, and is a piece of cargo Milton has taken on from the reformers: under it lurks the dogma of the original sin of mankind and how it was transmitted. The dogma has had many different explanations, and the far-reaching idea of redemption was swiftly tied to it, begetting many knotty arguments ever since the time of Christ. The original sin idea goes back, of course, to the Book of Genesis or earlier. In one of the apocryphal books of the Bible it is transformed to 'We have all been the Adam of our own souls,' but that solution was not within Milton's kind of orthodoxy, and in sticking to the sense of natural roots and what grew from them he appealed at once to a readership battered into submission by preachers. Here Beelzebub goes on speaking (390–416) and offers hope to the devils, paving the way for sending out Satan to explore.

> . . . we may chance
> Re-enter heaven; or else in some mild zone
> Dwell not unvisited of heaven's fair light
> Secure, and at the brightening orient beam
> Purge off this gloom; the soft delicious air,
> To heal the scar of these corrosive fires
> Shall breathe her balm. . . .   (396–402)

The devils worry over this audacious expedition, but Satan speaks (430–66) and at least in a metaphor we are granted some relief from hellishness: birds twitter for a moment (494) and herds bleat. The parliament breaks up with a procession of peers (507) and Satan as emperor, whom 'A globe of fiery seraphim enclosed/With bright emblazonry, and horrent arms' (512–13) until he addresses himself alone to his expedition. As Satan makes off on his business the devils disport themselves; Homer and Josephus and Greek mythology offer us their entertainment; the sixth form (as it were) of the devils play music and discuss philosophy (546–69), while the adventurous explore the classical Underworld with its rivers and the Serbonian bog (592), which to Milton is as mythic and antique as the rest, although it was a real place in Egypt. 'Damiata and Mount Casius old' are famous in Italian romantic epics, though they were real, of course, but then the Styx and the Acheron, which Homer treats as mythic, were real Greek rivers. The idea (600) that devils are sent to this region for a freeze between roastings is a queer one, and must be older than our poet, but where did he get it? His entire geography of Hell is as visual as a wall painting, even to the ford 'Medusa with Gorgonian terror guards' (611).

> . . . through many a dark and dreary vale
> They passed, and many a region dolorous,
> O'er many a frozen, many a fiery alp,
> Rocks, caves, lakes, fens, bogs, dens, and shades of death,
> A universe of death . . .   (618–22)

The summary is brilliant but the long dangling sentence muses on (614–28), to end with 'Gorgons and Hydras, and Chimeras dire'.

Satan explores as human explorers do, and he comes to the gate of Hell, where the guards are Sin and Death. Milton refers us to Scylla, and the 'night-hag' who goes with Lapland witches, but Sin and Death are a sufficiently nasty couple, and the conflict of Sin with Satan is as pleasantly horrible as any ghost story. The revelation of identities is the point of all this, and it is delayed. Sin is the daughter of Satan and mother of Death, as Basil maintained in a commentary on Genesis which Milton seems to have read. Andreini in his *L'Adamo* and old Phineas Fletcher in *The Purple Island* make similar attempts at genealogy. Here the dialogue, being inherently absurd, seems to

me by turns feeble and disgusting. Still, in some sense it carries the
story on, though Sin describing how she gave birth to Death is by no
means canonical. There must have been an appetite for these gruesome allegories (681–870). Satan nastily cajoles her, she as nastily
unlocks the gate for him.

> Illimitable ocean without bound,
> Without dimension, where length, breadth, and highth
> And time and place are lost; where eldest Night
> And Chaos, ancestors of Nature, hold
> Eternal anarchy, amidst the noise
> Of endless wars, and by confusion stand. . . .   (892–7)

Yet the journey of Satan through the waste from this point to the
throne of Chaos is very capably described and full of interest of one
kind or another; he is, we are told, like a gryphon in pursuit of an
Arimaspian, which will mean more to readers of Herodotus than it
does to the man in the street. Chaos and Night have a string of
mythical and abstract attendants (960–67) who stand about while he
gets directions and 'springs upward like a pyramid of fire'. Death and
Sin help him with the engineering of a bridge from Hell to this world,
until far away (1047) he sees Heaven, 'With opal towers and battlements adorned/Of living sapphire, once his native seat', and 'fast by
hanging in a golden chain' he sees the earth. It may or may not rotate,
but it must somehow be balanced and it does not seem to occur to
Milton that it could move around the sun.

He begins again at the opening of his third book with an invocation
addressed to God as Light, which I have already noticed. He is
relieved, as the reader is, that the long treatment of Hell and the
devils is over, and Wisdom may displace chaos. The heavenly Muse
taught him 'to venture down/The dark descent, and up to reascend'.
Does this refer to the fable of Orpheus? Or to something in his
personal and inner life (as I suspect) or in Neoplatonic religion? He
revisits the Light but light does not revisit his eyes (21–3). Still, he
wanders wherever the Muses haunt, and chiefly Sion, and remembers
Homer and Tiresias,

> Then feed on thoughts, that voluntary move
> Harmonious numbers; as the wakeful bird

> Sings darkling, and in shadiest covert hid
> Tunes her nocturnal note.

To him, of course, the nightingale is a familiar bird, at Horton or at Hammersmith, let alone in Italy. The remarkable introduction to this book ends (55) and God and the Son converse. Milton did believe in God, but not in the Son, whom he would wish to translate into other terms, as he does in the first few lines of this book. For that reason, if for no other, Milton's Son is somewhat stilted as an epic character. God explains human freedom, taking the Jesuit or common-sense view as against the Dominican view of the nature of divine foreknowledge of free decisions (112–19) and deliberately setting aside Calvinist predestination. These theological conundrums ignored, we may proceed; and the angels are cheered by ambrosial fragrance and new joy while the Son shows 'love without end, and without measure grace'. The Son wonders whether God's plan for the consequences of the Fall is not too drastic, but he is told 'man shall not quite be lost, but saved who will' (173) and conscience can be God's umpire (195). But who is to pay 'the rigid satisfaction, death for death'? This line (212) must be one of the most terrible Milton ever wrote: he takes for granted that an absolute justice must govern the repair of mankind. He may secretly reject this idea, but even in *De Doctrina* he refers to 'repayment of the required price', and theological textbooks would agree with him. At this point Heaven is silent but the Son makes his offer.

> . . . Thou at the sight
> Pleased, out of heaven shalt look down and smile,
> While by thee raised I ruin all my foes . . .   (256–8)

God agrees, saying 'in thee/As from a second root shall be restored,/ As many as are restored', and goes on to foretell the Last Judgement, new Heaven and new earth. At this the angels (344) make loud, jubilant noises. One cannot but recommend Empson's book, *Milton's God*, on the theological difficulties of all this: I doubt whether it has ever been fully and convincingly answered. But it is better at the moment to read on about the angels.

> . . . down they cast
> Their crowns inwove with amarant and gold,

Immortal amarant, a flower which once
In Paradise, fast by the tree of life
Began to bloom, but soon for man's offence
To heavn removed where first it grew, there grows,
And flowers aloft shading the fount of life ...   (351–7)

The angels sing hymns to the Trinity (372–415) of great beauty
and traditional argument: but we must return to Satan, the space
explorer, and the middle lands or limbos that Milton partly invents,
partly picks up here or there and partly satirizes (474–5). In the
middle of all this (481–3) come the ten spheres – seven planetary,
the eighth holding the 'fixed' stars – then the crystal sphere, the last
or outermost 'that first moved'. These spheres were an attempt
to explain how the universe could move in the odd way it seemed to
move, by something like clockwork. The theory is not worth the
space it would take to explain it here, and Milton scarcely notices the
theory. It grew more and more complicated as new features were
incorporated in the model to account for newly observed phenomena,
until it fell out of use at last in about 1600. Milton still speaks of
alchemists with respect (600–605).

... by their powerful art they bind
Volatile Hermes, and call up unbound
In various shapes old Proteus from the sea,
Drained through a limbeck to his native form.

As he points out, he is describing a sort of wonderland. Satan sees an
angel, 'the same whom John saw also in the sun', who turns out to be
the archangel Uriel (648). Satan disguises himself as 'a stripling
Cherub' and asks for directions, which Uriel delivers at great length.
Then Satan 'throws his steep flight in many an airy wheel', and lands
on a mountain called Niphates.

In Book 4, Satan arrives on earth and gives his great address to the
sun (32–113). He is still a prey to passions, and Uriel keeps an eye on
him, observing his fierce gestures and 'mad demeanour'. Eden is
described (132f.) and the smell of fruit like the smell of spices past
Mozambique: 'and many a league/Cheered with the grateful smell old
Ocean smiles'. Satan cannot see a near way in so he jumps the wall
and sits 'like a cormorant' (196) on top of the highest, tallest tree, the
Tree of Life. Milton then pretends to give his Paradise a precise

location, compromising between a number of theories on the subject (209–16), and noting the trees of Life and of Knowledge. A big river runs southwards, to disappear underground then spring up to water the garden. The rivers are a bit hard to grasp, but Milton is concerned

> How from that sapphire fount the crisped brooks
> Rolling on orient pearl and sands of gold,
> With mazy error under pendant shades
> Ran nectar, visiting each plant, and fed
> Flowers worthy of Paradise . . .   (237–41)
> Groves whose rich trees wept odorous gums and balm,
> Others whose fruit burnished with golden rind
> Hung amiable, Hesperian fables true,
> If true, here only . . .   (248–51)

There are flocks, wild flowers, vines and waterfalls falling into lakes; there are birds and airs, 'while universal Pan/Knit with the Graces and the Hours in dance/Led on the eternal spring'. Once started, the store of classical allusion comes pouring out, Proserpine and Ceres, Daphne by the Orontes, the Castalian spring and, finally, a wondrous amalgam,

> . . . that Nyseian isle
> Girt with the river Triton, where old Cham,
> Whom Gentiles Ammon call and Libyan Jove,
> His Amalthea and her florid son
> Young Bacchus . . .   (275–9)

Here Milton introduces Adam and Eve. He is a little over-careful to make sure we take them seriously in every way. Since they are naked, Adam has shoulder-length hair, and Eve's hair is long enough to veil her beauties, but only down to the waist: it is important that they are unashamed. They are hand in hand, 'the loveliest pair/That ever since in love's embraces met', playing as lovers do, while all the animals frisk around them. 'The unwieldy elephant/To make them mirth used all his might, and wreathed/His lithe proboscis', and the stars 'that usher evening rose'. Whatever was once to be said by the evening star, Satan now makes a grumbly speech (358–92), like that of a demon king announcing his plans. Adam (411–39) repeats God's orders to Eve, and Eve (440–91) remembers her idyllic creation. Adam and Eve sleep like Jupiter and Juno (499ff.), and Satan makes another envious monologue

(505–35). Meanwhile at the only (eastern) gate of Paradise Uriel comes to report to Gabriel and his squad of angels.

> Now came still evening on, and twilight grey
> Had in her sober livery all things clad . . .   (598–9)

The ten lines that follow this are among the most exquisite that even Milton ever composed. The birds go to sleep,

> . . . all but the wakeful nightingale;
> She all night long her amorous descant sung;
> Silence was pleased: now glowed the firmament . . .   (602–4)

Adam and Eve retire, he explains the stars, and at last they lie together. Beetles and worms sensibly keep off (704–5) while Adam and Eve make love. The angels on night duty (780) search the garden and find the devil in the form of a toad trying to invade Eve's dreams, so they bring him to Gabriel. The encounter might have ended in a battle, but it does not. All this has lasted 239 lines, and unless tactics require them it is hard to see what purpose they serve. It is not just the beauty and innocence of Adam and Eve that have reassured us of their security; it is their normality. They are humans, like us, and all the mythical creatures fade a little into the shadows. Milton adores them and is enthusiastic about their coupling. But he also manifestly enjoys the animals in Paradise, the fruit trees and the water everywhere. His only rival in this is his friend Andrew Marvell.

In Book 5 Adam and Eve are warned by Raphael, who explains to them the history of the devil. But the book begins in an idyll once again.

> Now Morn her rosy steps in the eastern clime
> Advancing, sowed the earth with orient pearl . . .

Adam wakes from his usual sleep, 'airy light from pure digestion bred', to hear the dawn chorus, but finds Eve distressed. He speaks to her as mildly as Zephyrus would to Flora, and the garden is as enticing as ever. She then recounts her tempting dream about the Tree of Knowledge. He tries to explain dreams (95–108), and she drops a tear or two and cheers up. They say their prayers 'in various style' and extempore (153–208). The prayer is mostly about nature, and Adam is charming on the subject; he includes the spheres and fixed stars, the four elements and heaven knows what else. As they start their morning's work, training and perhaps pruning the fruit trees and the vine, God calls to Raphael, 'the sociable spirit, that deigned/To travel with Tobias' and secure his marriage. Raphael is to warn Adam, so that his sin, if he commits it, will be the worse. Raphael hastens to Paradise (260–65), which is like a tiny spot in the moon seen by Galileo or like the first view of a Greek island. To the birds he appears to be a phoenix,

> as that sole bird
> When to enshrine his relics in the sun's
> Bright temple, to Aegyptian Thebes he flies.   (272–4)

Arriving, he returns to his usual shape of a six-winged seraph. 'Like Maia's son he stood' (285) is surely Shakespearian, like the phoenix. So we come into the garden at noon, 'a wilderness of sweets' (294). Adam calls Eve and they prepare to entertain Raphael to a meal so arcane as to be mystical. It appears to include grape juice and rhubarb: 'and from sweet kernels pressed/She tempers dulcet creams' (346–7). It is all much better than long processions of horses and 'grooms besmeared with gold'. Eve is like one of the goddesses that Paris chose between; their home is like Pomona's cave, with a turf table and mossy seats. The entertainment reminds one of what Philemon and Baucis offered the gods in Ovid's *Metamorphoses*. A lecture from the angel on the spiritual and the physical interrupts this, however, until cheerfulness returns. They then (461) get down to serious talk: Raphael is a Neoplatonist and expounds how all things come from God and return to God (469–505). At Adam's request he explains free obedience. Adam is more pleased than when 'cherubic songs by night from neighbouring hills/Aerial music send ...' (547–8). Raphael, being pressed, now tells Adam and Eve all about the mysterious life of the angels (563–907) and their mystical dances, 'regular/Then most, when most irregular they seem' (623–4), and the whole leisurely tale of the fall of Lucifer, which is not over when the book ends. This story is elaborately planned, and is brought in here because there was no one before Adam and Eve who did not already know it. The *Odyssey* and the *Aeneid* both contain these long backward perspectives. Whether this device is perfectly successful the reader of *Paradise Lost* must judge. It does add a touch of Homeric confusion, like a speech by ancient Nestor.

Book 6 carries straight on to the end of the war. Milton is

determined that it shall seem no light matter, no brief episode, no cataclysmic, instantaneous event. It is in this book that the devil invents artillery and the angels, surprised at the time, reply by throwing mountains at them. This farce is Spenserian. The book begins with a pretty dawn, an imitation of dawn in Heaven, perhaps, 'within the mount of God', but there are then marches as in the real world, though on the whole the war is a complete nonsense, freakishly imagined by a man with no experience of war who seeks to entertain with creatures in whom he does not believe, any more than we do. The saints fight in a 'cubic phalanx', which is a Greek military formation said to have been used by Cromwell (399). Satan's gun-powder (475–95) is a better moment. It was a device of literature in Ariosto, Daniel, Valvasone and probably many others: Shakespeare alludes to it. Milton enlivens his silly scene with jokes (607–29). All the same, as light conversation it is brilliant; it is perhaps in this book that Milton comes closest to Cowley.

Here the figure of Satan confirms the vivid impression he has already made of being a super-hero, so heroic that he has few other characteristics: he is taller, grander and more powerful than Achilles, Odysseus and Agamemnon combined: this unhappy legacy of the heroic ethos misunderstood vitiates the literary epic from Virgil onwards. Nevertheless, virtues may be found in the book's digres-sions, and in the pastoral and idyllic treatment of Eden, which are clearly by the writer of *Lycidas*. One must remember that Milton in Italy had already connected greatness with the heroic dimension, and was intent at that time on chronicling King Arthur's wars in the Underworld. Satan is the epic hero misconceived and exaggerated. In a similar way, the God of Milton is Zeus exalted to a super-god and, by being personally responsible for everything that happens, rather like the Zeus of Cleanthes in his prayer, becomes in a sense satanic.

Book 7 opens with the invocation of Urania, the heavenly muse, sister of Holy Wisdom. 'Half yet remains unsung' of Raphael's instruction (21) but the second half is earthly.

> More safe I sing with mortal voice, unchanged
> To hoarse or mute, though fallen on evil days,
> On evil days though fallen, and evil tongues;
> In darkness, and with dangers compassed round,

> And solitude; yet not alone, while thou
> Visit'st my slumbers nightly, or when morn
> Purples the east: still govern thou my song,
> Urania, and fit audience find, though few.

He wants to be protected from 'Bacchus and his revellers', that is from rhapsodic or dithyrambic poetry which apparently he has always, or at least since *Comus*, felt to be a temptation (32–9). If this inhibition prevented him from being an English Virgil, then it is a great pity. Adam enquires about the Creation and about the birth 'of Nature from the unapparent deep', which carries an overtone of genuine mystery (84–108). Raphael agrees to instruct him within limits (120–24), and begins by reciting God's speech (139) on Creation: 'necessity and chance/Approach not me, and what I will is fate' (172–3). In these words it is possible that Milton actually recalls the paradoxical sublimities of the hymn of Cleanthes, which so impressed Paul, though Fowler thinks that this speech of God is intended to contradict what Satan says in Hell (1, 116–17). The account of Creation then unfolds, with a procession that includes some winged chariots kept in an armoury between two bronze mountains (Zech. 6: 1) for just such occasions. The Word (217) calms the waves of the abyss outside Heaven, rides out into chaos, and takes the golden compasses (Prov. 8: 27), which Blake found here but Milton found in the Bible, and so sets limits to the world.

> . . . darkness profound
> Covered the abyss; but on the watery calm
> His brooding wings the spirit of God outspread,
> And vital virtue infused . . .   (233–6)

Creation proceeds with the same steady and thrilling solemnity. Milton follows Genesis quite closely, and the result (contrary to what one might expect) is wonderful, 'both when first evening was, and when first morn'. The world is built in a crystalline circumfluent ocean, mountains and land appear and the rivers find their places. Grass, fruit and sweet smells (2 Esd. 6: 44), and 'the corny reed' follow.

> and the humble shrub,
> And bush with frizzled hair implicit: last
> Rose as in dance the stately trees, and spread

Their branches hung with copious fruit; or gemmed
Their blossoms: with high woods the hills were crowned,
With tufts the valleys and each fountain side,
With borders long the rivers. . . .   (322–8)

It is a place fit for the gods; there is no rain, for mist sees to the watering and God created all plants and flowers before they came up: a question that had puzzled Sir Thomas Browne. God then creates the lights, first the sun, then

Hither as to their fountain other stars
Repairing, in their golden urns draw light,   (364–5)
                    . . . the grey
Dawn, and the Pleiades before him danced
Shedding sweet influence . . .   (373–5)

So, following Genesis, the Creation unrolls, and its abundance is enthralling. The sea is filled with fish and the birds go soaring away, 'with clang despised the ground' (422),

the swan with arched neck
Between her white wings mantling proudly, rows
Her state with oary feet . . .   (438–40)

The most surprising thing about Milton's version of the Creation is not the ingenuity of turns of phrase like the swan (as a state barge) but the discipline of the whole performance. There are no digressions, not even for the earth as a seat of gods, and he lingers too long over nothing. Only when man is to be created does God speak (519). It is curious that he refers to Sin and her black attendant Death (546–7) as if the grotesque scene in Book 2 had not yet been elaborated. If this formal set-piece of the Creation came early in the composition of *Paradise Lost*, which would explain its central position, then it was a sparkling beginning. Milton lingers a little as Heaven celebrates the new created world. On the seventh day, the Sabbath, he makes it clear (594) that God and the angels were not bound by any Presbyterian rules of sabbatarianism: the music in heaven is baroque and the incense cloudlike (595–600).

Book 8 is the last of Raphael's visitation, but in the first edition Books 7 and 8 were a single book; a brief transition or pause was added in the second. Adam wants to know more about astronomy and such matters, so Eve goes out because she would sooner hear it all from Adam than from their visitor (50–57). Raphael is doubtful about the knowledge Adam is asking for, and mordant about cycles and epicycles, substitutes Copernican theory. Milton is determined to discuss astronomical theory in verse, and this is where he does it: better than Manilius, one may consider. Adam (180) is pleased with his explanation; he sees that daily life and not pure scientific progress is his vocation. But Raphael missed the sixth day of creation and asks Adam about that: Adam does his best (250ff.). His account of his first experiences is curiously beautiful. He meets God who gives him Paradise, and the animals are paraded for him. Adam feels lonely all the same.

> What call'st thou solitude, is not the earth
> With various living creatures, and the air
> Replenished, and all these at thy command
> To come and play before thee, know'st thou not
> Their language and their ways, they also know,
> And reason not contemptibly; with these
> Find pastime . . .   (369–75)

Still, Adam persists in wanting more than would content a scientist, and God gives in. 'Thus far to try thee, Adam, I was pleased' (437). He puts Adam to sleep but lets him dream the birth of Eve as it is happening. Adam wakes sad to lose the dream of Eve but there she stands:

> . . . To the nuptial bower
> I led her blushing like the morn: all heaven,
> And happy constellations on that hour
> Shed their selectest influence; the earth
> Gave sign of gratulation, and each hill;
> Joyous the birds; fresh gales and gentle airs
> Whispered it to the woods, and from their wings
> Flung rose, flung odours from the spicy shrub,
> Disporting, till the amorous bird of night
> Sung spousal, and bid haste the evening star
> On his hill top, to light the bridal lamp.   (510–20)

Adam and the angel then become somewhat metaphysical about male supremacy and Eve's position; this is not Milton's most effective vein.

Raphael takes a Neoplatonic position, and may represent what is left of the Heavenly Love of the early drafts, with Adam as Earthly Love: but, if so, it is scarcely apparent on a normal reading. They progress to the discussion of what is love in heaven (615–17). Adam hopes that Raphael will continue to be a friend to men and often return.

> So parted they, the angel up to heaven
> From the thick shade, and Adam to his bower.

Book 9 opens with the last of those solemn invocations, the first three of which are as good as any verse Milton wrote: he must now turn his attention to Sin, Death and Misery (12), an argument he thinks more heroic than the wrath of Achilles or of Turnus, or of Poseidon against Odysseus: he must mean the wrath of Satan, not of God, but in neither case is his argument comparable with the antique examples:

> If answerable style I can obtain
> Of my celestial patroness, who deigns
> Her nightly visitation unimplored,
> And dictates to me slumbering, or inspires
> Easy my unpremeditated verse,
> Since first this subject for heroic song
> Pleased me long choosing, and beginning late ...   (20–26)

He admits he is not inclined by nature to write of wars or chivalrous romances. He has a higher argument,

> sufficient of itself to raise
> That name, unless an age too late, or cold
> Climate, or years damp my intended wing
> Depressed, and much they may, if all be mine,
> Not hers who brings it nightly to my ear.   (43–7)

He is right to suspect that true epic verse was unattainable in London in the mid-seventeenth century, but right also to maintain his path. What he hoped for his name he has after all attained, at least for nearly three hundred years, which is something. But now it is night (52) and Satan is on the prowl. He enters Paradise like an underground river and rises in mist. He has searched from Maeotis to the Ob (78) and decides his best chance is 'the wily snake' (91) but first comes a monologue (99–178) of complaints. It is well devised but rhetorical in the same way as parts of Ovid's *Metamorphoses*, a book that long before had become part of Milton's mind. Now it is dawn (193), and Adam and Eve join the dawn chorus. Eve suggests (205) they divide their work, though Adam has his high-minded doubts:

> Love not the lowest end of human life.
> For not to irksome toil, but to delight
> He made us, and delight to reason joined.   (241–3)

Eve knows about the devil because she overheard Raphael 'as in a shady nook I stood behind'. This swift piece of footwork keeps the plot logical at least. The high-mindedness which they share is thought by commentators to mark the style of tragedy, but readers may find it rebarbative. Phrases like 'Go; for thy stay, not free, absents thee more' (372) may be felt to confirm the tragic impression. Narrative returns after line 384.

> Thus saying, from her husband's hand her hand
> Soft she withdrew, and like a wood-nymph light
> Oread or dryad, or of Delia's train,
> Betook her to the groves, but Delia's self
> In gait surpassed and goddess-like deport,
> Though not as she with bow and quiver armed,
> But with such gardening tools as art yet rude,
> Guiltless of fire had formed, or angels brought.
> To Pales, or Pomona thus adorned,
> Likeliest she seemed . . .   (385–94)

These vignettes are pretty and logic is preserved, but the drama is delayed, and when Satan finds Eve alone (424), Milton for once overdoes his picture (424–33) of Eve among the flowers. The serpent enjoys the spectacle, however. It is like going into the country from a smelly city, Milton says, and all the nicer for a pretty girl (445–54). She is so beautiful she 'with rapine sweet bereaved/His fierceness of the fierce intent it brought' (461–2). Is it Milton or only Satan who now exclaims 'Thoughts, whither have ye led me . . .'? (473) The serpent is described as a fine animal, not fabulous (495–505), though he is as lovely as a long list of classical mythic references can make him (505–10).

At last Satan as serpent speaks to her (532–48), and she is seduced.

This passage is written with an extraordinary discretion, so that we feel it as drama, enjoy it as poetry and admire it as literature, all at once. Satan on the tree:

> When from the boughs a savoury odour blown,
> Grateful to appetite, more pleased my sense
> Than smell of sweetest fennel or the teats
> Of ewe or goat dropping with milk at even . . .   (579–82)

Whether or not this is a joke (Satan thinks like a snake), it is also extremely sensuous: more so than anything else in *Paradise Lost*. The seduction is accomplished and 'the wily adder, blithe and glad' leads Eve off to his secret place and to the Tree. Satan is like an orator of Athens or Rome in the days of freedom 'where eloquence/Flourished, since mute' (671–2) and makes a highly rhetorical speech of fifty or so lines. First she muses (745–79), then she falls, and then (795–833) she addresses the tree. All this is not as convincing as Genesis, in spite of the beauty of the serpent and his language. Adam has woven some flowers to crown her hair, 'as reapers oft are wont their harvest queen'. Eve brings him a branch of the fruit (856–85); he is horrified but he loves her still (896–916) and he eats (996–7).

> They swim in mirth, and fancy that they feel
> Divinity within them breeding wings . . .   (1009–10)

but lust and shame follow at once. It must be said that the love scene that follows (1034–45), from Eve's eye darting contagious fire to their dewy sleep, has gained in passion what it has lost in innocence.

> O might I here
> In solitude live savage, in some glade
> Obscured, where highest woods impenetrable
> To star or sunlight, spread their umbrage broad
> And brown as evening: cover me ye pines,
> Ye cedars, with innumerable boughs . . .   (1084–9)

They get leaves to cover themselves but now they reproach each other, 'and of their vain contest appeared no end'.

Book 10 brings back Sin and Death. The heavens and the elements are altered, Adam and Eve upset and in the end repenting. First the angels on guard get into trouble, but God tells them to calm down, and the Son agrees with his plan (68–84). Evening is as bewitching, as it always is in Milton (92–5), and the story follows Genesis, only at greater length. At times Milton even fits pieces of the Bible into his verse (175–81). Meanwhile Sin and Death (230) feel a new vigour and splendidly torment the earth (272–324) to make a bridge from earth to Hell. They meet Satan (327) and enjoy their conversation, and 'the blasted stars looked wan' (412). Satan returns to Hell and slips in among the devils, where he makes a godlike and spectacular appearance (443–55). In rush 'the great consulting peers,/Raised from their dark divan', and he speaks (460–503). Suddenly all the devils hiss, being transformed into snakes, adorned with a magnificent catalogue (524–31) of ancient snakes. God raises for them a tree of fruit but it is bitter ashes to them (565–7). Sin and Death have another scene, but this book has lost all credibility: a learned digression on snakes in the ancient world cannot restore it, nor can Sin and Death. God speaks, the angels triumph and normal life seems to return – only to dissolve in disturbances of the stars and winds. Adam grieves (720–844) and reproaches Eve (867–908). She makes a shorter speech (914–36), which is more moving. They long for death, and she thinks of suicide, which Adam tells her is no solution (1013–96), suggesting instead (1068–78) that they capture and domesticate fire. They weep and are penitent.

Book 11 reveals the future: first their prayers are heard and the Father agrees to the Son's plea for man. The angels assemble at a trumpet blast (76–82), although Heaven is as pale somehow as Virgil's Elysium. Michael and some angels are sent down, with more eyes than Argus, the hundred-eyed watchdog killed by Hermes,

> . . . and more wakeful than to drowse,
> Charmed with Arcadian pipe, the pastoral reed
> Of Hermes, or his opiate rod. . . .   (131–3)

They find Adam and Eve in a better mood, more practical and more hopeful: so 'down from a sky of jasper' (209) they alight in Paradise. The archangel now wears 'a military vest of purple', brighter than any ancient purple: 'Iris had dipped the woof' (244). He tells Adam he has to leave and take up farming. Eve grieves (267–85) in moderate and beautiful language. Adam tells Michael that if he were left in Paradise, he could build altars wherever God once appeared (296–333):

> On this mount he appeared; under this tree
> Stood visible, among these pines his voice
> I heard, here with him at this fountain talked:
> So many grateful altars I would rear
> Of grassy turf, and pile up every stone
> Of lustre from the brook, in memory,
> Or monument to ages, and thereon
> Offer sweet smelling gums and fruit and flowers . . . (320–27)

Michael assures him God will not disappear, and invites him up a hill while Eve sleeps. The view is extensive, and Milton tells us how thrilling it is, naming the exotic names (388–411), and as he mouths name after name he gives expression to something as deep in him as religion may be. Adam sees a vision of Cain murdering Abel, whom he hits in the midriff with a stone (445). (Cowley wrote that it was in the head, but the midriff is perhaps Homeric.) Adam then sees death by a catalogue of gruesome diseases (480–90). Michael warns him to watch his diet (530–33) and shows him the sons of Cain, tent dwellers, musical instrument makers, a metal-worker (Gen. 4: 10–22) and a wedding (580–97), which Michael warns is a folly. Still, it is described straightforwardly as beautiful. Adam then sees a vision of strife that recalls the Shield of Achilles passage in the *Iliad*, yet all this is biblical (Enoch is there, 700). Finally he sees Noah's Ark and the Flood. It may well be that without these visions we would not grasp the consequences of Adam's Fall. At this stage of Book 11 (797–806), Milton is thought to refer to his own world, and the line 'shall with their freedom lost all virtue lose' does have a familiar ring, but I am not convinced of his intention, and the world he deplores makes no mention whatever of the events of 1649–60.

> . . . then shall this mount
> Of Paradise by might of waves be moved
> Out of his place, pushed by the horned flood,
> With all his verdure spoiled, and trees adrift
> Down the great river to the opening gulf,
> And there take root an island salt and bare,
> The haunt of seals and orcs, and sea-mews' clang.   (829–35)

It is, of course, a cursed island, and it takes up line 751, 'Where luxury late reigned, sea monsters whelped/And stabled'. The Flood now follows, and the end of the Flood, the rainbow.

The last of these twelve books, separated by some skilful surgery in the second edition, goes further with the prophecy of Raphael, who expounds biblical history down to Babel. Adam's reactions are moralizing, and Raphael (94–6) explains tyranny. Biblical history continues at a jog-trot, to reach Abraham and his mighty nation (120–49) and some more geography. We meet Moses and see Sinai (227) and hear of the Messiah (244) but there is something lacklustre about the last book: even the birth of Christ cheers it up (360–67) only for a few lines. Adam addresses the Virgin, and Michael gives him rudimentary instruction in the Redemption and the Crucifixion (413–15). This jejune exposition of Christianity goes on in speech after speech without any striking poetry until the pair of them descend from their mountain, when the poetry at last explodes like a firework. Adam finds Eve, but she knows from dreams what he has been doing,

> . . . and from the other hill
> To their fixed station, all in bright array
> The cherubim descended; on the ground
> Gliding meteorous, as evening mist
> Risen from a river o'er the marish glides,
> And gathers ground fast at the labourer's heel
> Homeward returning. . . .   (626–32)
> They hand in hand with wandering steps and slow,
> Through Eden took their solitary way.   (648–9)

CHAPTER TWELVE

THE GREAT POET

MAYBE THE LAST eerie symbol was unconscious, but to compare angels with marsh lights or ground mist is to return us to common day. If Milton did not truly believe in his angels, if they were a fiction, then his great poem culminates in a sad few lines. And Paradise a barren island frequented by sea monsters. As in the first book, the body of Satan weltered in the waves like a whale, like Leviathan, like an orc? So that a fisherman might in error anchor on the great basking bulk? Part of the structure of *Paradise Lost* is hidden or submerged, and we shall not attempt to uncover it. There are about a dozen phrases in it so cramped, so arthritic with Latinity, that they are almost impossible to unpick, but they do make sense in the end. There are perhaps half a dozen lines in the standard text that are badly unmetrical and could easily be lopped, but that also is not our business: it is the life of Milton and the progression of his mind that we want to explore. This is the most artificial of poems: he deliberately invented a language for it, as he had elaborated the language of his Latin verse and the language of his *Lycidas*.

One of the secrets of this great poem is his use of direct, vernacular words and phrases for its best effects. He has learnt while he was hiding from his poem, hiding mostly in public business but also in his somewhat juvenile public debates, which are often or always redolent of Cambridge – even the Rota is like a school debating society – to clinch a sonnet in a line or two, and it is those closures that are the building bricks of his 'epic style'. Once he had learnt it there is no doubt that he felt secure in his formula: we are told that he wrote the four books of *Paradise Regained* with a speed that astonished everyone. Certainly the style included growls and rumbles better suited to Hell and the devils than to Paradise, and Latinisms and a few archaisms that astonish now more than they did then. 'Meteorous' was not a current word, nor was 'marish'. Milton seems to have invented 'meteorous';

Pope and Johnson copy him, and then Wrangham in the same century speaks of 'the glazed and meteorous eyes of the eighth Henry'; the Greek word that it comes from is the one Socrates uses where he placidly remarks 'nothing is more in mid-air than the gods'. Milton's word order is tricky and now unusable. But for the underlying vernacular diction consider this (5, 644–6):

> . . . the face of brightest heaven had changed
> To grateful twilight (for night comes not there
> In darker veil) . . .

Only 'grateful' in the sense of pleasing is unusual, and in the next line 'roseate dews disposed/All but the unsleeping eyes of God to rest'. What does surprise one is the plot, and to that Sin and Death those lugubrious characters offer a clue. They are repellent and (Milton acknowledges) incestuous; it is possible there is at least a hint that Eve was implicated in their sexual activities, in a story which was currently persistent in the margins of biblical commentary. This was, after all, the period of the Protestant phobia about witches. These characters belong to the imagination of the age, not to Milton's. Their strong visual quality might have arisen from a painting, like the syphilitic Pain and serpent-tailed Pleasure in an allegory by Bronzino. But Milton's introduction of these horrible low-life characters into his story is disastrous: when they become victorious they appear emasculated; as a thread running through the epic they are ridiculous; and they sort strangely with Satan, who is too heroic to fit their company. If we subtract Sin and Death, then most of the epic is based on straight warfare between Heaven and Hell. God's plans and Satan's do not matter much, because no one's plans in epic poems ever work out precisely: that is why it is unpleasant in God always to be producing the ace of trumps from up his sleeve. The warfare is all very well, and no worse as a spectacular effect than the ingenious Pandaemonium like a vast beehive, but the invention of artillery is too funny a joke to fit a story of heroism, nor is bombardment heroic, nor is using superior strength to throw mountains about.

When you subtract the visions at the end and the prophecies, which trail on to the Redemption shown in so few words it makes no strong impression, you begin to wonder how else the poem could have ended except by a mere reference to Christianity. The true climax is the Fall, which is delayed long enough (to Book 9). The professorial Archangel on the rhomb and so on (8, 130) is not really part of the story of Eden, but if we accept that the universe and all Creation and all nature and the devil or serpent are part of it, then the extent of the plan appears less leisurely or less unnecessarily extensive. It seems to me that the entire plot is merely a string in the end to tie together the things Milton chooses to write about: he might have done better to write an *Odyssey* than a combination of so many and such different features, but as it is we get glimpses of a mind as remarkable as any in his century, and a poet as astonishing and as satisfying as any in English. His mind can grasp the emmet (ant) and bee (7, 485f.), and so can his verse, as easily as the elephant and the Chinaman. He is intimate as well as monumental. The poetry can dart in any direction, but essentially he is a poet of Paradise and of passionate human love, into which Satan's conniving serpent voice fully enters. *Paradise Lost* is a remarkable performance, and it repays the study it requires.

Andrew Marvell was overwhelmed, and wrote a defence of Milton in Part 2 of *The Rehearsal Transpos'd* (1673), making it clear that the poet was still a public issue, and Marvell's subtler verse tribute to his friend appeared in the second edition (1674). Still, by the seniority of his friendship he should be heard first. His first reaction is to mistrust the plot. 'When I beheld the poet blind, yet bold', he fears that old Milton 'would ruin (for I saw him strong)/The sacred truths to fable and old song'. How could he cram it all into a poem? As he reads the poem he likes it but fears for its success in the field where 'lame faith leads understanding blind'. In the end he feels that Milton has not missed any thought that is proper to the subject, nor put in anything unfitting:

> . . . Thou singest with so much gravity and ease;
> And above human flight dost soar aloft
> With plume so strong, so equal, and so soft.

Marvell is right about the sublimity and strong, equal wingbeat over a variety of material: this poem is 'sublime', although Milton was better at humans than at God, or angels, or devils.

> Well mightest thou scorn thy readers to allure
> With tinkling rhyme, of thine own sense secure . . .

Marvell here delivers a gleeful attack on Dryden, who wanted to turn *Paradise Lost* into a play, who loves to rhyme, 'And like a pack-horse tires without his bells'. Milton attacked rhyme in the preface to this edition of *Paradise Lost* as 'the invention of a barbarous age, to set off wretched matter and lame metre ... the jingling sound of like endings'. Indeed, he made the splendid boast that *Paradise Lost* was 'an example set, the first in English, of ancient liberty recovered to heroic poem from the troublesome and modern bondage of rhyming'. As he said, there were Spanish and Italian examples, as well as dramatic verse in the last age, and it is true that the skill and salt of his blank verse depend on an internal vigour and a springing quality that he learnt in Italian. The quarrel with Dryden was not serious: in principle Dryden agreed with him, and wished at the end of his life that he had translated the *Aeneid* into unrhymed heroic verse: as for his Miltonic opera *The State of Innocence* (c. 1673), it was never performed, though it was published (1677), and his last play in rhyming verse was *Aureng-Zebe* (1675); he venerated Milton, and when Lord Buckhurst sent him a copy of *Paradise Lost* in 1669 he said, 'that Poet has cut us all out and the ancients.' What Dryden's opera would have been like may be grasped at once from his version of Satan's soliloquy about invading Eve's dreams.

> So now they lie, secure in love, and steep
> Their sated senses in full draughts of sleep.
> By what sure means may I their bliss invade?
> By violence? No; for they're immortal made.
> Their Reason sleeps; but mimic Fancy wakes ...

This clever and yet pitiful stuff justifies Marvell's rage, if anything could, but Milton himself is not known to have raged. Aubrey says Dryden 'went to him to have leave to put his *Paradise Lost* into a drama in rhyme. Mr Milton received him civilly and told him he would give him leave to tag his verses' (a tag being a metal point on the end of a ribbon). Marvell seems to know this story, since he says, 'Their fancies like our bushy-points appear,/The poets tag them ...'

The first we hear of the complete poem *Paradise Lost* is when Milton showed the manuscript to Thomas Ellwood, the Quaker: Ellwood used to call on Milton, 'which I seldom failed of doing whenever occasion drew me to London'. In 1665 there was a bad outbreak of plague in London. It began in April, and by June there were 590 dead in a month, by July 4,129 in a month, in August over 20,000 and in September 26,230. Pits were dug for the dead in Tothill Fields and in Finsbury, and Defoe says that the sick would jump into them still alive. Milton left London as soon as he could. 'I was desired by my quondam master Milton,' says Ellwood, 'to take an house for him in the neighbourhood where I dwelt, that he might get out of the City, for the safety of himself and his family, the pestilence then growing hot in London. I took a pretty box for him in Giles-Chalfont, a mile from me, of which I gave him notice.' This is Milton's cottage at Chalfont St Giles, which still exists, but Ellwood then went to prison. When he got out Milton, whom he found installed in the village, lent him *Paradise Lost* to read at home. He brought it back and said it was all very fine, but what about *Paradise Regained*? This worked in Milton, and in the end he wrote another long poem.

There is a little more to say about the cottage. It was some twenty-three miles from London by Uxbridge or by Rickmansworth, and four from Beaconsfield. Masson thought it an extremely sleepy, lost sort of place: Milton's Cottage, as it came to be called, was the last one in the village towards Beaconsfield: 'small, irregular, two tenements full of dark closets'; the glass in the windows was set in lozenges.

Meanwhile the plague went on until near Christmas of 1665, but in the new year it halted. Some time in very earliest spring, probably in March, Milton and his family returned to London, but in the first week of September that year came the Great Fire of London. There are maps printed to show the devastation: Bread Street, among other neighbourhoods, was burnt down; indeed, apart from the Tower and Leadenhall Street and Cripplegate Street in the north-east of the city, the whole Roman city of London which lay between the Tower and St Paul's was destroyed and, far to the west beyond Paul's, the whole of Ludgate and most of Fleet Street, whatever lay between Holborn (nearly) and the river, was wholly devastated. In Milton's direction the fire did not destroy any of those new streets that lay north of the walls. Where it had raged, it went on smouldering and smoking and stinking until the following March, and the wind-blown leaves from burnt books were found as far away as Windsor. If Milton had not already written his long poem, he might have had something to add to his Hell: but the true monument of the Fire of London is a poem by Dryden in which that poet swallows Milton whole.

The manuscript of Book 1 of *Paradise Lost* survives in New York, and it is some help with the history of the text. A scribe or a secretary wrote it, and more than one hand peppered it with minute corrections, and yet uniformity of spelling and punctuation were not achieved. For this last matter, which sheds a fascinating side-light on Milton's poetry, one must consult that brilliant book *Milton's Punctuation* by Mindele Treip (1970). The manuscript does not furnish us with any exciting new readings, but it carries the *imprimatur* of the Revd T. Tomkins, the new vicar of St Mary, Aldermary, and at twenty-eight chaplain to the archbishop, whose chaplains traditionally censored books. It was probably Tomkins, as senior censor, who disapproved of the effect of eclipses on the fears of kings, which Toland said nearly sank *Paradise Lost* (1, 597–9). Samuel Simmons of the Gold Lion, Aldersgate Street, was the printer; his contract allowed Milton £5, with £5 more when it had sold 1,300 copies, £5 for a second impression and £5 for a third: no impression was to be more than 1,500 copies. Tonson (d. 1767), whose treasure the Book 1 manuscript was, acquired this contract around 1683; a tailor in Oxford Street had it after that for arrears of rent and sold it for £25; Pickering's bought it at auction for £45 3 shillings, then it was owned by Sir T. Lawrence and at last by the poet Samuel Rogers, who paid 100 guineas and gave the old contract to the British Museum.

Between April and August 1667, *Paradise Lost* was in the press: when it came out it must have seemed a majestic and antique undertaking: its rivals among new books were Dryden's *Annus Mirabilis* and his essay *Of Dramatick Poesie*, and a book by Cowley's friend Sprat on the Royal Society. Milton's poem was advertised to be sold by two booksellers to the east of the burnt city and one to the west. In quarto it cost 3 shillings, and it was reissued in 1668 and 1669 with six different title pages altogether. The Argument (all the arguments to all the books as a continuous story printed together) and the printer's note to readers and Milton's note on 'The Verse' appeared in the fourth issue. We know that Milton called on Simmons and was paid his money. The second edition (1674) was in octavo. That had complimentary Latin verses by Samuel Barrow and English ones by Andrew Marvell. Other editions of various kinds appeared after his death; the first one with a commentary was the sixth (1695), and the first to dispute the text and offer a long list of emendations was by the perverse classical scholar Richard Bentley (1732), answered in Newton's edition (1749). The heaviest and most pregnant with learning is H. J. Todd's in six volumes (1801). The most curious of all Milton editions is the Italian poems (only) printed with the *Pervigilium Veneris* at Cape Town in 1911, but 'L'Allegro' and 'Il Penseroso' set to music (Charles Jennens, 1748) and *Paradise Lost* in Latin by G. Hogaeus, bound in vellum and printed in London, run it close. Hogaeus, by putting the poem 'in paraphrase' into Latin, may be the reason why the Roman Inquisition denounced Milton as an adherent of the Arian heresy.

In 1667 Milton had seven years to live; Clarendon was driven into exile in October; Louis XIV was offering £200,000 for a Roman Catholic declaration by Charles II, but £800,000 a year if he would fight the Dutch. The divorce Bill for Lord Roos or Ross was passed in April 1670. Milton's friends and enemies were still divided as if the war of angels and devils were to be replayed. Sir George Hungerford told a story of which the details may be confused but which is probably true in essentials. Old Sir John Denham, who had survived the war on the royalist side, wandered one day into the House of Commons. 'What have you got there, sir?' 'The noblest poem that ever was wrote in any language or in any age.' One can believe that this dashing and generous view was taken by Denham, who is another of the poets of that period who are still not praised, though they have virtues that might merit it. We are told that Waller was another admirer. Not much follows from that; he was thought the king of poetry at that moment, though now his laurels are dustier; still it is pleasing to catch a benevolent whisper of his friendship with Milton. Milton, of course, may have been a useful ally under the Commonwealth, as he was to the musical and corrupt Sir R. Howard, for example, though Howard prospered under all regimes. Milton told him he preferred republics to kings for their frugality. The opposition view of Milton was of 'that serpent Milton, a dead dog, a canker worm, a petty schoolboy scribbler' (Bishop Hacket of Lichfield). Yet Aubrey says he was 'visited much by the learned, more than he desired', and Richardson says Charles II offered him his job back as Latin Secretary after Fanshawe died. He is said to have answered to his wife, 'You as other women would ride in your coach: for me, my aim is to live and die an honest man.' This story is usually thought to be incredible: it is unlikely but not incredible.

In 1669 he published a book about grammar and in 1670 a *History of Britain*. The grammar is an old teacher's obsession. It is original, like nearly every other work of his, but one would have to be an English grammarian oneself to be seriously interested in it. Late the next year came the *History* that dated back perhaps even longer. (He had written four books in 1648 and later added two more.) The censor cut it severely. It runs smoothly and well enough to make a pleasing read today. He intended 'with plain and lightsome brevity to relate well and orderly things worth the noting' and not to delay the smooth run of things with controversies and quotations, but he was really too lively for modern tastes. Boadicea was 'a distracted woman with as mad a crew at her heels', and the ancient Britons 'painted their skins with several portraitures of beast bird and flower', as they now ornament their skirts 'with ribbons and gewgaws'. The longest piece the censor removed went because Milton had used modern and highly sensitive terms to analyse the state of the British in Roman times.

The censor cut five or six pages from the opening of Book 3 where Milton is asking how, when liberty so long desired had been left like a bridle in their hands, the British did not take it. Here he talks of a Parliament, 'the superficial zeal and popular fumes' that soon evaporated, with neglect of the Commonwealth, of 'some who had been called from shops and warehouses, without merit' to sit on Supreme Councils and Committees 'of justice delayed and soon after denied', and of sequestrations and 'thieves in office'. This account sounds as if his thoughts had strayed to the 1650s; his account of religion follows, and there we are undoubtedly in modern times. Finally 'the People which had been kept warm awhile with the counterfeit zeal of their Pulpits, after a false heat, became more cold and obdurate than before, some turning to lewdness, some to flat Atheism ...' We are given his doctrine of liberty, how 'sought out of season, in a corrupt and degenerate age' it reduced Rome to worse slavery than ever. Britain, he says, is fruitful in good soldiers but not in good governors. 'Hence did their Victories prove as fruitless as their losses dangerous; and left them still conquering under the same grievances that men suffer conquered.' He then returns to Gildas, Zosimus and Ethelwerd. It must rank as certain that Milton in the offending pages intended to convey his mature judgement of the last thirty years, but because he must continue his pretence of discussing the remote past it is not always certain to what extent he means to blame his own party.

The next year, 1671, he published *Paradise Regained* and *Samson Agonistes* with Tomkyns. The poem was licensed on 2 July 1670 and registered with the Stationers in September. That autumn it was advertised for sale, though no copy dated before 1671 has been found. The proof-reading may have taken a long time. Milton told Mr Ellwood, 'This [*Paradise Regained*] is owing to you, for you put it into my head by the question you put to me at Chalfont, which before I had not thought of.' Once again, Milton is concerned with visions on a mountain, but the entire epic, which is four books of 502, 486, 443 and 639 lines, that is, 2,070 altogether, is of a simpler construction than *Paradise Lost*. It is about the temptations of Christ as Luke tells the story (4: 1–13), though it follows Matthew in putting them after the forty days' fast. In this poem Satan is less knowing and less intelligent than he was in *Paradise Lost*, and Christ has a contemplative quality. *Paradise Regained* has been the subject of much excited controversy in this century, not much of it fruitful. The poem itself has always been a favourite of mine, and it does not surprise me to read that if Milton was told it was less great than *Paradise Lost*, he was furious. It is a different poem in another mode, and if it is lighter, then there are moods in which one prefers that, but it is more usual to reread *Paradise Lost*.

Book 1 is about 'Eden raised in the waste wilderness' by Christ's reversal of the Fall, and the Spirit is invoked, as usual, 'to tell of deeds/Above heroic, though in secret done'. The preaching of John the Baptist 'with a voice/More awful than the sound of trumpet' opens the narrative, and after a mere thirty lines 'Heaven opened, and in likeness of a dove/The Spirit descended'. Satan hears this 'nigh thunder-struck',

> . . . nor rests, but in mid air
> To council summons all his mighty peers,
> Within thick clouds and dark tenfold involved,
> A gloomy consistory . . .   (39–42)

Satan first addresses them with the splendid greeting, 'O ancient powers of air and this wide world ...', but then spoils it a little by explaining why he prefers to say air and not Hell. He tells them that the prophecy of Eve crushing the serpent's head is about to be fulfilled. He knows Christ's mother is mortal but his father is God: a dogma Milton could toy with but did not believe. This is a major speech (44–99) but discussion does not follow. The devils who are now 'Regents and potentates, and kings, yea gods/Of many a pleasant realm and province wide' (117–18) leave action to Satan, who 'directs/His easy steps; girded with snaky wiles' to Jordan, while God speaks to Gabriel: the verse is biblical but well balanced and better than anyone else's biblical verse. 'So they in heaven their odes and vigils tuned ...' (182), and Christ enters the desert, 'And with dark shades and rocks environed round' begins his meditations with a discussion of his nature and vocation and his nativity, with 'thy star, new-grav'n in heaven' (196–293).

> Full forty days he passed, whether on hill
> Sometimes, anon in shady vale, each night
> Under the covert of some ancient oak,
> Or cedar to defend him from the dew,
> Or harboured in one cave, is not revealed ...   (303–7)

Suddenly we meet an old man gathering sticks or searching for a sheep, straight out of Giles Fletcher (*Christ's Victory*, 2, 15). Milton has always been extremely good at these scenes (314–18) and this one is masterly: the old man is Satan, of course. His conversation with Christ is equally enchanting, though Christ answers laconically. It becomes at once (342) the first temptation, to turn stones into bread. One has the sense the entire epic could be over in 500 lines, but theological arguments take time: Christ tells him he is 'never more in hell than when in heaven' in the manner of Marlowe and of *Paradise Lost* (1, 255), and what is more,

> ... henceforth oracles are ceased,
> And thou no more with pomp and sacrifice
> Shall be inquired at Delphos or elsewhere,
> At least in vain, for they shall find thee mute.   (456–9)

One can feel for the nervous twitch that makes Milton explain himself in the last line quoted, because he suspects (rightly) that oracles did not at once die out and Plutarch did not relate the event to the birth of Christ. But it is a pleasure to get a whiff of Milton's old style, so close to Shakespeare's. But now Satan melts to thin air,

> ... for now began
> Night with her sullen wing to double-shade
> The desert, fowls in their clay nests were couched;
> And now wild beasts came forth the woods to roam.   (499–502)

   This poem is brief in its treatment, has fewer characters and less of the planet in it. But there is a fineness about its sound which ramifies into other aspects of its execution. Book 2 begins with a series of the long pendent sentences we have been used to, and with Andrew and Simon

> Now missing him their joy so lately found,
> So lately found, and so abruptly gone,
> Began to doubt, and doubted many days,
> And as the days increased, increased their doubt ...   (9–12)

Their conversation is in a fisherman's cottage by a creek of the Jordan (I nearly wrote the Thames), 'Where winds with reeds, and osiers whisp'ring play'. They are sad but trusting, and go to see Mary (60) whose words are scarcely consoling. Meanwhile Christ is wandering in the desert 'with holiest meditations fed', and Satan goes off gloomily to report to the other devils. 'Princes, heaven's ancient Sons ...'; the greeting goes on for more than twenty lines, but the message is gloomy: 'So spake the old serpent doubting ...'; in fact he is unable to shine in this poem. Belial, 'the dissolutest spirit that fell', suggests trying women as a temptation, but Satan rebukes him, and the words 'In wood or grove by mossy fountain-side,/In valley or green meadow' (184–5) introduce a great string of classical names. The speech (173–234) is applauded: 'beauty stands/In the admiration only of weak minds' (he means female beauty). Satan takes off to the desert with some select spirits and finds Christ soliloquizing (245–59). Christ then sleeps and dreams of how Elijah and Daniel were fed.

> Thus wore out night, and now the herald lark
> Left his ground-nest, high tow'ring to descry

The Morn's approach, and greet her with his song:
As lightly from his grassy couch uprose
Our Saviour, and found all was but a dream . . .   (279–83)

He comes at once to a pretty country scene: a grove inviting rest at noon. But there, in different clothes, as custom sometimes dictated in paintings of the Temptations, is Satan; he argues about food again, and Christ makes brief answers. He produces a fine dinner (339–67) with pretty waiters and an orchestra. There are a number of old themes here and a number of lovely lines, such as 'All these are spirits of air, and woods, and springs,/Thy gentle ministers' (374–5), but Christ is scornful: 'Thy pompous delicacies I contemn' (390). Satan points out that Christ lacks means; Christ dissents with biblical, then classical (446), arguments. He also recalls Shakespeare (459–61) on crowns.

Book 3 continues this argument, and Satan, who is just a little winded, comes back with strong counter-arguments about glory. Glory follows wealth, as it does in Book 2 of *The Faerie Queene*, although, as the poet Pope noticed, one might expect it among the pinnacles of the Temple as vainglory. Christ's reply is that glory is only praise, and the people who praise are only a rabble; conquerors are destroyers and enslavers. This speech (44–107) has a swelling rhetoric about it. Satan, checked here, makes another attack (150–80): why should Christ not fight the Romans and sit on David's throne? 'So shalt thou best fulfil, best verify/The prophets old, who sung thy endless reign' (177–8). This, as David Daube pointed out, is an argument that would have been of great interest to Jews in the time of Christ and must really have exercised him. Christ rests his resignation in the Father's decree. Satan becomes frenzied in his rhetoric (207–209) and finally takes Christ up the high mountain (252). The earth and its kingdoms, as Satan shows it to Christ with a history lesson (253–309), is a fine set-piece ending in an army 'in rhombs and wedges, and half-moons, and wings'. We are then allowed to see the vision without further comment: it strays into the country of the *Orlando Innamorato* of Boiardo. Satan then resumes his argument (347–85), and Christ rebukes him. All the same, the story from Boiardo about Abrican and Albracca and the city of Gallaphrone was a thrilling moment.

Book 4 is the last and a little longer than the others: it is also the climax of the poem in a way that Book 12 of *Paradise Lost* is not, unless the orc island and the marish are the climax. This book continues the same set of visions, but turns at once to Rome, because Satan 'Still will be tempting him who foils him still' (13). The view is from another part of the mountain, and the geography disturbs Milton.

> By what strange parallax or optic skill
> Of vision multiplied through air, or glass
> Of telescope, were curious to inquire . . .   (40–42)

Milton is the poet of the parallax and the rhomb, and obsessed with the telescope since his blindness; there is something peculiarly personal about his raising questions like these that cannot be answered. The *camera lucida* and *camera oscura* were invented in his lifetime, but does he really think Christ used a telescope, or is this all a joke? Yet the commentaries assure us that two Italian writers on scripture had seriously suggested that he did, or that what he saw was a mirage, and soon we have Satan talking of his 'airy microscope' (57). Milton's wonders of pagan Rome, 'turrets and terraces, and glittering spires ... cedar, marble, ivory or gold' are essentially a Renaissance vision; he rolls the grand words, 'praetors', 'proconsuls' and so on over on his tongue as he does the exotic geography: Meroe (where he is wrong about the shadows) and 'the realm of Bocchus to the Blackmoor sea' (72). The details he throws in are as enticing as the exotic can be: 'Dusk faces with white silken turbans wreathed'. He allows the Romans their traditional attainment of 'civility of manners, arts, and arms' but then speaks of the throne of Tiberius as a pigsty ready to be purged. Christ answers that the Roman luxury, the 'gorgeous feasts/On citron tables or Atlantic stone', do not attract him as they do us. He discusses the luxurious drinks and the political decadence of the Roman people: what wise man would seek to free 'These thus degenerate, by themselves enslaved,/Or could of inward slaves make outward free?' (144–5). This severe analysis foreshadows the views of Mommsen.

Satan makes his offer (159–69) and Christ spurns it (171–94). Satan can still stand on his dignity: angels and men are both Sons of God after all, but Satan is named by 'tetrarchs of fire, air, flood, and on the earth/Nations besides from all the quartered winds,/God of this world . . .' (201–3). He then turns Christ to the cult of wisdom, and to Athens. These lines showed Akenside a way forward for English poetry, and inspired Tennyson to a similar musical imitation; they are certainly remarkable.

> See there the olive-grove of Academe,
> Plato's retirement, where the Attic bird
> Trills her thick-warbled notes the summer long,
> There flowery hill Hymettus with the sound
> Of bees' industrious murmur oft invites
> To studious musing; there Ilissus rolls
> His whispering stream . . .　(244–50)
> Aeolian charms and Dorian lyric odes,
> And his who gave them breath, but higher sung,
> Blind Melesigenes thence Homer called,
> Whose poem Phoebus challenged for his own.
> Thence what the lofty grave tragedians taught . . .　(257–62)

This stream of eloquent enthusiasm passes on through the orators who 'shook the Arsenal and fulmined over Greece' to philosophy, 'From heaven descended to the low-roofed house/Of Socrates', and dies out like a river in the sand with the variety of philosophic schools. It has lasted nearly fifty lines (236–84), all spoken by Satan. Christ replies that light from God is enough; he criticizes the sects of philosophy though not the hero philosopher, the contemplative:

> Or if I would delight my private hours
> With music or with poem, where so soon
> As in our native language can I find
> That solace? . . .　　　　　　　　　　　(331–4)

Milton may be hinting at his own language, but he also means Hebrew from which he believes that Greek learnt its beauties; that was an old theory dating from the tricky Josephus and commonly accepted. Does he think that Greek poetry really 'Will far be found unworthy to compare/With Sion's songs, to all true tastes excelling'? Is it relevant that he wanted to please Mr Ellwood, a very bad religious poet indeed, who wrote verses in the manner of Wither? Does Milton believe the orators are lesser figures than the Hebrew prophets?

> In them is plainest taught, and easiest learnt,
> What makes a nation happy, and keeps it so,
> What ruins kingdoms and lays cities flat ...   (361–3)

Satan is at a loss: all he can now do is warn Christ of a painful future (368–93). Christ, tired 'after his airy jaunt', goes to sleep in a complicated but beautiful sentence (404–7), but Satan gives him bad dreams and a most stormy night, 'from many a horrid rift abortive poured/Fierce rain with lightning mixed, water with fire/In ruin reconciled ...' (411–13) until the Shakespearian dawn 'came forth with pilgrim steps in amice grey' (426–38); nature cheers up, but Satan arrives again to mock. He assures Christ that the night's natural effects are 'harmless, if not wholesome, as a sneeze'; they are signs and prodigies to warn Christ to accept Satan's offer (481–3). Christ answers briefly, and Satan swells with rage (499) and, being still in doubt (as Milton was) about Christ's divinity, he takes hold of him 'and without wing/Of hippogrif bore through the air sublime' (541–2) to the Temple, 'far off appearing like a mount/Of alabaster, topped with golden spires'. He puts Christ on the top and challenges him to jump (551–9). Christ repels him and he finally collapses like Antaeus, the earth-born giant whom Hercules strangled in mid-air. This popular Renaissance story seems to come with the place, Irassa in Libya, from Pindar's ninth Pythian ode: and the 'swelling epithets thick-laid' at 343, unworthy to compare with Sion's songs, may well be suggested by the same ode (64–5) where they apply to Antaeus. It is interesting that this climax is classical.

> So Satan fell and straight a fiery globe
> Of angels on full sail of wing flew nigh,
> Who on their plumy vans received him soft
> From his uneasy station, and upbore
> As on a floating couch through the blithe air ...   (581–5)

They comfort Christ, feed him and sing him songs (596–635). Satan is to fall 'like an autumnal star/Or lightning' (619–20). That star has a long history: it begins in the *Iliad* as the glitter of the spear point of Achilles. Christ 'home to his mother's house private returned'. Modesty and privacy are themes of the whole poem. In some ways, in its smooth verse, its straight narrative, its seldom embroidered texture, *Paradise Regained* embodies Milton's self-criticism after the luxury, pomp and variety and maybe the lushness of *Paradise Lost*, but it is also a deliberately different and more contemporary style. It is astonishing that Milton can write an epic poem about how Paradise was regained in which nothing happens to anyone but Christ, who is not crucified and does not rise from the dead: he simply resists temptation. Yet it is a remarkable poem in its own way, and the plain and virtuous Christ is close to the Redeemer of the Gospel.

At the same time Milton published *Samson Agonistes*, a tragedy in the Greek style, 1,758 lines long: Euripides usually lasts a little under 1,700 lines. The originality of *Samson*, with its biblical theme and its English verse, is awe-inspiring: nothing goes before it, and it has never been imitated. Italian analogies are inexact and Buchanan's *Baptistes* is not worth mentioning. The Elizabethan influences of *Comus* and the epics are here almost completely pruned: Milton has put himself to school to Euripides and Sophocles, though his usual very close reading of the Bible – here, in particular, three or four chapters of Judges – is still a key to what he writes. Dramatically, *Samson* has faults that would render it intolerable to modern audiences. As a poem, however, it has long been taken for Milton's final and perhaps greatest moral statement. This idea, and the identification of its characters with Milton himself and those he knew, have been used in attempts to date *Samson Agonistes*: they have become preposterous, and W. R. Parker's counter-effort to give the play a date early in the poet's blindness found some supporters, though now the balance of scholarly opinion, in this case following the balance of probability, has returned to a late date. The poetry does seem to speak with the full weight of the experience of life of the ageing poet. On the other hand, there are reasons for suspecting that this play, or something like it, had been in his mind a long time: perhaps for twenty years. The choral lyrics have suggested a connection with Milton's ode to Rouse (1647), since he explains them in similar terms, but they are so original (the lyrics) or eccentric (ode to Rouse) that they are hard to argue from. The Trinity manuscript suggests some major publication was planned in 1653; as to that, we know only that it did not appear. I have noticed most of the hints in their places and was seriously tempted to accept the earlier date. Yet for a poet to adopt a new style in old age is difficult to imagine: for him to work out one earlier and then simply drop it is almost inconceivable. The weight of suffering in *Samson Agonistes* is not a dating factor. Milton may also have kept the play half-elaborated for years. But the maturity of the poetry is undeniable. Edward Phillipps thought the date 'cannot certainly be concluded'.

Milton had in mind the *Oedipus at Colonus* of Sophocles, a thrilling and daring model, but his title contains a sardonic joke: it means 'Samson the Champion', or 'Samson contends'. The play opens with his monologue 'before the Prison in Gaza', which tells us all we should know and feel about the blinded hero: his words are very terrible, worse than the invocation in Book 3 of *Paradise Lost*.

> O dark, dark, dark, amid the blaze of noon,
> Irrecoverably dark, total eclipse
> Without all hope of day!
> O first-created beam, and thou great word,
> Let there be light, and light was over all;
> Why am I thus bereaved thy prime decree?
> The sun to me is dark
> And silent as the moon,
> When she deserts the night,
> Hid in her vacant interlunar cave.   (80–89)

The monologue is the strongest piece of poetry in the play, and the best piece of blank verse since the death of Shakespeare. The chorus (of the tribe of Dan from the town where he was born) break in on his solitude (115) in language with iron in it: 'Chalybean-tempered steel, and frock of mail/... The gates of Azza, post, and massy bar' (Azza is an alternative for Gaza, and a moment's trial of 'Gaza' will show why 'Azza' was used). Their lamentation continues until line 175, where a dialogue with Samson begins. He explains his marriage outside the community as a divine plan. His true purpose (Judg. 14: 4) was to pick a quarrel with the Philistines. He muses over the same subject of liberty as in the *History of England* and in *Paradise Regained*:

> But what more oft in nations grown corrupt,
> And by their vices brought to servitude,
> Than to love bondage more than liberty,
> Bondage with ease than strenuous liberty;
> And to despise, or envy, or suspect

> Whom God hath of his special favour raised
> As their deliverer . . . ? (268–74)

The chorus plunge into the still deeper argument of God's justice and human reason, which they then apply (322–5) like moral theologians to the case of Samson's marriage. Samson's old father, Manoa, then arrives (326–8) and can hardly recognize him. He grieves and Samson comforts him. This involves Samson in a passionate denunciation of the woman

> who also in her prime of love,
> Spousal embraces, vitiated with gold,
> Though offered only, by the scent conceived
> Her spurious first-born . . . (388–91)

'By the scent of gold' is what he means: he ends with a cool, Greek-sounding analysis of his own slave-like degeneracy which might be pure Euripides (414–19). Manoa warns him he is to figure today in the festival of the fish-god Dagon (whom Milton used in *Paradise Lost* as a devil or god, though he does not figure in these chapters of Judges). Samson agrees he has disgraced God, but says God will strike. His father wants to ransom him (481–3) but he refuses. Manoa goes further and speaks severely of suicide (508–15). It may well be that this discussion had in 1660 or in 1653 been real to Milton: it has a Roman ring, and a resonance which is not in *De Doctrina Christiana*, though that is doctrinally similar. Samson says he was tempted and fell, though he was a better hero than the Anakim, the giants of Hebron. The chorus, as tiresomely eloquent as any Greek chorus, remark that drink was not the problem (541–6), and Samson answers with a fine bit of Euripidean English (547–52). Nature within him seems 'in all her functions weary of herself' (596). His grief moves into lyric verse of great power, in which he speaks of

> Dire inflammation which no cooling herb
> Or med'cinal liquor can assuage,
> Nor breath of vernal air from snowy alp.
> Sleep hath forsook and given me o'er
> To death's benumbing opium as my only cure. . . . (626–30)

The chorus take up the chant, singing of how God 'with hand so various,/Or might I say contrarious' (668–9) deals with man, and into this Milton insinuates his own case. Suddenly Dalila, Samson's Philistine wife, arrives like a ship in full sail, with 'An amber scent of odorous perfume' (720) and weeping. She makes a conciliatory speech of sixteen lines but Samson calls her a hyena. She pours out excuses at greater length but Samson calls her sorceress. This rather pointless argument goes on, with a bit of Grotius's political theory (888–94) to give it substance. She sees he is implacable, but boasts she will be famous, 'my tomb/With odours visited and annual flowers' (986–7). She leaves him, and the chorus now deplore her; they discuss love with Samson and in doing so introduce the curious word 'Paranymph' for best man (1020). Harapha of Gath, a giant from 2 Sam.: 21, then arrives (1065–75), renowned 'as Og or Anak and the Emims old'. The two of them are longing to fight each other and the conversation goes accordingly, full of words like 'brigandine' and 'vantbrace', and lines about 'chafed wild boars and ruffled porcupines' (1138), but Harapha retires 'in a sultry chafe'. Samson is happy to risk death, and 'O how comely it is and how reviving', say the chorus, when God inspires 'plain heroic magnitude of mind'. In this scene Milton veers perhaps towards an Italian or romance manner, but within the limits of tragedy. A public officer comes to summon Samson but Samson refuses to perform, though now that his hair has grown again he could. He begins, in fact, to see his way. The officer comes a second time and Samson goes with him, leaving the chorus. Manoa arrives to tell them his plans to free Samson, but as he does so they hear shouts and a noise of ruin. A messenger brings them the news, which he lets out little by little, until his formal narrative (1596–659). Samson has brought down the roof on the Philistines and on himself. The narrative is clear and strong. The chorus says virtue is like a phoenix, in the metre of *The Phoenix and the Turtle*.

> Like that self-begotten bird
> In the Arabian woods embossed,
> That no second knows nor third,
> And lay erewhile a holocaust . . .
> A secular bird ages of lives.   (1699–707)

This strange chant with its magical closure (in choriambic dimeter) restores to the play whatever of mystery it had lost since the first monologue: lost inevitably through a rational treatment. It rises awe-inspiringly to the height of its theme, and at last justifies the books of Italian theory with which Milton had (as it seemed) preposterously stuffed his head. It is both a tragedy and a heroic poem. Manoa speaks the lament for his son, turning everything to triumph, which a Greek play would not quite do.

> Nothing is here for tears, nothing to wail
> Or knock the breast, no weakness, no contempt,
> Dispraise, or blame; nothing but well and fair,
> And what may quiet us in a death so noble.   (1721–4)

Manoa will bury his son and plant trees and set up games in his honour: 'the virgins also shall on feastful days/Visit his tomb with flowers'. The final line is from Aristotle on the effect of tragedy, how it purges the mind by pity and terror: 'and calm of mind all passion spent.'

As a dramatic vehicle the play does not really work. The characters of Dalila and Harapha have too little to do but goad, and there is not much real plot; poor old Manoa changes attitude amazingly, and only Samson and the chorus have solid existence. But the verse is remarkable, and in places as good as anything this poet had ever composed. Our inability to date it means we can only surmise that at the very end of his career, quite close to the time of his death, the poet put all his powers into an enterprise as original as was ever produced, and that in this demanding task he was largely successful.

His aim was 'to vindicate tragedy from the small esteem or rather infamy which in the account of many it undergoes at this day ... brought in without discretion corruptly to satisfy the people'. This was clearly a headlong attack against the Restoration theatre and its patrons and authors. It was ignored as it was bound to be, and yet was he not right? His only excuse for this curmudgeonly action is his greatness, and his wide experience of poetry. It is a matter for consternation that he can never have expected *Samson* to be performed, and that he was attempting to alter the course of theatrical history by an action at once dogmatic and despairing. That, alas, is not untypical of his life. Dr Johnson's attack on the play is memorable, but not quite just. The Doctor complained it had a beginning and an end, but no middle, no connection between them. Dalila and Harapha are well drawn, after all, and represent psychological if not logical steps, as Samson's father does too, in producing or evoking his final heroic mood. I wish I knew whether the silent pause in which he summons up his strength before suicide was prayer or something physical, but we are not meant to know. He was a Worthy, a popular hero who could not be plucked free of tradition.

In the next two years Milton published his *Logic* (1672) and *True Religion* (1673). Milton's version of logic would have been progressive in the 1630s, and it is possible that in English universities the logic-chopping was so antiquated that it was still useful. Hobbes said that Milton and Salmasius were both good Latinists and both rotten logicians, which up to a point is true. Milton hated Hobbes for some reason.

The book on *True Religion* seems to be acknowledged by no printer and claims no licence. It was a plain, simple pamphlet of sixteen pages, which tactically advocated toleration for Nonconformists, and no popery. Protestantism was the Word of God and the only safe guide, while popery was the only heresy or at least the greatest. He accepted the doctrine of Consubstantiation; Anabaptism was scriptural; the Arians and Socinians accepted Bible and Creed; predestination was not a mortal mistake. This may not be intellectually very fastidious, but at least it is tolerant. It is not surprising to find Marvell and Milton such close allies at this time, and if *True Religion* appears to us a political position and not the doctrinal statement we had expected, that is more easily explained from the close ally of a political man, as Marvell had become – as they had both become.

It used to be thought that Milton was publishing such obscure works as his grammar and his logic and his most readable history of England at this period because he needed money, but that is doubtful. He wanted to get them out of the way, and to present himself fully as all that he had been. In November 1673 he published his expanded collected minor poems, and included with them his *Treatise on Education* to Hartlib. The early poems, Latin and English, were now called *Poems, etc. upon Several Occasions*, and Milton included all the private sonnets that he could, the ode 'To Rouse' (1647), a fable against a landlord, a Latin exercise written at school fifty years before and the little translation of an ode of Horace which is so perfect. It is not datable with any certainty, and scholars have plumped for 1626 and 1655. Carey tries to tie it to an elegy in Latin to Diodati rejecting love, and so to 1629, but it is really as mysterious as *Samson Agonistes*. The only link I can suggest is to the early Horatian poems of Fanshawe: it has an ante-bellum or a Cambridge quality.

In the next year Milton produced his private Latin letters: *Epistolae Familiares*. He had wanted to include his Latin State letters, which would have added weight, but this was not allowed by some official, as we are told by his possibly over-careful publisher Brabazon Aylmer. Milton therefore produced his own *Prolusiones Oratoriae* instead, so as to make up a solid-looking book. There are bits and pieces of Latin prose, mostly from Cambridge, which cast some light on his college activities, his Neoplatonism and his rhetorical exercises, but they seem to me to be worthless. The Latin State documents did not see the light of day until the 1690s brought political change, when they were published by Edward Phillipps, with the three sonnets to Vane, Fairfax and Cromwell like a political credo at the beginning. One must greatly wonder whether Milton's late views on liberty and responsibility derived from Cromwell's, or whether the poet's views had influenced the great man's. Meanwhile he must have been excited by the second edition of *Paradise Lost* (1674) with its verses by Marvell and by Sam Barrow.

At the same time, Milton employed a young man called Daniel Skinner, who left Cambridge with a BA in 1673, to copy out his Latin State letters, and the 169 pages of *De Doctrina Christiana*. We do not know when that was composed, but it was written in tranquillity; my own impression is that this very full and remarkable statement of his personal theology was arrived at late in life. We know that in this late period of his life he attended no church; in fact, the last evidence that he did attend one, after his reply to the sermon on 'Fear God and the King' in April 1660, was his marriage in 1663.

Since Milton's theological work requires a new chapter, this is perhaps the appropriate moment to observe the results of the poet's third marriage, which were wholly good. Elizabeth looked after him, saw his great poems through to publication and quietly ordered his household. A letter written by Thomas Birch in 1750 records what was said a century later: that Mrs Milton treated Milton's daughters by his first marriage severely, and when she moved the poet to Artillery Walk she bound two of them as apprentices to workers in gold and silver lace, without Milton's knowledge. This sounds contradictory, since it is hard to believe they could go away and become working girls without his making any enquiry where they had gone or without his paying a fee for them as apprentices. But at least they did go, that seems certain, and the old man's life was doubtless the more peaceful for their going.

His wife is also, in the same letter, said to have forced the youngest daughter to leave his family. That seems quite untrue; she appears to have gone to Ireland freely as companion to a lady and to have married there a weaver called Abraham Clarke in Milton's lifetime. As for the other two, Milton told the rector of Ipswich, who visited him in July 1674, that 'the portion due from Powell I leave to the unkind children I had by her, but I have received no part of it. They shall have no other benefit of my estate, they have been very undutiful to me'. His third wife was present when he said this, and he was calm and without passion. It is therefore no surprise that his will, which was spoken not written, to his brother Christopher, was disputed: but his point about the Powell family never having paid his wife's dowry was true, and that dowry might traditionally have gone to his daughters. At about the same time his maid Elizabeth Fletcher heard him say to his wife at supper, 'God a'mercy, Betty, I see thou wilt perform according to thy promise, in providing for me such dishes as I think fit while I live, and when I die thou knowest I have left thee all.' Maybe he spoke as a joke, but the provision was clear enough, and repeated a number of times. As for the money the daughters claimed after Milton's death, he had declared quite peaceably, and more than once, that he had made provision for them in his lifetime, and 'had spent the greatest part of his estate in providing for them'.

A problem arises about dates. As Parker pointed out, we know that Milton moved from Jewin Street to Bunhill, that is to Artillery Lane, only from Edward Phillipps, but the two elder sisters and the youngest all seem to have left home in about 1670, and other evidence suggests that at his death the move to the house 'opposite the Artillery garden wall' was recent. Aubrey seems to think so, and so does the young Jacob Tonson, a publisher. Richardson says that in about 1670 Milton was not living at home at all but lodging with the bookseller Edward Millington, possibly to be near publishers. There is plenty of room for conjecture, but a quarrel with the daughters is not impossible; he could have told his wife he would come home when she had got rid of them or, more probably, he could have been lodging while he moved house, as Parker supposed. We know at least that the Bunhill house was a small one, while the Jewin Street house, which in 1665 attracted hearth-tax for eight fireplaces, was twice the size. Edward Phillipps is not at all reliable about dates (Parker, 1125–6), but the choice is to accept his date for Milton's last move, or the confusions and probabilities of the other witnesses. Edward was away from home, first of all as tutor to John Evelyn's household, and then as tutor at Wilton.

Meanwhile Milton's life had reached its end with the astounding series of *Paradise Lost* in a second edition (1674) and *Paradise Regained* and *Samson Agonistes* (1671). His last political pronouncement was *The Election of the King of Poland* (1674), a pamphlet of a dozen pages of such a lucidity and brilliance, and so unexpected, that no one else can be credited with it. It was accepted in 1698 as Milton's, and also by Toland. It is an apparently anonymous translation of an account of the Polish election of a new king, Jan Sobietzski, John III of Poland. The parallels with Cromwell, and with the English situation in 1674, when the King's death would bring in James II, a Catholic monarch, unless some stratagem like election prevented him, were obvious. Indeed, in less than ten years, in 1683, the *Propositions* of Hobbes and Milton were burnt at Oxford. No translator was named, but the prose breathes the breath of Milton, and he is certain to have done it. The new king was elected on 22 May, so as journalism this pamphlet was up to the minute. It is probable enough that Milton was paid by Brabazon Aylmer as publisher: the pamphlet makes inspiriting reading. At that time, Milton's Russian history must also have been in his hands. Milton had written that before he lost his sight, and it reads with the excitement and spirit of a young man: it appeared as the *History of Muscovy* (1682). *Muscovy* and *The Election* must be the best of Milton's prose writings except *Areopagitica*. His prose style is victorious but they are not often reprinted, nor is it often remembered how far Milton's serious interest in the world extended.

CHAPTER THIRTEEN

THEOLOGY

THERE IS NO WAY to date Milton's long book about Christianity except by the handwriting of Daniel Skinner, his amanuensis: evidently it was either composed or, more likely, fair-copied late in his life, and he seems to have intended, since English publication was out of the question in his last years, to have it printed abroad. That was a common enough device and he had recently used it. Skinner's hand suggests the 1670s, and the secrecy is explained by the revolutionary contents of the book. But it is important to know at what stage he worked out his theological views in such detail. The interest he had as a teacher or tutor in German and Dutch declarations on doctrinal matters suggests that in the early 1640s, when Milton was in his thirties, his mind was busy about these things, and perhaps the experience of teaching was a force in persuading him towards clarity, the most surprising and pleasing quality of this final statement.

He must have begun dissenting, at least inwardly, from the doctrine of the Church of England at the time when he decided against ordination. At Hammersmith and Horton his view must have hardened, and he opposed Laud with a certain savage bitterness. At Cambridge he appears to have been mildly intractable, but also puzzled, and was still so in the letter he wrote perhaps to Thomas Young, which is in the Trinity notebook. We should suppose, then, that he was argumentative and anti-clerical and probably a scornful extreme Protestant before his beard had grown. All this is not surprising in a young man who had Thomas Young for a tutor. Probably a little later he knew Edward Calamy, vicar of St Mary's, Aldermanbury (1639–62). He remembered the livery halls of Cripplegate as magnets for the wildest independence: Curriers' Hall for the Seventh Day Baptists, Glovers' Hall for Baptists (and later Wesleyans and Sandemanians) and so on, let alone the Anabaptists at Cradle Court, and Dr Doolittle's congregation later housed in Monkwell

Street (1671) in the first Nonconformist chapel ever built in the City of London, where Bunyan preached.

St Giles, where Milton's father was buried, was also the church where Cromwell was married. Bunhill was known to Aubrey as the 'Fanatiques' burial ground', and Gordon and Dewhirst on the ward of Cripplegate (1985) trace the extremes of this area around which Milton hovered, and where he came to rest, far back into the sixteenth century. At Bread Street he was brought up to Nonconformity, as we have seen, with an element of political hope about it that attracted him though he lived through its failure. His doctrinal vigour and clarity should not be counted as an intellectual quality exactly; it was no more essential to his mind than the puzzled mathematics and optics of his poetry: he was after all a pre-Newtonian muser. But the clarity about doctrines comes from the amount of argument that had been devoted to the subject for over a century. It is to be found among the Jesuits and at the Council of Trent; Izaak Walton knows and respects it in an English bishop. Milton can put it on like an overcoat, that is all. He learnt it at Cambridge, where a medieval tradition had preserved it as a late flower of scholasticism.

The fate of Milton's book about Christian doctrine was a curious one. Aylmer sensibly refused to touch it. At first it was taken to Elzevir in Amsterdam, but the British government discovered this and approached Elzevir about it. The matter then hung fire; Daniel Skinner, the young man in charge of the manuscript, wanted a job under the British government, and entered into negotiations for one, involving Milton's State letters, which seem to have worried the government much more. Sir J. Williamson refused to license any English edition of those and refused to allow an advertisement in the *Gazette* for the authentic edition produced in Holland; what is more, he demanded to see any further Milton papers. Skinner got a job of a kind under Sir Leoline Jenkins at Nijmegen, and set off with a stern warning from Sir J. Williamson against permitting his book to be printed; this warning was also put in writing to Sir Leoline Jenkins. In November 1676 Skinner was cornered: the State letters in Latin had suddenly appeared in October, and he now wanted only to withdraw.

On 20 October, Daniel Elzevier wrote to Williamson that he had now seen the theology manuscript and thought it had better be suppressed. He had 'since then' given the papers back to the boy, and he assured Williamson that he had never contemplated a 'Collected Works' by John Milton. That, of course, must have been the deepest fear of the British government, but tormenting the Church of England was quite bad enough. Skinner's father had now sent him to France to learn better French. He still hoped to be taken on by Williamson as a diplomat. It is quite untrue, he says, that Elzevir had sent back his Milton papers. Elzevir replied in a letter of excuses to Skinner's father: 'It had begun to freeze . . . I shall send them to you.' Meanwhile the Master of Trinity (Isaac Barrow) demanded that young Skinner should return at once, but in March Skinner was thinking of Italy. In May 1669, however, he was admitted a major fellow of Trinity. Who knows whether, behind all these pressures, the hand of the government was not moving?

The 'Christian Doctrine' manuscript was returned, but no one ever read it again until 1825, when it was found as a parcel still in its wrapping paper, addressed to 'Mr Skinner, Merchant', in a cupboard in Whitehall where Williamson's secretary, Pitt, had put it. Luckily, when it was found George IV ordered the work to be printed, as it was by Sumner, a librarian and a clergyman who became Bishop of Winchester and was a brother of the Archbishop of Canterbury. Sumner's edition is excellent and his notes pertinent: indeed, the edition is beyond praise. It is a pity perhaps that it stayed in Latin and is now available only in immensely expensive American complete editions of Milton. The person who did most for it, in an article that rocked England, and was so much and so universally discussed that it initiated the great age of such articles, was Macaulay. Richard Sumner's 1826 edition calls the document (in Latin) 'dragged out from the darkness of the public records' by order of George IV, and offers facsimiles of 'Cromwell, our chief of men', and 'Methought I saw my late espoused saint'. In the last year the first translation has appeared, I believe by John Carey.

From the beginning of the treatise Milton makes brisk statements like 'As for myself, I stick to the Holy Scripture alone, and I belong to no other ecclesiastical party or sect whatsoever.' He is to address the question, 'What the doctrine of Christ is and how many parts it has. This teaching is what Christ divinely made known to all ages, even if it was not so known from the beginning'. So far so good: Milton's manner is reverent, and his doctrine so far unsurprising: at the worst it is no worse than that of poor Chillingworth, who died after the siege of Arundel. The teaching of Christ was for the glory of God and the salvation of men: and we demand that Christians should believe the Scriptures.

The parts of this doctrine or teaching are the knowledge of God, and charity or the religious cult of God. As it turns out, the first part is what preoccupied Milton. By page eleven he has got to Conscience, and without any trace of Neoplatonism, which he has outgrown or forgotten, or perhaps thinks irrelevant to this sternly theological logic. With no God, he announces, there would be no distinction between good and evil. This seems a queer point of view, but let us not argue, only (like Dante) observe and pass on. In the Scripture, we are informed, there is nothing indecorous nor unworthy, since it is God talking about himself. This might to modern readers seem even queerer, but it was once widely believed, and if all Scripture is equally decorous and worthy, then the picker and chooser has a wide field of choice. Milton had exercised his in *Samson Agonistes*. God has given himself to us as an object to be contemplated. He is Jehovah, Jah and Ehie: he who is, was and shall be. (We are told this is in Hebrew.) The true God is by his nature the most simple Spirit, and in him there is no composition, no substance and no person. Suddenly in a sentence, when Milton has been innocently pondering Hebrew roots, the Trinity goes overboard. God is immense, infinite, immutable, incorruptible and everywhere omnipotent. He is one; he lives, knows and wills. He is supremely happy, truthful, faithful and just: wonderful and incomprehensible.

In Chapter 4 we come to predestination and election. Here he takes refuge in the *Odyssey* (1, 7, and 1, 32–4) and warns us that man makes his own sufferings and blames the justice of Zeus. In Chapter 5 he deals with the Son and the Spirit. He notices that Catholics say the Trinity cannot be proved from Scripture. Milton says he imposes his view on no one, and no one need be angry with him. They should judge this book without prejudice. The Son is not the Father (and here he expends some scorn on emanations and spirations). Generation creates what is external to God, and if the Son is generated then he is 'one with the Father' only as we are with him. Only the Father is to be called God. God is called Elohim, which is a plural word but it does not mean more than one God: let no one be deceived but look at Judges 13: 21–2. He deals very fully with this question in fifty-two pages (57–109); indeed, he may be said to beat it into the ground.

In Chapter 6 (110–23) we reach the Holy Spirit. God and angels and the mind of man may all be called 'spirit' and he goes through the arguments like a knife through butter. Chapter 7 is more rewarding, since it covers Creation. What was God doing before the world was created? One would be an idiot to enquire and not much brighter if one attempted an answer. This sentence depends on Latin word order, which I have preserved, and maybe the question mark is illegitimate and should just be a comma. Creation is what God the Father has by his word and spirit – that is, by his will – produced to show the glory and power of his goodness. Consider Genesis 1: 2: God's power is not a person. All is created not from nothing but from himself. Many Greek and some Latin fathers think that angels existed long before this physical world, and that the fall of the angels probably took place before this world. It was an apostasy in which many thousands turned away and were driven from Heaven. The world and all that is in it and the whole human race are visible things, *visibilia*. Here the Latin is no longer perspicuously clear.

Chapter 8 discusses Providence. His examples of it are all biblical, 'hardening, spurring, blinding'. Miracles are to show God's power and confirm our faith and make heavier the condemnation of unbelievers. Chapter 9 brings us to the special government of angels: the devils have princes and keep rank, and of these bad angels many wander the earth and air and the heavens. Can he have believed, or at least half-believed, all that I take for pure fiction in *Paradise Lost*? I think that he had a sneaking half-belief in it all. Good angels, he says, are not as the Papists pretend: he then allows for the military actions of angels. After this perplexing chapter comes Chapter 10 on man after the Fall, including the sabbath, marriage and polygamy, which he stoutly defends. On death he quotes Euripides: 'And whence each one came into his body,/Thither departs his spirit to the air,/His body to the earth'. I am not clear that this is a perfectly Christian or a scriptural text: it makes one wonder whether Milton did not prefer the classics, in the end.

He goes on to tell us about redemption and how it works, and how Christ is God-man, *Theanthropos*. He tells us of saving faith and being grafted on to Christ, but I am not sure how much all that can mean to him after that dash of cold water from Euripides, let alone if he has already decided there is no Son, no Spirit, only an incomprehensible God. But there it is (Chapters 21–2), written down in order. With the visible Church (332f.), he notes there can be no Pope on earth. The duties of the visible Church are pure doctrine, true cult of God, true Gospel charity, as far as men can judge these things, and a right administration of the Seals. By the Seals he means the bread and baptism, normally called sacraments. The ordinary ministers of his Church and its Seals can be any believer, though special ministers are sent by God to found and to reform Churches. One can hear Laud's teeth grinding from his grave. What have funerals and weddings got to do with any clergy? he asks. Surely if you can circumcise, then you can baptize. As for Scripture, we are all capable of interpreting that.

He discusses (351) scholarly doubts about the editors of Scripture. His answer is that you believe in all Scripture because of the inward persuasion of the Spirit himself working on each of the faithful: *propter ipsum Spiritum unicuique fidelium intus persuadentem.* It is like the Samaritans, he subtly argues, who believed in Christ first because of what the woman said and then because of Christ himself and his words. Neither of these arguments is, in fact, original: the second is patristic but the first, I suspect, was first proposed by Calvin, who was still a formidable intellectual influence. So everything (Milton says) is to be referred to the Spirit, even the unwritten word, as Scripture itself witnesses. Written or unwritten human traditions will not stand. We cannot trust our elders or antiquity, not even the venerable Church, unless we mean the mystical and heavenly Church.

He discusses the particular Churches (354) in carefully general terms. He is clear that the election of ministers is a right of the people, and the people or their ministers should not rely on magistrates or their edicts for money. (We have come back to the tithe problem.) What should they live on then? On what the prophets and the apostles lived on. As he proceeds to the details of Church discipline he has perhaps less of importance to say, but wherever he is not original he at least gives an admirably lucid case-history of what happened in the mind of an intelligent, hard-working, scholarly man between 1630 and 1670. On the end of the world he recommends a book by Zanchius, *De Fine Saeculi.* The Last Judgement will be a self-judgement by one's own conscience in whatever light it has been given. Christ will not come in the flesh, contrary to the view of Junius on Daniel (7: 13) but we shall be glorified with things created in heaven and on earth for our use and our delight.

The second book, 'On the Religious Cult of God' (387–536), is just under 150 pages long, less than half the length of the first book. War is all right, as he has always said it was, but he deeply disapproves of superstition and hypocrisy, and it does not occur to him that these matters may be connected. We have no need for a liturgy because we simply follow the Spirit. He thought private groans were permissible but that prayers should be quiet. There ought to be no dead languages in public prayer, and tautology and futility were to be avoided both in private and in public. All places were fine for prayer and all times, but morning, evening and noon were to be preferred. He did at least think that fasting was a private matter and should not therefore be publicly imposed. On the whole, this second book is banal and thin compared to the first.

There is no English poet about whom there are so many major mysteries. W. R. Parker spent a lifetime trying to unravel them, but he did not always succeed. Indeed, near the end of his *Milton* he groups together the important unanswered questions just about Milton's last few years. Starting with the composition dates of *Samson Agonistes* and *Paradise Regained*, they range through his relations with his bookseller friend Millington, his contribution to the Roos case, Deborah's marriage, his relations with Daniel Skinner (who is not related to Cyriack) and the day of his death. But for every period of his life there are at least equally dark problems: we do not know enough about Cambridge, or about Thomas Young, or about when Milton heard of Diodati's death, or what he did in Venice, or what classics he read when, or whether he was serious about the law. We do not really know how he got mixed up with Cromwell, what he really thought of mob rule in churches, or if he had any views about Diggers and Levellers. We do not know for certain whether or when he became disillusioned with Cromwell, or whether the King really offered to re-employ him.

One might argue that his old pre-war life as a poet was distracted by theology but held together by the series of sonnets, which move from one tone to another, until in his blindness he composes his *Paradise Lost*: but then how explain the stage of charming Horatian sonnets to Lawrence and to Cyriack Skinner that form a plateau on their own and, more astonishing still, the final bursting out of *Paradise Regained* and of *Samson Agonistes*? In this perspective, I do not think that his *Christian Doctrine* has taken up too much of our time, but it may have taken up too much of his, and so may his pamphlets about Smectymnus, which are the equivalent of letters to the *Church Times*. But their importance is that they drew him into politics and into *Areopagitica*, the central issue of most of his life after all, in which his theological treatise is only one of many incidents.

Had none of it happened, had Lady Derby lived for ever, as it were, would he have gone on happily writing works like *Comus*? I doubt it, and he doubted *Comus*, as the publication history shows. He was determined to write an epic, a heroic narrative, and we must simply be thankful that we already had the ode 'On the Morning of Christ's Nativity', 'L'Allegro' and 'Il Penseroso' and *Lycidas*, and I suppose *Comus* and 'Arcades', and that when he finally chose his subject, it had room for the idyllic scenes of natural wonders and, above all, for the thrilling growth of human passion that *Paradise Lost* allows. In the same way we must be grateful to Thomas Ellwood because out of his casual remark came Milton's idealized but wonderfully beautiful Athens.

He was a proud man, proud of his learning as he was of his art, and no doubt proud of his hard-hitting style, which is paralleled in many deadly theological writings of the Elizabethan generation. And that was doubtless where he got his style, from the Marprelate controversy and other works inflated by the same *odium theologicum* that filled his own hot-air balloon. Only remember that as late as 1836 William Carpenter writes in all honesty, 'these works are written with beautiful simplicity and earnestness, and should be studied by all who wish to understand the principles of religious liberty'. It is already hard to remember or imagine what English life under an established Church of the old kind was like, but Milton was surely right to struggle as he did; his quarrel was not with the King, however guilty the King may have been, so much as with the persecuting Church, the whole monolithic establishment of his youth and his old age: 'their seizing of pots and pans from the poor, who have as good right to tithes as they; from some the very beds; their suing and imprisoning . . .' (*The Best Means of Removing Hirelings*).

There remains the problem of his relations with women, not his patronesses like Lady Ranelagh, who retired to Dublin the same year as Deborah went with the lady she called Merian, nor the ladies he flirted with in verses in middle life, but his wives and daughters. His first wife begged him to take her back after the Civil War; he did so, and behaved decently enough to her family, but the circumstances were obviously dictated by the times, and that division must have remained, though there is no evidence of any further quarrel with that wife, who bore him four children, the last a son who would not live long. He did retain a grudge about her unpaid dowry: that was a family arrangement, and he was just about it, if not merciful. He quarrelled with the daughters by being too demanding in his blindness. The two elder daughters hated him and his third wife, of whose marriage they heard not from him but from the maid. It is small wonder that he came to dislike them. With the third his relations were more ambiguous and are obscure to us.

His second wife he adored, and with his third wife he was clearly on the pleasantest of terms. His brother stood up for his 'nuncupatory' or verbal will when it came to court: indeed, his clear and sturdy evidence makes one think him a better lawyer than anyone but James II, who made him a Lord Justice, seems to have believed. Milton the poet was too proud a man to defend himself publicly over such things as his intimate humanity with his wives or what was said in his bed-chamber. That he was a passionate lover and had been an innocent one we can fairly deduce from his description of the two conditions in *Paradise Lost*. He appears to have valued his last wife most for the way she looked after him, and every account we have of his last years suggests that she made him very happy indeed. He was vulnerable and could be made unhappy, certainly, as we can see from his delicate retelling of the story of Anteros from Plato's *Phaidros* (255d) and from other passages in his divorce writings; his third wife's kind treatment of him becomes all the more striking. As for polygamy without polyandry, of which he never entertained the possibility, it appears to me a crazy whim based on the Bible, as so many follies of the seventeenth century were, from tithes to regicide. It goes without saying that he was no champion of women's rights; he never seriously discussed women preachers, but he would I think have accepted them, if he had accepted any preachers at all.

There is no sign that he did, in his last years; he sat in the sun like a tranquil, happy secularist. Writers of his life like Richardson (1734) already speak of him as if he had been a Chinese sage: 'Had he lived in ancient Rome or Athens, what a lustre would his name have been clothed with.' Toland says he died worth £1,500, besides all his goods. Books and music were his governing passions to his dying day. He was not a big eater or drinker, 'played much upon an Organ he kept in the house, and had a Pully to swing and keep him in motion. But the love of Books exceded all his other Passions'. In summer he got up at four and in winter at five, but in the evenings he would be in bed at nine.

His dress in old age was a coat of coarse grey cloth worn with broad linen bands. He sat in an elbow-chair, sometimes outside his front door and often with his leg hanging over one arm. He was of middle height and well proportioned, with light-brown hair, regular features, pink cheeks and eyes that were bright blue in age but had been hazel in his youth. He was a pleasant talker, cheerful and affable. We know that he composed his poetry during the long nights of winter, and that when his secretary came for dictation he described the process as being 'milked'. In the evenings he would read poetry; he is said to spent early morning hours and Sundays at his Hebrew Bible, but we do not know how long he kept up this devout habit or how well he read Hebrew: he tends to use the same few quotations repeatedly. He sang a great deal. John Phillips says that his blindness came from a *gutta serena*, and that he died in 'a fit of the Gout, but with so little pain or emotion that the time of his expiring was not perceived by those in the room'.

Milton's death occurred in November 1674, and he was buried, as his father had been, in St Giles, Cripplegate, attended by his friends. The church is not easily found, surrounded as it is by school playgrounds and paved deserts, and Milton's bones were long ago dug up and sold as relics. Yet it is appropriate that he should lie in a Christian church, devastated by fire, by bombing and the vicissitudes of ecclesiastical fashion. This church was where Cromwell had married, and the monument of the topographical genius, the map-maker John Speed, guards the walls.

Milton, Toland tells us, 'as he looked upon true and absolute Freedom to be the greatest Happiness of this Life, whether to Societies or single Persons, so he thought Constraint of any sort to be the utmost Misery: for which Reason he used to tell those about him the entire Satisfaction of his Mind, that he had constantly employed his Strength and Faculties in the defence of Liberty, and in direct opposition to Slavery . . . he would say to his Friends, that the divine Properties of Goodness, Justice, and Mercy, were the adequate rule of human actions.'

Translations of the Latin and Italian Poems of Milton by William Cowper

ELEGIES

ELEGY I
To Charles Deodati

At length, my friend, the far-sent letters come,
Charged with thy kindness, to their destin'd home,
They come, at length, from Deva's Western side,
Where prone she seeks the salt Vergivian tide.
Trust me, my joy is great that thou shouldst be,
Though born of foreign race, yet born for me.
And that my sprightly friend, now free to roam,
Must seek again so soon his wonted home.
I well content, where Thames with refluent tide
My native city laves, meantime reside,   10
Nor zeal nor duty, now, my steps impell
To reedy Cam, and my forbidden cell,
Nor aught of pleasure in those fields have I,
That, to the musing bard, all shade deny.
'Tis time that I a pedant's threats disdain,
And fly from wrongs, my soul will ne'er sustain.
If peaceful days, in letter'd leisure spent,
Beneath my father's roof, be banishment,
Then call me banish'd, I will ne'er refuse
A name expressive of the lot I chuse.   20
I would, that, exiled to the Pontic shore,
Rome's hapless bard had suffer'd nothing more.

He then had equall'd even Homer's lays,
And Virgil! thou hadst won but second praise:
For here I woo the muse, with no controul;
And here my books – my life – absorb me whole.
Here too I visit, or to smile, or weep,
The winding theatre's majestic sweep;
The grave or gay colloquial scene recruits
My spirits, spent in learning's long pursuits;   30
Whether some senior shrewd, or spendthrift heir,
Suitor, or soldier, now unarm'd, be there,
Or some coif'd brooder o'er a ten years' cause,
Thunder the Norman gibb'rish of the laws.
The lacquey, there, oft dupes the wary sire,
And, artful, speeds th' enamour'd son's desire.
There, virgins oft, unconscious what they prove,
What love is, know not, yet, unknowing, love.
Or, if impassion'd Tragedy wield high
The bloody sceptre, give her locks to fly   40
Wild as the winds, and roll her haggard eye,
I gaze, and grieve, still cherishing my grief,
At times, e'en bitter tears yield sweet relief.
As when from bliss untasted torn away,
Some youth dies, hapless, on his bridal day,
Or when the ghost, sent back from shades below,
Fills the assassin's heart with vengeful woe,
When Troy, or Argos, the dire scene affords,
Or Creon's hall laments its guilty lords.
Nor always city-pent, or pent at home,   50
I dwell; but, when spring calls me forth to roam,
Expatiate in our proud suburban shades
Of branching elm, that never sun pervades.
Here many a virgin troop I may descry,
Like stars of mildest influence, gliding by.
Oh forms divine! Oh looks that might inspire
E'en Jove himself, grown old, with young desire!
Oft have I gazed on gem-surpassing eyes,
Outsparkling every star, that gilds the skies.
Necks whiter than the ivory arm bestow'd   60

By Jove on Pelops, or the milky road!
Bright locks, Love's golden snare! these falling low,
Those playing wanton o'er the graceful brow!
Cheeks too, more winning sweet than after show'r
Adonis turn'd to Flora's fav'rite flow'r!
Yield, heroines, yield, and ye who shar'd th' embrace
Of Jupiter in antient times, give place!
Give place, ye turban'd fair of Persia's coast!
And ye, not less renown'd, Assyria's boast!
Submit, ye nymphs of Greece! ye, once the bloom   70
Of Ilion! and all ye, of haughty Rome,
Who swept, of old, her theatres with trains
Redundant, and still live in classic strains!
To British damsels beauty's palm is due,
Aliens! to follow them is fame for you.
Oh city, founded by Dardanian hands,
Whose towering front the circling realm commands,
Too blest abode! no loveliness we see
In all the earth, but it abounds in thee.
The virgin multitude that daily meets,   80
Radiant with gold and beauty, in thy streets,
Outnumbers all her train, of starry fires,
With which Diana gilds thy lofty spires.
Fame says, that wafted hither by her doves,
With all her host of quiver-bearing loves,
Venus, preferring Paphian scenes no more,
Has fix'd her empire on thy nobler shore.
But lest the sightless boy inforce my stay,
I leave these happy walls, while yet I may.
Immortal Moly shall secure my heart   90
From all the sorc'ry of Circæan art,
And I will e'en repass Cam's reedy pools
To face once more the warfare of the schools.
Meantime accept this trifle! rhimes though few,
Yet such, as prove thy friend's remembrance true!

ELEGY II

ON THE DEATH OF THE UNIVERSITY
BEADLE AT CAMBRIDGE

Composed by Milton in the seventeenth year of his age.

Thee, whose refulgent staff, and summons clear,
    Minerva's flock long time was wont t' obey,
Although thyself an herald, famous here,
    The last of heralds, Death, has snatch'd away.
He calls on all alike, nor even deigns
To spare the office, that himself sustains.

Thy locks were whiter than the plumes display'd
    By Leda's paramour in antient time,
But thou wast worthy ne'er to have decay'd,
    Or Æson-like to know a second prime,   10
Worthy, for whom some goddess should have won
New life, oft kneeling to Apollo's son.

Commission'd to convene, with hasty call,
    The gowned tribes, how graceful wouldst thou stand!
So stood Cyllenius erst in Priam's hall,
    Wing footed messenger of Jove's command!
And so Eurybates, when he address'd
To Peleus' son Atrides' proud behest.

Dread queen of sepulchres! whose rig'rous laws
    And watchful eyes, run through the realms below,   20
Oh, oft too adverse to Minerva's cause!
    Too often to the muse not less a foe!
Chuse meaner marks, and with more equal aim
Pierce useless drones, earth's burthen, and its shame!

Flow, therefore, tears for him, from ev'ry eye,
    All ye disciples of the muses, weep!
Assembling, all, in robes of sable dye,
    Around his bier, lament his endless sleep!
And let complaining elegy rehearse,
In every school, her sweetest, saddest verse.   30

ELEGY III
ON THE DEATH OF THE BISHOP OF WINCHESTER
Composed in the Author's seventeenth year.

Silent I sat, dejected, and alone,
Making, in thought, the public woes my own,
When, first, arose the image in my breast
Of England's sufferings by that scourge, the Pest!
How death, his fun'ral torch and scythe in hand,
Entering the lordliest mansions of the land,
Has laid the gem-illumin'd palace low,
And levell'd tribes of nobles, at a blow.
I, next, deplor'd the fam'd fraternal pair,
Too soon to ashes turn'd, and empty air!   10
The heroes next, whom snatch'd into the skies,
All Belgia saw, and follow'd with her sighs,
But thee far most I mourn'd, regretted most,
Winton's chief shepherd, and her worthiest boast!
Pour'd out in tears I thus complaining said:
'Death, next in pow'r to him, who rules the dead!
Is't not enough that all the woodlands yield
To thy fell force, and ev'ry verdant field;
That lilies, at one noisome blast of thine,
And ev'n the Cyprian queen's own roses, pine;   20
That oaks themselves, although the running rill
Suckle their roots, must wither at thy will;
That all the winged nations, even those,
Whose heav'n-directed flight the future shows,
And all the beasts, that in dark forests stray,
And all the herds of Proteus are thy prey.
Ah envious! arm'd with pow'rs so unconfin'd!
Why stain thy hands with blood of human kind!
Why take delight, with darts, that never roam,
To chase a heav'n-born spirit from her home?'   30
    While thus I mourn'd, the star of evening stood,
Now newly ris'n above the western flood,
And Phœbus from his morning-goal again

Had reach'd the gulphs of the Iberian main.
I wish'd repose, and, on my couch reclin'd
Took early rest, to night and sleep resign'd.
When – Oh for words to paint what I beheld!
I seem'd to wander in a spacious field,
Where all the champaign glow'd with purple light
Like that of sun-rise on the mountain height;   40
Flow'rs over all the field, of ev'ry hue
That ever Iris wore, luxuriant grew.
Nor Chloris, with whom am'rous Zephyrs play,
E'er dress'd Alcinous' garden half so gay.
A silver current, like the Tagus, roll'd
O'er golden sands, but sands of purer gold,
With dewy airs Favonius fann'd the flow'rs,
With airs awaken'd under rosy bow'rs.
Such, poets feign, irradiated all o'er
The sun's abode on India's utmost shore.   50
    While I, that splendour, and the mingled shade
Of fruitful vines, with wonder fixt survey'd,
At once, with looks, that beam'd celestial grace,
The seer of Winton stood before my face.
His snowy vesture's hem descending low
His golden sandals swept, and pure as snow
New-fallen shone the mitre on his brow.
Where'er he trod a tremulous sweet sound
Of gladness shook the flow'ry scene around:
Attendant angels clap their starry wings,   60
The trumpet shakes the sky, all æther rings,
Each chaunts his welcome, folds him to his breast,
And thus a sweeter voice than all the rest:
'Ascend, my son! thy father's kingdom share!
My son! henceforth be free'd from ev'ry care!'
    So spake the voice, and at its tender close
With psaltry's sound th' angelic band arose.
Then night retired, and chas'd by dawning day
The visionary bliss pass'd all away.
I mourn'd my banish'd sleep, with fond concern;   70
Frequent to me may dreams like this return!

ELEGY IV
TO HIS TUTOR, THOMAS YOUNG
CHAPLAIN TO THE ENGLISH FACTORY AT HAMBURGH
Written in the Author's eighteenth year.

Hence my epistle – skim the deep – fly o'er
Yon smooth expanse to the Teutonic shore!
Haste – lest a friend should grieve for thy delay
And the Gods grant, that nothing thwart thy way!
I will myself invoke the king, who binds,
In his Sicanian echoing vault, the winds,
With Doris and her nymphs, and all the throng
Of azure gods, to speed thee safe along.
But rather, to insure thy happier haste,
Ascend Medea's chariot, if thou may'st;   10
Or that, whence young Triptolemus of yore
Descended, welcome on the Scythian shore.
The sands, that line the German coast, descried,
To opulent Hamburga turn aside!
So called, if legendary fame be true,
From Hama, whom a club-arm'd Cimbrian slew!
There lives, deep-learn'd and primitively just,
A faithful steward of his Christian trust,
My friend, and favorite inmate of my heart,
That now is forced to want its better part!   20
What mountains now, and seas, alas! how wide!
From me this other, dearer self divide,
Dear, as the sage renown'd for moral truth
To the prime spirit of the Attic youth!
Dear, as the Stagyrite to Ammon's son,
His pupil, who disdain'd the world he won!
Nor so did Chiron, or so Phœnix shine
In young Achilles' eyes, as he in mine.
First led by him thro' sweet Aonian shade,
Each sacred haunt of Pindus I survey'd;   30
And favor'd by the muse, whom I implor'd,
Thrice on my lip the hallow'd stream I pour'd.

But thrice the sun's resplendent chariot roll'd
To Aries, has new ting'd his fleece with gold,
And Chloris twice has dress'd the meadows gay,
And twice has summer parch'd their bloom away,
Since last delighted on his looks I hung,
Or my ear drank the music of his tongue:
Fly, therefore, and surpass the tempest's speed!
Aware thyself, that there is urgent need!   40
Him, entering, thou shalt haply seated see
Beside his spouse, his infants on his knee;
Or turning, page by page, with studious look,
Some bulky father, or God's holy book;
Or minist'ring (which is his weightiest care)
To Christ's assembled flock their heavenly fare.
Give him, whatever his employment be,
Such gratulation, as he claims from me!
And, with a down-cast eye, and carriage meek,
Addressing him, forget not thus to speak!   50
    If, compass'd round with arms thou canst attend
To verse, verse greets thee from a distant friend.
Long due, and late, I left the English shore;
But make me welcome for that cause the more:
Such from Ulysses, his chaste wife to cheer,
The slow epistle came, tho' late, sincere.
But wherefore this? why palliate I the deed,
For which the culprit's self could hardly plead?
Self-charged, and self-condemn'd, his proper part
He feels neglected, with an aching heart;   60
But thou forgive – delinquents, who confess
And pray forgiveness, merit anger less;
From timid foes the lion turns away,
Nor yawns upon or rends a crouching prey;
Even pike-wielding Thracians learn to spare,
Won by soft influence of a suppliant prayer;
And heav'n's dread thunderbolt arrested stands
By a cheap victim, and uplifted hands.
Long had he wish'd to write, but was withheld,
And writes at last, by love alone compell'd;   70

For fame, too often true, when she alarms,
Reports thy neighbouring-fields a scene of arms;
Thy city against fierce besiegers barr'd,
And all the Saxon chiefs for fight prepar'd.
Enyo wastes thy country wide around,
And saturates with blood the tainted ground;
Mars rests contented in his Thrace no more,
But goads his steeds to fields of German gore,
The ever verdant olive fades and dies,
And peace, the trumpet-hating goddess, flies,   80
Flies from that earth which justice long had left,
And leaves the world of its last guard bereft.

   Thus horror girds thee round. Meantime alone
Thou dwell'st, and helpless in a soil unknown;
Poor, and receiving from a foreign hand
The aid denied thee in thy native land.
Oh, ruthless country, and unfeeling more
Than thy own billow-beaten chalky shore!
Leav'st thou to foreign care the worthies, giv'n
By providence, to guide thy steps to Heav'n?   90
His ministers, commission'd to proclaim
Eternal blessings in a Saviour's name!
Ah then most worthy, with a soul unfed,
In Stygian night to lie for ever dead!
So once the venerable Tishbite stray'd
An exil'd fugitive from shade to shade,
When, flying Ahab, and his fury wife,
In lone Arabian wilds, he shelter'd life;
So, from Philippi, wander'd forth forlorn
Cilician Paul, with sounding scourges torn;   100
And Christ himself, so left, and trod no more,
The thankless Gergesenes' forbidden shore.

   But thou take courage! strive against despair!
Quake not with dread, nor nourish anxious care!
Grim war indeed on ev'ry side appears,
And thou art menac'd by a thousand spears;
Yet none shall drink thy blood, or shall offend
Ev'n the defenceless bosom of my friend.

For thee the Ægis of thy God shall hide,
Jehovah's self shall combat on thy side.   110
The same, who vanquish'd under Sion's tow'rs
At silent midnight, all Assyria's pow'rs;
The same who overthrew in ages past,
Damascus' sons that lay'd Samaria waste;
Their king he fill'd and them with fatal fears
By mimic sounds of clarions in their ears,
Of hoofs, and wheels, and neighings from afar,
Of clashing armour, and the din of war.
    Thou, therefore, (as the most afflicted may)
Still hope, and triumph, o'er thy evil day!   120
Look forth, expecting happier times to come,
And to enjoy, once more, thy native home!

ELEGY V
On the Approach of Spring
Written in the Author's twentieth year.

Time, never wand'ring from his annual round,
Bids Zephyr breathe the spring, and thaw the ground;
Bleak winter flies, new verdure clothes the plain,
And earth assumes her transient youth again.
Dream I, or also to the spring belong
Increase of genius, and new pow'rs of song?
Spring gives them, and, how strange soe'er it seems,
Impels me now to some harmonious themes.
Castalia's fountain, and the forked hill
By day, by night, my raptur'd fancy fill,   10
My bosom burns and heaves, I hear within
A sacred sound, that prompts me to begin.
Lo! Phœbus comes, with his bright hair he blends
The radiant laurel wreath; Phœbus descends;
I mount, and, undepress'd by cumb'rous clay,
Through cloudy regions win my easy way;
Rapt through poetic shadowy haunts I fly:
The shrines all open to my dauntless eye,

My spirit searches all the realms of light,
And no Tartarean gulphs elude my sight.   20
But this ecstatic trance – this glorious storm
Of inspiration – what will it perform?
Spring claims the verse, that with his influence glows,
And shall be paid with what himself bestows.
   Thou, veil'd with op'ning foliage, lead'st the throng
Of feather'd minstrels, Philomel! in song;
Let us, in concert, to the season sing,
Civic, and sylvan heralds of the spring!
   With notes triumphant spring's approach declare!
To spring, ye Muses, annual tribute bear!   30
The Orient left, and Æthiopia's plains,
The Sun now northward turns his golden reins;
Night creeps not now; yet rules with gentle sway,
And drives her dusky horrors swift away;
Now less fatigued, on his ætherial plain
Bootes follows his celestial wain;
And now the radiant centinels above,
Less num'rous, watch around the courts of Jove,
For, with the night, force, ambush, slaughter fly,
And no gigantic guilt alarms the sky.   40
Now haply says some shepherd, while he views,
Recumbent on a rock, the redd'ning dews,
This night, this surely, Phœbus miss'd the fair,
Who stops his chariot by her am'rous care.
Cynthia, delighted by the morning's glow,
Speeds to the woodland, and resumes her bow;
Resigns her beams, and, glad to disappear,
Blesses his aid, who shortens her career.
Come – Phœbus cries – Aurora come – too late
Thou linger'st, slumb'ring, with thy wither'd mate!   50
Leave him, and to Hymettus' top repair!
Thy darling Cephalus expects thee there.
The goddess, with a blush, her love betrays,
But mounts, and driving rapidly, obeys.
Earth now desires thee, Phœbus! and t' engage
Thy warm embrace, casts off the guise of age;

Desires thee, and deserves; for who so sweet,
When her rich bosom courts thy genial heat?
Her breath imparts to ev'ry breeze that blows,
Arabia's harvest, and the Paphian rose.   60
Her lofty fronts she diadems around
With sacred pines, like Ops on Ida crown'd;
Her dewy locks, with various flow'rs new-blown,
She interweaves, various, and all her own,
For Proserpine, in such a wreath attired,
Tænarian Dis himself with love inspired.
Fear not, lest, cold and coy, the nymph refuse!
Herself, with all her sighing Zephyrs, sues;
Each courts thee, fanning soft his scented wing,
And all her groves with warbled wishes ring.   70
Nor, unendow'd and indigent, aspires
The am'rous Earth to engage thy warm desires,
But, rich in balmy drugs, assists thy claim,
Divine Physician! to that glorious name.
If splendid recompense, if gifts can move
Desire in thee (gifts often purchase love),
She offers all the wealth, her mountains hide,
And all that rests beneath the boundless tide.
How oft, when headlong from the heav'nly steep
She sees thee playing in the western deep,   80
How oft she cries – 'Ah Phœbus! why repair
Thy wasted force, why seek refreshment there?
Can Tethys win thee? wherefore shouldst thou lave
A face so fair in her unpleasant wave?
Come, seek my green retreats, and rather chuse
To cool thy tresses in my chrystal dews,
The grassy turf shall yield thee sweeter rest;
Come, lay thy evening glories on my breast,
And breathing fresh, through many a humid rose,
Soft whispering airs shall lull thee to repose!   90
No fears I feel like Semele to die,
Nor let thy burning wheels approach too nigh,
For thou can'st govern them, here therefore rest,
And lay thy evening glories on my breast!'

Thus breathes the wanton Earth her am'rous flame,
And all her countless offspring feel the same;
For Cupid now through every region strays,
Bright'ning his faded fires with solar rays,
His new-strung bow sends forth a deadlier sound,
And his new-pointed shafts more deeply wound; 100
Nor Dian's self escapes him now untried,
Nor even Vesta at her altar-side;
His mother too repairs her beauty's wane,
And seems sprung newly from the deep again,
Exulting youths the Hymeneal sing,
With Hymen's name roofs, rocks, and vallies, ring;
He, new-attired, and by the season drest,
Proceeds, all fragrant, in his saffron vest.
Now, many a golden-cinctur'd virgin roves
To taste the pleasures of the fields and groves, 110
All wish, and each alike, some fav'rite youth
Hers, in the bonds of Hymeneal truth.
Now pipes the shepherd through his reeds again,
Nor Phillis wants a song, that suits the strain;
With songs the seaman hails the starry sphere,
And dolphins rise from the abyss to hear;
Jove feels himself the season, sports again
With his fair spouse, and banquets all his train.
Now too the Satyrs, in the dusk of eve,
Their mazy dance through flowery meadows weave, 120
And neither god nor goat, but both in kind,
Sylvanus, wreath'd with cypress, skips behind.
The Dryads leave their hollow sylvan cells
To roam the banks, and solitary dells;
Pan riots now; and from his amorous chafe
Ceres and Cybele seem hardly safe,
And Faunus, all on fire to reach the prize,
In chase of some enticing Oread, flies;
She bounds before, but fears too swift a bound,
And hidden lies, but wishes to be found. 130
Our shades entice th' Immortals from above,
And some kind pow'r presides o'er every grove;

And long, ye pow'rs, o'er every grove preside,
For all is safe, and blest, where ye abide!
Return, O Jove! the age of gold restore –
Why choose to dwell, where storms and thunder roar?
At least, thou, Phœbus! moderate thy speed!
Let not the vernal hours too swift proceed,
Command rough Winter back, nor yield the pole
Too soon to Night's encroaching, long controul!   140

ELEGY VI
To Charles Deodati

Who, while he spent his Christmas in the country, sent the Author a poetical epistle, in which he requested that his verses, if not so good as usual, might be excused on account of the many feasts, to which his friends invited him, and which would not allow him leisure to finish them, as he wished.

With no rich viands overcharg'd, I send
Health, which perchance you want, my pamper'd friend;
But wherefore should thy muse tempt mine away
From what she loves, from darkness into day?
Art thou desirous to be told how well
I love thee, and in verse? verse cannot tell,
For verse has bounds, and must in measure move;
But neither bounds nor measure knows my love.
How pleasant, in thy lines describ'd, appear
December's harmless sports, and rural cheer!   10
French spirits kindling with cærulean fires,
And all such gambols, as the time inspires!
   Think not that wine against good verse offends;
The Muse and Bacchus have been always friends,
Nor Phœbus blushes sometimes to be found
With ivy, rather than with laurel, crown'd.
The Nine themselves ofttimes have join'd the song,
And revels of the Bacchanalian throng;
Not even Ovid could in Scythian air
Sing sweetly – why? no vine would flourish there.   20
What in brief numbers sung Anacreon's muse?
Wine, and the rose, that sparkling wine bedews.

Pindar with Bacchus glows – his every line
Breathes the rich fragrance of inspiring wine,
While, with loud crash o'erturn'd, the chariot lies
And brown with dust the fiery courser flies.
The Roman lyrist steep'd in wine his lays
So sweet in Glycera's, and Chloe's praise.
Now too the plenteous feast, and mantling bowl
Nourish the vigour of thy sprightly soul;   30
The flowing goblet makes thy numbers flow,
And casks not wine alone, but verse, bestow.
Thus Phœbus favors, and the arts attend,
Whom Bacchus, and whom Ceres, both befriend.
What wonder then, thy verses are so sweet,
In which these triple powers so kindly meet.
The lute now also sounds, with gold in-wrought,
And touch'd, with flying fingers, nicely taught,
In tap'stried halls, high roof'd, the sprightly lyre
Directs the dancers of the virgin choir.   40
If dull repletion fright the Muse away,
Sights, gay as these, may more invite her stay;
And, trust me, while the iv'ry keys resound,
Fair damsels sport, and perfumes steam around,
Apollo's influence, like aethereal flame,
Shall animate, at once, thy glowing frame,
And all the Muse shall rush into thy breast,
By love and music's blended pow'rs possest.
For num'rous pow'rs light Elegy befriend,
Hear her sweet voice, and at her call attend;   50
Her, Bacchus, Ceres, Venus, all approve,
And, with his blushing mother, gentle Love.
Hence to such bards we grant the copious use
Of banquets, and the vine's delicious juice.
But they, who demi-gods, and heroes praise,
And feats perform'd in Jove's more youthful days,
Who now the counsels of high heaven explore,
Now shades, that echo the Cerberean roar,
Simply let these, like him of Samos live,
Let herbs to them a bloodless banquet give;   60

In beechen goblets let their bev'rage shine,
Cool from the chrystal spring, their sober wine!
Their youth should pass, in innocence, secure
From stain licentious, and in manners pure,
Pure as the priest, when rob'd in white he stands,
The fresh lustration ready in his hands.
Thus Linus liv'd, and thus, as poets write,
Tiresias, wiser for his loss of sight!
Thus exil'd Chalcas, thus the bard of Thrace,
Melodious tamer of the savage race!   70
Thus train'd by the temp'rance, Homer led, of yore,
His chief of Ithaca from shore to shore,
Through magic Circe's monster-peopled reign,
And shoals insidious with the siren train;
And through the realms, where grizzly spectres dwell,
Whose tribes he fetter'd in a gory spell;
For these are sacred bards, and, from above,
Drink large infusions from the mind of Jove!
   Would'st thou (perhaps 'tis hardly worth thine ear)
Would'st thou be told my occupation here?   80
The promised King of peace employs my pen,
Th' eternal cov'nant made for guilty men,
The new-born Deity with infant cries
Filling the sordid hovel, where he lies,
The hymning angels, and the herald star,
That led the Wise, who sought him from afar,
And idols on their own unhallow'd shore
Dash'd, at his birth, to be revered no more!
   This theme on reeds of Albion I rehearse:
The dawn of that blest day inspired the verse;   90
Verse, that, reserv'd in secret, shall attend
Thy candid voice, my critic, and my friend!

ELEGY VII
Composed in the Author's nineteenth year.

As yet a stranger to the gentle fires,
That Amathusia's smiling queen inspires,

Not seldom I derided Cupid's darts,
And scorn'd his claim to rule all human hearts.
'Go, child,' I said, 'transfix the tim'rous dove!
An easy conquest suits an infant love;
Enslave the sparrow, for such prize shall be
Sufficient triumph to a chief like thee!
Why aim thy idle arms at human kind?
Thy shafts prevail not 'gainst the noble mind.'   10
   The Cyprian heard, and, kindling into ire,
(None kindles sooner) burn'd with double fire.
   It was the spring, and newly risen day
Peep'd o'er the hamlets on the first of May;
My eyes too tender for the blaze of light,
Still sought the shelter of retiring night,
When Love approach'd, in painted plumes arrayed;
Th' insidious god his rattling darts betray'd,
Nor less his infant features, and the sly,
Sweet intimations of his threat'ning eye.   20
   Such the Sigeian boy is seen above,
Filling the goblet for imperial Jove;
Such he, on whom the nymphs bestow'd their charms,
Hylas, who perish'd in a Naiad's arms.
Angry he seem'd, yet graceful in his ire,
And added threats, not destitute of fire.
'My power,' he said, 'by others' pain alone,
'Twere best to learn; now learn it by thy own!
With those, who feel my power, that power attest!
And in thy anguish be my sway confest!   30
I vanquish'd Phœbus, though returning vain
From his new triumph o'er the Python slain,
And, when he thinks on Daphne, even he
Will yield the prize of archery to me.
A dart less true the Parthian horseman sped,
Behind him kill'd, and conquer'd as he fled:
Less true th' expert Cydonian, and less true
The youth, whose shaft his latent Procris slew.
Vanquish'd by me see huge Orion bend,
By me Alcides, and Alcides' friend.   40

At me should Jove himself a bolt design,
His bosom first should bleed transfixt by mine.
But all thy doubts this shaft will best explain,
Nor shall it reach thee with a trivial pain;
Thy Muse, vain youth! shall not thy peace ensure,
Nor Phœbus' serpent yield thy wound a cure.'
　　He spoke, and, waving a bright shaft in air,
Sought the warm bosom of the Cyprian fair.
　　That thus a child should bluster in my ear,
Provok'd my laughter, more than mov'd my fear.　　　　50
I shunn'd not, therefore, public haunts, but stray'd
Careless in city, or suburban shade,
And passing, and repassing, nymphs, that mov'd
With grace divine, beheld where'er I rov'd.
Bright shone the vernal day, with double blaze,
As beauty gave new force to Phœbus' rays.
By no grave scruples check'd, I freely eyed
The dang'rous show, rash youth my only guide,
And many a look of many a fair unknown
Met full, unable to controul my own.　　　　　　　　60
But one I mark'd (then peace forsook my breast) –
One – oh how far superior to the rest!
What lovely features! such the Cyprian queen
Herself might wish, and Juno wish her mien.
The very nymph was she, whom when I dar'd
His arrows, Love had even then prepar'd!
Nor was himself remote, nor unsupplied
With torch well-trimm'd and quiver at his side;
Now to her lips he clung, her eye-lids now,
Then settled on her cheeks, or on her brow.　　　　　70
And with a thousand wounds from ev'ry part
Pierced, and transpierced, my undefended heart.
A fever, new to me, of fierce desire
Now seiz'd my soul, and I was all on fire,
But she, the while, whom only I adore,
Was gone, and vanish'd, to appear no more.
In silent sadness I pursue my way;
I pause, I turn, proceed, yet wish to stay,

And while I follow her in thought, bemoan
With tears, my soul's delight so quickly flown.   80
When Jove had hurl'd him to the Lemnian coast,
So Vulcan sorrow'd for Olympus lost,
And so Oeclides, sinking into night,
From the deep gulf look'd up to distant light.
 Wretch that I am, what hopes for me remain,
Who cannot cease to love, yet love in vain?
Oh could I once, once more behold the fair,
Speak to her, tell her, of the pangs I bear,
Perhaps she is not adamant, would show
Perhaps some pity at my tale of woe.   90
Oh inauspicious flame! – 'tis mine to prove
A matchless instance of disastrous love.
Ah spare me, gentle pow'r! – If such thou be,
Let not thy deeds, and nature, disagree.
Spare me, and I will worship at no shrine
With vow and sacrifice, save only thine.
Now I revere thy fires, thy bow, thy darts:
Now own thee sov'reign of all human hearts.
Remove! no – grant me still this raging woe!
Sweet is the wretchedness, that lovers know: 100
But pierce hereafter (should I chance to see
One destin'd mine) at once both her, and me.

 Such were the trophies, that, in earlier days,
By vanity seduc'd, I toil'd to raise,
Studious, yet indolent, and urg'd by youth,
That worst of teachers! from the ways of truth;
Till learning taught me, in his shady bow'r,
To quit love's servile yoke, and spurn his pow'r.
Then, on a sudden, the fierce flame supprest,
A frost continual settled on my breast,   110
Whence Cupid fears his flames extinct to see,
And Venus dreads a Diomede in me.

EPIGRAMS[1]

ON THE INVENTOR OF GUNS

Praise in old times the sage Prometheus won,
Who stole æthereal radiance from the sun;
But greater he, whose bold invention strove
To emulate the fiery bolts of Jove.

TO LEONORA SINGING AT ROME[2]

Another Leonora once inspir'd
Tasso, with fatal love to phrenzy fir'd,
But how much happier, liv'd he now, were he,
Pierc'd with whatever pangs for love of thee!
Since could he hear that heavenly voice of thine,
With Adriana's lute of sound divine,
Fiercer than Pentheus' tho' his eye might roll,
Or idiot apathy benumb his soul,
You still, with medicinal sounds, might cheer
His senses wandering in a blind career;   10
And sweetly breathing thro' his wounded breast,
Charm, with soul-soothing song, his thoughts to rest.

TO THE SAME

Naples, too credulous, ah! boast no more
The sweet-voic'd Siren buried on thy shore,

1. The Poems on the subject of the Gunpowder Treason I have not translated, both because the matter of them is unpleasant, and because they are written with an asperity, which, however it might be warranted in Milton's day, would be extremely unseasonable now [C.].
2. I have translated only two of the three poetical compliments addressed to Leonora, as they appear to me far superior to what I have omitted [C.].

That, when Parthenope deceas'd, she gave
Her sacred dust to a Chalcidic grave,
For still she lives, but has exchang'd the hoarse
Pausilipo for Tiber's placid course,
Where, idol of all Rome, she now in chains,
Of magic song, both gods, and men, detains.

THE COTTAGER AND HIS LANDLORD

A FABLE

A peasant to his lord pay'd yearly court,
Presenting pippins, of so rich a sort
That he, displeas'd to have a part alone,
Remov'd the tree, that all might be his own.
The tree, too old to travel, though before
So fruitful, wither'd, and would yield no more.
The 'squire, perceiving all his labour void,
Curs'd his own pains, so foolishly employ'd,
And 'Oh,' he cried, 'that I had liv'd content
With tribute, small indeed, but kindly meant!   10
My av'rice has expensive prov'd to me,
Has cost me both my pippins, and my tree.'

TO CHRISTINA, QUEEN OF SWEDEN

WITH CROMWELL'S PICTURE

Christina, maiden of heroic mien!
Star of the North! of northern stars the queen!
Behold what wrinkles I have earn'd, and how
The iron casque still chafes my vet'ran brow,
While following fate's dark footsteps, I fulfil
The dictates of a hardy people's will.
But soften'd, in thy sight, my looks appear,
Not to all Queens or Kings alike severe.

MISCELLANEOUS POEMS

On the Death of the Vice-Chancellor
A PHYSICIAN

Learn, ye nations of the earth,
The condition of your birth,
Now be taught your feeble state!
Know, that all must yield to fate!

If the mournful rover, Death,
Say but once – 'resign your breath!'
Vainly of escape you dream,
You must pass the Stygian stream.

Could the stoutest overcome
Death's assault, and baffle doom,　　　　　10
Hercules had both withstood,
Undiseas'd by Nessus' blood.

Ne'er had Hector press'd the plain
By a trick of Pallas slain,
Nor the chief to Jove allied
By Achilles' phantom died.

Could enchantments life prolong,
Circe, sav'd by magic song,
Still had liv'd, and equal skill
Had preserv'd Medea still.　　　　　20

Dwelt in herbs, and drugs, a pow'r
To avert man's destin'd hour,
Learn'd Machaon should have known
Doubtless to avert his own.

Chiron had surviv'd the smart
Of the Hydra-tainted dart,

And Jove's bolt had been, with ease,
Foil'd by Asclepiades.

Thou too, sage! of whom forlorn
Helicon and Cirrha mourn,   30
Still had'st filled thy princely place,
Regent of the gowned race;

Had'st advanc'd to higher fame
Still, thy much-ennobled name,
Nor in Charon's skiff explor'd
The Tartarean gulph abhorr'd.

But resentful Proserpine,
Jealous of thy skill divine,
Snapping short thy vital thread
Thee too number'd with the dead.   40

Wise and good! untroubled be
The green turf, that covers thee!
Thence, in gay profusion, grow
All the sweetest flow'rs, that blow!

Pluto's consort bid thee rest!
Œacus pronounce thee blest!
To her home thy shade consign!
Make Elysium ever thine!

On the Death of the Bishop of Ely
Written in the Author's seventeenth year.

My lids with grief were tumid yet,
And still my sullied cheek was wet
With briny tears, profusely shed
For venerable Winton dead;
When Fame, whose tales of saddest sound
Alas! are ever truest found,
The news through all our cities spread
Of yet another mitred head

By ruthless fate to death consign'd,
Ely, the honour of his kind!   10
At once, a storm of passion heav'd
My boiling bosom, much I griev'd
But more I rag'd, at ev'ry breath
Devoting Death himself to death.
With less revenge did Naso teem,
When hated Ibis was his theme;
With less, Archilochus, denied
The lovely Greek, his promis'd bride.
    But lo! while thus I execrate,
Incens'd, the minister of fate,   20
Wond'rous accents, soft, yet clear,
Wafted on the gale I hear.
    'Ah, much deluded! lay aside
Thy threats, and anger misapplied!
Art not afraid with sounds like these
T' offend, where thou canst not appease?
Death is not (wherefore dream'st thou thus?)
The son of Night and Erebus:
Nor was of fell Erynnis born
On gulphs, where Chaos rules forlorn: 30
But sent from God; his presence leaves,
To gather home his ripen'd sheaves,
To call encumber'd souls away
From fleshly bonds to boundless day,
(As when the winged hours excite,
And summon forth the morning-light)
And each to convoy to her place
Before th' Eternal Father's face.
But not the Wicked – them, severe
Yet just, from all their pleasures here   40
He hurries to the realms below,
Terrific realms of penal woe!
Myself no sooner heard his call,
Than, scaping through my prison-wall,
I bade adieu to bolts and bars,
And soar'd, with angels, to the stars,

Like him of old, to whom 'twas giv'n
To mount, on fiery wheels, to Heav'n.
Bootes' waggon, slow with cold,
Appall'd me not; nor to behold   50
The sword, that vast Orion draws,
Or ev'n the Scorpion's horrid claws.
Beyond the Sun's bright orb I fly,
And, far beneath my feet, descry
Night's dread goddess, seen with awe,
Whom her winged dragons draw.
Thus, ever wond'ring at my speed,
Augmented still as I proceed,
I pass the planetary sphere,
The Milky Way – and now appear   60
Heav'n's chrystal battlements, her door
Of massy pearl, and em'rald floor.
    But here I cease. For never can
The tongue of once a mortal man
In suitable description trace
The pleasures of that happy place;
Suffice it, that those joys divine
Are all, and all for ever, mine!'

NATURE UNIMPAIRED BY TIME

Ah, how the human mind wearies her self
With her own wand'rings, and, involv'd in gloom
Impenetrable, speculates amiss!
Measuring, in her folly, things divine
By human; laws inscrib'd on adamant
By laws of man's device, and counsels fixt
For ever, by the hours, that pass, and die.
    How? – shall the face of nature then be plough'd
Into deep wrinkles, and shall years at last
On the great Parent fix a sterile curse?   10
Shall even she confess old age, and halt
And, palsy-smitten, shake her starry brows?

Shall foul Antiquity with rust and drought,
And Famine, vex the radiant worlds above?
Shall Time's unsated maw crave and ingulph
The very Heav'ns, that regulate his flight?
And was the Sire of all able to fence
His works, and to uphold the circling worlds,
But, through improvident and heedless haste,
Let slip th' occasion? – so then – all is lost –   20
And in some future evil hour, yon arch
Shall crumble, and come thund'ring down, the poles
Jar in collision, the Olympian king
Fall with his throne, and Pallas, holding forth
The terrors of the Gorgon shield in vain,
Shall rush to the abyss, like Vulcan hurl'd
Down into Lemnos, through the gate of Heav'n.
Thou also, with precipitated wheels,
Phœbus, thy own son's fall shalt imitate,
With hideous ruin shalt impress the deep   30
Suddenly, and the flood shall reek, and hiss,
At the extinction of the lamp of day.
Then too, shall Hæmus, cloven to his base,
Be shattered, and the huge Ceraunian hills,
Once weapons of Tartarean Dis, immers'd
In Erebus, shall fill himself with fear.

   No. The Almighty Father surer lay'd
His deep foundations, and providing well
For the event of all, the scales of Fate
Suspended, in just equipoise, and bade   40
His universal works, from age to age,
One tenour hold, perpetual, undisturb'd.

   Hence the Prime mover wheels itself about
Continual, day by day, and with it bears
In social measure swift the heav'ns around.
Not tardier now is Saturn than of old,
Nor radiant less the burning casque of Mars.
Phœbus, his vigour unimpair'd, still shows
Th' effulgence of his youth, nor needs the god
A downward course, that he may warm the vales: 50

But, ever rich in influence, runs his road,
Sign after sign, through all the heav'nly zone.
Beautiful, as at first, ascends the star
From odorif'rous Ind, whose office is
To gather home betimes th' ethereal flock,
To pour them o'er the skies again at eve,
And to discriminate the night and day.
Still Cynthia's changeful horn waxes, and wanes,
Alternate, and with arms extended still,
She welcomes to her breast her brother's beams.   60
Nor have the elements deserted yet
Their functions: thunder with as loud a stroke
As erst, smites through the rocks, and scatters them.
The east still howls, still the relentless north
Invades the shudd'ring Scythian, still he breathes
The winter, and still rolls the storms along.
The king of ocean, with his wonted force,
Beats on Pelorus, o'er the deep is heard
The hoarse alarm of Triton's sounding shell,
Nor swim the monsters of th'Ægean sea   70
In shallows, or beneath diminish'd waves.
Thou too, thy antient vegetative power
Enjoy'st, O Earth! Narcissus still is sweet,
And, Phœbus! still thy favourite, and still
Thy fav'rite, Cytherea! both retain
Their beauty, nor the mountains, ore-enrich'd
For punishment of man, with purer gold
Teem'd ever, or with brighter gems the Deep.
  Thus, in unbroken series, all proceeds;
And shall, till wide involving either pole,   80
And the immensity of yonder heav'n,
The final flames of destiny absorb
The world, consum'd in one enormous pyre!

ON THE PLATONIC IDEA
AS IT WAS UNDERSTOOD BY ARISTOTLE

Ye sister pow'rs, who o'er the sacred groves
Preside, and thou, fair mother of them all,
Mnemosyne! and thou, who in thy grot
Immense reclin'd at leisure, hast in charge
The archives, and the ord'nances of Jove,
And dost record the festivals of heav'n,
Eternity! – Inform us who is He,
That great original by nature chos'n
To be the archetype of human kind,
Unchangeable, immortal, with the poles   10
Themselves coæval, one, yet ev'ry where,
An image of the god, who gave him being?
Twin-brother of the goddess born from Jove,
He dwells not in his father's mind, but, though
Of common nature with ourselves, exists
Apart, and occupies a local home.
Whether, companion of the stars, he spend
Eternal ages, roaming at his will
From sphere to sphere the tenfold heav'ns, or dwell
On the moon's side, that nearest neighbours earth;   20
Or torpid on the banks of Lethe sit
Among the multitude of souls ordain'd
To flesh and blood, or whether (as may chance)
That vast and giant model of our kind
In some far distant region of this globe
Sequester'd stalk, with lifted head on high
O'ertow'ring Atlas, on whose shoulders rest
The stars, terrific even to the gods.
Never the Theban seer, whose blindness prov'd
His best illumination, him beheld   30
In secret vision; never him the son
Of Pleione, amid the noiseless night
Descending, to the prophet-choir reveal'd;
Him never knew th' Assyrian priest, who yet

The ancestry of Ninus chronicles,
And Belus, and Osiris far-renown'd;
Nor even thrice great Hermes, although skill'd
So deep in myst'ry, to the worshippers
Of Isis show'd a prodigy like him.
    And thou, who hast immortaliz'd the shades   40
Of Academus, if the schools receiv'd
This monster of the fancy first from thee,
Either recall at once the banish'd bards
To thy republic, or thyself evinc'd
A wilder fabulist, go also forth.

To His Father

Oh that Pieria's spring would thro' my breast
Pour its inspiring influence, and rush
No rill, but rather an o'erflowing flood!
That, for my venerable Father's sake
All meaner themes renounc'd, my muse, on wings
Of duty borne, might reach a loftier strain.
For thee, my Father! howsoe'er it please,
She frames this slender work, nor know I aught,
That may thy gifts more suitably requite;
Though to requite them suitably would ask   10
Returns much nobler, and surpassing far
The meagre stores of verbal gratitude:
But, such as I possess, I send thee all.
This page presents thee in their full amount.
With thy son's treasures, and the sum is nought;
Nought, save the riches that from airy dream
In secret grottos, and in laurel bow'rs,
I have, by golden Clio's gift, acquir'd.
    Verse is a work divine; despise not thou
Verse therefore, which evinces (nothing more)   20
Man's heav'nly source, and which, retaining still
Some scintillations of Promethean fire,
Bespeaks him animated from above.

The Gods love verse; th' infernal Pow'rs them selves
Confess the influence of verse, which stirs
The lowest deep, and binds in triple chains
Of adamant both Pluto and the Shades.
In verse the Delphic priestess, and the pale
Tremulous Sybil, make the future known,
And he who sacrifices, on the shrine   30
Hangs verse, both when he smites the threat'ning bull,
And when he spreads his reeking entrails wide
To scrutinize the Fates invelop'd there.
We too, ourselves, what time we seek again
Our native skies, and one eternal now
Shall be the only measure of our being.
Crown'd all with gold, and chaunting to the lyre
Harmonious verse, shall range the courts above,
And make the starry firmament resound.
And, even now, the fiery spirit pure   40
That wheels yon circling orbs, directs, himself,
Their mazy dance with melody of verse
Unutt'rable, immortal, hearing which
Huge Ophiuchus holds his hiss suppress'd,
Orion soften'd, drops his ardent blade,
And Atlas stands unconscious of his load.
Verse grac'd of old the feasts of kings, ere yet
Luxurious dainties, destin'd to the gulph
Immense of gluttony, were known, and ere
Lyæus delug'd yet the temp'rate board.   50
Then sat the bard a customary guest
To share the banquet, and, his length of locks
With beechen honours bound, propos'd in verse
The characters of heroes, and their deeds,
To imitation, sang of Chaos old,
Of nature's birth, of gods that crept in search
Of acorns fall'n, and of the thunder bolt
Not yet produc'd from Etna's fiery cave.
And what avails, at last, tune without voice,
Devoid of matter? Such may suit perhaps   60
The rural dance, but such was ne'er the song

Of Orpheus, whom the streams stood still to hear,
And the oaks follow'd. Not by chords alone
Well touch'd, but by resistless accents more
To sympathetic tears the ghosts themselves
He mov'd: these praises to his verse he owes.
 Nor thou persist, I pray thee, still to slight
The sacred Nine, and to imagine vain
And useless, pow'rs, by whom inspir'd, thyself
Art skilful to associate verse with airs   70
Harmonious, and to give the human voice
A thousand modulations, heir by right
Indisputable of Arion's fame.
Now say, what wonder is it, if a son
Of thine delights in verse, if so conjoin'd
In close affinity, we sympathize
In social arts, and kindred studies sweet?
Such distribution of himself to us
Was Phœbus' choice; thou hast thy gift, and I
Mine also, and between us we receive,   80
Father and son, the whole inspiring God.
 No! howsoe'er the semblance thou assume
Of hate, thou hatest not the gentle Muse,
My Father! for thou never bad'st me tread
The beaten path, and broad, that leads right on
To opulence, nor did'st condemn thy son
To the insipid clamours of the bar,
To laws voluminous, and ill observ'd;
But, wishing to enrich me more, to fill
My mind with treasure, led'st me far away   90
From city-din to deep retreats, to banks
And streams Aonian, and, with free consent,
Didst place me happy at Apollo's side.
I speak not now, on more important themes
Intent, of common benefits, and such
As nature bids, but of thy larger gifts
My Father! who, when I had open'd once
The stores of Roman rhetorick, and learn'd
The full-ton'd language of the eloquent Greeks,

Whose lofty music grac'd the lips of Jove,   100
Thyself didst counsel me to add the flow'rs,
That Gallia boasts, those too, with which the smooth
Italian his degen'rate speech adorns,
That witnesses his mixture with the Goth;
And Palestine's prophetic songs divine.
To sum the whole, whate'er the heav'n contains,
The earth beneath it, and the air between,
The rivers and the restless deep, may all
Prove intellectual gain to me, my wish
Concurring with thy will; science herself,   110
All cloud remov'd, inclines her beauteous head,
And offers me the lip, if, dull of heart,
I shrink not, and decline her gracious boon.

   Go now, and gather dross, ye sordid minds,
That covet it; what could my Father more?
What more could Jove himself, unless he gave
His own abode, the heav'n, in which he reigns?
More eligible gifts than these were not
Apollo's to his son, had they been safe,
As they were insecure, who made the boy   120
The world's vice-luminary, bade him rule
The radiant chariot of the day, and bind
To his young brows his own all-dazzling wreath.
I therefore, although last and least, my place
Among the learned in the laurel grove
Will hold, and where the conqu'ror's ivy twines,
Henceforth exempt from the unletter'd throng
Profane, nor even to be seen by such.
Away, then, sleepless Care, Complaint away,
And, Envy, with thy 'jealous leer malign!'   130
Nor let the monster Calumny shoot forth
Her venom'd tongue at me. Detested foes!
Ye all are impotent against my peace,
For I am privileg'd, and bear my breast
Safe, and too high, for your viperean wound.

   But thou! my Father! since to render thanks
Equivalent, and to requite my deeds

Thy liberality, exceeds my power,
Suffice it, that I thus record thy gifts,
And bear them treasur'd in a grateful mind!   140
Ye too, the favourite pastime of my youth,
My voluntary numbers, if ye dare
To hope longevity, and to survive
Your master's funeral, not soon absorb'd
In the oblivious Lethæan gulph
Shall to futurity perhaps convey
This theme, and by these praises of my sire
Improve the Fathers of a distant age!

To Salsillus

A ROMAN POET, MUCH INDISPOSED

The original is written in a measure called *Scazon*, which signifies
limping, and the measure is so denominated, because, though in
other respects Iambic, it terminates with a Spondee, and has
consequently a more tardy movement.

   The reader will immediately see that this property of the Latin
verse cannot be imitated in English [C.].

My halting Muse, that dragg'st by choice along
Thy slow, slow step, in melancholy song,
And lik'st that pace, expressive of thy cares,
Not less than Diopeia's sprightlier airs,
When, in the dance, she beats, with measur'd tread,
Heav'n's floor, in front of Juno's golden bed;
Salute Salsillus, who to verse divine
Prefers, with partial love, such lays as mine.
Thus writes that Milton then, who wafted o'er
From his own nest, on Albion's stormy shore,   10
Where Eurus, fiercest of th'Æolian band,
Sweeps, with ungovern'd rage, the blasted land,
Of late to more serene Ausonia came
To view her cities of illustrious name,
To prove, himself a witness of the truth,
How wise her elders, and how learn'd her youth.
Much good, Salsillus! and a body free

From all disease, that Milton asks for thee,
Who now endur'st the languor, and the pains,
That bile inflicts, diffus'd through all thy veins,   20
Relentless malady! not mov'd to spare
By thy sweet Roman voice, and Lesbian air!
     Health, Hebe's sister, sent us from the skies,
And thou, Apollo, whom all sickness flies,
Pythius, or Pæan, or what name divine
Soe'er thou chuse, haste, heal a priest of thine!
Ye groves of Faunus, and ye hills, that melt
With vinous dews, where meek Evander dwelt!
If aught salubrious in your confines grow,
Strive which shall soonest heal your poet's woe,   30
That, render'd to the Muse he loves, again
He may enchant the meadows with his strain.
Numa, reclin'd in everlasting ease,
Amid the shade of dark embow'ring trees,
Viewing with eyes of unabated fire
His loved Ægeria, shall that strain admire:
So sooth'd, the tumid Tiber shall revere
The tombs of kings, nor desolate the year,
Shall curb his waters with a friendly rein,
And guide them harmless, till they meet the main.   40

To Giovanni Battista Manso

Marquis of Villa

Milton's Account of Manso

Giovanni Battista Manso, Marquis of Villa, is an Italian nobleman of the highest estimation among his countrymen, for genius, literature, and military accomplishments. To him Torquato Tasso addressed his Dialogues on Friendship, for he was much the friend of Tasso, who has also celebrated him among the other princes of his country, in his poem entitled, Gerusalemme Conquistata, book xx.

> *Fra cavalier magnanimi, e cortesi,*
> *Risplende il Manso.*

During the Author's stay at Naples, he received at the hands of the Marquis a thousand kind offices and civilities, and, desirous not to appear ungrateful, sent him this poem a short time before his departure from that city.

These verses also to thy praise the Nine,
Oh Manso! happy in that theme design,
For, Gallus and Mæcenas gone, they see
None such besides, or whom they love as thee,
And, if my verse may give the meed of fame,
Thine too shall prove an everlasting name.
Already such, it shines in Tasso's page
(For thou wast Tasso's friend) from age to age,
And, next, the Muse consign'd, (not unaware
How high the charge,) Marino to thy care,   10
Who, singing, to the nymphs, Adonis' praise,
Boasts thee the patron of his copious lays.
To thee alone the poet would entrust
His latest vows, to thee alone his dust;
And thou with punctual piety hast paid,
In labour'd brass, thy tribute to his shade.
Nor this contented thee – but lest the grave
Should aught absorb of their's, which thou could'st save,
All future ages thou hast deign'd to teach
The life, lot, genius, character of each,   20
Eloquent as the Carian sage, who true
To his great theme, the life of Homer drew.
  I, therefore, though a stranger youth, who come

Chill'd by rude blasts, that freeze my Northern home,
Thee dear to Clio, confident proclaim,
And thine, for Phœbus' sake, a deathless name.
Nor thou, so kind, wilt view with scornful eye
A muse scarce rear'd beneath our sullen sky,
Who fears not, indiscreet as she is young,
To seek in Latium hearers of her song.   30
We too, where Thames with his unsullied waves
The tresses of the blue-hair'd Ocean laves,
Hear oft by night, or, slumb'ring, seem to hear,
O'er his wide stream, the swan's voice warbling clear,
And we could boast a Tityrus of yore,
Who trod, a welcome guest, your happy shore.
  Yes – dreary as we own our Northern clime,
E'en we to Phœbus raise the polish'd rhyme,
We too serve Phœbus; Phœbus has receiv'd,
(If legends old may claim to be believ'd)   40
No sordid gifts from us, the golden ear,
The burnish'd apple, ruddiest of the year,
The fragrant crocus, and to grace his fane,
Fair damsels chosen from the Druid train;
Druids, our native bards in antient time,
Who gods and heroes prais'd in hallow'd rhyme!
Hence, often as the maids of Greece surround
Apollo's shrine with hymns of festive sound,
They name the virgins, who arriv'd of yore,
With British off'rings, on the Delian shore,   50
Loxo, from giant Corineus sprung,
Upis, on whose blest lips the future hung,
And Hecaerge, with the golden hair,
All deck'd with Pictish hues, and all with bosoms bare.
  Thou, therefore, happy sage, whatever clime
Shall ring with Tasso's praise in after-time,
Or with Marino's, shalt be known their friend,
And with an equal flight to fame ascend.
The world shall hear how Phœbus, and the Nine,
Were inmates once, and willing guests of thine.   60
Yet Phœbus, when of old constrain'd to roam

The earth, an exile from his heavenly home,
Enter'd, no willing guest, Admetus' door,
Though Hercules had ventur'd there before.
But gentle Chiron's cave was near, a scene
Of rural peace, cloth'd with perpetual green,
And thither, oft as respite he requir'd
From rustic clamours loud, the god retir'd.
There, many a time, on Peneus' bank reclin'd
At some oak's root, with ivy thick entwin'd,   70
Won by his hospitable friend's desire
He sooth'd his pains of exile with the lyre.
Then shook the hills, then trembled Peneus' shore,
Nor Oeta felt his load of forests more;
The upland elms descended to the plain,
And soften'd lynxes wonder'd at the strain.
   Well may we think, O dear to all above!
Thy birth distinguish'd by the smile of Jove,
And that Apollo shed his kindliest pow'r,
And Maia's son, on that propitious hour,   80
Since only minds so born can comprehend
A poet's worth, or yield that worth a friend.
Hence, on thy yet unfaded cheek appears
The ling'ring freshness of thy greener years,
Hence, in thy front, and features, we admire
Nature unwither'd, and a mind entire.
Oh might so true a friend to me belong,
So skill'd to grace the votaries of song,
Should I recall hereafter into rhyme
The kings, and heroes of my native clime,   90
Arthur the chief, who even now prepares,
In subterraneous being, future wars,
With all his martial knights, to be restor'd,
Each to his seat, around the fed'ral board,
And Oh, if spirit fail me not, disperse
Our Saxon plund'rers, in triumphant verse!
Then, after all, when, with the past content,
A life I finish, not in silence spent,
Should he, kind mourner, o'er my death-bed bend,

I shall but need to say – 'Be yet my friend!'   100
He, too, perhaps, shall bid the marble breathe
To honour me, and with the graceful wreath,
Or of Parnassus, or the Paphian isle,
Shall bind my brows, – but I shall rest the while.
Then also, if the fruits of Faith endure,
And Virtue's promis'd recompense be sure,
Borne to those seats, to which the blest aspire
By purity of soul, and virtuous fire,
These rites, as Fate permits, I shall survey
With eyes illumin'd by celestial day,   110
And, ev'ry cloud from my pure spirit driv'n,
Joy in the bright beatitude of Heav'n!

ON THE DEATH OF DAMON

THE ARGUMENT

Thyrsis and Damon, shepherds and neighbours, had always pursued
the same studies, and had, from their earliest days, been united in
the closest friendship. Thyrsis, while travelling for improvement,
received intelligence of the death of Damon, and after a time,
returning and finding it true, deplores himself, and his solitary
condition, in this poem.

By Damon is to be understood Charles Deodati, connected with
the Italian city of Lucca by his father's side, in other respects an
Englishman; a youth of uncommon genius, erudition and virtue.

Ye nymphs of Himera (for ye have shed
Erewhile for Daphnis, and for Hylas dead,
And over Bion's long-lamented bier,
The fruitless meed of many a sacred tear)
Now, through the villas lav'd by Thames, rehearse
The woes of Thyrsis in Sicilian verse,
What sighs he heav'd, and how with groans profound
He made the woods, and hollow rocks, resound,
Young Damon dead; nor even ceas'd to pour
His lonely sorrows at the midnight hour.   10
   The green wheat twice had nodded in the ear,
And golden harvest twice enrich'd the year,
Since Damon's lips had gasp'd for vital air

The last, last time, nor Thyrsis yet was there;
For he, enamour'd of the Muse, remain'd
In Tuscan Fiorenza long detain'd,
But, stor'd at length with all, he wish'd to learn,
For his flock's sake now hasted to return,
And when the shepherd had resum'd his seat
At the elm's root, within his old retreat,   20
Then 'twas his lot, then, all his loss to know,
And, from his burthen'd heart, he vented thus his woe.
   'Go, seek your home, my lambs; my thoughts are due
To other cares, than those of feeding you.
Alas! what deities shall I suppose
In heav'n, or earth, concern'd for human woes,
Since, Oh my Damon! their severe decree
So soon condemns me to regret of thee!
Depart'st thou thus, thy virtues unrepaid
With fame and honour, like a vulgar shade?   30
Let him forbid it, whose bright rod controuls,
And sep'rates sordid from illustrious souls,
Drive far the rabble, and to thee assign
A happier lot, with spirits worthy thine!
   Go, seek your home, my lambs; my thoughts are due
To other cares, than those of feeding you.
Whate'er befall, unless by cruel chance
The wolf first give me a forbidding glance,
Thou shalt not moulder undeplor'd, but long
Thy praise shall dwell on ev'ry shepherd's tongue;   40
To Daphnis first they shall delight to pay,
And, after him, to thee the votive lay,
While Pales shall the flocks, and pastures, love,
Or Faunus to frequent the field, or grove;
At least, if antient piety and truth,
With all the learned labours of thy youth.
May serve thee aught, or to have left behind
A sorrowing friend, and of the tuneful kind.
   Go, seek your home, my lambs; my thoughts are due
To other cares, than those of feeding you.   50
Yes, Damon! such thy sure reward shall be;

But ah, what doom awaits unhappy me?
Who, now, my pains and perils shall divide,
As thou wast wont, for ever at my side,
Both when the rugged frost annoy'd our feet,
And when the herbage all was parch'd with heat;
Whether the grim wolf's ravage to prevent,
Or the huge lion's, arm'd with darts we went?
Whose converse, now, shall calm my stormy day,
With charming song, who now beguile my way?   60

   Go, seek your home, my lambs; my thoughts are due
To other cares, than those of feeding you.
In whom shall I confide? Whose counsel find
A balmy med'cine for my troubled mind?
Or whose discourse, with innocent delight,
Shall fill me now, and cheat the wint'ry night,
While hisses on my hearth the pulpy pear,
And black'ning chesnuts start and crackle there,
While storms abroad the dreary meadows whelm,
And the wind thunders thro' the neighb'ring elm.   70

   Go, seek your home, my lambs; my thoughts are due
To other cares, than those of feeding you.
Or who, when summer suns their summit reach,
And Pan sleeps hidden by the shelt'ring beech,
When shepherds disappear, nymphs seek the sedge,
And the stretch'd rustic snores beneath the hedge,
Who then shall render me thy pleasant vein
Of Attic wit, thy jests, thy smiles, again?

   Go, seek your home, my lambs; my thoughts are due
To other cares, than those of feeding you.   80
Where glens and vales are thickest overgrown
With tangled boughs, I wander now alone,
Till night descend, while blust'ring wind and show'r
Beat on my temples through the shatter'd bow'r.

   Go, seek your home, my lambs; my thoughts are due
To other cares, than those of feeding you.
Alas! what rampant weeds now shame my fields,
And what a mildew'd crop the furrow yields!
My rambling vines, unwedded to the trees,

Bear shrivell'd grapes, my myrtles fail to please, 90
Nor please me more my flocks; they, slighted, turn
Their unavailing looks on me, and mourn.
   Go, seek your home, my lambs; my thoughts are due
To other cares, than those of feeding you.
Ægon invites me to the hazel grove,
Amyntas, on the river's bank to rove,
And young Alphesibœus to a seat
Where branching elms exclude the mid-day heat.
"Here fountains spring – here mossy hillocks rise:"
"Here Zephyr whispers, and the stream replies." – 100
Thus each persuades, but, deaf to ev'ry call,
I gain the thickets, and escape them all.
   Go, seek your home, my lambs; my thoughts are due
To other cares, than those of feeding you.
Then Mopsus said, (the same who reads so well
The voice of birds, and what the stars foretell,
For he by chance had noticed my return)
"What means thy sullen mood, this deep concern!
Ah Thyrsis! thou art either craz'd with love,
Or some sinister influence from above; 110
Dull Saturn's influence oft the shepherds rue;
His leaden shaft oblique has pierc'd thee through."
   Go, go, my lambs, unpastur'd as ye are,
My thoughts are all now due to other care.
The nymphs amaz'd, my melancholy see,
And "Thyrsis!" cry – "what will become of thee?
What would'st thou, Thyrsis? such should not appear
The brow of youth, stern, gloomy, and severe;
Brisk youth should laugh, and love – ah shun the fate
Of those, twice wretched mopes! who love too late:" 120
   Go, go my lambs, unpastur'd as ye are,
My thoughts are all now due to other care.
Ægle with Hyas came, to sooth my pain,
And Baucis' daughter, Dryope the vain,
Fair Dryope, for voice and finger neat
Known far and near, and for her self-conceit;
Chloris too came, whose cottage on the lands,

That skirt the Idumanian current, stands;
But all in vain they came, and but to see
Kind words, and comfortable, lost on me.   130

    Go, go, my lambs, unpastur'd as ye are,
My thoughts are all now due to other care.
Ah blest indiff'rence of the playful herd,
None by his fellow chosen, or preferr'd!
No bonds of amity the flocks enthrall,
But each associates, and is pleas'd with all;
So graze the dappled deer in num'rous droves,
And all his kind alike the zebra loves;
The same law governs, where the billows roar,
And Proteus' shoals o'erspread the desert shore;   140
The sparrow, meanest of the feather'd race,
His fit companion finds in ev'ry place,
With whom he picks the grain, that suits him best,
Flirts here and there, and late returns to rest,
And whom if chance the falcon make his prey,
Or hedger with his well aim'd arrow slay,
For no such loss the gay survivor grieves;
New love he seeks, and new delight receives.
We only, an obdurate kind, rejoice,
Scorning all others, in a single choice,   150
We scarce in thousands meet one kindred mind,
And if the long-sought good at last we find,
When least we fear it, Death our treasure steals,
And gives our heart a wound, that nothing heals.

    Go, go, my lambs, unpastur'd as ye are,
My thoughts are all now due to other care.
Ah, what delusion lur'd me from my flocks,
To traverse Alpine snows, and rugged rocks!
What need so great had I to visit Rome,
Now sunk in ruins, and herself a tomb?   160
Or, had she flourish'd still as when, of old,
For her sake Tityrus forsook his fold,
What need so great had I t' incur a pause
Of thy sweet intercourse for such a cause,
For such a cause to place the roaring sea,

Rocks, mountains, woods, between my friend and me?
Else, had I grasp'd thy feeble hand, compos'd
Thy decent limbs, thy drooping eye-lids clos'd,
And, at the last, had said – "Farewell – ascend –
Nor even in the skies forget thy friend!" 170
   Go, go, my lambs, untended homeward fare,
My thoughts are all now due to other care.
Although well-pleas'd, ye tuneful Tuscan swains!
My mind the mem'ry of your worth retains,
Yet not your worth can teach me less to mourn
My Damon lost. – He too was Tuscan born,
Born in your Lucca, city of renown!
And wit possess'd, and genius, like your own.
Oh how elate was I, when stretch'd beside
The murm'ring course of Arno's breezy tide, 180
Beneath the poplar grove I pass'd my hours,
Now cropping myrtles, and now vernal flow'rs,
And hearing, as I lay at ease along,
Your swains contending for the prize of song!
I also dar'd attempt (and, as it seems,
Not much displeas'd attempting) various themes,
For even I can presents boast from you,
The shepherd's pipe, and ozier basket too,
And Dati, and Francini, both have made
My name familiar to the beechen shade, 190
And they are learn'd, and each in ev'ry place
Renown'd for song, and both of Lydian race.
   Go, go, my lambs, untended homeward fare,
My thoughts are all now due to other care.
While bright the dewy grass with moon-beams shone,
And I stood hurdling in my kids alone,
How often have I said (but thou had'st found
Ere then thy dark cold lodgment under ground)
Now Damon sings, or springes sets for hares,
Or wicker work for various use prepares! 200
How oft, indulging fancy, have I plann'd
New scenes of pleasure, that I hop'd at hand,
Call'd thee abroad as I was wont, and cried –

What hoa! my friend – come, lay thy task aside,
Haste, let us forth together, and beguile
The heat, beneath yon whisp'ring shades awhile,
Or on the margin stray of Colne's clear flood,
Or where Cassibelan's grey turrets stood!
There thou shalt cull me simples, and shalt teach
Thy friend the name, and healing pow'rs of each,   210
From the tall blue-bell to the dwarfish weed,
What the dry land, and what the marshes breed,
For all their kinds alike to thee are known,
And the whole art of Galen is thy own.
Ah, perish Galen's art, and wither'd be
The useless herbs, that gave not health to thee!
Twelve evenings since, as in poetic dream
I meditating sat some statelier theme,
The reeds no sooner touch'd my lip, though new,
And unassay'd before, than wide they flew,   220
Bursting their waxen bands, nor could sustain
The deep-ton'd music of the solemn strain;
And I am vain perhaps, but I will tell
How proud a theme I chose – ye groves farewell!
    Go, go, my lambs, untended homeward fare,
My thoughts are all now due to other care.
Of Brutus, Dardan chief, my song shall be,
How with his barks he plough'd the British sea,
First from Rutupia's tow'ring headland seen,
And of his consort's reign, fair Imogen;   230
Of Brennus and Belinus, brothers bold,
And of Arviragus, and how of old
Our hardy sires th' Armorican controll'd,
And of the wife of Gorlois, who, surpris'd
By Uther, in her husband's form disguis'd,
(Such was the force of Merlin's art) became
Pregnant with Arthur of heroic fame.
These themes I now revolve – and Oh – if Fate
Proportion to these themes my lengthen'd date,
Adieu my shepherd's reed – yon pine-tree bough   240
Shall be thy future home, there dangle thou

Forgotten and disus'd, unless ere long
Thou change thy Latian for a British song;
A British? – even so – the pow'rs of man
Are bounded; little is the most he can;
And it shall well suffice me, and shall be
Fame, and proud recompence enough for me,
If Usa, golden-hair'd, my verse may learn,
If Alain bending o'er his chrystal urn,
Swift-whirling Abra, Trent's o'ershadow'd stream,   250
Thames, lovelier far than all in my esteem,
Tamar's ore-tinctur'd flood, and, after these,
The wave-worn shores of utmost Orcades.
   Go, go, my lambs, untended homeward fare,
My thoughts are all now due to other care.
All this I kept in leaves of laurel-rind
Enfolded safe, and for thy view design'd;
This, and a gift from Manso's hand beside,
(Manso, not least his native city's pride)
Two cups, that radiant as their giver shone,   260
Adorn'd by sculpture with a double zone.
The spring was graven there; here slowly wind
The Red-sea shores with groves of spices lin'd;
Her plumes of various hues amid the boughs
The sacred, solitary Phœnix shows,
And watchful of the dawn, reverts her head,
To see Aurora leave her wat'ry bed.
   – In other part, th' expansive vault above,
And there too, even there, the God of love;
With quiver arm'd he mounts, his torch displays   270
A vivid light, his gem-tipt arrows blaze,
Around, his bright and fiery eyes he rolls,
Nor aims at vulgar minds, or little souls,
Nor deigns one look below, but aiming high
Sends every arrow to the lofty sky,
Hence forms divine, and minds immortal, learn
The pow'r of Cupid, and enamour'd burn.
   Thou also Damon (neither need I fear
That hope delusive) thou art also there;

For whither should simplicity like thine   280
Retire, where else such spotless virtue shine?
Thou dwell'st not (thought profane) in shades below,
Nor tears suit thee – cease then my tears to flow,
Away with grief! on Damon ill-bestow'd!
Who, pure himself, has found a pure abode,
Has pass'd the show'ry arch, henceforth resides
With saints and heroes, and from flowing tides
Quaffs copious immortality, and joy,
With hallow'd lips! – Oh! blest without alloy,
And now enrich'd with all, that faith can claim,   290
Look down, entreated by whatever name,
If Damon please thee most (that rural sound
Shall oft with echoes fill the groves around)
Or if Deodatus, by which alone
In those etherial mansions thou art known.
Thy blush was maiden, and thy youth the taste
Of wedded bliss knew never, pure and chaste,
The honours, therefore, by divine decree
The lot of virgin worth, are given to thee;
Thy brows encircled with a radiant band,   300
And the green palm-branch waving in thy hand,
Thou in immortal nuptials shalt rejoice,
And join with seraphs thy according voice,
Where rapture reigns, and the ecstatic lyre
Guides the blest orgies of the blazing quire.'

AN ODE ADDRESSED TO MR JOHN ROUSE,

LIBRARIAN, OF THE UNIVERSITY OF OXFORD

ON A LOST VOLUME OF MY POEMS, WHICH HE DESIRED ME TO REPLACE, THAT HE MIGHT ADD THEM TO MY OTHER WORKS DEPOSITED IN THE LIBRARY

This Ode is rendered without rhime, that it might more adequately represent the original, which, as Milton himself informs us, is of no certain measure. It may possibly for this reason disappoint the reader, though it cost the writer more labour than the translation of any other piece in the whole collection [C.].

STROPHE

My two-fold book! single in show,
    But double in contents,
Neat, but not curiously adorn'd,
    Which, in his early youth,
A poet gave, no lofty one in truth,
Although an earnest wooer of the Muse –
Say while in cool Ausonian shades
    Or British wilds he roam'd,
Striking by turns his native lyre,
    By turns the Daunian lute,   10
    And stepp'd almost in air, –

ANTISTROPHE

Say, little book, what furtive hand
Thee from thy fellow-books convey'd,
What time, at the repeated suit
    Of my most learned friend,
I sent thee forth, an honour'd traveller,
From our great city to the source of Thames,
    Cærulian sire!
Where rise the fountains, and the raptures ring,
    Of the Aonian choir,   20
Durable as yonder spheres,
And through the endless lapse of years
    Secure to be admir'd?

Now what God, or Demigod
For Britain's antient Genius mov'd
(If our afflicted land
Have expiated at length the guilty sloth
Of her degen'rate sons)
Shall terminate our impious feuds,
And discipline, with hallow'd voice, recall?   30
Recall the Muses too,
Driv'n from their antient seats
In Albion, and well nigh from Albion's shore,
And with keen Phœbean shafts
Piercing th' unseemly birds,
Whose talons menace us,
Shall drive the Harpy race from Helicon afar!

ANTISTROPHE

But thou, my book, though thou hast stray'd,
Whether by treach'ry lost,
Or indolent neglect, thy bearer's fault,   40
From all thy kindred books,
To some dark cell, or cave forlorn,
Where thou endur'st, perhaps,
The chafing of some hard untutor'd hand,
Be comforted –
For lo! again the splendid hope appears
That thou may'st yet escape
The gulphs of Lethe, and on oary wings
Mount to the everlasting courts of Jove!

STROPHE III

Since Rouse desires thee, and complains   50
That, though by promise his,
Thou yet appear'st not in thy place
Among the literary noble stores,
Giv'n to his care,
But, absent, leav'st his numbers incomplete:

He, therefore, guardian vigilant
  Of that unperishing wealth,
Calls thee to the interior shrine, his charge,
Where he intends a richer treasure far
Than Iön kept (Iön, Erectheus' son   60
Illustrious, of the fair Creüsa born)
In the resplendent temple of his God,
Tripods of gold, and Delphic gifts divine.

   ANTISTROPHE
Haste, then, to the pleasant groves,
  The Muses' fav'rite haunt;
Resume thy station in Apollo's dome,
    Dearer to him
Than Delos, or the fork'd Parnassian hill!
    Exulting go,
Since now a splendid lot is also thine,   70
And thou art sought by my propitious friend;
  For there thou shalt be read
  With authors of exalted note,
The antient glorious lights of Greece and Rome.

   EPODE
Ye, then, my works, no longer vain,
  And worthless deem'd by me!
Whate'er this steril genius has produc'd
Expect, at last, the rage of envy spent,
 An unmolested happy home,
Gift of kind Hermes, and my watchful friend, 80
 Where never flippant tongue profane
  Shall entrance find,
And whence the coarse unletter'd multitude
  Shall babble far remote.
 Perhaps some future distant age,
Less ting'd with prejudice, and better taught,
  Shall furnish minds of pow'r
  To judge more equally.

Then, malice silenced in the tomb,
  Cooler heads and sounder hearts,   90
  Thanks to Rouse, if aught of praise
I merit, shall with candour weigh the claim.

A TRANSLATION OF THE ITALIAN POEMS

SONNET

Fair Lady! whose harmonious name the Rhine,
  Through all his grassy vale, delights to hear,
  Base were indeed the wretch, who could forbear
To love a spirit elegant as thine,
That manifests a sweetness all divine,
  Nor knows a thousand winning acts to spare,
  And graces, which Love's bow and arrows are,
Temp'ring thy virtues to a softer shine.
When gracefully thou speak'st, or singest gay,
  Such strains, as might the senseless forest move,   10
Ah then – turn each his eyes, and ears, away,
  Who feels himself unworthy of thy love!
Grace can alone preserve him, ere the dart
Of fond desire yet reach his inmost heart.

SONNET

As on a hill-top rude, when closing day
  Imbrowns the scene, some past'ral maiden fair
  Waters a lovely foreign plant with care,
Borne from its native genial airs away,
That scarcely can its tender bud display,
  So, on my tongue these accents, new, and rare,
  Are flow'rs exotic, which Love waters there.
While thus, O sweetly scornful! I essay
Thy praise, in verse to British ears unknown,
  And Thames exchange for Arno's fair domain;   10
So Love has will'd, and ofttimes Love has shown
  That what he wills, he never wills in vain.
Oh that this hard and steril breast might be,
To Him, who plants from heav'n, a soil as free!

CANZONE

They mock my toil – the nymphs and am'rous swains –
'And whence this fond attempt to write,' they cry,
'Love songs in language, that thou little know'st!
How dar'st thou risk to sing these foreign strains?
Say truly. Find'st not oft thy purpose cross'd,
And that thy fairest flow'rs here fade and die?'
Then with pretence of admiration high –
'Thee other shores expect, and other tides,
Rivers, on whose grassy sides
Her deathless laurel leaf, with which to bind   10
Thy flowing locks, already Fame provides;
Why then this burthen, better far declin'd?'
  Speak, Muse! for me. – The fair one said, who guides
My willing heart, and all my fancy's flights,
'This is the language, in which Love delights.'

SONNET
TO CHARLES DIODATI

Charles – and I say it wond'ring – thou must know
  That I, who once assum'd a scornful air,
  And scoff'd at love, am fallen in his snare,
(Full many an upright man has fallen so)
Yet think me not thus dazzled by the flow
  Of golden locks, or damask cheek; more rare
  The heart-felt beauties of my foreign fair;
A mien majestic, with dark brows, that show
The tranquil lustre of a lofty mind;
  Words exquisite, of idioms more than one,   10
And song, whose fascinating pow'r might bind,
  And from her sphere draw down the lab'ring Moon,
With such fire-darting eyes, that should I fill
My ears with wax, she could inchant me still.

SONNET

Lady! It cannot be, but that thine eyes
  Must be my sun, such radiance they display,
  And strike me ev'n as Phœbus him, whose way
Through horrid Lybia's sandy desert lies.
Meantime, on that side steamy vapours rise
  Where most I suffer. Of what kind are they,
  New as to me they are, I cannot say,
But deem them, in the lover's language – sighs.
Some, though with pain, my bosom close conceals,
  Which, if in part escaping thence, they tend   10
To soften thine, thy coldness soon congeals.
  While others to my tearful eyes ascend,
Whence my sad nights in show'rs are ever drown'd,
Till my Aurora comes, her brow with roses bound.

SONNET

Enamour'd, artless, young, on foreign ground,
  Uncertain whither from myself to fly,
  To thee, dear Lady, with an humble sigh
Let me devote my heart, which I have found
By certain proofs, not few, intrepid, sound,
  Good, and addicted to conceptions high:
  When tempests shake the world, and fire the sky,
It rests in adamant self-wrapt around,
As safe from envy, and from outrage rude,
  From hopes and fears, that vulgar minds abuse,   10
As fond of genius, and fixt fortitude,
  Of the resounding lyre, and every Muse.
Weak you will find it in one only part,
Now pierc'd by Love's immedicable dart.

Selected entries from
Flagellum Parliamentarium

an anonymous mansucript report on the Parliament of 1661
once attributed to Marvell, and surely written by an acquaintance of Milton

Nevil a court cully

Sir R Braham a bankrupt member in pension

Sir T Dolman flattered with the belief of being a Secretary of State

Sir J Trelawney a private foresworn cheat in the Prize Office, with the
profits of which he bought the place of Comptroller to the Duke of
York.

Sir S Fox once a Link-boy, then a singing-boy at Salisbury, then a serving
man; and permitting his wife to be common beyond sea, at Restoration
was made Paymaster to the Guards, where he has cheated £100,000, and
is one of the Green Cloth.

Sir J Trevor once the great instrument of Cromwell, and has got by
rebellion £1500 per annum out of the Lord Derby's estate. He has been
Envoy in France and is now Secretary of State.

Sam Sandys had a £1000 lick out of the Bribe pot.

E Waller, commissioner for plantations worth £500 per annum

Sir Sol. Swale high sheriff of Yorks. preserved by the court for making two
forged wills. Sent his sons beyond the sea to be Papists.

John Birch an old Rumper who formerly bought nails at Bristol, where
they were cheap, and carried them into the West to sell at Exeter and
other places, but marrying a rich widow got into the House, and is
now Commissioner in all Excises, and is now one of the Council of
Trade

Sir T Clifford Bribe master general

Sir John Northcott, an old Roundhead, now the Lord of Bath's cully

Peter Prideaux a secret pensioner of £200 a year, and his daily food

Sir W Church a pimp to his own daughter

Viscount Mandeville a Bedchamber pimp

Lord Arran had £5000 a year given him in Ireland, and a regiment

H Clerk hath had a lick of the Bribe-pot

W Ashburnham, not born to a farthing, now a cofferer

Thomas Morrice a broken stocking-seller is promised some estate in
    Ireland under pay of the Bribe-master Clifford, who has advanced him
    fifty pound

Note: This selection, some of it unfair, some no doubt libellous, is from a list of 178
members (1661–78), ed. 1827.

INDEX